CHILDREN'S THINKING

Robert S. Siegler
Carnegie-Mellon University

Prentice-Hall, Englewood Cliffs, New Jersey 07632

Library of Congress Cataloging-in-Publication Data

SIEGLER, ROBERT S. (date)
    Children's thinking.

    Bibliography: p.
    Includes index.
    1. Cognition in children.   I. Title.
BF723.C5S54   1986   155.4′13   85-19205
ISBN 0-13-132622-8

        *Editorial/production supervision and
            interior design: Shirley Stern*
        Cover design: Diane Sax
        Cover photo: Diane Stanford
        Manufacturing buyer: Barbara Kittle

to Alice

Printed in the United States of America

10 9 8 7 6 5 4 3

ISBN 0-13-132622-8   01

PRENTICE-HALL INTERNATIONAL (UK) LIMITED, *London*
PRENTICE-HALL OF AUSTRALIA PTY. LIMITED, *Sydney*
PRENTICE-HALL OF CANADA INC., *Toronto*
PRENTICE-HALL HISPANOAMERICANA, S.A., *Mexico*
PRENTICE-HALL OF INDIA PRIVATE LIMITED, *New Delhi*
PRENTICE-HALL OF JAPAN, INC., *Tokyo*
PRENTICE-HALL OF SOUTHEAST ASIA PTE. LTD., *Singapore*
EDITORA PRENTICE-HALL DO BRASIL, LTDA., *Rio de Janeiro*
WHITEHALL BOOKS LIMITED, *Wellington, New Zealand*

CONTENTS

4   TOOLS FOR STUDYING CHILDREN'S THINKING   96

FIVE SPECIFIC ASPECTS OF CHILDREN'S THINKING

5   PERCEPTUAL DEVELOPMENT   134

A BIG PICTURE OF CHILDREN'S THINKING

PREFACE

Children's thinking inherently fascinates many people. All of us were children once; most of us either have or expect to have our own children some day. The ways in which children think are at the same time both familiar and foreign. We remember some of the ways in which we thought at younger ages and have impressions of the thinking of many other children as well. Children's thinking seems reasonable most of the time, and occasionally it seems surprisingly insightful. At other times, though, children reason in ways that are difficult for adults to comprehend. It is fairly well known, for example, that most 5-year-olds believe that by pouring water into a differently-shaped container the amount of water is changed.

Until recently, many of the most intriguing aspects of children's thinking were inaccessible to our understanding. For example, philosophers argued for hundreds of years whether infants see the world as a "booming, buzzing confusion" or in much the same way that older children and adults do. Only in the past few years, with the development of revealing experimental methods, has the answer become clear. Even newborns see certain aspects of the world quite clearly, and by four months of age, infants' perception closely resembles that of adults. This and other discoveries about children's thinking are the subject matter of the book.

Who would be interested in this type of book? Anyone who is curious about children should find some interesting facts and ideas in it. Anyone sufficiently motivated to take an undergraduate or graduate course in this area should find a great deal to intrigue the imagination and stimulate further interest in children's thinking.

While writing this book, I found that Carnegie-Mellon University was a unique, exciting place to be. One reflection of the friendly, intellectual atmosphere is the amount of professional help and high-quality comments I received. David Klahr and James Staszewski reviewed all ten of the chapters and made innumerable constructive suggestions about how to improve them. John Anderson, Patricia Carpenter, Carl Granrud, and Brian MacWhinney also read and offered useful comments on one or more chapters. Of course, good colleagues are not limited to any one university. Keith Humphrey, Kevin Miller, Marion Perlmutter, and James Stigler all commented in helpful ways on one or more chapters, as did several anonymous reviewers. I am confident that their suggestions moved the book in the right direction; only readers can judge just how far in the right direction it evolved.

Thanks go to those who helped prepare the manuscript. Jean Barr, Winsome Ho, and Patricia Roble patiently typed more drafts than any of us cares to remember. Special thanks to Rebecca Alden, who worked with me from the beginning to the end of the writing process, and was always up to the challenge of doing whatever it took to get things done. Thanks also to John Isley, Shirley Stern, and Susan Willig, Prentice-Hall people, who helped greatly with encouragement and wise advice. Finally, thanks to my children, Aaron, Beth, and Todd for greatly enriching my understanding of children's thinking, and to my wife, Alice, for keeping things going on the home front during the many times that I was preoccupied with the book. I hope that the text is worthy of all the confidence they have shown in me.

ACKNOWLEDGMENTS

I would like to thank the following individuals and publishing companies for permission to reproduce material in this book:

ACADEMIC PRESS

Figure 3–1   Atkinson, R. C. & Shiffrin, R. M. (1968).   Human memory: A proposed system and its control processes. In K. W. Spence & J. T. Spence (Eds.), *Advances in the Psychology of learning and motivation research and theory, Vol. 2.* Reprinted by permission of Academic Press.

Figure 4–7   Vurpillot, E. (1968).   The development of scanning strategies and their relation to visual differentiation. *Journal of Experimental Child Psychology, 6,* 632–650. Reprinted by permission of Academic Press.

Figures 5–3 and 5–4   Banks, M. S. & Salapatek, P. (1981).   Infant pattern vision: A new approach based on the contrast sensitivity function. *Journal of Experimental Child Psychology, 31,* 1–45. Reprinted by permission of Academic Press and M. S. Banks.

Table 7–2   Spilich, G. J., Vesonder, G. T., Chiesi, H. L., & Voss, J. (1979). Text processing of domain-related information for individuals with high and low domain knowledge. *Journal of Verbal Learning and Verbal Behavior, 18,* 275–290. Reprinted by permission of Academic Press.

Table 8–3   Keil, F. C. & Batterman, N. (1984).   A characteristic-to-defining shift in the development of word meaning. *Journal of Verbal Learning and Verbal Behavior, 23,* 221–236. Reprinted by permission of Academic Press and F. C. Keil.

AMERICAN PSYCHOLOGICAL ASSOCIATION

Figure 7–4   Chi, M. T. H. & Koeske, R. D. (1983).   Network representation of a child's dinosaur knowledge. *Developmental Psychology, 19,* 29–39. Reprinted by permission of the American Psychological Association and M. T. H. Chi.

Figure 9–1   Groen, G. J. & Parkman, J. M. (1972).   A chronometric analysis of simple addition. *Psychological Review, 79,* 329–343. Reprinted by permission of the American Psychological Association.

UNIVERSITY OF CHICAGO PRESS

Figure 1–2   Keating, D. P. & Bobbitt, B. L. (1978).   Individual and developmental differences in cognitive processing components of mental ability. *Child Development, 49,* 155–167. Reprinted by permission of the University of Chicago Press.

Figure 8–3   Younger, B. A. & Cohen, L. B. (1983).   Infant perception of correlations among attributes. *Child Development, 54,* 858–867. Reprinted by permission of the University of Chicago Press.

AMERICAN ASSOCIATION FOR THE ADVANCEMENT OF SCIENCE

Figure 4–5A and B   Shepard, R. N. & Metzler, J. (1971).   Mental rotation of three-dimensional objects. *Science, 171,* 701–703. Reprinted by permission of the American Association for the Advancement of Science and R. N. Shepard.

RANDOM HOUSE

Figure 5–5   Lamb, M. E. & Campos, J. J. (1982).   *Development in infancy: An introduction.* Reprinted by permission of Random House and M. E. Lamb.

CAMBRIDGE UNIVERSITY PRESS

Figure 6–1   Newport, E. L. (1982).   Task specificity in language learning. Evidence from speech. In E. Wanner & L. R. Gleitmen (Eds.), *Language acquisition: The state of the art.* Reprinted by permission of the Cambridge University Press.

Quotation in chapter 7:   Bartlett, F. C. (1932).   *Remembering.* Reprinted by permission of the Cambridge University Press.

LAWRENCE ERLBAUM, INC.

Figure 9–4A and B   Siegler, R. S. & Shrager, J. (1984).   A model of strategy choice. In C. Sophian (Ed.), *Origins of cognitive skills.* Reprinted by permission of Lawrence Erlbaum, Inc.

1
HOW DO CHILDREN PROCESS INFORMATION?

When did the sun begin? *When people began living.* Who made it? *God.* How did God do this? *He put a real lot of light bulbs in it.* Are these light bulbs still in the sun? *No.* What happened to them? *They burnt out. No, they stay good a long time.* So are the light bulbs still in it? *No. I think he made it out of gold. And he lit it with fire.* (Conversation with my son, 1985).

What do these answers, advanced by my younger son one week before his fifth birthday, tell us about the way in which he views the world? Can we attribute his explanations to a simple lack of knowledge about astronomy and physics? Or do they indicate a fundamental difference between young children's reasoning and that of older children and adults? An adult who did not know the origins of the sun would not ascribe its origins to God putting light bulbs in it. Nor would an adult link the origins of the sun to the fact that people began to be alive. Do these differences mean that children generally reason in more literal and self-centered ways than adults? Or do they just reflect a child grasping at straws when he does not even know the kind of explanation that would be acceptable?

For hundreds of years, people who have interacted with children have wondered about these and related questions. Where do children's ideas come from? Do infants see the world in the same way as adults? Why do societies throughout the world first send children to school between ages 5 and 7? A

TABLE 1-1   Chapter Outline

---

century ago, people could speculate about these issues, but now we have concepts and methods that magnify our ability to observe, describe, and explain the process of development. As a result, our understanding of children's thinking is growing rapidly.

This first chapter has two main goals. One is to introduce some central issues and ideas about children's thinking. The other is to introduce the information-processing approach, the perspective on children's thinking that will be emphasized in this book. The discussion initially focuses on what "children's thinking" involves and what the information-processing approach is. The next section places current ideas about children's thinking in historical perspective. Finally, the overall organization of the book is considered, both the content of each chapter and the central themes that recur in many chapters. The organization is outlined in Table 1-1.

WHAT IS CHILDREN'S THINKING?

Defining children's thinking sounds like a trivial task. We all know what children are, we all know what thinking is, and combining the terms poses no special problems. Providing a concrete definition of children's thinking turns out to be far from a trivial task, however. No sharp boundary divides activities that involve thinking from those that do not. Similarly, no particular age marks the end of childhood.

Listing examples of thinking turns out to be easier and more fruitful than formally defining the term. The first activities that come to mind when we think about thinking refer to higher mental processes: problem solving, reasoning, creativity, conceptualizing, remembering, classifying, symbolizing, planning, reading, writing, and so on. Other examples of thinking involve more basic processes, processes at which even young children are skilled: using language and perceiving objects and events in the external environment, to name two. Still other activities might or might not be viewed as types of thinking. These include being socially skillful, having a keen moral sense, feeling appropriate emotions, and so on. The qualities in this last group involve thought processes, but they also involve many other, nonintellectual features. In this book we will give these boundary areas some attention, but the spotlight will be on problem solving, memorizing, using language, perceiving, and the other more purely intellectual activities.

All types of thinking involve both products and processes. The products of thinking are the observable end states, what children know at different points in development. The processes of thinking are the initial and intermediate steps, often accomplished entirely inside people's heads, that produce the products. In studying children's understanding of causality, for example, we might ask them what causes rain. An older and a younger child both might answer that clouds do. However, the older child's answer might be based on observing that dark clouds usually appear in the sky before and during a storm, whereas the younger child might simply be parroting what his parents told him. The product of the two children's thinking—their statement that clouds cause rain—would be identical, but the processes that led to the answer would differ. Both processes and products must be part of any reasonable definition of thinking. However, this book will emphasize processes, because focusing on them usually yields deeper understandings of development.

Some of the most interesting parts of children's thinking are the parts where children differ most markedly from adults. DeVries (1969) provided a particularly compelling example of such a difference. She was interested in 3- to 6-year-olds' understanding of the difference between appearance and reality. The children were presented an unusually sweet-tempered cat named Maynard and were allowed to pet him. When the experimenter asked what Maynard was, all of them knew that he was a cat. Then the experimenter put a mask on Maynard's head, in plain sight of the children. The mask was that of a fierce-looking dog. The experimenter asked, "Look, it has a face like a dog. What is this animal now?"

DeVries found that many of the 3-year-olds thought that Maynard had become a dog. They refused to pet him and said that under his skin he had a dog's bones and a dog's stomach. In contrast, most 6-year-olds argued that a cat could not turn into a dog, and that the mask did not change the animal's identity.

The reasons why such thinking is interesting are easy to see. It is simply stunning that a human being, even a very young one, would think that a cat could turn into a dog. Overemphasizing such differences, however, can create an imbalanced view of *cognitive development* (another term for children's thinking). Even young children demonstrate surprisingly adultlike reasoning in many situations. Considering such developmental similarities, as well as developmental differences, is essential for a comprehensive understanding of children's thinking. Both will be given substantial attention throughout the book.

Defining "children" should be and is considerably easier than defining "thinking." The only issue is where to draw the boundary between childhood and other periods of life. We will consider infants and adolescents, as well as preschoolers and elementary school students, as falling within the category of children. This will allow broader depiction of cognitive development than would otherwise be possible.

A final crucial aspect of children's thinking may not be apparent from the name: Children's thinking inherently involves change. How children think at particular points in development is interesting in and of itself, but the most interesting part of development, at least for me, is the changes that occur. Comparing infants with adolescents, it is easy to appreciate the huge magnitude of these changes. More subtle, but just as intriguing, is the question of how the changes occur. What processes could imaginably transform the mind of a newborn baby into the mind of an adolescent? This is the central mystery of cognitive development.

WHAT IS THE INFORMATION-PROCESSING APPROACH?

Fifteen years ago, the information-processing approach barely existed as an identifiable strategy for studying children's thinking. Today it seems to be *the* leading approach. How can this growth be explained?

At the heart of the approach's success is the richness and appropriateness of its view of thinking as information processing. It has several appealing qualities: a dramatic metaphor for children's efforts to know their world, a set of elegant and precise experimental methods, and a number of provocative central issues. Most important, it has stimulated a number of intriguing discoveries about how children think. Each of these features of the approach will be discussed in depth in later chapters. To provide an overview of what is to follow, we also will briefly introduce each of these topics here. It should not be a matter of concern if many of the terms and concepts are unfamiliar. They are mentioned now precisely so that they will not be quite as unfamiliar when they appear later.

An Overview of the Information-Processing Approach

The central metaphor.   The information-processing approach to development is based on a flattering, almost heroic, view of children's thinking. This model speaks directly to the essential tension within cognition: the tension produced by children being severely limited in the material they can take in at any one time, yet also of constantly striving and often succeeding in devising means for overcoming these processing limitations.

In what sense is children's processing capacity limited? To get a feel for this, consider what it would be like to try to apply the quadratic equation without pencil, paper, or calculator. Almost everyone would have trouble remembering all the partial results. Executing some of the individual processes, such as calculating square roots, also would be difficult.

To overcome these memory and processing limitations, children use a variety of *strategies*. They use memory strategies such as *rehearsal* (repeating material over and over before recalling it, as when trying to remember a telephone number) to overcome their limited capacity to retain newly presented information. They use external memory aids such as books to overcome their limited knowledge. They use problem-solving strategies, such as dividing problems into parts, to overcome their limited capacity to arrive at wise decisions. The conflicts among the setting of goals, the memory and processing limitations that make it difficult to attain them, and the strategies children devise to overcome the limitations highlight the drama inherent in children's efforts to know the world.

Methods for studying thinking. Another reason for the growth of the information-processing approach to children's thinking is its arsenal of powerful methods. *Protocol analyses* use children's verbal comments in the course of solving problems to indicate which strategies they are using. *Error analyses* focus on patterns of correct answers and errors to reveal the nature of children's conceptual understanding. *Eye-movement analyses* examine exactly where children look to determine the processes by which they process visual information. *Chronometric methods* employ patterns of reaction times (the times needed to complete various tasks) to measure the time children need to execute various information processes.

These methods have several characteristics in common. Each is oriented toward testing models of thinking. Each uses a rich data base, in which many pieces of data are collected each minute. In each approach, the data *pattern* is of the greatest interest, rather than how often children in the experiment are correct or how fast they perform.

Useful languages for characterizing cognition. Another advantage lies in the precision and versatility of information-processing languages for characterizing thinking. Standard spoken languages such as English and French are among the greatest of all human creations, but as flexible and powerful as they are, they are not ideal for all purposes. For example, suppose that you wanted to describe what a 6-year-old girl knew about the concept of "fairness." You could make a list of the qualities she associated with the term: Being fair is being good, being fair is two people having exactly as much as each other, being fair is taking turns, and so on. Such a list would not easily include the relations among all the different parts of the girl's knowledge of fairness, however. Nor would it easily specify what kinds of knowledge guide her behavior under various conditions where the concept of fairness comes into play.

Because of these limits of natural languages, a variety of special languages have been developed for describing thinking. Some, such as *flow diagrams,* are familiar because they are used in other contexts as well. Others, such as *semantic networks,* are less familiar, but were formulated especially for the difficult problem of describing complex concepts such as "fairness."

Some of the languages that have been found to be useful for describing children's thinking are computer languages. These can be especially useful for testing theories about cognitive development. Consider one case in which they were used to test a theory about how young children learn to count. Gelman and Gallistel (1978) hypothesized that even preschoolers understand the principles underlying counting, and that knowing the principles helps children acquire skill at counting. These principles included such essentials as the necessity of each object being labeled with one and only one number and the special quality that the last number in a counting sequence represents the size of the entire set that was counted ("How many are there? One, two, three, four, five, *six.*") As will be discussed later in the book, Gelman and Gallistel convincingly demonstrated that young children possess considerable knowledge about counting. But questions still remained. What does it mean to say that a child understands a principle? What does such understanding have to do with the skill children show in counting?

Greeno, Riley, and Gelman (1984) formulated a computer simulation of preschoolers' counting that answered these questions. The simulation embodied understanding of the counting principles described by Gelman and Gallistel, thus specifying what it could mean for children to understand them. This meaning differed somewhat from what might have been expected. In particular, the model suggested that children did not know the principles in any explicit form. They could not state them even if asked. However, the principles did guide the children's counting behavior. The simulation also illustrated just where the principles were most important. They were particularly crucial for solving novel counting problems, such as being asked to count a row of five objects in a way that would make the leftmost object the fourth one counted. Overall, the simulation helped to clarify the theory and demonstrated its ability to explain important aspects of children's counting skill.

This example also illustrates how building models of children's thinking on particular tasks is useful not just for suggesting ideas about the particular task, but also for suggesting more general ideas about the nature of development. Gelman and Gallistel (1978) demonstrated that the largest improvement between ages 3 and 5 years in children's counting was in their ability to solve novel counting problems, such as making the leftmost object the fourth one counted. The Greeno et al. model indicated that ability to solve such problems depends on adequate planning capabilities. The empirical finding and the model together suggest that improving ability to plan ahead might more generally contribute to improvements in children's problem solving during the preschool years.

Issues raised. The information-processing approach to children's thinking also has attracted adherents because of the issues it addresses. These issues focus on children's *representations* of information and the processes by which they transform the representations. The term "representation" refers to the ways in which knowledge is organized in the mind. Children's representations of objects and events are not literal copies of objects and events in the environment. Rather, they are subjective and reflect what children already know. For example, a 5-year-old who saw the contents of a glass of water poured into a taller, thinner glass might represent only the heights of the water in the two glasses, and might totally ignore the cross-sectional areas of the glasses. Children use a variety of mental processes to manipulate the contents of their mental representations. For example, when they read stories, they continually integrate new information with previous information so they can maintain a coherent representation of what is happening in the story and what might happen next.

Many interesting questions have been raised by this emphasis on representations and processes. Do children represent information in terms of verbal statements, spatial images, or in some third form that can be translated into both verbal and spatial codes? Are mental processes performed *serially* (one after another) or *in parallel* (simultaneously)? Do we represent in different form information that enables us to *know how* to do something than information that allows us to *know that* something is true? Information-processing theories have provided new frameworks within which to consider these questions; information-processing languages have provided new ways of asking the questions; information-processing methods have provided new procedures for gathering data relevant to them.

Describing a single example in detail may bring home the importance of these theories, methods, and issues. Brown and Burton (1978) were interested in children's subtraction. In particular, they wanted to know whether children's subtraction errors were due to complete lack of knowledge of the correct procedure or to various "bugs" existing in basically correct rules. They used a sophisticated error analysis method to investigate the question. That is, they presented problems in which particular bugs, hypothesized to be common sources of errors, would lead to specific erroneous answers. If a child's errors consistently met the expected pattern, and the child consistently answered correctly problems on which that bug would not lead to mistakes, then the view of a bug existing in a basically correct approach would be supported.

Brown and Burton found that many children's errors were produced by such bugs. Consider the pattern in Table 1-2. At first glance, it is difficult to draw any conclusion about this boy's performance, except that he is not very good at subtraction. With further analysis, however, his performance becomes entirely understandable. His three errors arose on problems where the top number included a 0; he answered correctly on the other two problems. This suggests that the difficulty involved specific problems with subtracting from 0, rather than general carelessness, ignorance, or lack of motivation.

Analysis of the three errors the boy made suggests the existence of two bugs that would produce these particular answers. When the problem required subtraction from zero, he simply wrote as the answer for that column the nonzero number in the same column as the zero. For example, in the problem 307 -- 182, he wrote 8 in the middle column as the answer to 0 -- 8. The boy's second bug involved not decrementing the number to the left of the zero (not reducing the 3 to 2 in 307 -- 182). This lack of decrementing is not surprising because, as indicated in the first bug, he has not in fact borrowed anything from this column. Thus, the three wrong answers, as well as the two correct ones, can be explained by assuming a basically correct subtraction procedure with two particular bugs. The explanation could be tested by presenting the boy additional problems that would lead to predictable errors and correct answers, and seeing how well the boy's performance fit the predictions.

The findings of Brown and his colleagues supported their theoretical claim that bugs in a basically correct procedure were the source of many children's difficulties in subtraction. Brown and Burton (1978) applied their assessment technique to the subtraction of 1300 Nicaraguan fourth, fifth, and sixth graders. At all three grade levels, roughly half the children whose performance was not consistently correct exhibited one or more specific bugs. Most of the bugs centered on problems where it was necessary to borrow from zero. The next most common bug was subtracting the smaller digit in a column from the larger, regardless of which number was supposed to be subtracted from which.

Brown and Burton also wrote a computer program, known as "Buggy," to teach prospective teachers how to detect their students' bugs. The program works in a tutorial fashion. It might first display the five problems and answers shown in Table 1-2. The teacher would be told to indicate when he or she knew what bug the student was using. The next task would be for the teacher to generate new problems and to answer them the way the bug would suggest. The program would give the teacher feedback on each of the generated answers. Finally, once the teacher generated five consecutive correct answers to his own problems, "Buggy" would design new problems where subtle differences between the teacher's understanding of the bug and the bug itself would be apparent. If the teacher answered these correctly, the program would offer congratulations for insight and persistence.

TABLE 1-2   Example of a Subtraction "Bug"

307	856	606	308	835
− 182	− 699	− 568	− 287	− 217
285	157	168	181	618

Brown and Van Lehn (1982) reported that teachers often failed at first in such tutorial sessions. Frequently, several bugs were consistent with the original five answers. Teachers tended to design new problems where children's answers would not reveal which bug they actually were using. That is, because several possible bugs would produce identical answers to the problems the teacher designed, a bug that was entirely consistent with the previous evidence might prove wrong in the final test phase. Working with "Buggy" helped teachers learn to design more revealing problems that allowed them to isolate the true bug. A number of teachers offered testimonials that using "Buggy" aided their ability to locate the sources of their students' errors.

KEY ISSUES ABOUT CHILDREN'S THINKING

What are the most important issues about children's thinking? Many different answers are possible, but there is widespread agreement that the following four issues are among the most important. Does children's thinking progress through qualitatively different stages? What processes cause developmental changes? How can cognitive development best be studied? What is the relation between children's and adults' thinking? Below, I introduce each of these issues.

Does Development Progress Through Stages?

When a girl misbehaves, her parents might console each other by saying "It's just a stage she's going through." When a boy fails utterly to learn something, his parents might lament, "I guess he just hasn't reached the stage where he can understand this." It is interesting to think about how the stage idea came to be applied to child development, what exactly it means to say that a child is in a stage, and whether children in fact progress through qualitatively distinct stages of thinking.

Charles Darwin usually is not thought of as a developmental psychologist. In many ways he was one, though. In his book *The Descent of Man*, Darwin discussed the development of reason, curiosity, imitation, attention, imagination, language, and self-consciousness. He was most interested in these topics in a comparative context, that is, in the development of such qualities from other animals to man. However, many of his ideas could be and were translated into concepts about the development that occurs in an individual's lifetime.

Perhaps Darwin's most influential observation was his most basic one: that over vast time periods, life progresses through a series of qualitatively distinct forms. This observation suggested to some (among them G. Stanley Hall, widely viewed as the father of developmental psychology) that in any given lifetime, development would progress through distinct forms or stages.

Hall and many other developmental theorists of his day further hypothesized that children would make the transition from one stage to the next quite suddenly. This stage approach directly contradicted speculations by associationist philosophers such as John Locke that children's thinking developed through the gradual influence of thousands of particular experiences. Associationists compared the developmental process to a building being constructed brick by brick. Stage theorists compared it to the metamorphosis from caterpillar to butterfly.

In the early part of the 20th century, James Mark Baldwin hypothesized a set of plausible stages of intellectual development. He suggested that children progressed from a sensorimotor stage, in which interactions with the physical environment were the dominant form of thought, to a quasilogical, a logical, and a hyperlogical stage. The idea that children progress through these stages receives a certain amount of support in everyday observations of children. Infants' interactions with the world do seem, at least at first, to emphasize perceptual impressions and motoric actions. At the other end of the developmental period, not until adolescence do people spend much time thinking about purely logical issues, such as whether the laws that apply to adolescents (laws about draft ages, driving ages, drinking ages, etc.) are logically consistent with each other. Baldwin's stage theory was ignored by most of his contemporaries, but exerted a strong influence on at least one later thinker: Jean Piaget.

Piaget, without question, added more to our understanding of cognitive development than any other individual. He made a huge number of fascinating observations about children's thinking. For example, the conversation with my son that I quoted at the beginning of this chapter was based on my wondering whether children in the 1980s still respond to questions about the origin of the sun like the children Piaget questioned in the 1920s. (They do.) Piaget also developed the stage notion to a much greater extent than Baldwin had and popularized the general idea of viewing human intellectual development in terms of stages. The chapter after this one focuses on what he found out about children's thinking and how well the stages he postulated describe and explain cognitive development.

Stages are a sufficiently complex idea that it is important to specify exactly what we mean when we say that children's thinking progresses through certain stages. Flavell (1971) noted four implications of the stage concept. First, stages imply qualitative changes. We do not say that a boy is in a new stage of understanding of arithmetic when he progresses from knowing 50 percent to knowing 100 percent of the multiplication facts. Instead, we reserve the term for situations where the child's thinking seems not only considerably better but different in kind. For example, when a girl makes up her first genuinely amusing joke, after several years of making up stories that are intended to be humorous but that are barely comprehensible, it seems like a qualitative change. Note the ambiguity of the term "seems like," however.

Perhaps the efforts had been improving slowly for a long time, but had not quite reached the threshold for what an adult recognizes as a joke.

A second implication of stages is that children make the transition from one stage to another on many concepts at the same time. When they are in Stage 1, they show Stage 1 reasoning in all of these concepts; when they are in Stage 2, they show Stage 2 reasoning on all of them. Flavell labeled this the *concurrence assumption*, because changes are believed to occur at the same time across a wide range of understandings, resulting in children thinking similarly across many different domains. When the parent in the above example said, "He's just not in a stage where he can understand this," the implication was that some more-or-less general deficiency would keep the child from understanding other concepts of comparable complexity.

Viewing children's thinking as progressing through a series of stages also has a third and a fourth implication that we will consider only briefly here. The third implication is that changes occur abruptly. Children are in Stage 1 for a prolonged period of time, enter briefly into a transition period, and then are in Stage 2 for a prolonged period. The fourth is that children's thinking is structured into a coherent organization rather than being composed of a large number of independent, unrelated ideas. Neither of these positions is controversial today, though for entirely different reasons. The view that important transitions in children's thinking are limited to certain transitional periods is no longer controversial because it almost certainly is wrong. Children's thinking is continually changing, and most changes seem to be gradual rather than sudden. The issue of whether children's thinking is structured is no longer controversial for the opposite reason; it is clear that children's thinking is coherently structured. The issues of whether children's thinking shows qualitative changes and whether their thinking shows similar patterns across many tasks remain controversial, however; these issues will be discussed in greater depth in the next chapter.

How Does Change Occur?

Above all, development involves change. Figure 1–1 illustrates some of the types of changes that occur. The illustration was developed by Aslin and Dumais (1980) to illustrate changes in perceptual development, but the classification applies to all changes in children's thinking. The left side of the figure illustrates three types of changes that can occur in the prenatal period: a particular capability can develop fully, partially, or not at all during this time. The right hand side depicts changes occurring after birth. An already-developed ability can either be maintained or can decline; an undeveloped ability can grow or stay undeveloped; and a partially-developed ability can grow, stay the same, or decline.

The diversity of these patterns multiplies even further when we realize that any given ability involves many components that may follow quite different developmental courses. For example, as will be discussed in Chapter

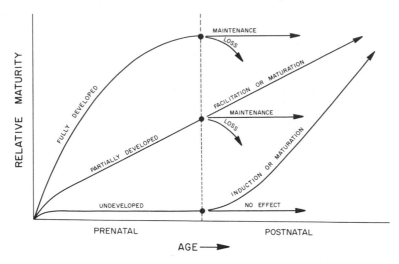

FIGURE 1-1   Illustration of several paths of developmental change.

5, infants can produce sounds that are not part of their native language and that they later will lose the capability of making. On the other hand, their facility in producing at will the sounds that are part of their native language increases tremendously after infancy. Thus, ability to produce sounds both declines and grows during childhood.

How can changes in children's thinking be explained? One type of explanation involves stages. Just as people often say that a child is in a particular stage of development, they also say that the child is (or is not) ready to move ahead. In school, for example, 5- and 6-year-olds are often tested to see if they are ready to learn to read. The idea of readiness corresponds to a deep insight into the nature of cognitive development: that when and what children learn depends on the fit between their general level of thinking, what they already know about the particular topic, and the complexity of the material they encounter. Hunt (1961) labeled this whole issue "the problem of the match."

Piaget described a plausible and appealing means by which changes in children's thinking might occur. He suggested that the basic mechanisms were *assimilation* and *accommodation*. Assimilation is the idea that people represent their experience in terms of their existing understandings. A 1-year-old girl given a round candle by her mother might think of it as a ball if she knew about balls and not about candles. Accommodation is the opposite tendency. Just as previous understandings influence acquisition of new information, the new information alters the previous understandings. The 1-year-old who was given the candle might notice that this "ball" was different from others in having a thin object protruding from it and in having an indentation around the thin object. This discovery might lay the groundwork for eventually learning that this round object was a candle, not a ball.

Information-processing theorists have analyzed changes at a somewhat more detailed level and have postulated four change mechanisms that seem to play large roles in cognitive development: *automatization, encoding, generalization,* and *strategy construction.* Automatization involves executing mental processes increasingly efficiently so that they require less and less attention. As children develop and have greater experience using a variety of mental processes, their processing becomes noticeably more efficient in many situations. This more efficient processing allows them to see connections among ideas and events that they otherwise would miss. For example, in the first few months of walking home from school, a 5-year-old girl might need to attend carefully to go in the right direction and cross the street at the right time. Later, her going home would become automatized, and she could pay greater attention to what other people were saying and learn more from them.

Encoding involves identifying the most informative features of objects and events and using the features to form internal representations. The importance of improved encoding in children's increasingly good understanding of the world is evident in the context of their learning to solve story problems in arithmetic and algebra. Often such stories include irrelevant as well as relevant information. The trick to solving the problems is to encode the relevant information and to ignore the irrelevant parts.

The third and the fourth change mechanisms, generalization and strategy construction, can be illustrated through a single example. After repeated experience with nonfunctioning televisions, lamps, toasters, and radios, a child might reach the generalization that when machines do not work, it often is due to their not being plugged in. On drawing this generalization, the child might form a strategy of always first checking the plug whenever any machine did not work. The child's construction of this strategy would rest on a base of reaching the generalization that plugs are often involved in machines not working, of encoding the plug as a distinct feature of the machine, and of automatizing processing sufficiently to note the relations among the seemingly different balky machines. As will be evident throughout the book, improvements in children's thinking in areas ranging from 2-year-olds' language learning to adolescents' computer programming depend heavily on these four change processes: automatization, improved encoding, generalization, and strategy formation.

How Can Development Best Be Studied?

Studying the thought processes of children, especially young ones, poses special difficulties. Consider some issues that have arisen in using one common method: the verbal report approach. Often, the quickest way of finding out some of the ways children think about a topic is simply to ask them relevant questions. The children's statements are often quite informative concerning how they solved problems, what factors they based decisions on, and why they thought a sequence of events occurred.

On the other hand, children's verbal statements can either overstate or understate their knowledge. If children repeat comments they have heard but not understood, their comments give a falsely favorable impression. If children understand a concept but are too inarticulate to explain it, their statements can give an overly negative impression of their competence. A final problem is that both children and adults often have incorrect impressions about their thinking, and thus produce a misleading picture.

These are compelling arguments and might at first seem irrefutable. However, good counterarguments also exist. Children's verbal statements often reveal their reasoning in a way no other evidence would. How else would we have found out that some children believe that the sun's origin is due to God putting light bulbs in it? In addition, other methods can supplement initial insights obtained from asking children about their thinking. Finally, all methods at times suggest misleading impressions, and it is not clear that verbal methods are worse offenders than other approaches.

Given these arguments and counterarguments, it is not surprising that children's thinking is studied using a wide range of methods, verbal and nonverbal. The ideal would be to find an approach that is as applicable to diverse content domains and as revealing as verbal statements, but that also can be used in all periods of development and that neither underestimates nor overestimates knowledge. Discovering such an ideal method may be like trying to touch a rainbow, however. The more we try to move toward it, the farther it recedes in the distance.

Relations Between Children's and Adults' Thinking

A Wordsworth poem states, "The child is father to the man." The proverb reflects the wisdom that there is a close connection between the way people think and act as children and the way they think and act as adults. One distinctive characteristic of the information-processing approach is a conscious effort to explore the relations between children's and adults' thinking and to use insights obtained in each area to better understand the other. It is easier to understand adults' thinking when we know how it acquired its mature form; it is easier to understand development when we know where the development is going. To illustrate just how this connection can add to understanding of how children think, I will describe a pair of studies conducted to reveal how adults' and children's short-term memory systems work.

S. Sternberg (1966) performed one of the best known of all psychological experiments. He presented college students with a set containing between one and six numbers. Then he presented one more number; the task was to determine whether the last number was one of those contained in the original set. The issue was how having more information (more numbers) already in short-term memory would influence the time needed to search through the content to answer the question.

Sternberg found that the more numbers there were in the original set, the longer it took to make the decision. Further, the time needed to make the decision increased by a constant amount for each additional number in the original set. That is, it took 430 milliseconds (500 milliseconds is half a second) to answer the question when there was one number in the original set, 470 milliseconds when there were two, 510 milliseconds when there were three, 550 when there were four, and so on. Sternberg interpreted this to mean that people performed the task by searching through their short-term memory one number at a time, with each additional number requiring about 40 milliseconds.

Keating and Bobbitt (1978) extended this research to intellectually gifted and intellectually average 9-, 13-, and 17-year-olds. Their experiment had the same theoretical goal as Sternberg's and used the same method. As shown in Figure 1–2, their results also resembled the findings with adults.

FIGURE 1-2   Memory scanning times of gifted and average-ability 9-, 13-, and 17-year-olds. Note the steeper slopes of the lines representing the performance of the 9- and to some extent the 13-year-old average-ability children. These steeper slopes indicate that these children are scanning the contents of their memories more slowly, since their solution times rise a greater amount for each additional item they are holding in memory (from Keating & Bobbitt, 1978).

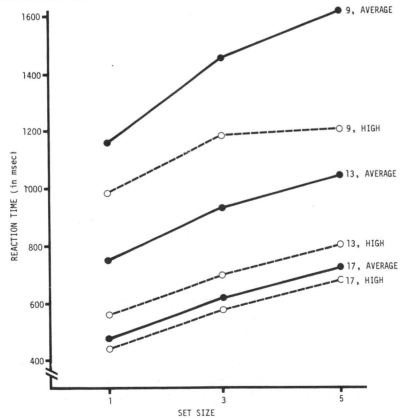

The greater the number of objects in the set, the longer it took children of all ages and abilities to decide whether the new number was a member of the original set. Looking at the slopes of the six lines, it is apparent that with age, the children's rate of searching through their short-term memories increased. The 9-year-olds required an extra 84 milliseconds for each additional number in the original set, but the 17-year-olds required only 60. The rate of development of gifted and average-intelligence children also differed. For average children, the time needed for each extra number in the original set declined greatly between ages 9 and 17. In contrast, the gifted 9-year-olds searched just as rapidly as the gifted 17-year-olds; their development on this skill was already adultlike by age 9.

What conclusions can be drawn from these results? At the most basic level, children and adolescents search through the contents of their short-term memories in the same way as adults. They seem to search one unit at a time and require a constant amount of time for each additional search. Development comes in how rapidly the searches are made. In general, older children search more rapidly than younger ones. However, by the middle of childhood, gifted children can search through their short-term memories at adultlike rates. This early ability to retrieve information rapidly from short-term memory may aid gifted children in seeing a wide variety of connections that other children do not see. In summary, the Keating and Bobbitt study illustrates how information about adults' thinking can illuminate our understanding of children's thinking.

THE BOOK'S ORGANIZATION

The organization of this book can be viewed either on a chapter-by-chapter basis or in terms of the central themes that recur in many chapters. Below, the book is described from each perspective.

The Chapter-by-Chapter Organization

The book is divided into three sections. The first section, which includes Chapters 1–4, explores broad perspectives on children's thinking, such as Piaget's theory of development. The second section, which includes Chapters 5–9, focuses on more specific aspects of children's thinking, such as how they perceive the world, how they use language to communicate, and how they learn reading, writing, and arithmetic. The third section includes only a single chapter, Chapter 10. It is a summing up of what has gone before and a look forward toward the questions and issues that promise to be most important in the future.

The first chapter, which you are just finishing, is an attempt to define the field that will be considered in this book and to introduce some of the ideas that are important within it. Chapter 2 is devoted to a set of observations and ideas about children's thinking that can fairly be said to have created the modern field of cognitive development. These are Jean Piaget's investigations. Piaget's observations, and his theoretical interpretations of what he saw, were what created initial interest in the field among whole generations of students and researchers, me among them. On topics ranging from how children infer the origins of the sun to how they order the weights of different objects, he saw much that other people had missed. In addition, Piaget observed children of an extremely wide age range, stretching from the first days of infancy into late adolescence. Thus, his observations provide a feel for many aspects of development in many parts of childhood.

The next two chapters of the book describe the information-processing perspective on children's thinking. In some ways this approach represents an extension of Piaget's approach; in other ways it represents an alternative to it. Chapter 3 focuses on theories of how children process information. The goal is to provide a framework for thinking about children's information processing as a whole and to address the questions of what develops and how development occurs. The theories of development that are discussed are chosen in large part because they propose interesting and plausible change mechanisms that seem to greatly influence cognitive development. Chapter 4 presents methods that have proven useful for finding out how children think and also languages that can clearly and concisely describe their thinking. Discovering how children think is an inherently difficult enterprise, because thought processes are hidden from view, because infants and young children cannot verbally convey to us much if anything about their thinking, and because standard spoken languages often cannot capture the complexity of thought. The methods and languages described in this chapter have greatly enhanced our insights into children's thinking and often have made their thought processes almost visible.

The second main section of the book examines five specific aspects of children's thinking: the development of perception, language, memory, concepts, and academic skills. Chapter 5 explores the development of perceptual processes. The emphasis is on the surprising number of visual and auditory skills children possess from early in infancy. By age 6 months, their visual and auditory worlds seem to be largely similar to those of adults. Chapter 6 examines language development. Here the discussion centers on what types of words children use first, when and how they learn grammar, how they acquire word meanings, and how they use all their knowledge to communicate with others. The chapter also includes discussions of how deaf children acquire sign language and whether children are biologically pre-programmed to learn languages in certain ways.

Chapter 7 is about the development of memory. Are developmental differences in memory due to differences in older and younger children's basic capacities, strategies, prior knowledge about the content they encounter, or all of the above? The chapter also focuses on whether some of these sources of memory development are particularly influential in particular periods of development. Chapter 8 is about conceptual development. Among the concepts whose development will be considered are cause and effect, number, and classification. Chapter 9 concerns the development of the three R's: reading, writing, and arithmetic. In the past, these areas often have been thought of as "educational" rather than "developmental." As we learn more about how children acquire cognitive skills, however, educational and developmental changes seem more and more closely related.

The third main section of the book is an attempt to summarize what we know about children's thinking at present and to speculate about what we may find out in the not-too-distant future. Among the topics receiving greatest emphasis in this chapter is how social factors influence children's thinking: the influence of the culture into which the child is born, the influence of parents and teachers, and the role of available technologies from abacuses to computers. These are among the least well understood topics relevant to children's thinking; they also are among the most important.

The Central Themes

This chapter-by-chapter organization provides one way of thinking about the material the book covers. Another way is to consider the themes that arise in many chapters. The following are eight of the most frequently recurring themes.

1. The two questions that stand out as the most basic in the study of children's thinking are "What develops?" and "How does development occur?"

2. Development is about change. Four change processes that seem to be particularly large contributors to cognitive development are automatization, encoding, generalization, and strategy construction.

3. A major challenge that children face is how to deploy limited processing resources to deal effectively with cognitively demanding situations.

4. Changes in children's thinking do not occur in a vacuum. What children already know about material they encounter influences not only *how much* they learn but also *what* they learn.

5. Knowledge of the adult cognitive system is useful for studying changes in children's thinking. It is much easier to study development when we know where the development is going.

6. Differences between age groups tend to be ones of degree rather than kind. Young children are more cognitively competent than they often are given credit for, and older children and adults are not quite so cognitively competent as we often think.

7. Children's thinking develops within a social context. Parents, peers, teachers, and the overall society influence what children think about, as well as how and why they come to think in particular ways.

8. We have learned quite a bit about cognitive development, but there is far more left to learn.

A good strategy for reading the rest of this book is to think over these themes now, and try to notice how they apply to different aspects of children's thinking as you encounter them in later chapters.

SUMMARY

For hundreds of years, people who have had contact with children have wondered about such questions as where the children's ideas came from and whether infants perceived the world in the same way as adults. Recent conceptual and methodological advances have greatly improved our ability to explore these and many other questions about children's thinking.

The information-processing approach is an increasingly popular way of thinking about children's thinking. At the heart of this approach is a dramatic metaphor of children trying to deal with all kinds of challenging environments with only limited processing resources to help them. To overcome these processing limits, they adopt a wide variety of strategies for remembering and for solving problems. The approach also raises a variety of important issues about children's thinking and offers useful theories, methods, and languages for addressing these issues. One example of the usefulness of the approach is work on subtraction "bugs." This work indicates that many of students' errors on multidigit subtraction problems reflect systematic misunderstandings rather than random missteps. A program based on this research teaches teachers how to diagnose the misunderstandings that lead to students' errors, which is an important first step toward clearing up the students' problems.

A number of the most important questions about children's thinking have long histories. Do children proceed through qualitatively different stages of thinking, or is development continuous? How do changes in children's thinking occur? What means are most effective for finding out about what children know and can learn? What is the relation between children's and adults' thinking? These continue to be among the most basic questions about cognitive development.

The book is organized into three sections. The first section discusses broad perspectives on children's thinking, such as those provided by Piaget's theory and by the information processing approach. The second section examines five specific aspects of children's thinking: perception, language, memory, conceptual understanding, and academic skills. The third section summarizes what is known about children's thinking and identifies questions and issues that seem critical for the future. The goal in all three sections is to identify general themes and ways of looking at development that apply across many areas of children's thinking, as well as describing particular aspects of how children think.

A number of themes also emerge as important throughout the book. Among these are the importance of the questions of what develops and how development occurs, the continuing challenge to children of coping with complex tasks while only having limited processing resources, the surprising cognitive competence of infants and young children, and the ways in which what children already know influence how they acquire new information.

RECOMMENDED READINGS

Brown, J. S., & van Lehn, K. (1982). Towards a generative theory of "bugs." In T. Romberg, T. Carpenter, & J. Moser (Eds.), *Addition and subtraction: A developmental perspective.* Hillsdale, NJ: Erlbaum. One of the best examples of how children's patterns of correct answers and errors can be used to determine their underlying reasoning. Also illustrates how analyses of children's thinking can be useful for teachers.

Flavell, J. H. (1971). Stage-related properties of cognitive development. *Cognitive Psychology, 2,* 421–453. An excellent analysis of the nature of stage models of development and how they differ from other models.

Gelman, R., & Gallistel, C. R. (1978). *The child's understanding of number.* Cambridge, MA: Harvard University Press. A thought-provoking demonstration that even a task as simple and straightforward as counting objects may reflect understanding of principles.

Keating, D. P., & Bobbitt, B. L. (1978). Individual and developmental differences in cognitive processing components of mental ability. *Child Development, 49,* 155–167. Clear, compelling illustration of the way in which theories and methods originally developed in the context of studying adults can add to our understanding of children's thinking as well.

2
PIAGET'S THEORY OF DEVELOPMENT

At age 7 months, 28 days, I offer him a little bell behind a cushion. So long as he sees the little bell, however small it may be, he tries to grasp it. But if the little bell disappears completely, he stops all searching.

I then resume the experiment, using my hand as a screen. Laurent's arm is outstretched and about to grasp the little bell at the moment I make it disappear behind my hand (which is open and at a distance of about 15 cm. from him). He immediately withdraws his arm, as though the little bell no longer existed. I then shake my hand . . . Laurent watches attentively, greatly surprised to rediscover the sound of the little bell, but he does not try to grasp it. I turn my hand over and he sees the little bell; he then stretches out his hand toward it. I hide the little bell again by changing the position of my hand; Laurent withdraws his hand (Piaget, 1954, p. 39).

What does this infant's odd behavior tell us? Piaget (1954) advanced one provocative interpretation: that Laurent did not search for the bell because he did not know that it still existed. In other words, his failure to search was due to his inability to mentally represent the bell's existence. It was as if the infant's thinking embodied the strongest possible version of the adage "Out of sight, out of mind."

This chapter is the only one in the book whose title includes a person's name as well as a content area. This is no accident. Jean Piaget's contribution to the study of cognitive development is a testimony to how much one man can do to shape an intellectual discipline. Before Piaget began his work, no recognizable field of cognitive development existed. Yet despite thousands of studies on children's thinking having been conducted in the interim, even Piaget's earliest research is still informative. What explains the longevity of Piaget's theory?

Perhaps the basic reason is that Piaget's theory communicates an almost tangible sense of what children's thinking is like. His descriptions feel right. Many of his individual observations are quite surprising, but the general trends that he detects appeal to our intuitions and to our memories of childhood.

A second important reason is that the theory addresses topics that have been of interest to parents, teachers, scientists, and philosophers for hundreds of years. At the most general level, the theory speaks to such questions as "What is intelligence?" and "Where does knowledge come from?" At a more specific level, the theory examines development of the concepts of time, space, number, and other ideas that are among the basic intellectual acquisitions of mankind. Placing the development of such fundamental concepts into a single coherent framework has made Piaget's theory one of the most significant intellectual achievements of our century.

A third reason for the theory's longevity is its exceptional breadth. The theory covers an unusually broad age span, the entire range from infancy through adolescence. It is possible to see concepts such as cause and effect evolving from rudimentary forms in infancy to more complex forms in middle childhood to even more complex forms in adolescence. The theory also encompasses an unusually broad variety of children's achievements at any given age. For example, it brings together 5-year-olds' scientific and mathematical reasoning, their moral judgments, their drawings, their idea of cause and effect, their use of language, and their memory for past events. One of the purposes of scientific theories is to point out the meaning underlying seemingly unrelated facts. Piaget's theory is especially strong on this dimension.

A fourth reason for the theory having endured is that Piaget had the equivalent of a gifted gardener's "green thumb" for making interesting observations. One of these observations was quoted at the outset of this chapter: the one concerning infants' failure to search for objects if they cannot see them. Many other surprising observations will be described throughout the chapter.

Because of the range and complexity of Piaget's theory, it seems worthwhile to approach it first in general terms and then in greater and greater depth. The first section of this chapter provides an overview of Piaget's theory. The second describes children's thinking during each of his four stages of development. The third focuses on his description of the development of several especially important concepts from birth through adolescence. The fourth section is an evaluation of the theory. Table 2–1 depicts this organization.

TABLE 2-1   Chapter Outline

AN OVERVIEW OF PIAGET'S THEORY

Piaget's theory is sufficiently broad and complex that it is easy to lose the forest for the trees. This section provides an overview of the forest.

The Theory as a Whole

To appreciate Piaget's theory, it is essential to understand the motivation behind it. This motivation grew out of Piaget's early interest in biology and philosophy. When he was 11 years old he published his first article, describing a rare albino sparrow he had observed. Between the ages of 15 and 18 he published several more articles, most of them about molluscs. The articles must have been impressive. When Piaget was 18, the head of a natural history museum, who had never met him but who had read his articles, wrote offering the position of curator of the mollusc collection at the museum. Piaget turned down the offer so that he could finish high school.

In addition to this early interest in biology, Piaget was keenly interested in philosophy. He was especially enthusiastic about epistemology, the branch of philosophy concerned with the origins of knowledge. Kant, an 18th-century philosopher who, like Piaget, was most interested in the origins of knowledge, received his closest attention.

The combination of philosophical and biological interests influenced Piaget's later theorizing in several ways. It led to the fundamental question underlying the theory; "Where does knowledge come from?" It also influenced the particular problems Piaget chose to study. He followed Kant in emphasizing space, time, classes, and relations as being central categories of knowledge. At the same time, he opposed Kant's position that these basic types of knowledge were innate to human beings; instead, he believed that children invented the concepts during their lifetimes. Perhaps most important, the joint interest in philosophy and biology suggested to Piaget that long-standing philosophical controversies could be resolved by the application of scientific methods. Just as Darwin attempted to answer the question, "How did people evolve?" Piaget attempted to answer the question, "How does knowledge evolve?"

With this background, we can consider the theory itself. At the most general level of analysis, Piaget was interested in intelligence. By this he meant a more general quality than what is measured on intelligence tests. He believed that intelligence influenced perception, language, morality—in fact, any act involving thinking. It produced both practical responses to particular situations and theoretical understandings of the nature of reality. It was basic to survival, as well as to the enjoyment of life. Piaget also believed that within a person's lifetime, intelligence evolves through a series of qualitatively distinct stages, with the evolution made possible by a set of developmental processes. Below, these stages and developmental processes are discussed.

The Stages of Development

Piaget's theory is a stage theory *par excellence.* As noted in Chapter 1, stage theorists make certain assumptions that distinguish their views from those of others. They assume that children's reasoning in earlier stages differs qualitatively from their reasoning in later ones. They also assume that at a given point in development, children reason similarly on many problems. Finally, they assume that after spending a prolonged period of time "in" a stage, children abruptly make the transition to the next stage. These assumptions have allowed stage theorists to paint a vivid picture of cognitive development.

Piaget's stage theory postulated that all children progress through four stages and that they do so in the same order: first the sensorimotor period, then the preoperational period, then the concrete operational period, and finally the formal operational period. The sensorimotor period typically spans the period from birth to roughly the second birthday, the preoperational period lasts roughly from age 2 to age 6 or 7, the concrete operational period extends from about age 6 or 7 to 11 or 12, and the formal operational period continues from approximately age 11 or 12 through adulthood and old age.

First consider the sensorimotor period, lasting from birth through age 2. At birth, children's cognitive system is limited to motor reflexes. Within a few months, however, children build on these reflexes to develop more sophisticated procedures. They begin to systematically repeat initially inadvertent behaviors, generalize their activities to a wider range of situations, and coordinate them into increasingly lengthy chains of behavior. Children's physical interactions with objects provide the impetus for this development.

The preoperational period encompasses the age range from 2 to 6 or 7 years. The greatest achievement of this period is the acquisition of representational skills: language, mental imagery, and drawing. Perhaps the most dramatic growth takes place in the area of language. Vocabulary increases one hundredfold between 18 and 60 months (McCarthy, 1954), and grammatical and sentence construction patterns become increasingly complex. In Piaget's view, however, preoperational children can use these representational skills only to view the world from their own perspective. They focus their attention too narrowly, often ignoring important information. They also cannot adequately represent transformations, instead being only able to represent static situations.

Concrete operational children (ages 6 or 7 to 11 or 12) can take other points of view, can simultaneously take into account more than one perspective, and can accurately represent transformations as well as static situations. This allows them to solve many problems involving concrete objects and physically possible situations. However, they do not consider all of the logically possible outcomes and do not understand highly abstract concepts.

Formal operations, attained at roughly age 11 or 12, is the crowning achievement of the stage progression. Children who achieve it are said to reason on the basis of theoretical possibilities as well as concrete realities. This broad perspective brings with it the potential for solving many types of problems that children in earlier stages could not hope to conquer. Piaget likened formal operational reasoners to scientists who devise experiments on the basis of theoretical considerations and interpret them within a logical framework. Their particular beliefs and attitudes may need to be revised, but their basic mode of thinking is sufficiently powerful that it will last a lifetime.

Developmental Processes

How do children progress from one stage to another? Piaget viewed three processes as crucial: *assimilation, accommodation,* and *equilibration.*

Assimilation.   Assimilation refers to the way in which people transform incoming information so that it fits within their existing way of thinking. To illustrate, when my older son was 2, he encountered a man who was bald on the top of his head and had long frizzy hair growing out from each side. To my embarrassment, on seeing the man, he gleefully shouted, "Clown, clown." The man apparently possessed the features that separate clowns from other people. Therefore, the boy perceived him in that light.

Inability to assimilate new information to existing ways of thinking sometimes prevents people from forming any meaningful representation of the new material. The music critic Bernard Levin's description of his initial reaction to a Bartok piece provides one such case. Levin noted that when he heard the premiere performance of Bartok's *Concerto for Violin and Orchestra*, early in Bartok's career, neither he nor other critics could make sense of it or later remember it in any detail. When he next heard the piece, almost 20 years later, it seemed eminently musical. Levin's explanation was that in the ensuing period, "I had come to hear the world with different ears" (*London Daily Telegraph*, June 8, 1977). In Piaget's terms, he initially was unable to assimilate the Bartok piece. Twenty years later, he was able to do so.

One interesting type of assimilation that Piaget described is *functional assimilation*, the tendency to use any mental structure that is available. If children or adults have a capacity, they seek to use it, especially when they first acquire it. Illustratively, when my older son was first learning to talk, he spent endless hours talking in his crib, even though no one else was present. He also would turn somersaults over and over again, despite considerable encouragement from his parents to stop. Piaget contrasted this source of motivation with behaviorists' emphases on external reinforcers as motivators of behavior. In reinforcement, the reason for engaging in an activity is the external reward that is obtained. In functional assimilation, the reason for engaging in the activity is the sheer delight children obtain from mastering new skills.

Accommodation.   Accommodation refers to the ways in which people adapt their ways of thinking to new experiences. Returning to the clown anecdote, after biting my lip to suppress a smile, I told my son that the man we had seen was not a clown, that even though his hair was like a clown's he wasn't wearing a funny costume and wasn't trying to make people laugh. I hope that the experience helped his concept of clowns to accommodate to the concept's generally accepted meaning.

Assimilation and accommodation mutually influence each other; assimilation is never present without accommodation and vice versa. On seeing a new object, an infant might try to grasp it as he has other objects (thus assimilating the new object to an existing approach). However, he also would have to adjust his grasp to conform to the shape of the object (thus accommodating his approach as well). The extreme case of assimilation is fantasy play, in which children gloss over the physical characteristics of objects and treat them as if they were what the children are momentarily interpreting them to be. The extreme case of accommodation is imitation, in which children minimize their interpretations and simply mimic what they see. Even at the extremes, elements of each process are present. A child at play still must recognize physical properties (chairs almost never are assimilated as teacups, even in fantasy play). Conversely, when we do not understand what we are doing, imitation often is imperfect (try to repeat verbatim a 15-word Arabic sentence).

Equilibration. Equilibration encompasses both assimilation and accommodation. It refers to the overall interaction between existing ways of thinking and new experience. It also is the keystone of developmental change within Piaget's system. Piaget saw development as the formation of ever more stable equilibria between the child's cognitive system and the external world. That is, the child's model of the world would increasingly resemble reality.

Piaget also suggested that equilibration takes place in three phases. First, children are satisfied with their mode of thought and therefore are in a state of equilibrium. Then they become aware of shortcomings in their existing thinking and are dissatisfied. This constitutes a state of disequilibrium. Finally, they adopt a more sophisticated mode of thought that eliminates the shortcomings of the old one. That is, they reach a more stable equilibrium.

To illustrate the equilibration process, suppose a girl thought that animals were the only living things (in fact, Richards and Siegler [1984] found that most 4- to 7-year-olds do think this). At some point she would hear plants referred to as being alive. This new information might create a state of disequilibrium, in which the girl was unsure what it meant to be alive. After all, plants share few obvious features with animals. Eventually she would discover commonalities between plants and animals that are critical to the meaning of being alive: the ability to grow and to reproduce, in particular. These discoveries would pave the way for a new understanding, in which the girl identified life with the ability to grow and to reproduce. The new understanding would constitute a more stable equilibrium, since further observations would not call it into question (unless the girl later became unusually interested in certain viruses and bacteria whose status as living things continues to be debated by biologists.)

The above overview of assimilation, accommodation, and equilibration might create an impression that these change processes apply solely to specific, short-term cognitive changes. In fact, Piaget was especially interested in their capacity to produce far-reaching, longer-term changes, such as the change from one developmental stage to the next. Illustratively, the particular realizations that frizzy hair that looks like a clown's does not make its bearer a clown, that things that do not move can still be alive, and that the sun looking like gold does not mean it is made of gold are part of a more general trend from preoperational to concrete operational reasoning. Children generalize the assimilations, accommodations, and equilibrations involved in these particular changes into a general shift from emphasizing external appearances to emphasizing deeper, enduring qualities.

Orienting Assumptions

The child as scientific problem solver.   The basic metaphor underlying Piaget's work was a likening of children's thinking to that of scientists solving problems. This metaphor emerges most clearly in the account of formal operations reasoning, in which preadolescents and adolescents are asked to solve classic physics problems. Even in infancy, however, the comparison is clear. When infants systematically vary the height at which they drop food from their highchair to the floor to see what will happen, Piaget detects the beginnings of scientific experimentation.

At least three considerations led Piaget to concentrate on problem solving. One was his views concerning what development was. Piaget viewed development as a form of adaptation to reality. A problem can be viewed as a miniature reality. The way children solved problems thus could lead to insights about how they adapted to all kinds of challenges that life posed to them.

A second reason why Piaget emphasized problem solving relates to his views about how and why development occurs. Equilibration only happens when some problem arises that disturbs a child's existing equilibrium. Thus, problems, which by their very nature challenge existing understandings, have the potential for leading to cognitive growth. If encountering problems is indeed a main motivator of cognitive growth, then an interest in cognitive growth would naturally lead to an interest in problem solving.

A third reason for Piaget's focus on problem solving concerns the insights that can be gained by observing children's reactions to unfamiliar situations. Piaget noted that everyday activities may be performed by rote and thus reveal little about children's reasoning. By contrast, to the extent that children are unfamiliar with problems, their solution strategies may reveal their own logic.

The role of activity.   Piaget emphasized cognitive activity as the means through which development occurs. Assimilation, accommodation, and equilibration all are active processes by which the mind transforms, and is transformed by, incoming information. As Gruber and Voneche (1977) noted, it was significant that Piaget titled one of his earliest books *The Child's Construction of Reality*. Within Piaget's approach, reality is not waiting to be found; children must construct it from their own mental and physical actions.

This distinction between a found reality and a constructed reality is analogous to the distinction between a Xerox copy of a picture of a bridge and an engineer's model of the forces operating on the bridge. The Xerox copy would simply reflect the superficial appearance of the bridge. The engineer's model would emphasize the relations among components and how they combined to distribute stresses. Piaget believed that children's mental representations, like the engineer's model, emphasize active functions and mechanisms.

Methodological assumptions. Early in his career, Piaget perceived the trade-off between the precision and replicability that accompany standardized experimental procedures and the rich descriptions and theoretical insights that can emerge from flexible interview procedures. He also recognized the trade-off between the developmental continuities that can be demonstrated by observing individual children over many years and the greater generality that may emerge from observing large groups of children at one point in time. Yet a third trade-off involved the unexpected information that can emerge from talking with children and having them explain their reasoning, and the possibility of underestimating young children's reasoning because of their inarticulateness.

Recognizing these trade-offs, Piaget used different methods to study different topics. His studies of infants, conducted early in his career, were based on intense and repeated observations of his own children, Jacqueline, Laurent, and Lucienne. His early studies of moral reasoning, causation, play, and dreams relied almost entirely on children's explanations of their reasoning. His later studies of numbers, time, velocity, separation of variables, and proportionality relied on a combination of children's interactions with physically present materials and their explanations of their reasoning.

Generally, when the choice was between richness and standardization, Piaget opted for richness. This choice may have led him astray at times. Some of his conclusions seem today to be due to his methods' underestimating children's knowledge. However, his choice of methods also resulted in many discoveries that no one else had made using more standardized procedures.

Possessing this overview of Piaget's theory, we now can examine the major trends that characterize his four hypothesized periods of development. The goal is to communicate the basic nature of children's thinking at different times in life. To present as clean a description as possible, I will avoid phrases such as "Piaget said," "Piaget believed," and "Piaget argued." These qualifying phrases should be understood, since many of the claims are controversial. Before getting into the controversies, though, we need to know just how Piaget saw children's thinking.

PIAGET'S STAGE MODEL OF DEVELOPMENT

The Sensorimotor Period (Birth to Roughly 2 Years)

Several years ago, at the first class meeting of a developmental psychology course I was teaching, I asked each student to name the five most important aspects of intelligence in infancy, early childhood, later childhood, and adolescence. A number of students commented that they found it odd to describe infants as having intelligence at all. By far the most frequently named characteristics of infants' intelligence were physical coordination, alertness, and ability to recognize people and objects. It was evidence of Piaget's genius that he perceived much more than this. He saw the beginnings of some of humankind's most sophisticated thought processes in infants' early flailings and graspings.

Piaget's account of the development of sensorimotor intelligence constitutes a theory within a theory. Infants are said to progress through six stages of intellectual development within a two-year period. This might seem like too large a number of stages for such a brief time span, but when we consider the immense cognitive differences between a newborn baby and a 2-year-old, the number does not seem unreasonable. With this introduction, we can consider the six stages of infant development.

Stage 1: Modification of reflexes (birth to roughly 1 month).   Newborn infants enter the world possessing many reflexes. They suck when objects are placed in their mouths, close their fingers around objects that come into contact with their hands, focus on the edges of objects with their eyes, turn their heads toward noises, and so on. These seemingly primitive responses constitute the building blocks of intelligence within Piaget's system.

Even within the first month after birth, infants begin to modify the responses to make them more adaptive. In the first days, they suck quite similarly regardless of the type of object that is in their mouth. Later in the first month, however, they suck differently on a milk-bearing nipple than on a harder, drier finger, and differently on both of them than on the side of their hand. Thus, even in the first month out of the womb, infants begin to accommodate to new situations.

Stage 2: Primary circular reactions (roughly 1 to 4 months).   By the second month, infants exhibit *primary circular reactions.* The term *circular* is used here in the sense of a repetitive cycle of events. In primary circular reactions, if infants inadvertently produce some interesting effect, they attempt to duplicate it by performing the same action. If they are successful, the new instance of the interesting outcome triggers another similar cycle, which in turn can trigger another cycle, and so on.

These primary circular reactions are possible because infants have begun to coordinate actions that they originally performed only as separate reflexes. In Stage 1, infants grasp objects that come into contact with their palms. They also suck on objects that come into their mouths. During Stage 2, infants put these actions together. They bring to their mouths objects that their hands grasp, and grasp objects with their hands that they are sucking on. Thus, the reflexes have already begun to serve as building blocks for more complex activities.

Primary circular reactions are more versatile than the earlier reflexes and allow infants to learn a great deal about the world. However, they also are limited in at least three ways. First, the 1- to 4-month-olds only try to reproduce the exact behavior that produced the original interesting event. Second, their actions are poorly integrated and have a large trial-and-error component. Third, they only try to repeat actions where the outcome involves their own bodies, as occurs in sucking a finger.

Stage 3: Secondary circular reactions (roughly 4 to 8 months). In this stage, infants become increasingly interested in outcomes occurring beyond the limits of their own bodies. For example, they become interested in batting balls with their hands and watching them roll away. Piaget labeled the activities *secondary circular reactions.* Like all circular reactions, these activities are repeated over and over. Unlike the primary circular reactions, though, the interesting outcome (such as the ball rolling away) occurs beyond the child's body. For Piaget, the external world was secondary in children's thinking to their own body—thus the name *secondary* circular reactions.

Infants also make considerable progress toward more efficiently organizing the components of their circular reactions between 4 and 8 months. Piaget described instances in which, after he started a mobile swinging, his children kicked their legs to continue the movement. As in the primary circular reactions, infants seemed only to be trying to reinstate the original amusing occurrences. However, they could do so more efficiently. They reacted more quickly to the original event and wasted less motion in trying to repeat it.

At this point it is tempting to conclude that infants understand the causal connection between their actions and the effects of their actions. Piaget was reluctant to credit them with this understanding, though. Rather, he thought that infants' activities were not sufficiently voluntary to say that they had independent goals. In the first month, infants' behavior simply involved reacting reflexively; between 1 and 8 months they would form goals directly suggested to them by immediate events in the environment; only after 8 months would they form true, mentally generated goals, independent of immediate events in the environment.

Stage 4: Coordination of secondary reactions (roughly 8 to 12 months). Infants approaching one year of age become able to coordinate two or more secondary circular reactions into an efficient routine. Piaget (1952) observed his son Laurent combine the two activities of knocking a barrier out of his way and grasping an object. When Piaget put a pillow in front of a matchbox that Laurent liked, the boy pushed the pillow aside and grabbed the box. In earlier stages, placing the pillow in front of the matchbox might have led the boy to forget entirely about the box.

This example also illustrates another major development that occurs as children approach their first birthday. They clearly understand that if they produce certain causes, particular effects must necessarily follow. Thus, the child knows that pushing the pillow aside will provide a clear path to the matchbox.

Stage 5: Tertiary circular reactions (roughly 12 to 18 months).   With the onset of *tertiary circular reactions*, shortly before 1 year of age, infants transcend the remaining limits on their circular reactions. They actively search for new ways to interact with objects, and actively explore the potential uses to which objects can be put. They deliberately vary both their own actions in producing the event and the objects on which they act. As implied by the "circular reaction" label, they still repeat their actions again and again. Unlike previously, though, they now deliberately vary both their own actions in producing the event and the objects on which they act. Thus, the activities involve similar rather than identical behaviors. The following description of Piaget's son Laurent gives a flavor for the developments in this period.

> He grasps in succession a celluloid swan, a box, etc., stretches out his arm, and lets them fall. He distinctly varies the positions of the fall. Sometimes he stretches out his arm vertically, sometimes he holds it obliquely, in front of or behind his eyes, etc. When the object falls in a new position (for example on his pillow), he lets it fall two or three times more on the same place, as though to study the spatial relation; then he modifies the situation (Piaget, 1951, p. 269).

These changes from primary to secondary to tertiary circular reactions show just how far infants come in the first year and a half. The primary circular reactions, first seen between 1 and 4 months, involve repetitions of events whose outcomes center on the infants' own bodies, such as putting their fingers in their mouths. The secondary circular reactions, first seen between 4 and 8 months, again involve repetition of an event that by chance produced an interesting outcome, but the interesting outcome is at least slightly removed from the infants' bodies (e.g., the ball rolling away from them). The tertiary circular reactions, first seen between 12 and 18 months, involve deliberate variations on the behavior whose outcome was originally interesting, and thus reflect clear goals.

These developments are useful for thinking about a broad range of developments in infancy. At first, infants' activities center on their own bodies; later, they increasingly center on the external world. Goals begin at a concrete level (dropping an object) and become increasingly abstract (varying the heights from which objects are dropped). Correspondence between intentions and behaviors becomes increasingly precise, and exploration of the world becomes increasingly venturesome.

Stage 6: Beginnings of representational thought (roughly 18 to 24 months). The developments in this age range could as easily be placed in the preoperational period as in the sensorimotor period. In the sensorimotor period, children can only act; they cannot form internal mental representations of objects and events. In the preoperational period, children can form such internal mental operations. The following description communicates almost literally the way in which representations are internalized during the last half of the second year. Piaget has been playing with his daughter Lucienne. The game involves hiding a watch chain inside an otherwise empty matchbox. Previously, he has left the matchbox open far enough that Lucienne could get the chain out, but now he has closed it far enough that the chain stays inside even when the matchbox is turned over.

> She looks at the slit with great attention; then, several times in succession, she opens and shuts her mouth, at first slightly, then wider and wider! Apparently, Lucienne understands the existence of a cavity subjacent to the slit and wishes to enlarge the cavity. The attempt at representation which she thus furnishes is expressed plastically, that is to say, due to inability to think out the situation in words or clear visual images, she uses a simple motor indication as "signifier" or symbol (Piaget, 1951; p. 338).

As Lucienne opens her mouth, symbolizing her desire for the opening in the matchbox to become wider, we can almost see her representation of the situation becoming internalized. That is, the representation is moving from her external actions to her mind. Such internalized representations are the hallmark of the preoperational period.

The Preoperational Period (Roughly 2 Years to 6 or 7 Years)

Miller (1983) nicely captured children's position as they complete the sensorimotor period and enter the preoperational period. She likened them to mountain climbers who, after a hard climb, discover that what they have climbed is merely a foothill to Mt. Everest. By the end of the sensorimotor stage, infants have become toddlers. They interact smoothly with objects and people in their immediate environment. These achievements may not be paralleled by the development of true internal representations, however. Sensorimotor-period children may be able to throw a ball, catch a ball, and even name it "ball," but cannot think about the ball unless it is present. The development of internal mental representations that allow children to think about objects in their absence is the key development of the preoperational period. It is termed the *semiotic function.*

The semiotic function. Piaget suggested that the earliest sign of internal representations is *deferred imitation,* the imitation of an activity hours or days after the activity occurred. It is an interesting phenomenon, because for children to imitate an activity long after it occurred, they must have formed a durable internal representation of the original activity. How else could they imitate it?

Not until late in the sensorimotor period do children exhibit deferred imitation. One of the best-known illustrations of this phenomenon involves a description of Piaget's daughter Jacqueline kicking and screaming in her playpen.

> At 1;4(3) [Piaget's notation for one year, four months, and three days] Jacqueline had a visit from a little boy of 1;6 whom she used to see from time to time, and who, in the course of the afternoon, got into a terrible temper. He screamed as he tried to get out of a playpen and pushed it backward, stamping his feet. Jacqueline stood watching him in amazement, never having witnessed such a scene before. The next day, she herself screamed in her playpen and tried to move it, stamping her foot lightly several times in succession (Piaget, 1951, p. 63).

Jacqueline had never, to her father's knowledge, engaged in these behaviors before. Thus, an internal representation of the playmate's tantrum must have helped her reproduce the scene.

Piaget distinguished between two types of internal representations: *symbols* and *signs*. The distinction is not identical to the standard English distinction between the two. Rather, it is the difference between idiosyncratic representations intended only for one's personal use (symbols) and conventional representations intended for communication (signs).

Early in the preoperational period, children make extensive use of idiosyncratic (symbolic) representations. They may choose a particular piece of cloth to represent their pillow or a popsicle stick to represent a gun. Typically, these personal symbols physically resemble the object they represent. The cloth's texture is similar to that of the pillow, and both are comforting; the popsicle's shape and texture are something like those of a gun barrel. Signs, by contrast, often do not resemble the objects or events they signify. The word *cow* does not look like a cow, nor does the numeral 6 have any inherent similarity to six objects.

As children develop, they make less use of the idiosyncratic symbols and more of the conventional signs. This shift is an important achievement, as it greatly expands their ability to communicate. The transition from personal to publicly accepted representations is not an easy one, however.

The difficulty is illustrated in Piaget's description of *egocentric communication*. Piaget applied the term "egocentric" to preschool-age children not to castigate them for being inconsiderate, but rather in a more literal sense. Their thinking about the external world is always in terms of their own perspective, their own position within it. Their use of language reflects this adherence to their own perspective, particularly their frequent use of idiosyncratic symbols that are meaningless to other people.

Although even very young children use signs as well as symbols, they at first do not use them consistently in a social manner. Figure 2–1 portrays an

FIGURE 2-1 Two young children more or less having a conversation—an example of egocentric communication.

instance of this frequently observed aspect of young children's conversations. Preschoolers sometimes speak right past each other, without appearing to pay any attention to what others are saying. Even attentive adults often cannot figure out what the children mean.

Between the ages of 4 and 7, speech becomes less egocentric. One of the earliest signs of progress can be seen in children's verbal quarrels. The fact that a boy's verbal statements elicit a playmate's disagreement indicates that the playmate is at least paying attention to a perspective other than his own.

Piaget suggested that mental imagery was, like language, an aspect of the semiotic function, since it allowed children to represent internally objects and events. He also suggested that the development of mental imagery resembled that of language. As children became able to describe situations verbally, they also became able to represent them as images. Further, he believed that the initial representations in both domains are limited to the child's own perspective. That is, they are egocentric.

Although language, mental-imagery, and many other skills grow greatly during the preoperational period, Piaget's heaviest emphasis was on what preoperational children cannot do. He viewed them as unable to solve many problems that were critical indicators of logical reasoning. Even the name, "*pre*operational", suggests deficiencies rather than strengths.

One of the limits on preschoolers' thinking has already been mentioned: their egocentrism. This trait is evident in their conversations and also in their ability to take different spatial perspectives. Piaget sat 4-year-olds down at a square table in front of a model of three mountains. The task was to choose which of several photographs corresponded to what children sitting at chairs at different points around the table would see. To solve the problem, children needed to recognize that their own perspective was not the only one possible and to mentally rotate the arrangement they saw to correspond to what the view would be elsewhere. This was impossible for most of the 4-year-olds; they could not identify what the view would be from the other positions.

A second related limit on preschoolers' thinking is that it centers on individual, perceptually striking features of objects, to the exclusion of other, less striking features. One good example of this *centration* is found on a task that Piaget developed to measure children's understanding of the concept of time. His interest in this concept has an interesting history.

In 1928, Albert Einstein posed a question to Piaget: In what order do children acquire the concepts of time and velocity? The question was prompted by an issue within physics. Within Newtonian theory, time is a basic quality and velocity is defined in terms of it (velocity = distance/time). Within relativity theory, in contrast, time and velocity are defined in terms of each other, with neither concept being more basic. Einstein wanted to know whether understanding of either or both concepts was present from birth; whether children understood one before the other; and if so, how initial understanding of one influenced subsequent understanding of the other.

Almost 20 years later, Piaget (1946a; 1946b) published a two-volume, 500-page reply to Einstein's query. Piaget concluded that children did not understand time, distance, or velocity in infancy or early childhood. Only in the concrete operations period would they finally grasp the three concepts.

To test this view, Piaget presented a task involving two toy trains running along parallel tracks in the same direction (Figure 2–2). After the cars stopped moving, Piaget asked the question, "Which train traveled for the longer time (or the faster speed, or the farther distance)?"

Most 4- and 5-year-olds focused entirely on a single dimension, usually the stopping point. They chose the train that stopped farther down the track as having traveled faster, for the longer time, and for the greater distance. Stated differently, they ignored when the trains started, when they stopped, and the total time for which they traveled.

The example illustrates another of the basic qualities of children's thinking in the preoperational period. They tend to focus on static states rather than transformations. The point where each train ended constitutes a static position, readily perceivable and available for repeated inspection. The dimensions of time, speed, and distance are more fleeting and, in the case of time and distance at least, not as easy to perceive. The single dimensions on which preoperational period children focus most often are static states; the dimensions they ignore often involve transformations.

Thus, 2- to 6-year-olds are viewed as having difficulty taking perspectives other than their own, as paying too much attention to individual, perceptually salient dimensions and ignoring other dimensions, and as focusing on static states rather than on transformations. All these descriptions suggest that such young children think about the world clearly, but too simply

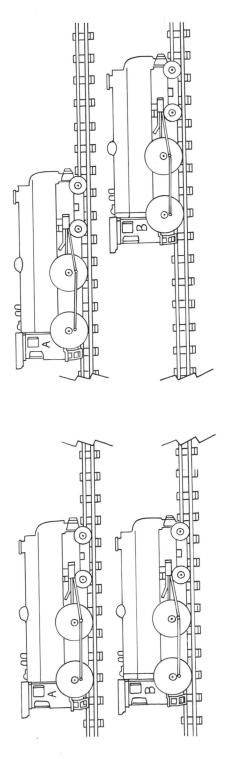

FIGURE 2-2 Train apparatus similar to the one used by Piaget to examine children's understanding of time. Children were asked which train traveled for the greater amount of time. Five-year-olds typically chose the train that stopped farther down the track as the one that traveled for more time. Thus, they would pick the bottom train in this figure as having traveled for the longer time.

and rigidly. They largely surmount these limitations in the next period of development.

The Concrete Operations Period (Roughly 6 or 7 Years to 11 or 12 Years)

The central development in the concrete operations period is the acquisition of *operations*. This is the achievement for which all development up to this time has been prelude. In the sensorimotor period, children learned to operate physically on the environment. In the preoperational period, they learned to internally represent static states. Finally, in the concrete operations period, they become able to manipulate mentally their internal representations, much as they earlier had become able to manipulate physical objects. These operations, or internalized actions as they are sometimes called, make children's thinking much more powerful.

Two crucial features of operations are that they are reversible and that they are organized with other operations into larger systems. Saying that an operation is reversible means that its steps can be executed in reverse order and the original situation recreated. Saying that operations are organized into larger systems means that the child integrates a number of different ways of looking at a problem and realizes their mutual implications for each other.

Understanding what operations are helps to clarify the close relation between the pre*operational* and the concrete *operational* periods. Piaget sometimes indicated that these two periods are best viewed as two parts of a larger stage, spanning the ages from 2 to 11 years. The preoperational period laid the groundwork for operations by enabling children to represent events internally. In the concrete operations period, children become able to manipulate the internal representations and thus realize the potential for flexible and powerful thinking that they make possible.

The importance of operations can most easily be illustrated in the context of conservation problems. Consider children's understanding of three interesting types of conservation: conservation of number, liquid quantity, and solid quantity. Although these three conservation problems differ among themselves in certain respects, all share a basic three-phase procedure (Figure 2–3). In the first phase, children see two or more identical objects or sets of objects—two identical rows of checkers, two identical glasses of water, two identical clay cylinders, and so on. Once the children agree that the two are equal on some dimension, such as the number of objects, the second phase begins. Here, one object or set of objects is transformed in a way that changes its appearance but does not affect the dimension of interest. Children might see the row of checkers lengthened, the water poured into a differently shaped glass, the clay cylinder remolded into a ball, and so on. Finally, in the third phase, children are asked whether the dimension of interest, which they earlier said was equal for the two choices, remains equal following the transformation of one of them. The correct answer invariably is "yes."

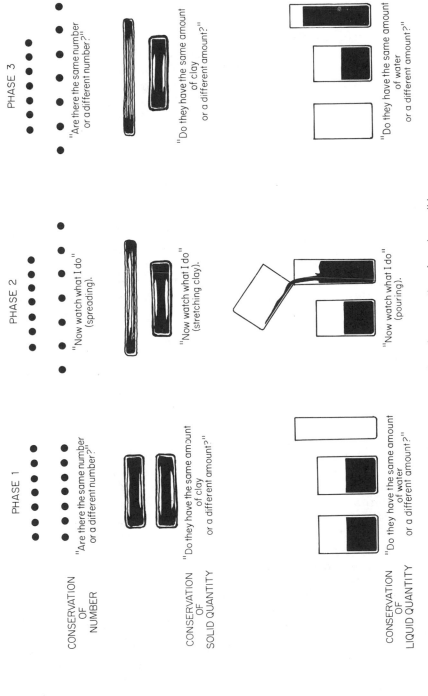

FIGURE 2-3 Procedures used to test children's understanding of conservation of number, solid quantity, and liquid quantity.

39

These problems seem trivially easy to adults and older children. However, 5-year-olds consistently answer them incorrectly. On number-conservation problems, they claim that the number of checkers in the longer row is greater (regardless of the actual numbers in each row). On conservation-of-liquid-quantity problems, they claim that the liquid quantity in the glass with the taller column of liquid is greater (regardless of the cross-sectional areas of the glasses). On conservation-of-solid-quantity problems, they believe there is a greater quantity of clay in the longer clay cylinder (again regardless of the cross-sectional areas).

Considering what children need to do to solve conservation problems makes understandable the 5-year-olds' difficulty. They must be able to mentally represent the spreading, pouring, or remolding transformation involved in the problem. They also must not focus all their attention on the perceptually salient dimension of height or length; they need to consider cross-sectional area and density as well. Finally, they need to realize that even though the transformed object may seem to have more of the dimension in question, it might not. That is, they need to understand that their own perspective can be misleading, and that they therefore need to take a nonegocentric attitude and approach the problem logically. Each of these is difficult for 5-year-olds to do.

In the concrete operations stage, children master all three conservation problems. They also master the train problem (Figure 2-2) that was used to measure understanding of time, distance, and velocity. Piaget explained their mastery of these and many other concepts in terms of the children now possessing mental operations. These operations allowed them to represent transformations as well as static states.

Children's explanations of their reasoning on conservation problems are especially revealing. When 5-year-olds are asked to explain why the amount of water has changed, they regularly point to the fact that the water in the new glass has reached a higher level. When 8-year-olds are asked to explain why the amount of water remains the same, they point to the nature of the transformation ("You just poured it"), to changes in the less-striking dimension offsetting the changes in the more-striking one ("The water in here is taller, but the water in here is wider), to the water looking different but really being the same, and to the reversible nature of the operation ("You could pour it back and it would be the same".) Interestingly, 5-year-olds will grant many of these same points. After seeing the water being poured back and forth, they realize that you could pour it back and it would look the same. They also agree that the water in the one glass is wider while the water in the other is taller, that it is the same water, and that all that was done to the water was to pour it. However, unlike older children, they do not see these facts as necessarily implying that the two glasses must have the same amount of water.

Although children in the concrete operations period become capable of solving many problems, certain types of abstract reasoning remain beyond them. Some of these problems involve reasoning in sophisticated ways about contrary-to-fact propositions ("If people could know the future, would they be happier than they are now?"). Others involve treating their own thinking as something to be thought about. To quote one adolescent, "I was thinking about my future, and then I began to think about why I was thinking about why I was thinking about my future" (Mussen, Conger, Kagan, & Geiwitz, 1979). Still others involve thinking about abstract scientific concepts such as force, inertia, torque, and acceleration. These types of ideas become possible in the formal operations period.

The Formal Operations Period (Roughly 11 or 12 Years Onward)

Formal operations resemble concrete operations in two important senses: Both involve mental operations and both are reversible. However, in formal operations, the particular reversible operations are organized into more elaborate systems, with the original reversible operations functioning as the basic unit within the more elaborate system. For this reason, formal operations often are described as being operations on operations. Simply put, thinking in this period is more abstract. The above story of the boy thinking about why he was thinking about why he was thinking about his thinking illustrates the aptness of this description.

Perhaps the most striking development during the formal operations period is that adolescents begin to see the particular reality in which they live as only one of several imaginable realities. This leads at least some of them to think about alternative organizations of the world and about deep questions concerning the nature of existence, truth, justice, and morality. As Inhelder and Piaget (1958) put it, "Each one has his own ideas (and usually he believes they are his own) which liberate him from childhood and allow him to place himself as the equal of adults" (pp. 340–41). From this perspective, it is no coincidence that many people first acquire a taste for science fiction during adolescence.

Where possible, formal operational reasoners not only consider many possibilities, they consider all possibilities. This allows them to achieve a broad overview, to plan in considerable detail what they are going to do, and to interpret whatever they do within the total context. In contrast, concrete operational children tend to reason on a case-by-case basis and to plan less thoroughly. This sometimes leads them to misinterpret what they see and to leap to conclusions too quickly.

All these differences between formal and concrete operational reasoners are evident in Inhelder and Piaget's (1958) descriptions of children's and adolescents' approaches to a chemistry problem. The task was to generate all possible combinations of the contents of four chemical beakers and then to infer what caused the mixtures sometimes to turn yellow. Concrete operational children typically generated a number of the possible pairs of the chemicals, then tried all four together, and then generated a few of the possible sets of three. They often repeated combinations they already had tried and left out other combinations altogether. In contrast, formal operational children first devised a systematic plan for generating all possible combinations of the chemicals. Then they used their plan to generate the combinations without redundancies or omissions.

The formal operational reasoners' more planful approach also helped them to draw a more appropriate conclusion about when and why the yellow color appeared. Concrete operations children often stopped trying combinations after they found a single combination that turned the solution yellow. They were content to say that that combination of chemicals was the cause. Formal operations children, who tried all sixteen possible combinations, eventually learned that two different combinations produced the yellow color. What these combinations had in common was the presence of two of the chemicals and the absence of a third. Therefore, these adolescents reached the correct conclusion that two of the chemicals were necessary to produce the change in color, that a third would prevent it from happening even if the first two were present, and that the fourth had no effect. Their focusing on the system of possible combinations allowed them to obtain the relevant data. Their identification of the relation between the events that actually produced the outcome of interest and the total set of events and outcomes allowed them to solve the problem.

THE DEVELOPMENT OF SOME CRITICAL CONCEPTS

The broad sweep of Piaget's descriptions of children's thinking emerges most clearly in his accounts of the development of particular concepts. Some concepts where his descriptions are especially interesting are conservation, classes, and relations. He traced the development of each of these from the earliest origins in the sensorimotor period, through more and more sophisticated refinements in the preoperational and concrete operational periods, to the highest level of mastery in the formal operations period. People do not usually think of infants' and young children's early understandings as having anything to do with their later thinking. Part of Piaget's genius was that he saw the connection.

Conservation

Conservation in the sensorimotor period.   During the sensorimotor period, children acquire a simple but important part of the conservation concept. This might be labeled the conservation of existence, though Piaget chose to call it *object permanence.* For adults, it is the most trivial of matters that objects do not just disappear from the world (although they sometimes seem to). When objects move away from our gaze, we move our eyes to track their paths. When they are hidden, we remove objects that might be covering them and look for them from different angles. Piaget observed that infants do not show such searching. He did not attribute their failure to do so to poor coordination or to loss of interest, but rather to their not understanding that the objects still existed. Piaget's account portrays infants' steadily growing understanding that objects do have a permanent existence through all six stages of the sensorimotor period.

In the first stage, from birth to 1 month, infants look at objects in their visual fields. However, if an object moves away, they do not follow it with their eyes. Thus, an infant will look at her mother's face if the face is directly above it, but will look quickly at something else if the mother moves aside. Next, between 1 and 4 months, infants continue looking at the place where an object disappeared, but do not actively attempt to find out where it went. If they are playing with a toy and drop it, they continue looking at their hand rather than looking at the floor. Between about 4 and 8 months, they anticipate where moving objects will go, and look for them there. However, if the object is completely covered, they do not attempt to retrieve it (as illustrated in the quotation at the beginning of this chapter).

In Stage 4 of the sensorimotor period, between 8 and 12 months, infants begin to search for objects that have disappeared. This indicates that they realize objects do have a permanent existence even if they cannot be seen. Under certain circumstances, however, 8- to 12-month-olds make an interesting mistake, known as the *Stage 4 error*. If they see an object hidden twice in succession under the same container, they retrieve the object from there each time. If they then see the same object hidden under a different container, however, they look under the original container. Even though they have just seen the object being placed under the new container, they ignore this information and search where they had found it earlier. It is as if this original container had assumed an independent status as a hiding place.

In Stage 5, between roughly 12 and 18 months, they stop making the Stage 4 error and search wherever they last saw the object hidden. However, they remain unable to deal efficiently with invisible displacements. When a toy is first hidden under a cover, and then the toy and cover together are hidden under a pillow, and then the cover is removed, the 12- to 18-month-old does not look under the pillow. By 18 to 24 months, however, babies understand even this type of complex displacement and immediately search in the right place.

I remember that when I first read about Piaget's research on object permanence, I found his account fantastic. I mean the term *fantastic* both in the sense of extremely interesting and in the sense of extremely improbable. It seemed to me much more likely that the infants below 8 months failed to search for objects either because they were not well enough coordinated to do so or because they had lost interest.

An experiment by Bower and Wishart (1972), however, renders unlikely both of my initial interpretations. Five-month-olds saw a toy hidden under a transparent cup. The large majority of infants retrieved it. Then the infants saw the same toy hidden under a cup they could not see through. Only 2 of 16 retrieved it. This experiment, in addition to ruling out motoric immaturity as an explantion for the lack of searching, also ruled out absence of motivation. If infants lacked sufficient interest in the toy to retrieve it, why would they retrieve it when it was hidden under the transparent cup? Thus, at least the most obvious alternative explanations to Piaget's account of the development of object-permanence concept can be ruled out.

Conservation in the preoperational and concrete operational periods. In the sensorimotor period, babies come to realize that the existence of objects is conserved over certain types of transformations. In the preoperational and concrete operational periods, children come to realize that certain qualities of objects also are conserved under transformations that may change their appearance. We discussed several of these earlier. Spreading out objects increases the length of the row but leaves unchanged the number of objects. Pouring water from one glass to a taller, thinner glass changes the height of the liquid but leaves unchanged the amount of water. By the end of the concrete operational period, children realize that a great many tangible dimensions are conserved over transformations that alter their appearances: number, amount, length, weight, perimeter, area, and so on.

Conservation in the formal operational period.   During the formal operations period, adolescents become able to conserve dimensions that themselves involve transformations (they understand transformations of transformations). One such problem, presented by Inhelder and Piaget (1958), involved conservation of motion. A spring-powered plunger shot balls of various sizes into motion. Children needed to predict where the balls would stop, to explain why some balls stopped earlier than others, and to explain why balls stopped at all.

Children's reasoning on this problem at different ages illustrated the types of reasoning that Piaget thought to be fundamental at those ages. Preoperational children often focus on only one dimension. They might consistently predict that a big ball will go farther because it is stronger. Concrete operational children begin to rethink the problem. Rather than focusing on what factors in the ball cause it to go farther, they begin to consider what factors inside and outside the ball cause it to stop. However, they are unable to consistently maintain the new perspective and frequently vacillate between it and the old one.

By the formal operations stage, children completely change their perspective. Their reasoning now is that objects in motion continue to move unless something interferes. Thus, motion is conserved. They also can conceptualize the problem in idealized terms ("If there were no air resistance. . ."). This way of thinking is a distinctive formal operations achievement because it involves conservation of a dimension, motion, that itself involves a transformation. In addition, it illustrates how adolescents proceed from the actual to the possible, since no adolescent has experienced an environment without air resistance or friction.

Classes and Relations

Another of Piaget's insights was seeing the connection between children's understanding of classes and relations. This connection can be illustrated with regard to numbers. What does it mean when we say that a girl understands the concept of "three"? She should be able to see what three balls, three cars, and three spoons have in common. That is, she should understand that they are all members of a certain class—the class of three-member sets. At the same time, she also should understand the relation of this class to other classes—larger than sets with two members and smaller than sets with four. As will be evident in the following account, Piaget viewed children as originally thinking of classes and relations as separate ideas, but eventually organizing them into a single, powerful system of operations.

Understanding of classes and relations in the sensorimotor period. Piaget contended that infants classify objects according to the objects' functions. He illustrated this point by describing his daughter Lucienne's reaction to a plastic parrot that sat atop her bassinet. Lucienne liked to make the parrot move by kicking her feet while lying in the bassinet. At 6 months of age she made similar kicking motions when she saw the parrot some distance away. By 7 months she abbreviated her motion, moving her feet in short distinct arcs when she was out of the bassinet. Piaget interpreted this as Lucienne thinking, "That's the parrot. It swings when I kick my feet." Far more sophisticated categories are seen as evolving from this initial functional classification.

Understanding of relations, like understanding of classes, is seen as developing out of sensorimotor actions. Piaget described his children at 3 and 4 months as being greatly amused by the relation between their actions and the consequences of those actions. The more vigorously they acted, the greater reaction they produced. More vigorous kicking produced more vigorous swinging of objects on the bassinet, more vigorous shaking of a rattle produced louder noises, and so on.

Toward the end of the first year, according to Piaget, infants also develop a crude notion of quantitative relations. In trying to repeat words, the 10-month-old Laurent roughly calibrated his number of syllables to his father's. When Piaget said "papa", Laurent did also. When his father said "papapapapapapa," Laurent said "papapapa." Piaget inferred that Laurent was trying to relate his own number of "papas" to his father's.

Understanding of classes and relations in the preoperational period. Children progress considerably in classificatory ability during the preoperational period. This progress is evident when children are asked to put together the objects that go together from among a group of blocks including large blue squares and triangles, small blue squares and triangles, large red squares and triangles, and small red squares and triangles. Thus, children could arrange the objects on the basis of size, color, or shape.

Early in the preoperational period, children might put together a small red square and a small blue square and then add a small red triangle, a large blue triangle, and a large red triangle. Their behavior gives the impression that they start out thinking about one quality (small size, in our example), but midway through the task start classifying on the basis of a different dimension (triangular shape, in the example). Later in the preoperational period, children classify on a consistent basis, so that all the objects in a group are there for the same reason.

Although children learn to solve this type of problem during the preoperational period, other classification problems remain difficult. The limitations of their reasoning are most evident when they need to consider competing bases of classification simultaneously, as in the *class inclusion* problem. On such problems, children might be presented eight toy animals, six of them cats and two dogs. They then would be asked, "Are there more animals or more cats?" Most children below age 7 or 8 answer that there are more cats, despite the number of cats inherently being less than or equal to the number of animals.

Piaget saw this behavior as stemming from preoperational children's tendency to focus on a single dimension to the exclusion of others. That is, to solve the problem, they would need to keep in mind that an object (Garfield) may simultaneously belong both to a subset (cats) and to a superset (animals). They focus either on all the animals being a particular type of animal (in which case they would compare the number of cats to the number of dogs), or on all the objects being animals (in which case there would be no comparison to make). Typically, they would reinterpret the question in a way that allowed them to compare the number of cats to the number of dogs and conclude that there were more cats.

Children's understanding of relations also grows considerably during the preoperational stage. However, their ability to ignore irrelevant relations and to concentrate on relevant ones remains limited. To illustrate both the growth and the remaining deficiencies, Piaget (1952) presented preoperational children the type of *seriation problem* shown in Figure 2–4. He asked them to arrange the sticks from shortest to longest in a single row. If they succeeded at this task, he presented them with a second problem. Here they needed to insert a new stick of medium length at the appropriate point in the row they had arranged.

Early in the preoperational stage, between ages 2 and 4, children encounter great difficulty creating correct orderings. As in Figure 2–4, they might arrange two subsets of the sticks correctly, but not integrate the two into a single overall ordering.

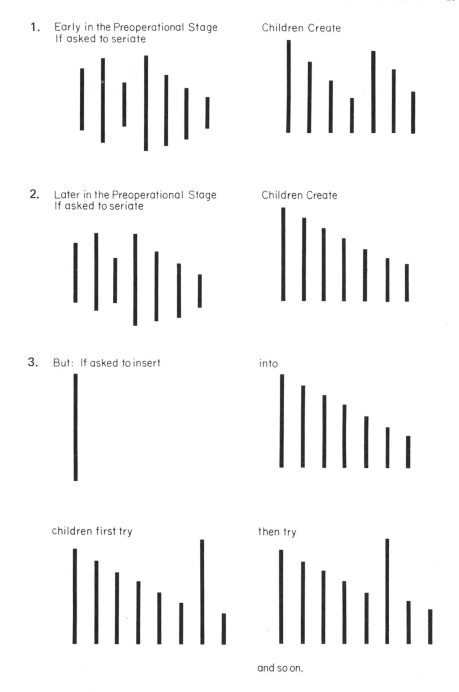

FIGURE 2-4 Typical responses to seriation problems of children early and late in the preoperational stage.

Later in the preoperational stage, children can correctly order the lengths of the original set of sticks. However, often they fail to find the correct place to insert the additional stick without extensive trial and error. Again, Piaget attributed such remaining difficulties to preoperational children's tendency to pay too much attention to a single dimension and to ignore other dimensions. In particular, they find it difficult simultaneously to view the new stick as being smaller than the one just larger than it and larger than the one just smaller than it.

Understanding of classes and relations in the concrete operations period. Piaget contended that with development, children come to treat classes and relations as part of a single, unified system. Children's attempts to solve *multiple classification problems* exemplify Piaget's views on this topic. One such problem is shown in Figure 2–5. Children see intersecting

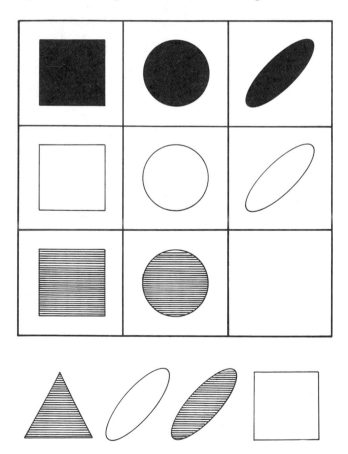

FIGURE 2-5 Type of matrix used to test children's understanding of multiple classification. The task was to decide which of the four objects at the bottom belonged in the empty square in the matrix (after Inhelder & Piaget, 1964).

rows of stimuli that vary along two dimensions, in this case shape (square, circular, or oblong) and color (black, white, or striped). They are asked to choose an object to put in the blank space so that all nine objects are ordered along the two dimensions. This requires that they attend to two different dimensions (shape and color) in classifying each object.

Inhelder and Piaget (1964) reported that 4- to 6-year-olds selected objects that included at least one of the desired dimensions on 85% of problems. However, they chose the single object that included both desired dimensions on only 15%. In other words, given the Figure 2–5 problem, they would choose a nonstriped oblong object or a striped square or circle far more often than the correct answer. By 9 or 10 years of age, the large majority of children correctly chose the striped oblong object, revealing an ability to consider classes and relations together.

Understanding of classes and relations in the formal operational period.   Formal operational reasoning enables adolescents to think about relations among relations and about classes of classes. For example, they might first generate a class of the most successful political leaders from each country in the world and then form a higher-order class of the types of countries where the successful leaders tended to be moral visionaries, efficient economic administrators, sly and ruthless infighters, nice guys, and so on.

Formal operational reasoning also leads adolescents to view the relations and classes that actually are relevant in a given situation as only a subset of the ones that could possibly be relevant. This type of reasoning was illustrated in the description of the chemical combinations problem earlier in the chapter. Formal operational adolescents not only planned a way to generate all possible combinations of the chemicals, but also interpreted the two combinations that produced the yellow color in the context of all of the possible combinations. In particular, only by comparing the two combinations that did produce the yellow color to the fourteen that did not could they realize that one of the chemicals actively prevented the color from changing.

A chronological summary.   It is easy to become confused among the numerous developmental changes Piaget described. Table 2–2 (see p. 50) places some of the most important changes in relation to each other and creates a better feel for which types of changes occur when in development.

AN EVALUATION OF PIAGET'S THEORY

How can we evaluate this rich and diverse theory of cognitive development? Some of the strengths of the theory were mentioned at the outset of the chapter. It provides us with a good feel for what children's thinking is like at different points in development. It addresses issues that parents, teachers,

TABLE 2-2   Children's Thinking at Different Ages: The Piagetian Model

STAGE OF DEVELOPMENT	RELEVANT AGE RANGE	TYPICAL ACHIEVEMENTS AND LIMITATIONS
Sensorimotor Period (Birth to 2 years)	Birth to 1 month	Modification of reflexes to make them more adaptive.
	1 to 4 months	Primary circular reactions and coordination of actions.
	4 to 8 months	Secondary circular reactions. No searching for hidden objects.
	8 to 12 months	Coordination of secondary circular reactions. Baby retrieves hidden objects but continues searching where objects were previously found rather than where they were last hidden.
	12 to 18 months	Tertiary circular reactions. Baby systematically varies heights from which to drop things.
	18 to 24 months	Beginning of true mental representations. Deferred imitation.
Preoperational Period (2 to 7 years)	2 to 4 years	Development of semiotic function. Growth of language and mental imagery. Egocentric communication.
	4 to 7 years	Good language and mental-imagery skills. Inability to represent transformations. Child focuses on single perceptual dimensions on conservation, class inclusion, time, seriation, and other problems.
Concrete Operational Period (7 to 12 years)	Whole period	Child can perform true mental operations, represent transformations as well as static states, and solve conservation, class inclusion, time, and many other problems. Child still has difficulty thinking of all possible combinations, as in the chemical problem, and of transformations of transformations.
Formal Operational Period (12 years through the rest of life)	Whole period	Adolescent can think about all possible outcomes, interpret particular events in terms of their relation to possible events, and understand abstract concepts such as conservation of motion and chemical interactions.

philosophers, and scientists have been interested in for hundreds of years. It covers a remarkably broad spectrum of developments in children's thinking. It covers the entire age span from infancy through adolescence. It includes uncountable interesting observations and discoveries.

With these clear virtues in mind we can consider three crucial questions. How accurately does the theory describe the specifics of children's reasoning at different ages? How useful are its stages as descriptions and explanations of children's thinking? How valid are its general trait characterizations of children's thinking, such as that preoperational period children are egocentric?

HOW ACCURATELY DOES THE THEORY DESCRIBE PARTICULAR ASPECTS OF CHILDREN'S THINKING?

Piaget's theory makes many specific claims about how children think and reason at different ages. How have these claims held up in the face of contemporary research?

The first issue to consider is whether other people can replicate Piaget's findings when they use similar methods. Piaget's claims about children's thinking were so surprising that many early experiments were conducted simply to replicate them. These replication experiments used larger, more representative samples of children and more standardized versions of Piaget's clinical method, but otherwise closely resembled his approach.

In general, the attempts to replicate were successful. Larger samples of American, British, Canadian, Chinese, and Australian aboriginal children tested in the 1960s and 1970s showed the same type of reasoning that Piaget's small samples of Swiss children had almost half a century earlier (Corman & Escalona, 1969; Dasen, 1973; Dodwell, 1960; Elkind, 1961a, b; Goodnow, 1962; Lovell, 1961; Uzgiris, 1964). Children in less-advanced societies reached the stages of reasoning later, but they eventually did show the expected type of reasoning. This was especially true for the sensorimotor, preoperational, and concrete operational periods. Formal operational reasoning seems to be exhibited by some adolescents, but only by a minority of them, even in advanced societies (Martorano, 1977; Neimark, 1975).

Can we accept these replications at face value? Perhaps the immature reasoning that children display in many situations is due not to their reasoning actually being immature, but rather to the verbal methods used by both Piaget and the replication studies underestimating their knowledge. As discussed in Chapter 1, the debate about the usefulness of verbal explanations data is a quite general one. Critics of such methods argue that young children's inarticulateness often creates a falsely pessimistic impression of their cognitive capabilities.

It now is apparent that use of verbal methods per se is not the cause of the young children's immature reasoning. When tested with nonverbal versions of Piaget's methods, they typically exhibit similar reasoning to that described by Piaget. I have been involved in one such series of experiments in which I employed a nonverbal method to examine a number of Piaget's tasks: the balance scale; conservation of liquid quantity; conservation of solid quantity; conservation of number, speed, time, and distance problems among them (Siegler, 1976, 1978, 1981; Siegler & Richards, 1979; Siegler & Vago, 1978). On each of these tasks, children reasoned much as would have been expected from Piaget's descriptions.

A third question is whether children possess conceptual understanding not revealed by Piaget's experiments. Here the situation is quite different. Throughout development, children seem to have basic understandings not evident in their performance on Piaget's problems. Many of the demonstrations of children's early understandings have been extremely clever. Consider Levin's (1977) experiment on 5-year-olds' understanding of the concept of time. When children were presented with two cars running along parallel tracks, they behaved much like the children described by Piaget; they chose whichever train stopped farther down the track as having traveled for the greater time. However, when they observed two cars traveling in circular paths, the children judged which traveled for more time very accurately. Thus, when the perceptually appealing stopping points were no longer such a large distraction, 5-year-olds displayed understanding that was not apparent in the situation previously used to measure their grasp of the concept of time.

Discoveries of unsuspected cognitive strengths in infants and young children have been one of *the* leading stories in the recent study of cognitive development. It is interesting to consider why these competencies are being discovered now. One reason is the development of new methods for finding out what children understand. These new methods will emerge as particularly important in Chapter 5, where we will consider infants' perceptual capabilities.

Another reason for the discoveries is that a broader range of children's thinking is being considered. The research of Gelman and her colleagues illustrates this trend (Gelman, 1972, 1978; Gelman & Gallistel, 1978; Miller & Gelman, 1983). Piaget focused on preschoolers' frequent failures on number conservation tasks and concluded that they do not grasp the concept of number. Gelman's research indicated that whether or not preschoolers grasp the concept of number, they know a great deal about numbers. They count accurately, and in a way that suggests understanding of the principles underlying counting; they know the effects that addition and subtraction have on small collections of objects; they know which numbers are bigger and which smaller; and so on. The number of insightful demonstrations of early competence is too large to review in any detail here. Examples include work on children's understanding of causality (Bullock, Gelman, and Baillargeon, 1982; Shultz, 1982), class inclusion (Markman & Seibert, 1976; C. Smith, 1979), conservation (McGarrigle & Donaldson, 1974; Markman, 1979), time (Levin, 1977, 1979; Wilkening, 1981), and object permanence (Baillargeon, 1984; Kelman & Spelke, 1983). In short, while Piaget's observations about children's thinking reveal a great deal about how they think, and while they can be replicated using both verbal and nonverbal methods, they tend to underestimate children's understanding.

How Stagelike Is Children's Thinking?

What does it mean to say that children's thinking progresses through a series of stages? Among the implications are that children's thinking changes qualitatively from one stage to another, that within any one stage their reasoning is similar across diverse problems, and that they are unable to learn to think in ways associated with the next higher stage until they are near that stage or in it (Brainerd, 1978; Flavell, 1971).

Qualitative changes.   Stage theories such as Piaget's imply that development is discontinuous and that transitions from one type of reasoning to another are qualitatively distinct. As noted in Chapter 1, the analogy is to development from caterpillar to butterfly rather than to the brick-by-brick construction of a house. How well does this analogy fit children's thinking?

In large part, the answer depends on what is meant by continuous and discontinuous development. When viewed from afar, many changes in children's thinking appear discontinuous; when viewed from closeup, the same changes often appear as part of a continuous gradual progression. Consider the way in which infants and young children search their environments. As noted in the discussion of the object concept, Piaget and a number of other researchers have found that infants younger than 7 or 8 months often do not search at all for objects hidden from their view. Older children almost always search for objects they see hidden. If we view the younger infants' lack of searching as implying that they do not realize that the objects continue to exist, then a conclusion of qualitative differences in thought seems justified.

Harris (1983) suggested an alternative interpretation, however, that was more consistent with an assumption of continuity. Infants might be quite sure that the missing object still exists, but fail to search because they simply do not know where the object might be. In this view, development involves becoming able to infer the location of hidden objects under a gradually increasing number of conditions rather than suddenly realizing that hidden objects continue to exist.

Even if we believe that infants do experience a sudden insight in realizing that objects do not simply disappear, it is still clear that, following this insight, they gradually expand their ability to locate hidden objects. That is, realizing that objects do not disappear forever when they are placed under containers is part of a more general cognitive trend—improved skill in searching the physical environment for lost or hidden objects. These searching skills develop over a long period; even 4-year-olds err on some hidden-object problems. Further, when older children err, their mistakes parallel those of younger children. When presented with three, rather than two, potential hiding places, infants, 1-year-olds, and 4-year-olds most often make the same type of errors. They look at locations where they have found the object previously rather than locations where they never have found it. The frequency of errors declines, but the type of errors remains the same. (For interesting articles on young children's abilities to search physical environments and find missing objects, see DeLoache, 1980, 1984; DeLoache & Brown, 1983; Perlmutter, 1980; Sophian, 1984; Wellman, Ritter, & Flavell, 1975; and Wellman & Somerville, 1980, 1984).

A branch of mathematics known as *catastrophe theory* provides justification for viewing development as both continuous and discontinuous. Catastrophe theory examines situations such as the collapse of bridges. The forces that lead to bridges collapsing often build up slowly over a period of years. The visible collapse, however, can be breathtakingly sudden. Analogously, despite the seeming abruptness of cognitive progress when a boy solves a problem one day that he could not solve the day before, the progress may be based on years of gradually accumulating experiences. In the boy, as in the bridge, the change can be viewed as either continuous or discontinuous.

Similar reasoning on different problems.   A central feature that differentiates stage theories such as Piaget's from other approaches is the stage theories' assumption of unities in reasoning. Saying that children are in a certain stage of reasoning implies that their reasoning across many tasks shares that stage's characteristics. Within Piaget's theory, an 8-year-old ideally would grasp all concrete-operations-level concepts—conservation of liquid quantity, class inclusion, seriation, and so on—and would fail to grasp all formal-operations-level concepts—thinking in terms of all possible combinations, conserving motion, and so on.

It has become increasingly apparent that this view does not accurately characterize children's thinking. Consider three concrete-operations-level conservation concepts: conservation of number, conservation of solid quantity, and conservation of weight ("If I remold this clay ball into a sausage, will it weigh the same as it did before?"). Theoretically, all of these should be mastered simultaneously; a child should understand either all or none of them. Actually, however, most children seem to master the number conservation task at around age 6, the solid quantity conservation task at around age 8, and the weight conservation task at around age 10 (Elkind, 1961a; Katz & Beilin, 1976; Miller, 1976). These data do not support the idea of concurrent development, even within the concept of conservation. Piaget named this phenomenon of children's differing understanding of related concepts—he called it *horizontal decalage*—but did not explain it.

Despite the evidence against the view that children generally reason similarly across many problems, potential consistencies of reasoning across different tasks continue to be of great interest. The motivation is rooted deeply in everyday observations of children's reasoning. There is something characteristic in 2-year-olds' reasoning that distinguishes it from 5-year-olds'; there is something about 5-year-olds' reasoning that distinguishes it from 10-year-olds'; and so on. That is, children of a given age do seem to reason in a characteristic way in different contexts.

In one attempt to address the issue, Flavell (1982) hypothesized that the amount of consistency of reasoning across tasks may depend on who, what, and when we observe. *Who* we examine may be important in that some children may exhibit more consistent reasoning across tasks than others. This possibility is suggested by findings that some people exhibit more consistency in personality traits than others (Bem & Allen, 1974; Carver & Scheier, 1981). *What* we investigate also may influence how much similarity we find. Children may show more similar reasoning within certain relatively self-contained areas, such as mathematics and music, than in other more-open domains.

When we observe may exert an especially large influence. Children seem to reason more consistently when they are just beginning to understand various concepts than when they better understand them. For example, 5-year-olds solve a large variety of problems by focusing exclusively on a single dimension. On conservation of liquid quantity, they predict that whichever glass has the taller liquid column has more water, regardless of the cross-sectional areas. On conservation of solid quantity, they predict that whichever clay sausage is longer also has more clay, again regardless of the cross-sectional areas. In judging amount of time, they focus entirely on spatial end points, ignoring the amount of time that has actually passed. In judging which side of a balance scale will tip, they rely entirely on relative amounts of weight, ignoring distance of the weights from the fulcrum. They exhibit similar reasoning with concepts as diverse as temperature, happiness, and morality. (Case, 1981; Ferretti, Butterfield, Cahn, & Kerkman, in press; Levin, Wilkening, & Dembo, 1984; Siegler, 1981; S. Strauss, 1982).

In contrast, children master these same concepts at very different ages. Even 9-year-olds generally can solve conservation of liquid and solid quantity problems; even college students often cannot solve balance-scale problems. Differing amounts of experience with the problems, differences in the ease of drawing analogies to other, better-understood problems, and differences in the complexity of the most advanced solution formulas contribute to these differences.

Another potential source of consistency in children's reasoning is the level of their most advanced reasoning (Fischer, 1980; Halford, 1985). This possibility might sound directly opposed to the one discussed above, but it actually is not. Children might not in general reason similarly across problems where they have specific knowledge, but all of their most advanced reasoning might be at the same level. For example, the most advanced thinking of 9-year-olds might involve single operations. This would mean that none of their thinking would involve operations on operations (as in the formal operations period). However, it would not mean that they could represent all transformations with the relevant operation. Whether they could do so would depend on how much experience they had had with the transformation, whether it occured in a familiar context, and so on. In sum, unities in children's reasoning may be most apparent in their early reasoning, when they have little knowledge of the concepts involved, and in the level of the most advanced reasoning of which they are capable.

Can development be accelerated?   Piaget's views concerning the possibility of accelerating cognitive development through training are among his most controversial. Some of his comments appear to rule out the possibility of any training being successful. Others suggest that training might at times be effective, but only if the child already possesses some understanding of the concept and if the training procedure involves active interaction with materials. Both types of statements indicate that many young children will not be able to benefit from any training technique, and that many types of training techniques will not benefit any children.

In fact, young children can learn more than Piaget thought they could, and can benefit from a greater variety of instructional techniques. Among the most convincing demonstrations are those of Brainerd (1973), Field (1977), Gelman (1969), Murray (1972), and Zimmerman and Rosenthal (1974). The findings dovetail with the unsuspected early competence that children have been found to have even without direct training. Not only do children understand more than previously thought, they also can learn more.

It is important not to throw out the baby with the bathwater, however. Although young children can learn to solve these problems, they often find doing so exceptionally difficult. Older children who cannot yet solve the same problems typically learn them much more easily. Similarly, although young children show beginning understanding of many important concepts even without training, they demonstrate the understanding in far fewer situations. The nature of their understanding also seems to differ in important ways from older children's understanding of the same concepts. Just how young children's existing understanding and learning abilities resemble and differ from older children's currently represents a much more intriguing and controversial issue than whether it is possible for children to be taught complex concepts at relatively young ages.

How Well Do Piaget's General Characterizations
Fit Children's Thinking?

In addition to describing children's thinking in terms of particular examples of their reasoning (5-year-olds think that the taller liquid column always has more water) and in terms of stages (type x thinking is typical of the preoperational period), Piaget characterized children's thinking in terms of intellectual traits. For example, he described preoperational-period children as being egocentric, precausal, semilogical, and perceptually oriented. These terms fit in some ways, but not in all. The characterization of preoperational children as egocentric illustrates many of the issues.

Recall from the discussion of egocentric communication that 2- to 4-year-olds often leave out critical information from what they say. They also often seem to ignore what other people say to them, and have trouble taking other people's point of view. These types of observations led Piaget to label their thinking "egocentric."

But consider other situations in which young children communicate nonegocentrically. If you ask 3-year-olds to show you their drawings, they hold the side with the artwork toward you. If they were completely egocentric, they would do the opposite, since they would assume that what they see is what you see. Similarly, preschoolers who have an experience with one adult later allude to the experience in conversations with that adult, but not in conversations with others. Again, if they assumed everyone knew what they did, they would have no reason to differentiate in this way (Menig-Peterson, 1975).

Conversely, people well beyond the preoperational period continue to be "at risk" for egocentrism (Flavell, 1985). A classic demonstration of this involved a situation analogous to a phone conversation. Two children were seated opposite each other at a table with a board between them preventing them from seeing each other. Each child could see the same set of pictures on the table, each picture containing an irregular design. The speaker had to describe the particular design he was thinking of in a way that would allow the listener to figure out which one was being described (Krauss & Glucksberg, 1969).

Not surprisingly, older children communicate which picture they have in mind more effectively than younger ones. More surprisingly, even 8- and 9-year-olds often have difficulty overcoming their knowledge of what they are referring to sufficiently to generate a description that will allow the other child to understand. Further, children well beyond the preoperational period experience difficulty knowing who is to blame for the missed communication—whether the message is inadequate or whether the listener simply failed to respond properly to it (See Ford, 1985; Patterson & Kister, 1981; Robinson & Robinson, 1981; Waters and Tinsley, 1985; and Whitehurst & Sonnenschein, 1981 for detailed discussions of egocentric communication). There seems little doubt that young children are egocentric in some important ways that older children are not. Attaching the label to any one group is too strong, though. It leads us to ignore both the ways that younger children's thinking is not egocentric and the ways that older children's thinking is.

The Current Status of Piaget's Theory

If Piaget's theory underestimates young children's reasoning abilities, overestimates adolescents' reasoning abilities, and describes children's thinking in terms such as egocentrism that are misleading as well as revealing, why pay so much attention to it? The simple reason is that with all of its shortcomings, the theory gives us a good feel for how children think. It also points us in the right direction for learning more about children's thinking. Piaget recognized previously unsuspected intelligence in infants' early activities. In making these discoveries, he raised the question of what other unsuspected capabilities infants might have, a question that underlies the remarkable recent discoveries about infants' perceptual development, which will be discussed in Chapter 5. Piaget recognized that children do not see the world as adults do. In this recognition he raised the questions of what mental processes lead them to see the world differently and how exactly they represent what they see. His estimate of the degree of unity in children's thinking may have been too high, but he discovered important unities that do exist and pointed to the importance of searching for more of them. Finally, Piaget's basic questions are the right ones: What capabilities do infants possess at birth, what capabilities do they possess at later points in development, and what developmental processes allow them to make the transitions? We will spend the remainder of the book trying to answer these questions.

SUMMARY

Piaget's theory remains a dominant force in developmental psychology despite the fact that much of it was formulated half a century ago. Some of the reasons for the approach's lasting appeal are the interesting topics it addresses, the large span of childhood it encompasses, and the reliability and interestingness of many of its observations.

At the most general level, Piaget's theory focused on the development of intelligence. Intelligence included four stages of development and several developmental processes. The purpose of all these was to organize experience in ways that allowed successful adaptation to the cognitive environment. This adaptation was achieved not simply through learning new responses, but rather through reorganizing existing systems of understandings.

The four main stages of development were the *sensorimotor, preoperational, concrete operational,* and *formal operational* periods. The sensorimotor occupies the age range between 0 and 2 years, the preoperational period between 2 and 6 or 7, the concrete operational period between 6 or 7 and 11 or 12, and the formal operational period from early adolescence to the end of life. Each of the periods includes large changes in understanding of such important concepts as conservation, classification, and relations.

The three major developmental processes are *assimilation, accommodation*, and *equilibration*. Assimilation refers to the means by which children interpret incoming information to make it understandable within their existing mental structures. Accommodation refers to the ways in which children's current means for understanding the world change in response to new experience. Equilibration is a three-stage process that includes assimilation and accommodation. First, children are in a state of equilibrium. Then, failure to assimilate new information leads to their becoming aware of shortcomings in their current understanding. Finally, their mental structure accomodates to the new information in a way that creates a more advanced equilibrium.

The sensorimotor period witnesses large improvements in many types of conceptual understanding. Infants acquire primary, secondary, and tertiary circular reactions in which their actions become more deliberate, more systematic, and extend farther beyond their bodies. They also acquire a simple form of conservation, the object concept, in which they realize that objects continue to exist even if they move out of sight and come to understand increasingly complex displacements. They also form simple understandings of classes and relations.

In the preoperational period children acquire the semiotic function, which allows them to acquire language and mental imagery. Despite this development, Piaget emphasized what preoperational children cannot do more than what they can. He noted that 5- and 6-year-olds usually fail conservation, class inclusion, and seriation problems. He attributed such failures to the children focusing on perceptual appearances rather than transformations, to their being egocentric, and to their centering on a single dimension rather than considering multiple variables simultaneously.

In the concrete operations period, children master many of the concepts they could not solve in the preoperational period. Their acquisition of true *operations* is what allows this cognitive progress. These operations allow them to represent transformations and to understand many concepts they could not previously grasp. The operations are reversible and are organized with other operations into larger systems. Among the concepts that children first grasp in this period are conservation of liquid and solid quantity, time, seriation, and class inclusion.

The formal operations period, according to Piaget, brings ability to think in terms of all possible outcomes, to interpret what they see in terms of these possibilities, and to plan ahead. Children in this stage become able to perform systematic experiments. They also think of causes in terms of all possible combinations of variables, a way of thinking made possible by sophisticated understanding of classes and relations. In sum, they think much like scientists.

Piaget made a number of controversial statements about what children know at different points in development, about stages of development they pass through, and about general traits that characterize their thinking. When given either the original or nonverbal versions of Piaget's problems, children reason much as he described them as doing. However, they appear to have important cognitive capabilities that he did not detect. His stage descriptions predict that children think in qualitatively different ways in different periods of development, that they reason similarly on many problems, and that they cannot learn modes of thought much more advanced than their current stage.

Each of these views contains a certain amount of truth, but also has certain problems. When viewed at a general level, many changes in children's thinking appear to represent qualitative shifts. However, when examined closely, the same changes often appear to be part of a gradual progression. In general, the consistency of reasoning that Piaget predicted children would show across many tasks has not been found. However, considerable consistency has been apparent in children's early conceptual understanding. Young children do not learn as rapidly as older children, but it is possible for them to learn a great many concepts that are well beyond their current understanding.

Piaget also described children in terms of general intellectual traits, such as egocentrism. These trait descriptions fit young children's thinking in many ways, but not in all ways. For example, although 5-year-olds are egocentric in some situations, they and even younger children behave non-egocentrically in other situations, and even older children and adults sometimes behave in an egocentric fashion. Thus, the trait descriptions seem to be in the right ball park, but to gloss over important exceptions. More generally, Piaget's theory continues to be of contemporary interest because it communicates a good feel for children's thinking and raises the right questions.

RECOMMENDED READINGS

Brainerd, C. J. (1978). The stage question in cognitive developmental theory. *Behavioral and Brain Sciences, 1*, 173–213. A fair but critical discussion of Piaget's theory in light of subsequent research.

DeLoache, J. S. (1984). Oh where, oh where: Memory-based searching by very young children. In C. Sophian (Ed.), *Origins of cognitive skills.* Hillsdale, NJ: Erlbaum. This chapter presents intriguing research documenting young children's ability to search for hidden objects. Especially interesting are the strategies that the 1- and 2-year-olds use to help themselves remember.

Gelman, R. (1978). Cognitive development. *Annual Review of Psychology, 29*, 297–332. A classic summary of the impressive understanding that preschoolers possess of such complex concepts as number, cause-and-effect, classification, and ordering.

Inhelder, B., & Piaget, J. (1958). *The growth of logical thinking from childhood to adolescence.* New York: Basic Books. One of the clearest presentations of Piaget's theoretical ideas, and some of the most interesting of Piaget's reasoning tasks. Emphasizes the development of formal operations, but also shows how understanding of the tasks develops during the preoperational and concrete operational periods.

Levin, I. (1982). The nature and development of time concepts in children: The effects of interfering cues. In W. J. Friedman (Ed.), *The developmental psychology of time.* New York: Academic Press. This chapter summarizes a first-rate series of studies on the development of the concept of time.

Piaget, J. (1952). *The child's concept of number.* New York: Norton. In this book, Piaget describes a number of his classic experiments: experiments on the conservation of liquid quantity, conservation of number, and seriation among them.

3
INFORMATION-PROCESSING
THEORIES OF DEVELOPMENT

> As a final point, we concentrated on "what develops" in keeping with the title of
> the volume. However, we would like to point out that an equally important
> question is how development occurs.... The problems of growth and change
> are quintessential developmental questions, and are of fundamental importance
> no less to the instructional psychologist who wishes to accelerate growth than to
> the theorist who seeks to understand development (Brown & DeLoache, 1978,
> p. 31).

Brown and DeLoache are not discussing trivial issues: "What
develops?" and "How does development occur?" are probably the two most
fundamental questions about children's thinking. Piaget's theory offers one
potential set of answers to the questions: that what develops is qualitatively
distinct levels of intelligence, and that development occurs through the
operation of assimilation, accommodation, and equilibration. As discussed
in Chapter 2, these answers seem to be generally in the right direction. As
also was discussed, though, the answers offered by Piaget's theory need to be
built upon, refined, and changed in certain ways before children's thinking
can be well understood. In this chapter we discuss a major attempt to provide such revisions, refinements, and rethinkings—the information-
processing approach.

Information-processing theories of development vary in a number of
ways, but all share certain fundamental views about how children think.

The basic assumption underlying them is that thinking *is* information processing. Rather than focusing on stages of development, they focus on the information that children represent, the processes that they use to transform the information, and the memory limits that constrain the amount of information they can represent and process. The quality of children's thinking, at any age, depends on what information they represent in a particular situation, how they operate on the information to achieve their particular goal, and how much information they can keep in mind at one time.

A second defining characteristic of information-processing theories of development is an emphasis on precise analysis of change mechanisms. Two critical goals are to identify the change mechanisms that contribute most to development and to specify exactly how these change mechanisms work together to produce cognitive growth. The flip-side of this emphasis on how development occurs is an emphasis on the cognitive limits that prevent it from occurring more rapidly than it does. Thus, information processing theories attempt to explain both how children of given ages have come as far as they have and why they have not gone farther.

What is the relation of information-processing approaches to alternative views, such as the Piagetian approach? The two approaches have quite a bit in common. Both try to identify children's cognitive capabilities and limits at various points in development. Both try to describe the ways in which children do and do not understand important concepts at different points in life and try to explain how later, more advanced understandings grow out of earlier, more primitive ones. Both emphasize the impact that existing understandings can have on children's ability to acquire new understandings.

The two approaches also differ in important ways, though. Information-processing theories place greater emphasis on specifying exactly how change mechanisms work. They also place greater emphasis on which processes are performed, in what order and for how much time, and on what information is represented in what form and for what period of time.

A final difference is that information-processing theories assume that our understanding of how children think can be greatly enriched by knowledge of how adults think. The underlying belief is that just as we can more deeply understand our own adult thinking when we appreciate how it developed during childhood, we also can better understand the development of children's thinking when we know where the development is heading. If we find that certain memory and reasoning processes are crucial to adults' thinking, we immediately wonder whether those processes are given at birth, whether they appear at some particular point in development, and whether particular experiences are crucial to their development. If we learn that adults' thinking is limited in certain ways, we immediately wonder whether children encounter similar, or even greater, obstacles.

We already have encountered instances of the usefulness of this perspective. Recall from Chapter 1, for example, how S. Sternberg's (1966) study of short-term-memory scanning in adults stimulated Keating and Bobbitt's (1978) study of short-term-memory scanning in intellectually gifted and average 9- to 17-year-olds (pp. 15–16). The adult work directly suggested an hypothesis about how children and adolescents might search through the contents of their memories. It also suggested a method for studying the issue and several dimensions along which children and adults might differ. As often is the case, knowledge of adults' thinking provided a background against which to understand, interpret, and appreciate the unique aspects of development.

Two information-processing theories that were originally developed to describe adults' thinking have contributed especially greatly to understanding of children: Atkinson and Shiffrin's and Newell and Simon's theories. Both of these provide visions of how the mind is organized, the types of processes involved in thinking, and the cognitive limits people must overcome. They are discussed early in this chapter because they provide plausible "big pictures" of how all people's minds are organized, children's as well as adults'.

Next we examine four information-processing theories intended to characterize how children's thinking differs from that of adults: R. Sternberg's, Case's, Klahr and Wallace's, and my own. No one of these theories covers the huge expanse of topics and ages encompassed by Piaget's theory. On the other hand, each of them provides more detailed and precise characterizations of what develops and how development occurs in the areas of their focus than does Piaget's theory. In addition, the four theories have an interesting relation to each other. Each theory emphasizes a particular change mechanism: One emphasizes automatization, one encoding, one generalization, and one strategy construction. As noted in the Chapter 1 discussion of change processes, these four mechanisms may work together to produce a large variety of cognitive developments. Taken as a group, the four theories can help us to understand the capabilities with which children begin life, the types of changes they undergo, and the heights they eventually attain. The chapter's organization is outlined in Table 3–1.

TABLE 3-1   Chapter Outline

I.   Theories of the Information-Processing System
    A.   Atkinson and Shiffrin's Theory
    B.   Newell and Simon's Theory

II.   Information-Processing Theories of Development
    A.   Sternberg's Theory
    B.   Case's Theory
    C.   Klahr and Wallace's Theory
    D.   Siegler's Theory

III. Summary

GENERAL THEORIES OF THE INFORMATION-PROCESSING SYSTEM

Theories of adults' information processing have contributed a number of ideas that are useful for understanding children's thinking. Atkinson and Shiffrin proposed a basic organization of the information-processing system that seems as applicable to children as to adults, emphasized the role of strategies within that system, and stimulated work on automatic processing. Newell and Simon noted the role of the task environment in determining what and how people think, emphasized encoding as a limiting factor on what strategies people could form, and introduced computer simulation as a tool for studying thinking. Below, we consider these ideas together with several discoveries about children's thinking that they have stimulated.

Atkinson and Shiffrin's Theory

The basic organization of the information-processing system.   Atkinson and Shiffrin (1968) distinguished between *structural features* and *control features* of people's information processing. Structural features are fixed characteristics of the system, such as memory capacity and speed of operation, that determine the absolute limits within which information processing occurs. Control processes are like computer software in that they indicate the exact sequence of processes to be performed and that they vary across different situations and different individuals.

Atkinson and Shiffrin hypothesized that the structural features of the information-processing system included three stores: the *sensory store* (also known as the *sensory register*), the *short-term store*, and the *long-term store*. As shown in Figure 3–1, information enters the system through the sensory store, then proceeds to the short-term store, and then proceeds to the long-term store. When a person reads a word, a pattern of horizontal, vertical, and oblique lines and curves enters the sensory register. Then the information moves to the short-term store, at which point the word's identity is discovered. Then the word is transferred to the long-term store, where it becomes part of the enduring representation of the sentence and paragraph being read.

Atkinson and Shiffrin further divided each of the three stores by the code of the entering information. The system included a visual sensory register, an auditory sensory register, a visual short-term store, an auditory short-term store, and so on. All three stores were viewed as limited in the speed with which they could perform basic processes. The sensory and short-term stores also were believed to be limited in capacity and in the durability of entering information.

Each of the structural units of the information-processing system is influenced by control processes. These control processes determine exactly what happens to information in a store. Unlike the structural features, control processes are learned. Infants, like adults, would have sensory, short-term, and long-term stores, but they would differ in which processes they

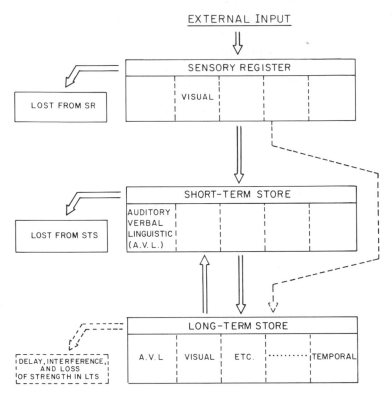

FIGURE 3-1   Atkinson and Shiffrin's model of the information-processing system (from Atkinson & Shiffrin, 1968).

could use to manipulate information within each store and how efficiently they could execute the processes. Also unlike structural features, control processes are specialized to meet the demands of particular situations. The capacity and speed with which each store can operate are the same regardless of the task, but different control processes are used to perform each task.

Atkinson and Shiffrin particularly emphasized the control process of *rehearsal* (for example, repeating a telephone number over and over to remember it). Rehearsal was important because it allowed people to overcome a structural limitation, the fading of information from the short-term store. As long as the person rehearsed an item, it would stay in the short-term store.

The way in which structural features and control processes work together in Atkinson and Shiffrin's model can be appreciated by examining the functioning of particular stores. Below we consider each store in turn.

The sensory store.   Sperling (1960) established several structural characteristics of the sensory store that influence processing of visual information. He presented college students a three-by-four matrix of letters for one-twentieth of a second. When asked immediately after the presentation to name the letters, the college students typically recalled four or five, about 40% of the list. Then Sperling changed the procedure in a small but important way. Rather than having the students recall all of the letters, he asked them to recall only the letters in one row. Since they could not anticipate the identity of the row, they needed to process all twelve letters, just as in the original format. However, requiring them to recite the contents of only one row eliminated the need to retain the information during the recitation period.

Sperling found that when the experimenter indicated which row to recall immediately after the display was shut off, the college students recalled 80% of the letters in the row. When the row's identity was indicated one-third of a second after the stimulus was turned off, their recall declined to 55%. When it was indicated one second after, performance declined to the original 40%. Sperling's interpretation was that a one-twentieth-second exposure was sufficient for letters to create a visual *icon* (a literal copy of the original stimulus), but that the icon faded within one-third of a second, and disappeared after one second.

This clever method has led to surprising discoveries about children's sensory memories. Simply put, the sensory memory of a 5-year-old seems to have as great a capacity as the sensory memory of an adult. Morrison, Holmes, and Haith (1974) briefly presented 5-year-olds and adults with an array of seven geometric figures. The screen then went blank, and after a one-twentieth-second delay, a marker pointed to one of the seven positions. The child or adult needed to name the object that had been in that position. Under these conditions, 5-year-olds' recall was as good as adults'. Thus, the capacity, of a 5-year-old's sensory memory appears to be equivalent to that of an adult.

The short-term store.   After information is processed in the sensory store, it moves to the short-term store. The short-term store is akin to the computer's central processor. It is here that information from the immediate environment and information from long-term memory are combined to perform whatever calculations are necessary. The active nature of the short-term store has led some investigators to refer to it as *working memory*. The short-term store also is often thought of as the conscious part of memory. People are not aware of the contents of either the sensory store or the long-term store, but they are conscious of much of the contents of the short-term store.

Atkinson and Shiffrin focused on the role of verbal rehearsal within the short-term store. One reason was the results of an experiment by Conrad (1964). Conrad presented a sequence of letters on a screen and asked college students to recall them. Despite the fact that people had seen the letters presented, rather than hearing them, most mistakes involved choosing letters that sounded similar rather than ones that were visually similar. This is evident in the confusion matrix in Table 3–2. The stimulus letter is the symbol students originally saw on a screen; the response letter is the letter they recalled. As can be seen, the students often confused letters whose names rhymed with each other. For example, when presented B, they frequently recalled P or V. In contrast, they rarely misrecalled the B's they had seen as F's or S's, letters that look like B but that do not sound like it. The most straightforward explanation of these confusion errors is that the students verbally rehearsed the sequence of letters on the screen and sometimes confused letters whose names had similar-sounding pronunciations.

Again, this method has also proved applicable to children. Conrad (1971) presented the same task to 5-year-olds that he earlier had presented to adults. Unlike the adults, the 5-year-olds did not confuse letters with similar-sounding names any more often than letters with dissimilar-sounding names. Conrad explained the difference between children and adults by pointing to differences in use of verbal rehearsal by the two groups. Since the young children did not rehearse very often, they were not especially prone to confuse letters whose names sound alike.

Considering Conrad's results together with the results of the experiment on the capacity of 5-year-olds' sensory stores points to a pervasive finding about children's thinking. The structural characteristics of children's memories, such as the capacity of the sensory store, tend to be similar or identical to those of adults. However, children and adults differ greatly in their use of control processes, such as rehearsal. Adults use sophisticated control processes more often than do young children, and tend to use higher-quality versions even when both groups employ superficially similar processes. This relation between children's and adults' thinking—similarity in structural features, large differences in control features—is so prevalent that it approximates the status of a law of cognitive development.

Atkinson and Shiffrin hypothesized several types of limits on the operations of the short-term store. One of these involved its capacity, the number of symbols it could include at one time. They proposed that short-term

TABLE 3-2   Recall Confusions (After Conrad, 1964)

		STIMULUS LETTER					
		B	P	U	F	S	X
	B	—	69	83	12	2	0
	P	102	—	40	15	7	7
Response Letter	U	56	30	—	21	11	5
	F	6	14	31	—	131	16
	S	7	11	9	37	—	5
	X	3	2	11	30	59	—

memory included approximately seven locations that could hold information. Additional information either would not enter the system or would push out existing information. This capacity limit was a limit on the number of meaningful units *(chunks)* rather than the number of physical units. A letter, a number, a word, or a very familiar phrase all would be viewed as a single chunk, because each was a single unit of meaning. One reason for viewing short-term store capacity as a limit on the number of chunks rather than on the absolute number of physical units was that both children and adults can retain in the short-term store three unrelated words with nine letters (e.g., hit, red, run) as easily as three unrelated letters (e.g., *q, f, r*).

Atkinson and Shiffrin also hypothesized that the rate at which information is lost from the short-term store limits cognitive functioning. Material in the store ordinarily passes out of it in 15 to 30 seconds. However, rehearsal can preserve it for a longer time. The longer the item is kept in the short-term store, the greater the probability that it will be transferred to the long-term store, where its maintenance would not require active effort.

The long-term store. Atkinson and Shiffrin made two main claims about the structural features of the long-term store. First, information in it does not decay. It remains there permanently, although people might have difficulty retrieving it on a given occasion. Second, events are not stored in all-or-none form. Rather, people store information in separable units and can retrieve each unit without retrieving others.

A memorable study by Brown and McNeil (1966) is one of the main sources of evidence for the conclusion that information is stored in fragmentary form. Brown and McNeil presented college students with definitions of words they might have heard but which would be unfamiliar. For example, they might provide the definition "a navigational instrument used in measuring angular distances, especially the altitude of the sun, moon, and stars at sea," and ask students to identify the word *(sextant)*.

Even students who couldn't remember the term often recalled related information. They said that the word sounded like *secant* and *sexton*, that it started with an *s*, that it ended with a *t*, and so on. These reports of partial information frequently were accompanied by the students saying that they were sure they knew the word, that they almost could remember it, and that they were sure with sufficient time they would remember it. Such comments led to the phenomenon being labeled the "tip-of-the-tongue" experience. From these results and similar findings, Atkinson and Shiffrin concluded that much information in the long-term store is fragmentary. People can remember pieces without remembering the whole.

I do not know of any formal research on the topic, but observations of my own children lead me to suspect that this description applies to children as well as to adults. For example, in trying to remember a friend who had moved away, my daughter recently said, "She was from South America, she had black hair, she was just as silly as I am, why can't I remember her name?" A few minutes later she succeeded in recalling the friend's name, Gabriella.

Further analyses of strategies.   Atkinson and Shiffrin's theory has stimulated more precise descriptions of people's strategies for enhancing their memories. Not only have new strategies been discovered, but previously discovered strategies have been found to include several variants that are useful for adapting to different situations. Craik and Watkins (1973), for example, divided rehearsal into two distinct types: *elaborative rehearsal* and *maintenance rehearsal.* Elaborative rehearsal involves making material more accessible for long-term recall by making it more meaningful. Maintenance rehearsal, in contrast, involves making material more accessible for immediate recall by repeating the sounds. The difference can be seen by imagining a 10-year-old boy who is looking up the phone number of either a good friend or someone he never expects to call again. Suppose the boy finds that the last four digits in the phone number are 1865. If this is the friend's number, the boy might engage in elaborative rehearsal by repeating the first three numbers and then thinking, "The last year of the Civil War." That is, he might elaborate the numbers in a way that could be helpful in remembering them on an enduring basis. On the other hand, if the number belonged to someone the boy never expected to call again, he might engage in maintenance rehearsal, just repeating the numbers. This would be effective for dialing the numbers immediately afterward, but would probably not lead to long-term retention.

Cuvo (1975) found that these two types of rehearsal have different developmental courses. Maintenance rehearsal is prominent early in the use of rehearsal (the first few years of elementary school), but increasingly is supplanted by elaborative rehearsal. The trend may be due to children's increasingly broad knowledge of the world allowing them to elaborate material that earlier they could only maintain. For example, in the 1865 example, a 12-year-old could associate the numbers to the war between the states, but a 7-year-old ordinarily would not have the knowledge to do so.

The role of automatic processing.   Another extension of Atkinson and Shiffrin's model has been to examine the role of automatic information processes, processes that transform information but are not under the individual's control. In one of the most interesting extensions, Hasher and Zacks (1984) suggested that automatic processing of frequency information underlies much of cognitive development. By frequency information they meant data on how often objects and events have been encountered. Hasher and Zacks noted that people retain this information even when they are not trying to. For example, people know the relative frequency with which letters of the alphabet appear, although no one tries to remember such trivia. Further, efforts to remember frequency information more effectively seem to have little effect. Recall of such information is influenced neither by instructions to try to remember it nor by practice in trying to remember it. Recall of frequency information also seems to be equivalent over a wide age range. Children as young as 5-year-olds are as proficient as college students in retaining this type of information.

Children's automatic retention of information about frequencies seems to contribute to cognitive development in many ways. When children form concepts, they must learn which features go together most frequently (learning the concept "bird" requires learning that flying, having feathers, having beaks, and living in trees frequently appear in the same animals). More subtle learning, such as learning of sex roles, also may depend on automatic processing of frequency information. Hasher and Zacks cited findings that only when children see a large difference in the frequency with which men and women engage in an activity do they imitate the same-sex models more than the different-sex ones (Perry & Bussey, 1979). Children are almost never conscious of gathering information about how often men engage in an activity and how often women do. Rather, they seem to acquire the information automatically and then base their behavior upon what they have observed.

Thus, processing of frequency information appears to be automatic from early in development, perhaps from birth. Other processes, however, may change from controlled to automatic as people gain experience with them. For example, when people first learn to drive a car with a stick shift, they ordinarily need to concentrate to change gears at the right time. A few weeks later, they shift effortlessly, often without even being aware that they are doing so. The process is known as *automatization.*

Spelke, Hirst, and Neisser (1976) demonstrated that sufficient practice can lead to automatization of even those processes that we think of as being inherently controlled. To make this point, they trained two people to simultaneously read passages and write down words that they heard dictated. Ordinarily, when people try to do these two tasks at the same time, performance on one or both suffers. This was the case for the two experimental subjects when they began the experiment. After six weeks of daily practice, however, they could read a book and write words simultaneously as efficiently as they could do either one alone. Apparently, the writing task had become automatized.

Newell and Simon's Theory

Newell and Simon (1972) contributed a number of insights that have proved invaluable for understanding children's thinking. Three of the most important have concerned the role of the task environment, the role of encoding, and the role of computer simulation.

The role of the task environment. Newell and Simon contended that people's information-processing capacities set only the broadest limits on their thinking, and that people's representations and processing of information were in large part attributable to the task they were trying to perform.

The reasons for their emphasis on the task environment are evident in the following description:

> We watch an ant make his laborious way across a wind-and-wave-molded beach. He moves ahead, angles to the right to ease his climb up a steep dunelet, detours around a pebble, stops for a moment to exchange information with a compatriot. Thus he makes his weaving, halting way back to his home. So as not to anthropomorphize about his purposes, I sketch the path on a piece of paper . . .
> Viewed as a geometric figure, the ant's path is irregular, complex, hard to describe. But its complexity is really a complexity in the surface of the beach, not a complexity in the ant. On that same beach another small creature with a home at the same place as the ant might well follow a very similar path (Simon, 1981, pp. 63–64).

Simon went on to argue that, as in the ant's journey across the beach, much of the complexity that we observe in people's thinking is really a reflection of the complexity of the environment. Only by analyzing in detail the demands of particular tasks can problem solving be understood, since so much of it is an effort to adapt to the task environment. In situations where people solve problems effectively, detailed analyses of what the task requires suggest which cognitive operations they use to do so. In situations where people cannot solve problems effectively, analyses of the task environment play a different but equally important role. By indicating what processing is required, such task analyses provide a background against which to evaluate exactly where the processing difficulty lies. Thus, understanding the task environment can help distinguish those actions that people take because the actions are adaptive on the task from those actions that they take because of limits on their information-processing capabilities.

Carver and Klahr (1985) illustrated how analyses of the task environment can lead to insights about children's problem solving. They presented 5-year-olds a puzzle in which a dog, a cat, and a mouse needed to find their way to a bone, a piece of fish, and a hunk of cheese respectively. To solve the puzzle, children needed to move all three animals to the location with the appropriate food. Superficially, the greater the number of moves needed to reach the goal of having all three animals in the right position, the harder the problem would seem.

A deeper analysis of the task environment, however, indicated that different problems would create varying degrees of conflict between the child's immediate goal of getting a given animal to the desired food and the child's broader goal of getting all three animals in the right positions. Some problems would require children to move an animal already at its goal away from the goal temporarily. These problems were more difficult for the preschoolers to solve than problems that required more moves but that did not entail any conflict among goals. Other problems required children to resist the opportunity to move an animal to a goal and instead to make a different move. These problems were even more difficult to solve than the problems that required the 5-year-olds to move a piece away from a goal it had already reached. The detailed analysis of the task environment and the conflicts it would create between narrow and broad goals enabled Carver and Klahr to identify the strategy that children were using (always try to increase the fit between the current and the desired arrangement of pieces) and to account for the pattern of difficulty among the problems.

The role of encoding. Newell and Simon's emphasis on the task environment goes hand in hand with their emphasis on the role of encoding. People cannot represent all features of the task environment; the world is simply too complex. Rather, they must be selective, and encode only the most important information. As discussed in Chapter 1, encoding involves identification of the critical information in a situation, and use of it to build internal representations. Often, children fail to encode important features of the task environment, because they do not know what the important features are, because they cannot comprehend them, or because they do not know how to encode them efficiently. This failure to encode critical elements can prevent children from learning from potentially useful experiences; if they are not taking in the relevant information, they cannot benefit from it.

Kaiser, McCloskey, and Proffitt (in press) provided one demonstration of the role of encoding in children's reasoning. They presented 4- to 11-year-olds and college students with a moving electric train carrying a ball on a flatcar. At a predesignated point, the ball dropped through a hole in the moving flatcar and fell several feet to the floor. The task was to predict the trajectory of the ball as it fell.

More than 70% of the 4- to 11-year-olds and a sizable minority of the college students predicted that the ball would fall straight down. After they advanced this hypothesis, the experimenter demonstrated what actually happened when the train ran and dropped the ball at a specified point (the ball fell in a parabolic trajectory). The children and the college students were faced with reconciling their predictions with the outcome they had seen. Their explanations revealed how their encoding of the event was influenced by their expectations. Some said that the ball actually had fallen straight down but that it was released from the train later than the experimenter said it was. Others said that the train gave the ball a push forward just before it was released. Interestingly, a number of the college students who encoded the ball as having gone straight down had previously taken and passed college physics courses. Apparently this experience was insufficient either to change their expectations or their encoding of what they saw.

Computer simulation. A third major contribution of Newell and Simon's work has been the introduction of computer simulation as a means for modeling people's thinking. They noted that computers, like people, manipulate symbols, and that programs can be written that seem to closely resemble people's thinking, both in the types of processes that are used and in the outcomes that are reached. Such programs allow precise specification of ideas about thinking, allow theories to be tested, and can lead to new discoveries. Even if we have already identified the relevant influences on how people solve some type of problem, stating the ideas precisely and integrating them into a single computer simulation often leads to unforseen insights.

Recently, work on computer simulation has been combined with work on computer assisted instruction to produce computer tutors. Anderson, Boyle, and Yost (in press) described one such system that helps high school students learn geometry. The computer tutor includes a simulation of an ideal geometry problem solver, designed to prove theorems in much the way that humans who are good at geometry do, and simulations of a variety of buggy theorem proving rules. These buggy geometry rules are approaches that students often use but that are only partially correct; they are akin to the buggy subtraction rules described in Chapter 1. As high school students solve geometry problems, the computer tutor matches their performance to both buggy and ideal rules; if a student's performance consistently matches a buggy rule, the computer provides an explanation of why that rule is incorrect and why another rule is preferable. The tutor also prompts students by suggesting an appropriate next step if they become confused and do not know what to do next.

Evaluation of the success of the geometry tutor is just beginning, but the early results are promising. Not only have students learned geometry to a level beyond that usually taught in high school courses, but at the end of the instructional program, the students have claimed to like geometry. Given that classroom geometry is usually rated the least liked of all school subjects (Hoffer, 1981), this positive attitude is especially encouraging.

INFORMATION-PROCESSING THEORIES OF DEVELOPMENT

In the remainder of this chapter we consider four theories of how information-processing capabilities develop: R. Sternberg's, Case's, Klahr and Wallace's, and my own. These theories are of particular interest when considered as a group, because together they illustrate four mechanisms that seem likely to play especially crucial roles in cognitive development: *automatization, encoding, generalization,* and *strategy construction.* Sternberg's theory is especially useful in suggesting how children construct strategies. Case's theory illustrates how automatization contributes to children's increasing ability to circumvent memory capacity limits. Klahr and Wallace's theory emphasizes children's ability to generalize, that is, to detect consistent relations and to extend them to new situations. My own theory emphasizes how increasingly effective encoding enables children to learn more effectively. Before discussing each theory in detail, it seems worthwhile to briefly consider each one so as to provide an overview.

Sternberg's theory focuses on how intelligence is produced by different types of information-processing components. He has been especially interested in linking children's general intelligence to their skill in using particular sets of components. For example, he has analyzed the types of components that distinguish gifted from average children, and those that distinguish average from retarded children.

Case adopts a general stage framework much like Piaget's. However, he suggests that cognitive growth stems from changes in the amount of information that can be retained in short-term memory. He attributes these changes to automatization of processing and to biological maturation.

Klahr and Wallace's theory focuses on the contribution of three processes to children's ability to draw general conclusions about the world: retention of experiences in a time line, detection of regular relations within the time line, and elimination of unnecessary processing. Their research resembles Newell and Simon's in its focus on problem solving and in its use of computer simulation as a tool for describing the course of cognitive activity.

My work emphasizes the relation between what children already know and their ability to learn more. The work focuses on such topics as how children represent their knowledge, why young children reason similarly across many problems, and how encoding influences ability to benefit from potentially useful learning experiences.

These theories reflect the contributions of both Piagetian and adult information-processing approaches, as well as a number of other influences. Table 3–3 lists some of these contributions. It also summarizes the goals of the theories and the mechanisms of development that they emphasize.

R. Sternberg's Theory

Since the beginning of the 20th century, intelligence has been characterized by a single number, the IQ score. This practice has several drawbacks: Intelligence tests may be culturally biased, they do not directly measure such critical capacities as the ability to learn and to create, and a single number is inherently inadequate to capture a quality as rich and complex as intelligence. IQ tests also have certain unique virtues, however. Scores on them are closely related to school performance at the time they are given; they predict later school performance quite well; and they provide a solid base from which to examine individual differences in cognitive functioning.

To preserve these virtues while reducing or eliminating the negative qualities, Sternberg has attempted to develop an information-processing analysis of intelligence. He has applied the analysis to diverse tasks and diverse groups of children and has related his results to those yielded by traditional intelligence tests.

TABLE 3-3 Overview of Information-Processing Theories of Development

THEORIST	GOAL OF THEORY	MAIN DEVELOPMENTAL MECHANISM(S)	INFLUENCES FROM PIAGET'S AND ADULT INFORMATION-PROCESSING THEORIES
Sternberg	To provide an information-processing analysis of the development of intelligence.	Strategy construction, based on the use of knowledge-acquisition components, metacomponents, and performance components.	Adult information-processing theories' emphasis on encoding, time course of processing, and dividing thinking into components.
Case	To unite Piagetian and information-processing theories of development.	Automatization and biologically based increases in working memory, both of which increase processing capacity.	Piaget's emphasis on stages of reasoning and on between-concept unities in reasoning. Adult information-processing theories' emphasis on short-term memory limits, automatization, and problem-solving strategies.
Klahr & Wallace	To formulate a computer simulation model of cognitive development.	Generalization, based on the workings of regularity detection, redundancy elimination, and the time line.	Piaget's emphasis on self-modification and on assimilation. Adult information-processing theories' emphasis on encoding and on computer simulation as a means for characterizing thinking.
Siegler	To understand the relation between children's knowledge and their ability to learn.	Encoding of meaningful attributes and relations, which allows construction of more advanced rules.	Piaget's emphasis on discrete levels of understanding and on assimilation. Adult information-processing theories' emphasis on encoding and on adaptation to the task environment.

Sternberg (1985) divided intelligence into three types of information-processing components: performance components, knowledge acquisition components, and metacomponents. Essentially, the metacomponents serve as a strategy construction mechanism, orchestrating the other two types of components into goal-oriented procedures. When the child already possesses sufficient understanding to solve a problem, only the metacomponents and the performance components are needed to construct a problem-solving strategy. The metacomponents select which performance components to use and the order in which to use them, and the performance components do the work of actually solving the problem. When the child does not yet possess sufficient understanding to solve the problem, the knowledge acquisition components also come into play. That is, the knowledge acquisition components obtain new information relevant to solving the problem and communicate this information to the metacomponents. Then the metacomponents combine the new and previous understanding to construct a problem-solving strategy from among the performance components.

Now we can analyze each of these types of components in greater detail. First consider performance components. These are processes that a problem solver uses to implement a decision to solve a problem in a particular way. Sternberg has identified four performance components that people use to solve a great many problems: encoding, inferring, mapping, and application.

The way in which these performance components work can be illustrated by thinking about analogy problems. Consider the problem

Turkey : Cranberry sauce :: Eggs: (1) Corn (2) Ham

The first step in solving this problem is to encode each term. This step involves identifying each term's attributes—for example, noting that turkey is a kind of food, that it is a meat, that it is a bird, that it is eaten on Thanksgiving, and so on. Next, inference is used to specify the relation between the first and second term, in this case that turkey is often eaten with cranberry sauce. Then mapping is used to establish the relation between the first and third terms, that turkey and eggs are both foods. Finally, application involves inducing a relation between the third term and one of the possible answers that parallels the relation between the first and second terms. Here, eggs go with ham in much the same way that cranberry sauce goes with turkey.

Sternberg and Rifkin (1979) found that 7-year-olds use the same components as adults to solve analogy problems. However, they differ in the amounts of cognitive resources they devote to each component. In particular, adults spend more time encoding the terms and then move quickly through the remaining steps. Seven-year-olds spend relatively (and absolutely) less time encoding, but more time on the other components. The children's strategy reduces the initial memory load, but ultimately lengthens the time needed to solve the problem. In addition, Sternberg and Rifkin found that amount of encoding time correlated highly with children's IQ. The higher their IQs, the more time they spent encoding. The linking of the information-processing construct of encoding with the psychometric construct of IQ is representative of the kinds of bridges between psychometric theory and information processing that Sternberg is building.

The second part of Sternberg's theory involves knowledge acquisition components. Sternberg has focused on three of these: selective encoding, selective combination, and selective comparison. Selective encoding involves sifting out relevant from irrelevant information. Selective combination involves integrating information in a meaningful way. Selective comparison involves relating newly encoded or combined information to previously stored information.

These constructs have proved especially useful for analyzing what makes a child intellectually gifted. Sternberg and Davidson (1983) tested use of each of the three types of knowledge-acquisition components on insight problems, problems much like the brain teasers that often appear in puzzle books. Their reason for using these problems was that knowledge-acquisition processes would be especially important on them, since such problems are new to everyone. The following was an example of the insight problems Sternberg and Davidson used: "If you have black socks and brown socks in your drawer, mixed in the ratio of 4 to 5, how many socks will you have to take out to be sure of having a pair of socks in the same color?" Another, harder, problem involved three fruit crates labeled "apples," "oranges," and "apples and oranges" respectively. The three crates did indeed include the three types of contents, but none of them included the contents that its label said it did. The question was whether, if you could ask about the contents of any one crate and find out which contents it included, you could deduce the contents of the other two.

The basic assumption underlying the experiment was that intellectually gifted children can execute knowledge-acquisition components more effectively than other children. They therefore would be expected not only to perform better on all problems but also to benefit less than intellectually average children from conditions that lessened the need for effective execution of knowledge acquisition processes. The reason was that they would execute the process effectively even without help.

The experimental procedures generated by this logic can be illustrated with regard to the selective encoding component. Its role in the socks problem cited above was tested by either including or omitting the irrelevant information about the 4-to-5 ratio of the two colors. If this information was present, children would need to ignore it and selectively encode only the essentials of the problem (the third sock is sure to match one or both of the others). If the irrelevant information were absent, skill in selective encoding would be less important because there would be fewer alternatives to encode.

Sternberg and Davidson's predictions were confirmed. Gifted children correctly solved the insight problems more often than nongifted children, and the hints were less essential for their success. This was the case for all three knowledge-acquisition components.

Then the investigators went a step further. They offered a Saturday morning course designed to train gifted and nongifted children in executing the three processes. The course included 14 hours of instruction, distributed over a 7-week period. At the end, children were given a posttest. The posttest included mathematical insight problems, hypothesized to require use of the knowledge-acquisition processes the children had been taught. It also included logical deduction problems, hypothesized to require different processes.

The nongifted children showed greater gains on the mathematical insight problems than the gifted children, which was consistent with the view that they were more in need of the instruction. Neither group showed gains on the logical deduction task, in accord with the view that this task required skills that were not part of the Saturday morning training program. In sum, gifted children's superior knowledge-acquisition components seemed to account for their superior performance on the insight problems.

The third part of Sternberg's theory involves metacomponents, components used to construct strategies. Metacomponents govern the use of the other components. They also are responsible for most aspects of developmental change. As Sternberg (1984) commented, "There can be no doubt that in the present conceptual scheme, the metacomponents form the major basis for the development of intelligence" (p. 172).

Just as Sternberg argued that superiority in the use of knowledge-acquisition components is especially important in intellectual giftedness, he argued that inferiority in the use of metacomponents is especially important in retardation. He focused on three ways in which inferior functioning of metacomponents might lead to intellectual retardation. One source would be inadequate choices of performance and knowledge-acquisition components for inclusion within strategies. Retarded people might possess sufficient capabilities to solve certain problems, but fail to use the capabilities because their metacomponents did not construct strategies with the right components.

Another potential problem was poor coordination between controlled and automatized problem-solving routines. For example, in reading, people need to move back and forth between the automatized programs used to recognize individual words and the controlled processes that often are used to integrate meanings in texts. Failure to move smoothly back and forth between these two modes can disrupt processing.

Finally, metacomponents are responsible for reacting to experience and making midcourse corrections in processing. Again, retarded individuals seem to be deficient in these skills. Experiments reported by Campione and Brown (1978) and by Butterfield, Siladi, and Belmont (1980) indicate that retarded children differ from nonretarded ones especially greatly in their ability to transfer, to draw on all their knowledge to solve problems, and to be sufficiently flexible to construct new strategies to adapt to changing task demands.

How should Sternberg's theory be evaluated? Two weaknesses can be noted. One is that the theory summarizes more than it predicts. It is not clear what types of evidence would be inconsistent with the approach. Another involves the role of metacomponents in the organization of the system. These are crucial parts of the overall theory, but their workings remain somewhat mysterious. On the other hand, the theory is exceptional in the breadth of phenomena and of populations to which it has proven applicable. It encompasses a large number of intuitively important aspects of development and organizes them in an easy-to-grasp way. It provides a plausible outline of how a strategy construction mechanism would operate. In short, it constitutes a useful framework within which to view development.

Case's Theory

Case's theory is an attempt to unite Piagetian and information-processing theories. It incorporates stages much like Piaget's, an emphasis on short-term memory limitations much like Atkinson and Shiffrin's, and a focus on problem-solving strategies much like Newell and Simon's. Its greatest emphasis is on how the biologically based growth of working memory capacity, together with automatization of processing, allows children to progressively overcome processing limits. The theory can be divided into two main parts: the developmental stages themselves and the transition processes that produce progress between stages.

Like Piaget, Case hypothesized that children progress through four developmental stages. Case characterized these stages in terms of the types of mental representations children can form while they are in them and the types of mental operations they can use. The first stage involved *sensorimotor operations*. Children's representations in this stage are composed of sensory input. The actions they produce in response to these representations are physical movements. In the *representational operations stage*, children's representations include durable concrete internal images, and their actions can produce additional internal representations. In the stage of *logical operations*, children represent stimuli abstractly; they can act on these representations with simple transformations. In the *formal operations stage*, children also represent stimuli abstractly but they are capable of performing complex transformations of the information. (Note: In all stages, children also produce representations and actions like those that were the most advanced possible in earlier stages.)

Examples may clarify the differences in the representations that become possible in different stages. A sensorimotor operation might involve a child seeing a frightening face (the sensory representation) and then hastily leaving the room (the motor action). A representational operation might involve the child producing a mental image of the same frightening face (the internal representation), and using the image to draw a picture of the face the next day (the representational action). A logical operation might involve a child realizing that two of his friends did not like each other (the abstract representation) and telling them that they all could have more fun if they all were friends (the simple transformation). A formal operation might involve the child realizing that such direct attempts at producing friendships rarely are effective (the abstract representation) and therefore leading all three into a situation in which they would need to unite to overcome some common danger, thus producing friendly feelings (the complex transformation). The resemblance to Piaget's stages of development should be clear.

The within-concept developmental sequence by which children were said to acquire understanding of particular concepts also resembled Piaget's views. These views are exemplified by Case's description of children's reasoning on the orange juice problem. This task involved two sets of small drinking glasses, each glass containing either orange juice or water. Children needed to predict which pitcher would taste more strongly of orange juice if the contents of the glasses in one set were poured into one pitcher and those in the other set into another. In other words, they needed to choose which pitcher would have the higher proportion of juice.

Case identified four strategies that children used on this task. Three- and 4-year-olds judged on the basis of the presence of orange juice. If only the glasses in one set contained orange juice, they predicted that that set's liquid would taste more strongly of orange juice. If both sets included orange juice, the children predicted that both would taste more strongly of it. Five and 6-year-olds predicted on grounds that seem more plausible to adults. They compared the number of glasses in each set that contained orange juice, and said that whichever set had more would have the stronger taste (regardless of the number of glasses in each set that had water). Seven- and 8-year-olds considered both the number of glasses containing orange juice and the number containing water. If one set had more orange juice than water, they said that that set would taste more like orange juice. If both or neither set had more orange juice than water, they said the two would taste the same. Finally, 9- and 10-year-olds subtracted the number of glasses containing water from the number containing orange juice, and chose whichever set had the greater remainder.

Where Case differs most clearly from Piaget, and shows the strongest influence of the information-processing approach, is in his account of transition mechanisms. Case hypothesized that children begin life with an innate kernel of processing capabilities. Among these capabilities are the potential for setting goals, for formulating problem-solving strategies to meet the goals, and for integrating different problem-solving strategies into more elaborate and effective strategies. These innate capabilities allow children to make a considerable amount of cognitive progress.

However, the innate capabilities do not allow children to make all kinds of cognitive progress. Whether they can make a given kind of progress depends, according to Case, on the fit between the child's short-term memory capacity and the capacity needed to make such progress. If the new acquisition demands no more memory capacity than the child possesses, then the acquisition will be possible; otherwise, it will not.

How do children ever surmount their short-term memory limits to acquire capabilities that require substantial capacity? The simplest explanation would be that with age, the capacity of short-term memory grows larger. Unfortunately, there is little evidence to support this proposition, and much evidence against it. For example, when adults and children first learn a new type of operation, such as counting in a foreign language, the adults' capacity for the new material is no greater than the children's (Case, Kurland, & Goldberg, 1982).

If the absolute capacity of short-term memory does not increase, how do children become able to hold more information in short-term memory? Case proposed two transition mechanisms by which this progress might occur. One was automatization. With practice, a cognitive operation that previously required all the capacity of the short-term store could be accomplished more efficiently. This would free up part of the short-term memory capacity for other processing. It may be useful to think of this view of short-term memory in terms of an analogy to a car's trunk. The capacity of a car's trunk does not change as the owner acquires experience in packing luggage into it. Nonetheless, the amount of material that can be packed into the trunk does change. Whereas the trunk at first might hold two or three suitcases, it might eventually come to hold four or five. As each packing operation is executed more efficiently, trunk space is freed for additional operations.

The second major transition process was biological maturation. Case (1985) hypothesized that degree of myelinization of the systems in the brain required for executing the operations characteristic of a given stage might determine the efficiency that was possible. Case noted that different systems within the brain are myelinated at different times during development. He perceived a correspondence between the timing of the myelinization of different systems of the brain and the timing of changes in efficiency of operations controlled by those parts of the brain. Thus, myelinization might account for transitions between stages, whereas automatization might account for transitions within stages.

Case's theory appears to have significance for practical as well as theoretical issues. Consider his analysis of missing addend problems. The problems are of the form $4 + ? = 7$. Although the task appears simple, and is part of most first-grade curricula, children find it a major obstacle. Many first-grade teachers find it so frustrating that they do not even try to teach it, despite its presence in their teaching manuals and in the children's textbooks (O'Hara, 1975).

After analyzing several correct and several commonly used incorrect strategies for solving missing addend problems, Case noted that most correct strategies required more short-term memory capacity than 6- and 7-year-olds usually possess. However, he also noted that the simplest correct strategy and the most demanding incorrect strategy made the same memory demands. The least demanding correct strategy, according to his analysis, was to count on from the one addend given in the problem and to note the number of counts required to reach the sum. On the problem $4 + ? = 7$, this simplest correct strategy would involve counting from 4 to 7 and keeping track of the number of counts needed to get from one to the other. The most demanding (and the most common) incorrect strategy was to first count up to the addend that was given and to then count on from there the number of times indicated by the sum. Illustratively on the problem $4 + ? = 7$, children would first count to 4, then count up 7 more times to 11, and finally answer that the missing addend was 11. Case reasoned that if 6-year-olds could learn the incorrect strategy, they also could learn the correct one.

The instructional strategy that Case used was straightforward. As shown in Figure 3–2, the first step was to illustrate that the equal sign = meant that entities on each side of the sign must be equivalent. The next step was to illustrate that the plus sign (+) meant to sum the entities adjacent to the sign. After the child finished working with the faces, the focus of the instruction shifted to direct consideration of problems involving numbers. In one part of this instruction, the experimenter demonstrated the incorrectness of children's existing strategy for solving missing addend problems involving numbers by having them compare the numbers on the two sides of the equal sign that their strategy yielded. This would allow them to see that on $4 + ? = 7$, the 11 that their strategy yielded was not equivalent to the 7 on the other side of the equal sign. Following this, the simplest correct procedure for solving missing addend problems (the counting-on strategy described in the previous paragraph) was introduced, one step at a time.

Case (1978) reported that his teaching strategy allowed 80% of kindergarten children to learn missing addend problems. This percentage represented a considerable improvement over the 10% of children who were able to learn such problems from the standard State of California arithmetic workbook. The procedure also enabled retarded children of mental age 6 to learn missing addend problems. Thus, Case's approach seems useful for applied as well as theoretical purposes.

Several criticisms of Case's theory have been voiced. Flavell (1984) noted that Case has not explicated the principles by which he determines how much short-term memory capacity a procedure requires. As a result, it is often difficult to evaluate whether the estimates are comparable from one task to the next. Further, his ideas about the role of myelinization in between-stage transitions are quite speculative at present. On the other hand, Case's theory is exceptional among information-processing approaches to development in its attempt to relate basic capacities, strategies,

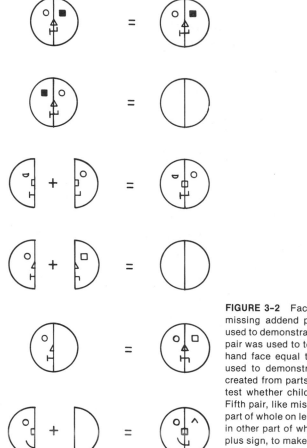

FIGURE 3-2 Faces used by Case (1978) to teach missing addend problem. First pair of faces was used to demonstrate meaning of equal sign. Second pair was used to test whether child can make right-hand face equal to left-hand face. Third pair was used to demonstrate that whole on right can be created from parts on left. Fourth pair was used to test whether child can create whole out of parts. Fifth pair, like missing addend problem, shows one part of whole on left and whole on right; task is to fill in other part of whole on left. Sixth pair introduces plus sign, to make problem even more like standard missing addend problems with numbers.

and learning. It has yielded compelling analyses of development on many tasks and has proved practically useful, as well. Also, there is a strong intuition among many researchers that improved ability to surmount memory limits does underlie much of cognitive development, though it is difficult to provide evidence that unambiguously supports the position. Thus, it seems that Case has taken a difficult but potentially rewarding path. To the extent that the effort succeeds, it will be a grand achievement.

Klahr and Wallace's Theory

Klahr and Wallace have been in the forefront of those urging more explicit specification of how change mechanisms operate. Klahr's (1982) critique of Piaget's proposed change mechanisms, assimilation, accommodation, and equilibration, reflects this view.

For 40 years now we have had assimilation and accommodation, the mysterious and shadowy forces of equilibration, the Batman and Robin of the developmental processes. What are they? How do they do their thing? Why is it after all this time, we know no more about them than when they first sprang on the scene? What we need is a way to get beyond vague verbal statements of the nature of the developmental process. (p. 80)

As an alternative, Klahr and Wallace advocated the writing of *self-modifying production systems*. These are computer simulations equipped with mechanisms that allow them to develop in response to their experience. The key developmental mechanism in Klahr and Wallace's theory was generalization. They divided generalization into three more particular representation and processing units: the *time line, regularity detection*, and *redundancy elimination*.

The time line contains the data on which generalizations are based. It is a record of all the situations the system has ever encountered, the responses it produced when confronted with those situations, the outcomes of the actions, and the new situations that arose. Its workings, as well as those of the other two mechanisms, can be explained in the context of Klahr and Wallace's theory of number conservation. (Recall from the chapter on Piaget's theory that number conservation is the task on which children are presented two rows of objects, and then, after seeing one row spread out or compressed, are asked if the rows still have the same number of objects.)

Table 3–4 illustrates the type of information that might be included in the time line's record of a single event. A child saw a group of cookies and discovered that there were three. The discovery was made by *subitizing* (simply looking at a group and perceiving the number of objects; people can subitize sets of one to four objects, but not larger sets). Next, the child transformed the spatial position of the cookies by picking them up in his hand. Finally, the child again subitized the collection of cookies and found that there still were three.

TABLE 3-4   A Portion of a Child's Time Line

(PREVIOUS PROCESSING EPISODES)	
—	—
—	—
—	—
87456.	Cookies on table
87457.	I subitized
87458.	There were three
87459.	I heard a bird
87460.	I picked up the cookies
87461.	I subitized the cookies
87462.	There were three again
—	—
—	—
—	—

Such detailed records of situations, responses, and outcomes might at first seem unnecessary. Why would it be useful to remember so much about each experience? In fact, the information could be invaluable for cognitive development. In many situations, children cannot know beforehand what will turn out to be relevant. If they retain detailed information that may or may not be relevant, they later may be able to draw unanticipated generalizations. If they retain only what they know to be relevant, however, they may miss much relevant information.

Is it realistic to think that children have a memory record similar to a time line? Observing the level of detail with which they remember certain information suggests that it is. Almost all parents have anecdotes to this effect. One of mine concerns a vacation on which my wife, our almost-2-year-old, and I were staying in a motel. We wanted to go to dinner, but could not find our room key. After 10 minutes of searching, I finally listened to my son long enough to understand what he was saying: "Under phone." As soon as I understood, I knew he was right. I had put it there (for reasons that I no longer remember). It seems likely that if he remembered this relatively inconsequential detail, he probably was remembering a great many other details as well. Hasher and Zacks' (1984) ideas about automatic processing of frequency information and of several other aspects of experience, such as spatial locations and time of occurrence, suggest the types of content that might be entered into the time line. Thus, at least to me, Klahr and Wallace's contention that children retain a detailed ledger of their experiences seems quite plausible.

The second key process, regularity detection, operates on the contents of the time line to produce generalizations about experience. This is accomplished by the system noting places in the time line where many features are similar and where variation in a single feature does not affect an outcome. In number conservation, regularity detection could produce at least three types of generalizations. One would involve generalizing over different objects. Regardless of whether two checkers, two coins, two dolls, or two cookies were spread, there still would be two objects. Children also could generalize over equivalent transformations. Spreading, compressing, piling up, and putting in a circle all preserve the initial number of objects. They also could generalize over different numbers of objects. The results of compressing a row are the same regardless of the number of objects in the initial arrangement.

The third crucial process in Klahr and Wallace's model, redundancy elimination, accomplishes a different type of generalization. It improves efficiency by locating processing steps that are unnecessary, thus reaching the generalization that a less complex sequence can achieve the same goal. In the number conservation example, children eventually would note that it is unnecessary to subitize after picking up the cookies. Since there were three cookies before, and since picking up objects does not affect how many there are, the numbers still must be the same. Klahr and Wallace hypothesized that the information-processing system eliminates redundancy by examining procedures within the time line and checking if the same outcome always occurs even if one or more steps are deleted. If so, the simpler procedure is substituted for the more complex one.

When does the information-processing system have time to detect regularities and to eliminate redundancies? Klahr and Wallace (1976) advanced one intriguing possibility: Perhaps children do it in their sleep. Other possibilities are that moments of quiet play, relaxation, or daydreaming are when children accomplish these functions.

Klahr and Wallace's approach, unlike stage theories, implies that different children develop skills in different orders. In the cognitive system's attempts at self-modification, there is no obvious reason why one type of regularity always should be detected before another type. In the number conservation context, it seems quite arbitrary whether children first detect that it does not matter if the rows of objects contain cookies or checkers or whether they first detect that it does not matter if the cookies are pushed together or stretched apart. Either of these discoveries could be made first or the two could be made simultaneously.

Another implication of Klahr and Wallace's theory relates to the idea of encoding. The way in which information is encoded in the time line shapes the learning that can later occur. Suppose, for example, that in a liquid quantity conservation experiment, a child encodes only the heights of the water in the glasses. Such a child would not be able to detect the regular relation between increments in the height of water and decrements in its cross-sectional area. The information about cross-sectional area simply will not be available in the time line.

Several limitations of Klahr and Wallace's theory should be mentioned. Although they proclaim the virtues of self-modifying computer simulations, neither they nor other investigators interested in children's thinking have yet written many of these (for one interesting example of such a model, see Wallace, Klahr, & Bluff, in press). In addition, Klahr and Wallace's work thus far has been more useful for explaining other researchers' results than for generating new findings. On the other hand, these comments do not detract from the potential of self-modifying computer simulations as models of development. In addition, even without well-worked-out self-modifying computer simulations, Klahr and Wallace's explanation of generalization in terms of the time line, regularity detection, and redundancy elimination is more precise and explicit than almost all other mechanisms of cognitive development that have been proposed. These are important virtues and may well foreshadow additional breakthroughs.

Siegler's Theory

My approach to children's thinking has focused on what children know about particular concepts, how they learn more about them, and how what they already know influences their subsequent learning. Three positions that are of central importance within the approach are that much of children's understanding is rule governed, that some of these rules are quite broadly applicable and produce important unities in children's reasoning, and that encoding exerts a large influence on children's construction of new knowledge.

First consider the generalization that much of children's knowledge is rule governed. Rules are "if . . . then" statements linking particular conditions to actions to be taken if those conditions hold true. They are a way of characterizing children's knowledge that is intermediate in its level of analysis between the extreme detail of behaviorists' stimulus-response descriptions and the generality of stage descriptions.

Rules are useful for representing a wide variety of children's understandings. Infants appear to have rules that guide their choices of where to look (Haith, 1979), toddlers have rules for generating past tense and plural forms in language (Berko, 1958), and older children and adolescents have rules for memorizing, solving problems, forming concepts, and so on. Children's thinking often follows these rules very consistently. For example, on over a dozen of Piaget's problems, the large majority of 5- to 17-year-olds has been found to follow one of a few rules on more than 90% of their responses (Siegler, 1981, 1983).

Describing children's thinking in terms of rules often yields intuitively reasonable portrayals of development. This property can be illustrated with regard to the concept of fullness. Siegler and Vago (1978) presented 6- and 10-year-olds pairs of differently shaped glasses, each containing some water and some unoccupied space, and asked the children which glass was more full. Most 6-year-olds used a height rule to solve such problems. If one glass had the taller liquid column, they consistently said that glass was fuller; if the two heights were equal, then they said the two glasses were equally full. Most 10-year-olds used a volume rule. If one volume was greater, then they said that glass was fuller; otherwise, they said the two were equally full. The volume rule seemed to be a natural outgrowth of the height rule, in that it required consideration of one new dimension (the cross-sectional area of water) as well as the previous dimension (the height of the water). Similarly, the correct rule for computing fullness seemed to be a natural outgrowth of the volume rule, since it requires consideration of the volume of unoccupied space in the glass as well as the volume of occupied space.

A second general conclusion within the theory is that children possess fall-back rules for dealing with unfamiliar problems. These fall-back rules lead children to reason similarly on quite diverse tasks. One example of a fall-back rule is evident in 5-year-olds' problem-solving approaches. As mentioned in the chapter on Piaget's theory, 5-year-olds focus on a single dimension on many problems. They consistently predict that the side of a balance scale with more weight will go down, that the glass with the taller liquid column must contain more water, that the larger object necessarily casts the larger shadow, that the train that stopped farther down the track traveled for more time, and so on.

It is tempting to conclude that these problem-solving approaches indicate that 5-year-olds can only consider a single dimension. This conclusion is almost certainly incorrect, however. When 5-year-olds speak, for example, they take into account many dimensions: how to pronounce words, how to order them into grammatical sentences, how to convey desired meanings, how loudly they need to talk to be heard, and so on.

An alternative explanation for 5-year-olds' frequent focus on a single dimension involves fall-back rules. Children may have certain standard forms of reasoning on which they rely when they lack detailed procedures for solving a problem. Five-year-olds may utilize a fall-back rule of the following form: If you lack direct information about how to solve a problem in which you need to judge which object has more x, then focus on the single seemingly most important dimension and choose the object with more of that dimension as having more x. Conceptualizing 5-year-olds' one-dimensional problem-solving strategies as reflecting such a fall-back rule suggests why children focus on a single dimension in some but not all situations. In familiar situations such as speaking, they rely on knowledge they have acquired for dealing with that particular situation. This knowledge may involve understanding of many different dimensions. In unfamiliar problem-solving situations, however, they rely on fall-back rules as a useful guide for how to proceed. The fall-back rules may not be perfect, but they do work in most situations.

The third general conclusion concerns the centrality of encoding in cognitive development. As noted in the discussion of Newell and Simon's theory, encoding involves identification of sets of features for internally representing objects and events in particular situations. The very idea of encoding implies that the nature of information processing is active rather than passive; some information is focused on, while other parts are ignored or processed only superficially (Craik & Lockhart, 1972). Thus, emphasizing encoding implies that the information-processing system is not simply a videocassette machine that blindly records experience. Rather, it is an active interpreter and organizer of experience.

Although the simplest way to think of encoding is to identify it with attention, the concept goes beyond attention to include the way in which we organize our experiences. This aspect of encoding can be seen in the contributions of great artists who change the ways entire cultures encode what they see and hear. An anecdote about Pablo Picasso illustrates this function. Picasso painted a portrait of Gertrude Stein, a writer well known in the 1920s and 1930s. An observer looked at the painting for several minutes and then commented that it did not look much like Stein. "No matter," Picasso is said to have answered. "It will."

Encodings are related to long-term memory representations, though the two are not identical. The difference stems from the fact that encodings are created at the time the stimulus is presented. Illustratively, Pellegrino and Glaser (1982) gave college students the analogy 15:19 :: 8:12 :: 5:?. It seems unlikely that college student's long-term memory representations of the number 19 included the property "is 4 more than 15" prior to presentation of this problem, though they would encode this information here. Complementarily, relevant information from long-term memory may be omitted from a particular encoding. Sternberg (1977) presented the analogy problem Washington:1 :: Lincoln:? The problem included the information that the correct answer was either 5 or 10. This problem is difficult not because the relevant information (Whose faces are on one-dollar and five-dollar bills?) is absent from most people's long-term memories, but because the relevant information is not included in their encoding of "Washington" and "Lincoln" in the context of this problem. An encoding, then, is a representation of information in a particular situation.

Although encodings are generally important in cognition, they seem likely to be especially important in producing cognitive development. Young children frequently find themselves in task environments about which they know little or nothing. Encoding the meaningful features of these situations is of far from trivial difficulty. Even mundane tasks illustrate the importance of improved encoding in allowing children to understand their world: learning to encode the first digit of school room numbers as indicating different information than the next two numbers (e.g., the 2 in Room 206); learning to encode the position of the hour and minute hands on a clock, rather than the position of the second hand, as communicating the important information about the time of day; and learning to encode those typographic features that are of practical importance in reading and to ignore those that serve only esthetic purposes.

An experiment on children's understanding of balance scales documented the way in which encoding contributes to children's steadily increasing ability to learn. The balance scale that was used is shown in Figure 3–3. Different amounts of weight could be placed on pegs at varying distances from the fulcrum. The task was to discover how the balance scale works.

Most 5-year-olds believe that the side of the balance with more weight will go down, regardless of the distance of the weight from the fulcrum. While this knowledge is one factor that influences children's ability to learn more about balance scales, Siegler (1976) found that it was not the only factor. In one experiment, 5- and 8-year-olds, who on a pretest had consistently indicated that the side with more weight would go down, were presented a series of balance-scale problems and allowed to see how the arm of the scale actually tipped on each problem. Then they were given a posttest to assess the effects of their experience. The goal was to determine whether different-age children using the same initial rule would derive the same or different lessons from potential learning experiences.

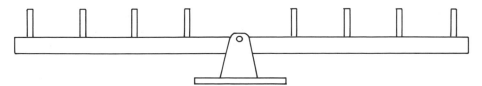

FIGURE 3-3 The balance scale. Metal disks could be placed on a peg on each side of the fulcrum. Children needed to decide which side of the balance would go down given the particular configuration of weights on pegs (from Siegler, 1976).

It turned out that the 5- and 8-year-olds derived different lessons from the experience. The majority of 8-year-olds benefited from observing the balance scale's activity. They adopted more advanced rules that reflected understanding of the importance of the weights' distance from the fulcrum. In contrast, the 5-year-olds made no progress. None of them adopted rules that reflected understanding of the role of distance from the fulcrum.

Why might 5- and 8-year-olds have reacted differently to the same experience? Detailed examination of a few children suggested that encoding of the balance-scale configuration played a crucial role. The 5-year-olds seemed to see each configuration solely in terms of two piles of weights, one on each side of the fulcrum. They did not view it as two piles of weights, one a certain distance to the right of the fulcrum and one a certain distance to the left. If 5-year-olds' encoding was limited in this way, their failure to learn the role of distance from the experience with the balance scale would be unsurprising. They simply would not be taking in the critical information.

Several sources of evidence supported this interpretation. One involved an encoding test that was given to both 5- and 8-year-olds who believed that the side of the balance with more weight would invariably go down. The 8-year-olds were found to notice and remember both the amounts of weight and the distances of the weights from the fulcrum, even though they did not use the distance information to predict which way the balance scale would tip. The 5-year-olds, however, noticed and remembered only the amounts of weight.

Following this, 5-year-olds were taught to encode both weight and distance. Then they were given the same experience observing the effects of different configurations of weights on pegs that previously had not helped other 5-year-olds. The instruction in encoding made a difference. Although 0% of 5-year-olds without encoding training had previously benefited from the experience with the balance scale, now 70% did.

A similar pattern emerged with very young children. When 3- and 4-year-olds were presented the balance-scale task (Siegler, 1978), all of the 3-year-olds and half of the 4-year-olds were found not even to consistently rely on weight. Their performance seemed entirely haphazard. When 3- and 4-year-olds were allowed to observe the activities of the balance scale, most of the older children learned, but none of the younger ones did. An encoding test indicated that 4-year-olds typically encoded the weight dimension, but that 3-year-olds did not. Finally, in the crucial test, after 3-year-olds were taught to encode the weight dimension, they were able to learn the weight rule from the same problems that had not helped their peers previously. Similar patterns have appeared on other concepts, such as time and projection of shadows (Siegler, 1983).

These results imply a cyclical view of cognitive development. First, children's predictive knowledge and encoding are at the same level. Then the children start to encode features of the world that they previously missed. This improved encoding heightens their ability to learn. When children encounter relevant experience, their improved encoding allows them to learn more advanced rules. Then the cycle can start again.

What is wrong with this approach? It does not explain in detail how encoding is done. It also does not explain why some dimensions, such as weight, are easier to encode than others, such as distance. Still, it would be disingenuous of me to appear pessimistic about it. The generalizations about much of children's thinking being rule governed and about the existence of fall-back rules appear consistent with many other investigators' findings (e.g., Brown & Burton, 1978; Case, 1985; Strauss, 1982). The role of encoding also has been documented in many situations (Chase, in press; Chi, Feltovich, & Glaser, 1981; Larkin, Heller, & Greeno, 1980). Further, the research carries an important educational implication. When children fail to learn, parents and teachers should examine whether the children are encoding the information they need to benefit from the experience. If the children's encoding is inadequate, teaching them to encode more effectively may help them to learn. Together with the other theories that have been described, the general approach may contribute positively to future understanding of children's thinking.

Developmental mechanisms work together.   In this chapter the contributions to cognitive development of automatization, encoding, generalization, and strategy construction have been discussed in the contexts of different theories. The separate discussions may have created an impression that the mechanisms operate in isolation, despite previous assurances to the contrary. In fact, all the mechanisms work together to contribute to the growth of children's thinking. A single development can reflect each of their contributions.

Consider a hypothetical process through which a girl might learn to attach an "ed" sound to verbs to indicate that the action occurred in the past. Early in the process of language development, all her mental resources would be needed just to perceive clearly words and phrases she heard (think of hearing conversation in a foreign language that you don't know or are just starting to learn). With greater experience listening to language, her processing of the words and phrases would become automatized, freeing up cognitive capacity for other types of processing. This free capacity would allow her to notice that similar meanings were expressed by words that sometimes ended with an "ed" sound and sometimes did not (e.g., like and liked; jump and jumped). This realization, in turn, would lead her to encode the "ed" sound as a separate unit, to find out just what it meant. She then could note the regular connection between the "ed" sound being present and the action having occured in the past. Finally, she could construct a new strategy based on the generalization: Whenever you want to indicate that an action occurred in the past, attach an "ed" to the end of the word describing the action. By working together in this way, automatization, encoding, generalization, and strategy construction may account for many improvements in children's thinking.

SUMMARY

All theories of development attempt to answer two questions: What develops? How does development occur? Information-processing theories of development have several additional distinguishing characteristics. Their basic assumption is that thinking is information processing. They emphasize precise analysis of change mechanisms. They also focus on which processes are performed, in what order, and for how much time. Finally, they look to findings about adults' thinking, as well as to findings about children's thinking, for ideas about the nature of cognitive development.

Two theories of adults' information processing, Atkinson and Shiffrin's model of memory and Newell and Simon's approach to problem solving, have especially influenced developmental research. Atkinson and Shiffrin's central distinction was between structural and control features of memory. Structural features are those aspects that are part of the inherent organization and that are the same for all individuals. Among these are the division of memory into sensory, short-term, and long-term stores. Control features are the flexible processes that vary among individuals, change with experience, and can be used to overcome the structural limitations of the memory system.

In Atkinson and Shiffrin's model, information enters the sensory store, in which it resides briefly. Then it moves to the short-term store, where it stays for a considerably longer, but still brief, time (about 15 seconds). Finally, it may move to the long-term store, in which it can reside indefinitely. Control processes influence the workings of each store. They influence what information enters the sensory register, what information is maintained in short-term memory by such means as rehearsal, and how people retrieve information from long-term memory. Atkinson and Shiffrin's theory has stimulated work indicating that children and adults differ much more in their use of control features than in the structural features of their memories, on children's and adult's automatic processing of frequency information, and on adaptive use of strategies.

Newell and Simon's theory of problem solving focused on the role of the task environment, the role of encoding of the critical information in the task environment, and the usefulness of computer simulations for modeling thought processes. The complexity of much of human cognition was, in their view, attributable to the need to adapt to complex task environments more than to the complexity of the cognitive system itself. The complexity of many tasks, together with people's limited information processing capacity, creates the need to encode selectively. Computer simulation is a tool for studying thinking that has proved useful both in promoting theoretical insights and for practical purposes, as illustrated by the geometry tutor.

Several information-processing theories of development have been formulated to make understandable how creatures as helpless and unknowledgeable as infants eventually attain the power and flexibility of the adult information-processing system. These theories have emphasized the roles of four mechanisms that seem especially important in producing cognitive development: strategy construction, automatization, generalization, and encoding.

Sternberg's theory has attempted to link information-processing ideas with earlier ideas developed in studying intelligence. He divided intelligence into three types of components: metacomponents, performance components, and knowledge-acquisiton components. Metacomponents function as a strategy construction mechanism, arranging the other two types of components into goal-oriented procedures. Performance components do the work of actually solving problems. Knowledge-acquisition components are used to obtain new information when no solution to a problem is immediately possible. The theory has been applied to diverse cognitive skills and to many populations, including gifted children and retarded children.

Case's theory is aimed at uniting Piagetian and information-processing theories. It suggests that one major obstacle to cognitive growth is limited short-term memory capacity. By automatizing their processing, and through biological maturation, children become able to perform increasingly difficult cognitive feats. Case's approach includes stages similar to Piaget's, a model of memory like Atkinson and Shiffrin's, and an emphasis on problem-solving strategies similar to Newell and Simon's. His approach has proved to be of practical value as well as theoretical interest—for example, in teaching young children how to solve missing addend problems.

Klahr and Wallace's theory focused on the developing system's capacity for drawing generalizations. In their analysis, generalization included three more particular processes: the time line, regularity detection, and redundancy elimination. The time line is a record of all the situations the system has encountered, the response to the situations, and the outcome.

Regularity detection operates on the data in the time line to generalize about experience. Redundancy elimination looks for parts of procedures that could be eliminated without changing the outcome of processing. Together, these mechanisms allow children to identify regular relations and to extend the realizations to new situations.

My own theory focuses on what children know about particular concepts, how they acquire new knowledge, and how their knowledge influences their learning. One conclusion that has emerged from the research is that much of children's knowledge can be described in terms of rules. Another is that children possess fall-back rules that they use when they have no direct knowledge about how to solve problems. A third is that differences in younger and older children's encoding accounts for at least some of the differences in their ability to learn. Inadequate encoding can make learning impossible by depriving the cognitive system of critical information. Improved encoding can improve children's ability to learn, which results in improved existing knowledge. The improved knowledge can, in turn, lead to further improvements in encoding, thus starting a new cycle of development.

RECOMMENDED READINGS

Case, R. (1985). *Intellectual development: A systematic reinterpretation.* New York: Academic Press. The most up-to-date presentation of Case's theory; an appealing synthesis of ideas from Piaget's and Newell and Simon's theories together with an emphasis on the role of short-term-memory limitations and automatization.

Klahr, D. (1984). Transition processes in quantitative development. In R. J. Sternberg (Ed.), *Mechanisms of cognitive development.* New York: Freeman and Company. A clear, incisive description of Klahr's theory. Especially interesting for the emphasis on change processes that might influence development.

Siegler, R. S. (1981). Developmental sequences within and between concepts. *Monographs of the Society for Research in Child Development, 46,* Whole No. 189. Describes the sequence of rules through which children come to understand a large number of complex problems such as conservation and the balance scale. Also focuses on the role of fall-back rules in determining when children will and will not center on a single dimension.

Simon, H. A. (1981). *The sciences of the artificial.* Cambridge, MA: MIT Press. A lucid presentation of the surprising similarities that unite cognitive psychology, architecture, computer science, and other fields. Page for page, one of the most worthwhile books I have ever read.

Sternberg, R. J. (1985). *Beyond IQ.* New York: Cambridge University Press. The most up-to-date presentation of Sternberg's deservedly-influential theory of human intelligence.

4
TOOLS FOR STUDYING CHILDREN'S THINKING

And although the arguing from Experiments and Observations by Induction be no Demonstration of general Conclusions; yet it is the best way of arguing which the Nature of Things admits of. . . . (Sir Isaac Newton, *Optics*.)

Studying thinking is not easy. There are many reasons why this is true, but two seem especially important. First, natural languages such as English often prove inadequate for precisely describing thought processes. If you try to describe exactly how you read, you quickly will realize the difficulty of characterizing even those mental activities of which you are conscious. Second, the most straightforward methods for studying thinking often prove unilluminating. We could study children's reading by examining the percentage of words they read correctly, but this would not teach us much about their reading processes. We probably would learn only that older children can read more and harder words than younger ones. Because of these shortcomings of commonsense techniques, researchers have invented a variety of specialized information-processing languages and methods for studying cognitive development. These can be thought of as tools for understanding children's thinking.

The central theme of this chapter is that choices of methods and languages are inherently related to each other, and that both choices influence, and are influenced by, prevailing theories. An example may help illustrate the linkages among theories, methods, and languages. Recall the discussion in the last chapter of Sternberg and Rifkin's (1979) model of how children solve analogy problems. First they encode the four terms in the analogy, then they infer the relation between the first two terms, then they establish a relation between the first and third terms, and finally they generate a relation between the third and fourth terms that parallels that between the first and second. Flow diagrams provide a fitting language for depicting such a model because flow diagrams, like the model, directly imply an ordered sequence of steps. First, children take the action in the square or diamond on top of the flow diagram, then they take the action in the square or diamond second from the top, and so on. It is not surprising, then, that Sternberg and Rifkin presented their model in the form of a flow diagram. The *chronometric analysis* (analysis of patterns of solution times) they used to test their ideas also fit well with the sequential nature of the model and the language. This method was based on the assumption that each successive execution of a process would add a fixed additional amount of time, an assumption that would be most likely if each new execution began after the previous one ended.

In sum, the availability of flow diagrams for representing information processing and of chronometric methods for collecting evidence created the conditions under which models such as Sternberg and Rifkin's might be formulated. As such models are formulated, they in turn stimulate the invention of new methods and languages for representing thinking that are even more precisely suited to testing and expressing them. Proceeding through this chapter, we will encounter many more connections between theories and models and the specialized languages and methods on which they are built.

The chapter is organized into two main sections. The first section focuses on languages for representing thinking. We will first consider the limits of standard spoken languages and then consider several languages designed to overcome these limits: flow diagrams, production systems, semantic networks, and scripts. The value of each of these languages will be illustrated in the context of current research on the development of problem solving, memory, and conceptual understanding. The second part of the chapter is about methods. We will examine methods for analyzing solution times, errors, eye movements, and verbal statements. The goal of each of these methods is to get inside children's heads—that is, to reveal knowledge and thought processes that are not easily apparent. Illustrations will involve reading, problem solving, and understanding of spatial relations. The organization of the chapter is outlined in Table 4-1.

TABLE 4-1   Chapter Outline

    I.   Languages for Representing Children's Thinking
        A.   The Limits of Natural Languages
        B.   Flow Diagrams
        C.   Production Systems
        D.   Semantic Networks
        E.   Scripts
        F.   Comparisons Among Languages
   II.   Methods for Studying Children's Thinking
        A.   Chronometric Analysis
        B.   Methods of Error Analysis
        C.   Analysis of Eye Movements
        D.   Protocol Analysis
  III.   Summary

LANGUAGES FOR REPRESENTING CHILDREN'S THINKING

The Limits of Natural Languages

Natural languages such as English, French, and Chinese are among the most profound accomplishments of human beings. They are not, however, well suited to all purposes. By their very natures, natural languages are compromises among different and sometimes conflicting purposes. A natural language must allow users to get across meanings, to express emotions, to be polite or informal, to make statements that are not intended to be taken literally, and so on. Precision of expression and brevity are only two among many goals. Frequently they are not the primary ones. In scientific contexts, however, precision and brevity are essential.

Different languages have different advantages. Every language facilitates communication of some types of information and makes difficult communication of other types. A verbal description of a scene involving several people in a room can precisely characterize the people's goals, though the verbal format is clumsy for describing their exact spatial positions. A picture of the same scene can clearly communicate spatial positions, but is poorly suited for specifying the goals. Family relationships (e.g., first cousin once removed) are difficult to express either verbally or in a photo, but can be captured quite nicely in a genealogical tree. Thus, different languages are useful for different purposes.

Each of the languages in the next section—flow diagrams, production systems, semantic networks, and scripts—has been found useful for one or more purposes that frequently arise in characterizing children's thinking. Flow diagrams are especially useful for depicting the sequence of thought processes that people go through in solving problems. Production systems are especially useful for expressing detailed hypotheses about the unobservable symbol manipulations that lead to visible behavior. Semantic networks are especially useful for describing people's static knowledge about the world, such as their information about the meanings of words and concepts. Scripts are especially useful for portraying knowledge that includes both sequences of actions and static information about the world, such as how to act at a doctor's office. Together, these languages provide a formidable arsenal for attacking the problems that arise in describing and explaining children's thinking.

Flow Diagrams

Among the languages for representing children's thinking that we will discuss in this chapter, flow diagrams are the simplest and most widely used. The boxes, diamonds, and arrows that appear in them have become quite well known. I will illustrate their use in the context of research on the balance-scale task.

As noted in the last chapter, the balance-scale apparatus involved a long arm sitting atop a fulcrum. Four pegs extended vertically from the arm on each side of the fulcrum. Metal weights with holes in the middle could be placed on any of these pegs. The arm of the balance could tip left or right or remain level, depending on how the weights were arranged. The task was to predict which (if either) side would go down if a lever, which could be set to hold the arm motionless, were released. (The balance scale that was used is depicted on page 91).

In Siegler (1976), I suggested that children's knowledge about the balance scale could be represented in terms of the four decision trees shown in Figure 4–1. Children using Rule I consider only the number of weights on each side of the fulcrum. If the numbers are the same, the children predict "balance." Otherwise, they predict that the side with the greater amount of weight will go down.

Children using Rule II also first consider whether the weights on the two sides are equal. If the weights are unequal, children say that whichever side has more weight will go down. However, if the weights are equal, they consider an additional variable: distance of the weights from the fulcrum. If the weights are equal, and the pile of weights on one side is farther from the fulcrum, Rule II children predict that that side will go down.

Children using Rule III always consider both weights and distances. If both weights and distances are equal, they say the scale will balance. If one side has more weight and the distances are equal, they say that the side with more weight will go down. If the weights are equal and one side has its weights farther from the fulcrum, they say that side will go down. However, if one side has more weight and the other side has its weight farther from the fulcrum, Rule III children do not know what to do. They realize that there is a conflict between the one side having more weight and the other having its weight farther from the fulcrum, but do not know how to resolve the conflict. Therefore, they muddle through, or guess which side will go down.

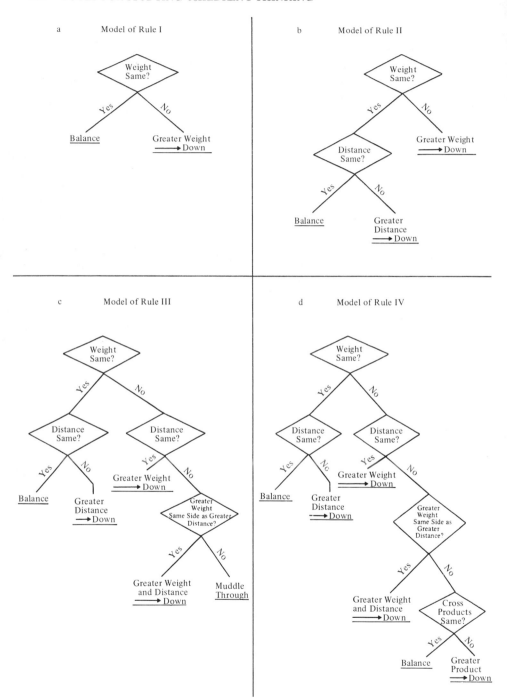

FIGURE 4-1   Rules for solving balance-scale problems (from Siegler, 1976).

Rule IV is the correct performance rule for the task. It is identical to Rule III in all respects except that it includes knowledge of what to do when one side has more weight and the other side's weight is farther from the fulcrum. Under these circumstances, Rule IV children compute the torques on each side. They do this by multiplying the number of weights on each side by the distance of those weights from the fulcrum. Then they compare the torques on the two sides and predict that the side with the greater torque will go down. Thus, if the left side of the balance's arm has three weights on the second peg from the fulcrum, and the right side has four weights on the first peg from the fulcrum, the torques would be six units on the left side and four units on the right side. Thus, the left side would go down.

This set of rules makes clear what is developing in understanding of balance scales. Between Rule I and Rule II, children begin to use the distance dimension to make predictions. Between Rule II and Rule III, children generalize their reliance on distance, from just considering it when weights are equal to always considering it. Between Rule III and Rule IV, children learn how to combine weight and distance in a mathematical formula that allows them for the first time to solve all types of balance-scale problems.

Using the rule models as a language for expressing ideas about children's understanding of balance scales also had another benefit. It allowed a choice to be made between two means that children could use to solve all problems. The method diagrammed in Rule IV involves computing torques only when one side has more weight and the other side's weights are more distant from the fulcrum. On other types of problems, children judge qualitatively, not bothering to calculate torques. For example, if presented a problem with two weights on the second peg on each side, a Rule IV user would say that equal weights and equal distances means that the two sides will balance.

This is not the only way children could consistently solve balance-scale problems. Another way would be to compute torques on all problems, regardless of whether weights or distances are equal. For example, if there were two weights on the second peg on each side of the fulcrum, children could multiply 2 × 2 on each side, see that the products were equal, and predict that the scale would balance.

Both approaches would produce consistently correct answers, but the two would produce different patterns of solution times. If children use the Rule IV model, they should solve problems more quickly where weights, distances, or both are equal on the two sides than problems where one side has more weight and the other has more distance. As shown in Figure 4–1, children using Rule IV try to find a qualitative solution before computing torques. In contrast, if children compute torques for all types of problems, there would be no reason to expect this pattern. All types of problems would be solved equally quickly.

In fact, the pattern implied by the Rule IV model was clearly evident. People who consistently performed correctly answered more quickly on every problem they were presented where weights, distances, or both were equal than on any problem where one side had more weight and the other side had its weights farther from the fulcrum. Thus, the rule models were useful in determining exactly how children solved the problems.

Production Systems

Production systems are a type of computer language that has proved especially useful for modeling thinking. Like other computer languages, they provide detailed descriptions of symbol-manipulating activities. Unlike most other computer languages, production systems' activities are directed by explicit goals built into the productions themselves. This incorporation of goals with activities aimed at achieving the goals makes production systems a more intuitively plausible language for representing thinking than many other computer languages. It was these advantages that led Klahr and Wallace (1976) to phrase their theory (Chapter 3) in the language of production systems.

One advance warning: Production systems are the most difficult language we will consider, and many people find them baffling. Getting a general sense of their uses and functioning is more important than understanding all the details. But—Catch-22—it is easier to understand their uses and functioning if you do understand the details.

As shown in Figure 4–2, production systems include two main parts: the *production system proper*, which is made up of all of the individual productions, and the *short-term memory*. The production system proper

FIGURE 4–2 Organization of production systems.

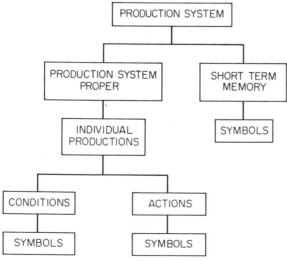

represents the system's knowledge for dealing with the world. Each production within it indicates what *action* the system will take should particular *conditions* arise. The short-term memory represents the system's knowledge about the momentary state of the world. Information about this current state enters the short-term memory either through the system perceiving some event in the external world or through the *firing* (operating) of a production. Both the contents of short-term memory and the conditions and actions in the individual productions are composed of symbols.

The production system as a whole operates in two-step cycles. The first step in each cycle involves a particular situation arising and being represented in short-term memory. The second step in the cycle involves the firing of a production within the production system proper in response to the state of the world represented in the short-term memory. The current goal is always the first element in short-term memory. Other than this, elements within short-term memory are ordered by how recently they entered the memory. The most recent entry is nearest the front.

Table 4–2, a simple production system for stopping and going at traffic lights, illustrates how production systems work. Each production, such as P1, P2, and P3, contains two sides: the *condition side* to the left of the arrow and the *action side* to the right of it. The condition side indicates when that production should fire; if all the symbols on the condition side of the production are included within the current short-term memory contents, then the production can fire. The action side indicates what actions will be taken if the production fires. Thus, production P1 in the traffic light example will fire if the short-term memory contents indicate that your goal is to go and you see a red light and you are moving. The action taken under these circumstances is that the goal in short-term memory is changed from going to stopping.

With this background, we can examine how the Table 4–2 production system works. As shown in the trace of the system's activities, the situation begins with the short-term memory containing a goal of going and the knowledge that the car is moving. These conditions do not subsume the entire condition side of any production, so no production fires. The driver just continues. Now suppose the driver sees a red light. The symbol "see red light" is inserted into the short-term memory. Now P1 applies, since the contents of short-term memory match all three of its conditions: The driver's goal is to go, he sees a red light, and the car is moving. When P1 fires, it changes the goal within short-term memory from going to stopping. The conditions required for P1 to fire no longer exist, since the goal is to stop rather than to go. However, the conditions required for P2 to fire are now in effect. P2 fires, which leads to the action of pressing on the brake until the car stops, and also to the representation of the state of the car in short-term memory being changed to "stopped."

Now the goal is to stop, the light is red, and the car is stopped. No production applies, so the driver does nothing. When the light switches to

TABLE 4-2 Production System for Driving a Car

PRODUCTIONS

P1: (Goal is to go) (See red light) (Are moving) – – – – – – → (Change goal to stop)

P2: (Goal is to stop) (See red light) (Are moving) – – – – – – → (Press brake until stopped)
(Change "are moving" to "are stopped")

P3: (Goal is to stop) (See green light) (Are stopped) – – – → (Change goal to go)

P4: (Goal is to go) (Are stopped) (See green light) – – – – → (Press gas pedal until moving)
(Change "are stopped" to "are moving")
(Delete "see green light")

P5: (Light changed to green) (See red light) – – – – – – – → (Change "red light" to "green light")
(Delete "light changed to green")

TRACE OF SYSTEM'S ACTIVITY

SHORT-TERM MEMORY CONTENTS	PRODUCTION THAT FIRES	EXTERNAL EVENTS
(Goal is to go) (Are moving)	– – –	– – –
(Goal is to go) (Are moving)	– – –	See red light
(Goal is to go) (See red light) (Are moving)	P1	– – –
(Goal is to stop) (See red light) (Are moving)	P2	– – –
(Goal is to stop) (See red light) (Are stopped)	– – –	– – –
(Goal is to stop) (See red light) (Are stopped)	– – –	See green light
(Goal is to stop) (Light changed to green) (See red light) (Are stopped)	P5	– – –
(Goal is to stop) (See green light) (Are stopped)	P3	– – –
(Goal is to go) (See green light) (Are stopped)	P4	– – –

green, however, the symbol "light changed to green" enters short-term memory. P5 fires. Now all the conditions for P3 are included in short-term memory, so it fires. Since the goal is now to go, and the car is stopped, P4 fires, and the car is again on its way.

A few years ago, my colleague David Klahr and I got into a good-natured argument in a class we were teaching together. Klahr pointed to the advantages of production systems, the language he uses to represent children's thinking. I did the same for flow diagrams, the language I usually use. As we continued the discussion during lunch, we realized that the pros and cons of these languages for studying children's thinking might be of interest to a wider audience. The end result was a 55-page article titled "The Representation of Children's Knowledge" (Klahr & Siegler, 1978). Our strategy was to show how a particular developmental model could be represented as a flow diagram or a production system and then to discuss the advantages and disadvantages associated with each representation.

Our specific focus was on the development of knowledge about balance scales. The rules I hypothesized for the balance scale were shown in Figure 4–1. The same rules are expressed as production systems in Table 4–3. First consider Model I. A child using this model considers only the amount of weight. P1 indicates that when the amount of weight on the two sides is the same, the child predicts "balance." P2 indicates that when one side has more weight, the child predicts that side will go down. The expression "Side X" in P2 indicates that X can take on the value of either left or right. Thus, in Model I, P2 can fire if either the left or right side has more weight than the other.

The first two productions in Model II are identical to those in Model I. However, this model also includes P3: When weights are the same on the two sides, and when one side's weights are more distant from the fulcrum, say that the side with the more distant weights will go down. This model introduces an important aspect of production systems: *conflict resolution principles*. The need for a conflict resolution principle arises because sometimes the symbols in the short-term memory match the condition sides of more than one production. In Model II, the condition sides of both P1 and P3 would be matched if the short-term memory contents included weights being the same and one side's weights being farther from the fulcrum. Some criterion must be adopted for deciding which production will operate in such situations.

One common criterion, the one used in the Table 4–3 production system, is that among the productions that could fire, the production whose condition side has the greatest number of elements will fire. For example, in Model II, any time all three conditions of P3 are included in the short-term memory contents, both conditions of P1 also must be included. If both P1 and P3 have their condition sides matched, P3 will fire, because it has a greater number of elements to match. The logic underlying this criterion is that the greater the number of conditions that match the short-term memory

TABLE 4-3 Production-System Models of Balance-Scale Rules

MODEL I

P1: (Goal is to predict) ————→ (Say "Balance")
    (Sides X and Y have same weight)

P2: (Goal is to predict) ————→ (Say "Side X down")
    (Side X has more weight)

MODEL II

P1: (Goal is to predict) ————→ (Say "Balance")
    (Sides X and Y have same weight)

P2: (Goal is to predict) ————→ (Say "Side X down")
    (Side X has more weight)

P3: (Goal is to predict) ————→ (Say "Side X down")
    (Sides X and Y have same weight)
    (Side X has greater distance)

MODEL III

P1: (Goal is to predict) ————→ (Say "Balance")
    (Sides X and Y have same weight)

P2: (Goal is to predict) ————→ (Say "Side X down")
    (Side X has more weight)

P3: (Goal is to predict) ————→ (Say "Side X down")
    (Sides X and Y have same weight)
    (Side X has greater distance)

P4: (Goal is to predict) ————→ (Muddle through)
    (Side X has more weight and less distance)

MODEL IV

P1: (Goal is to predict) - - - - - - - - - - - → (Say "Balance")
(Sides X and Y have same weight)

P2: (Goal is to predict) - - - - - - - - - - - → (Say "Side X down")
(Side X has more weight)

P3: (Goal is to predict) - - - - - - - - - - - → (Say "Side X down")
(Sides X and Y have same weight)
(Side X has greater distance)

P4': (Goal is to predict) - - - - - - - - - - - → (Interrupt goal of predicting)
(Side X has more weight and less distance) (Goal = Compute torques)
(Torques are unknown)

P5: (Goal is to compute torques) - - - - - - - - - - - → (Torque on Side X) = (Weight on Side X) times (Distance on Side X)
(Torque on Side Y) = (Weight on Side Y) times (Distance on Side Y)
(Delete goal of computing torques)
(Reactivate goal of predicting)

P6: (Goal is to predict) - - - - - - - - - - - → (Say "Side X goes down")
(Torque on Side X > Torque on Side Y) (Stop)

P7: (Goal is to predict) - - - - - - - - - - - → (Say "The two sides balance")
(Torque on Side X = Torque on Side Y) (Stop)

contents, the more that production must be specifically relevant to the demands of the situation.

Model III's first three productions are identical to those of Model II. The fourth production is new. It indicates that if one side has both more weight and less distance, then the system must muddle through or guess.

Model IV involves a number of changes from Model III, all of which stem from the system having learned the concept of torques. The old P4 is changed into the new P4′ by making three changes. The condition side now stipulates that torques must be unknown; the action side stipulates that rather than muddling through, the system should interrupt the currently unattainable goal of predicting which side will go down; and the action side stipulates that the system should establish the goal of performing the torque computations. P5 performs these computations, deletes the goal of computing torques, and reactivates the goal of predicting which side will go down. P6 indicates that if the torque on one side is greater than that on the other, then the side with the greatest torque will go down. P7 indicates that if the torques on the two sides are equal, the scale will balance.

Now we can examine the way in which these models solve a balance-scale problem. Suppose that a child is shown a balance-scale configuration with two weights on the third peg to the left of the fulcrum and four weights on the first peg to the right of it. In Model I, P2 would fire since the right side has more weight. The model would predict (incorrectly) that the right side would go down. Model II would go through the same process and reach the same conclusion as Model I. Model III would recognize that although the right side has more weight, it also has less distance. Therefore P4 would fire, and the system would muddle through. In Model IV, P4′ would fire, establishing the goal of computing torques on each side and interrupting the goal of predicting. Then P5 would compute the torques and reactivate the goal of predicting. Finally, P6 would fire, since the torque on the left side (six units) is greater than that on the right side (four units).

Writing models of knowledge about balance scales in both flow-chart and production-system forms provided a basis for directly comparing the two languages. On one dimension, the languages are equivalent; the two models make identical predictions about children's performance on the balance-scale task. The flow diagrams have an obvious advantage in readability. No special background is required to follow them, whereas considerable background is necessary to understand the production systems. Another advantage of the flow diagrams is that a higher percentage of their components is testable. It is difficult to see how definitive tests could ever be made about some of the symbol manipulations that occur in production systems.

On the other hand, the production system specifies in greater detail the memory contents and encodings that the investigator believes to underlie behavior. Illustratively, the production systems make clear that to execute Model IV, children must interrupt their original goal of predicting in order to pursue another goal (computing torques), but at the same time must maintain the original goal in memory so that they can eventually complete the task of predicting. The flow diagrams are less clear on this point. Also, a production system that runs on a computer thereby demonstrates its sufficiency to produce the behavior in question. A flow diagram lacks this test. On simple tasks such as the balance scale, both production-system and flow-diagram models clearly are sufficient to produce the desired behavior. On more complex tasks, however, it is sometimes unclear whether flow-diagram models are sufficient.

Klahr and I concluded that when great detail and demonstrated sufficiency are the primary goals, production systems are more useful. When testability and readability are the paramount considerations, flow diagrams have the advantage. Then we went back to doing our research pretty much as we had before, he using production systems and I using flow diagrams. But we knew better why we did it that way.[1]

Semantic Networks

Flow diagrams and production systems are especially useful for representing the time course of information processing. They imply a sequence of steps taken one after another. With many types of knowledge, however, we do not wish to imply any particular time course. For example, we may wish to characterize children's understanding of a concept such as "time" or "density." The important characteristics of such a representation are how well it illustrates the components of the concept and how well it illustrates their organization. Semantic networks are particularly apt languages for expressing such information.

Semantic networks are composed of *propositions*, which resemble simple declarative sentences. Ordinary verbal statements often include several propositions. For example, the sentence "The quick red fox jumped over the lazy brown dog" can be decomposed into seven propositions:

1. There was a fox.
2. The fox was quick.
3. The fox was red.
4. The fox jumped over something.
5. The something that was jumped over was a dog.
6. The dog was lazy.
7. The dog was brown.

[1]A year and a half after drawing this conclusion, it has become apparent that the discussion had a long-term benefit that was not immediately apparent. It helped me decide that a computer simulation was a good means of formalizing my ideas about how children learn arithmetic. The simulation is described in Siegler and Shrager (1984). In that case, the time and effort needed to write a simulation seemed justified by the benefits of proving that the model was sufficient to account for a large range of children's behavior in learning arithmetic. Writing the simulation also led to predictions about children's arithmetic learning that I had not previously formulated. Thus, the discussion seems to have been even more useful than I realized at the time.

A semantic network representation of the sentence would include each of these propositions.

As discussed in the chapter on Piaget's theory, a central issue in the study of cognitive development is why children understand some words and concepts before others. Sometimes the order of acquisition can be explained by the children being more familiar with certain words and concepts, but at other times it cannot. Semantic networks make possible detailed analyses of words and concepts that can help to explain these sequences.

Gentner (1975) examined why children consistently understand some verbs before others. The terms that interested her were possessive verbs such as *give, take, buy, sell, lend,* and *borrow.* Informal observation indicated that 3-year-olds often understand some of these terms, though even 8-year-olds do not understand others. Therefore, Gentner decided to express each word's meaning as a semantic network to see how the networks required to describe the later-acquired terms differed from those needed to describe the earlier-acquired ones.

Gentner noted that all possessive verbs can be described within the same framework, because all of them include a number of relations in common. She labeled these common relations *semantic primitives.* Among the semantic primitives that are useful for describing possessive verbs are transfer, contractual relation, and cause.

Representations of the verbs *give* and *sell* are shown in Figure 4–3. As shown in Figure 4–3A, *give* implies an agent, a recipient, and a transfer of an object from a source to a goal. In the sentence "John gave the ball to Mary," John would be the agent (the person who caused the transfer), Mary the recipient (the goal of the transfer), and the ball the object being given. Looking farther down in Figure 4–3A, John would also be the source in the transfer, Mary the goal, and the ball the object being transferred.

Turning to Figure 4–3B, *sell,* like *give,* involves an agent and a recipient. However, it entails two objects. As shown near the bottom of the figure, *sell* also involves two transfers that are linked by a contractual arrangement between two experiencers. Within these transfers, an unspecified object is transferred from its source to its goal, and another object (money) is transferred from its source to its goal.

Consider how the Figure 4–3B diagram could be used to represent the sentence "John sold the ball to Mary." Looking at the top of the figure, the two objects being transfered are the ball ($Z1$) and money ($Z2$). Now focusing near the bottom of the figure, the ball is transferred from John (X) to Mary (Y); money is transferred from Mary to John.

Gentner asked 3- to 8-year-olds to have dolls act out sentences containing possessive verbs. For example, she asked them to have the Jimmy doll give the ball to the Susie doll. As Gentner predicted on the basis of the semantic networks, children understood *give* and *take,* which involve one transfer, earlier than *buy* or *sell,* which involve two. Also as she predicted, 3-to 5-year-olds frequently thought that *sell* meant *give* and that *buy* meant

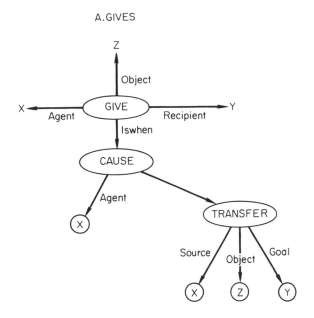

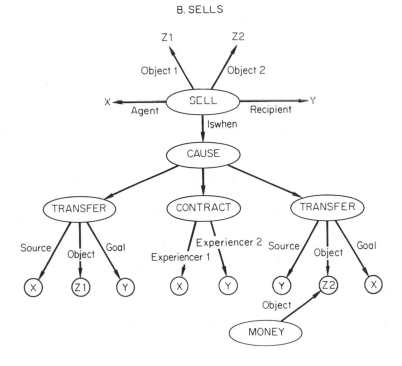

FIGURE 4-3 Semantic network analysis of *gives* and *sells* (after Gentner, 1975).

take. For a child who did not know about the exchange of money inherent in the first term in each pair, the meanings of the two terms in each pair would be identical. Finally, children understood *buy* earlier than *sell*. Gentner suggested that since the representations of these two verbs were similar, the earlier understanding of *buy* was due to children's greater familiarity with the buyer role than the seller role.

Scripts

Scripts and the related languages of plans, frames, schemata, and story grammars attempt to capture knowledge of a more amorphous kind than ordinarily would be depicted by the other languages we have discussed. My choice of scripts to illustrate this class of languages is to some degree arbitrary and to some degree due to a quite interesting developmental hypothesis arising from the script representation: Nelson's (1978) suggestion that even young children have detailed and abstract representations of events that arise frequently in their everyday lives. Before we can examine how this hypothesis grew out of the script representation, we need to know more about how scripts work.

Scripts have been defined as "predetermined sequences of actions that characterize situations" (Schank, 1975). Less stiffly, they can be thought of simply as the way things usually go. They include information about the range of situations in which the script might apply, about actors and events that must appear in these situations, about the actors' purposes and activities, and about distinctions between the script and related ones. Scripts also include slots that may be occupied by a restricted range of actors and events. Illustratively, it is acceptable to say that the halfback, fullback, or even tackle ran for the touchdown in a football game, but not acceptable (without considerable explanation) to say that the goalie or referee did. Thus, slots function as variables that can assume some range of values.

Schank (1975) popularized the script representation. His basic idea was that many scripts can be built from a small number of *acts*. Thus, the acts' role is similar to that of the semantic primitives in Gentner's network representation of the possessive verbs. In each case, the central assumption is that complex meanings can be reduced to combinations of a small number of simpler meanings. The acts that Schank described included such common functions as physically transporting oneself, transferring ownership or possession, eating, grasping, attending, and speaking.

Schank described how these acts could be combined into a script for eating at a restaurant. The restaurant script was organized into four phases: entering the restaurant, ordering, eating, and leaving. Each phase included several acts. For example, the eating phase involved a transfer of responsibility for the plates of food from the cook to the waitress, a corresponding physical transfer, another transfer of responsibility for the plates of food from the waitress to the customer and a corresponding physical transfer, and, last but not least, the eating of the food. Schank noted that this script is specific to restaurants in which people sit down at tables and order food from a waitress. Only a few points (entering the restaurant, receiving food, eating, and paying) are inherent to all restaurants. He also noted, however, that other types of restaurants and other activities can be described by the same eleven acts.

But what does all this have to do with children's thinking? The answer provides another illustration of how languages can influence theoretical views. Schank and Katherine Nelson were colleagues at Yale University. As Nelson became familiar with Schank's script representation, she thought that here was a kind of knowledge that was abstract and symbolic but that even preschoolers might possess (contrary to Piaget's view that preoperational children do not have abstract representations). To test whether young children do indeed possess this abstract information, Nelson compared preschoolers' knowlege of eating situations to Schank's restaurant script. In particular, she asked 4-year-olds at a day care center to describe what happened when they ate at home, at the day care center they attended, and at McDonald's.

The children demonstrated a fairly abstract understanding in numerous ways. Virtually all of them mentioned those events in Schank's restaurant script that applied to all three eating situations. They rarely mentioned events that were not part of the script but that still were likely to occur. For example, they seldom commented on people coming into and leaving McDonald's, though this doubtlessly is part of every visit they make to the restaurant. Finally, the few inaccurate statements that children made tended to be intrusions from the general restaurant script. For example, most children said that people paid for their meals at McDonald's after eating rather than before, a statement true of most restaurants but not McDonald's.

These observations support Nelson's hypothesis that even young children have general notions, akin to scripts, about what goes on in commonly encountered situations. The point is not that Nelson could never have developed her hypothesis without Schank's script notion; she might have had similar thoughts anyway. By her own account, however, the script representation stimulated her to think of the issues in a particular way, a way that directly influenced her ideas and the experiment she performed.

Comparisons Among Languages

Flow charts, production systems, semantic networks, and scripts differ in numerous ways. What are the advantages and disadvantages of each of them? Table 4–4 lists some of each language's pluses and minuses. The table classifies the languages along three dimensions: their typical degree of specificity, their typical level of readability, and the type of knowledge that the languages fit most naturally. Note that these differences are not absolute.

TABLE 4-4 Comparisons Among Four Representational Languages

	TYPICAL DEGREE OF SPECIFICITY	TYPICAL LEVEL OF READABILITY	TYPE OF KNOWLEDGE THAT LANGUAGE IS MOST USEFUL FOR REPRESENTING
Flow Diagrams	Medium	High	Fixed procedures and decision rules
Production Systems	Very high	Low	Fixed procedures and decision rules
Semantic Networks	High	Medium	Static knowledge, general world knowledge
Scripts	Medium	Medium	Combinations of fixed procedures and general world knowledge

Any type of information *can* be described by any of the languages at any level of specificity. Nonetheless, each language seems best suited for expressing particular types of information at particular levels of detail.

When researchers want to express detailed hypotheses about people's knowledge, they usually employ semantic networks and/or production systems. The price of this specificity is some loss of readability. Even for quite knowledgeable readers, following semantic networks and production systems can be challenging. The complexity may be unavoidable, however. Human knowledge is interconnected in so many ways, and the symbol manipulation process is so complicated, that languages well designed to express this complexity may be necessary to capture what is happening. Production systems and semantic networks allow as clear a description of these complex interconnections as currently is possible.

The languages also differ in the types of knowledge that they describe most naturally. Semantic networks seem most useful for modeling *declarative knowledge*—concepts such as time and density, and general knowledge about the world, such as that there are five pennies in a nickel and five nickels in a quarter. Such concepts and facts are used in a variety of circumstances (buying objects, making change, doing arithmetic problems). Therefore, it is desirable that they be available for use in many contexts. Semantic networks enable concepts to be accessed for many purposes, since all concepts are linked to all other concepts. Models of long-term memory therefore have found semantic networks a convenient language for representing knowledge (Anderson, 1983).

Production systems and flow charts also can be used to model declarative knowledge, but more often have been used to model *procedural knowledge*. This is knowledge about how to execute specific sequences of behavior, such as how to play songs on the piano, ski, or multiply. People do not seem to have many access paths to the components of such knowledge (try, for example, to name the fifth number in your telephone number without proceeding through the first four). On the other hand, people can execute the components of these procedures smoothly and in rapid sequence (it is not difficult to find the fifth number when reciting the entire phone number or when dialing). In representing procedural knowledge, therefore, efficient execution seems more important than multiple access routes. Production systems and flow charts, which proceed in fixed orders with one step eliciting the next, seem compatible with this demand.

Semantic networks, production systems, and flow diagrams seem most useful for depicting knowledge at a relatively specific level. In contrast, scripts seem most useful for representing event sequences at a more general level. The reason is that scripts are intended to capture a sense of the way the world ordinarily functions, a level of analysis that must allow considerable variability. Scripts and the related languages of frames, plans, schema, and story grammars seem useful for characterizing activities in which procedural and declarative knowledge both are necessary: activities such as interpreting fairy tales (Mandler & Johnson, 1977; Stein & Glenn, 1979), knowing how to act at a doctor's office (Bower, 1979), and understanding how Ernie cons Bert on Sesame Street (Bruce & Newman, 1978). Taken as a group, then, scripts, semantic networks, production systems, and flow diagrams allow us to represent diverse types of knowledge in a precise and revealing fashion.

METHODS FOR STUDYING CHILDREN'S THINKING

Having considered information-processing languages for representing knowledge, we now can examine methods for obtaining evidence about what thought processes to represent. Among the most useful methods for studying thinking are chronometric, error-analysis, eye-movement, and protocol-analysis techniques. One important theme in considering all four of these methods is their emphasis on the *pattern of data* rather than on its absolute level. For example, in considering solution times, the pattern across different problems is the key consideration, rather than the absolute speed of performance.

Another quality that unites all these methods is their ability to yield useful data about the thinking of individual children, as opposed to simply revealing group tendencies. Averaging over groups sometimes is necessary to reveal subtle patterns, but it is also dangerous. Consider a situation in which half of 8-year-olds are using a rule that solves only half of a certain type of problem, and the other half are using a rule that solves all of that type of problem. Averaging the performance of all the 8-year-olds might suggest that they are using a rule that yields above-chance but imperfect performance. In fact, such a rule would fit none of the individual children's thinking. This is not simply a theoretical problem; cases have arisen where conclusions that fit the data from an entire group quite well fit none of the group members individually (e.g., Estes, 1956). The emphasis of chronometric, error-analysis, eye-movement, and protocol-analysis methods on the patterns of data produced by individuals guards against this problem.

Chronometric Analysis

Mental processes take time. This assumption may seem uncontroversial. People obviously spend long periods thinking about which chess move to make and how to solve physics problems. Even on simple cognitive tasks where people seem to recall answers immediately, however, they actually require varying amounts of time. Adults as well as children take longer to add 3 + 2 than 3 + 1, for example (Groen & Parkman, 1972). The amounts of time needed to solve different problems frequently provide clues to people's solution processes. Therefore, chronometric methods—methods that analyze patterns of solution times—have achieved great popularity.

The most commonly used chronometric method is the *subtractive technique*. Researchers employ this approach to determine the time people take to perform a single mental process. In the approach's original form, the investigator devised two tasks that he or she thought differed only in the need to perform a particular process. For example, the first task might require processes A, B, and C, and the second task only processes A and B. The difference between solution times on the two tasks was interpreted as an index of the time necessary to perform process C. Thus, if the first task took five seconds and the second task four seconds, the conclusion would be that process C took one second.

This approach had been used sporadically since the early days of psychology. Sternberg (1966), however, had an insight that multiplied the power of the subtractive-factors approach. As long as investigators compared only two tasks, any difference between the tasks might explain differences in solution times. Sternberg's insight was that devising several versions of the basic task, with the versions differing only in how many times it was necessary to execute the process of interest, could yield higher-quality information about the time needed to perform the process. If, in the above example, processes A, B, and C together took five seconds, and process C accounted for one second of that time, then a task that required processes A and B and two repetitions of process C should require six seconds; a task that required processes A and B and three repetitions of process C should require seven seconds; and so on (Sternberg's application of this method to memory scanning, and Keating and Bobbitt's [1978] subsequent use of it with children, was discussed in Chapter 1, page 15).

Figure 4–4 shows an idealized version of the type of data that would be expected when using the subtractive technique. As shown, the method yields a slope and an intercept. The slope indicates the amount of time needed to perform the process of interest. In this case, each additional repetition of process C adds exactly one second to the total solution time. The subtractive technique's power stems from the fact that such a linear slope has far fewer explanations than a single difference between two tasks. There are many reasons why one task might take longer than another, but few explanations for such a regular *pattern* of increments.

As noted, the subtractive method yields an intercept as well as a slope. The intercept indicates the amount of time occupied by all factors other than the process of interest. For example, encoding what the problem is and pressing a button to answer the problem would take a certain amount of time even if we were not directly interested in them in a particular experiment. In the Figure 4–4 illustration, the processes measured in the intercept take four seconds. The importance of knowing the intercept as well as the slope is that the two together yield predicitions concerning the absolute amount of time new problems will take. For example, in Figure 4–4, we could predict that a version of the task that required four executions of process C would take eight seconds (four seconds for the intercept plus four seconds for the four executions of process C).

Shepard and Metzler's (1971) investigation of how people think about

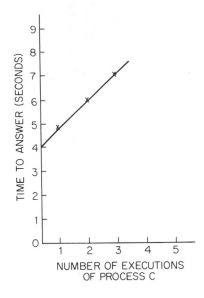

NUMBER OF EXECUTIONS
OF PROCESS C

FIGURE 4-4 An illustration of the chronometric technique with hypothetical data.

spatial transformations exemplifies the potential for elegance of the subtractive technique. These researchers presented college students a series of slides, each slide showing two Lego-like figures (Figure 4–5A). One of these figures, the standard stimulus, was said to be in an upright position. The other, the comparison stimulus, was rotated anywhere from 0 to 180 degrees relative to the standard stimulus. On half of the problems, the comparison stimulus was

FIGURE 4-5A Example of standard (top) and comparison (bottom) stimuli used by Shepard and Metzler. *Science, 171,* 701–703. © by the AAAS.

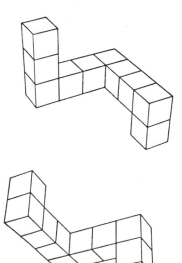

identical to the standard; on the others it was a mirror image. The task was to decide if the two stimuli were identical or if they were mirror images.

Shepard and Metzler believed that people would perform this task by mentally rotating the comparison stimulus until it was upright and then comparing it to the standard stimulus to see if the two figures were identical. If people followed this strategy, and if the rate of rotation was constant, their solution times would follow a predictable pattern. They would take longer to compare the figures when the comparison stimulus was rotated 80 degrees than when it was rotated 60, longer when it was rotated 60 degrees than when it was rotated 40, and longer when it was rotated 40 degrees than when it was rotated 20. More important, they would require the same additional time for 80- versus 60-degree rotations as they would for 60- versus 40-and for 40- versus 20-degree ones. As shown in Figure 4–5B, the results supported this expectation. The college students seemed to rotate the comparison stimulus at a consistent rate until it was in the same orientation as the standard and then check whether the two forms were identical.

Kail, Pellegrino, and Carter (1980) wondered whether children would be able to perform such complex spatial transformations, and if so, whether they would perform them in the same way as adults. Therefore, they tested fourth graders and college students on a similar mental rotation task. They found that the children showed the same pattern of solution times as the adults (Figure 4–5C). The main developmental change was in the rate of rotation. The 9-year-olds rotated the figures at 102 degrees per second. Adults rotated at 166 degrees per second. Thus, as is often the case in experiments comparing children's and adult's memorial and perceptual proc-

FIGURE 4-5B Adults' solution times at varying angular differences between standard and comparison stimuli (after Shepard & Metzler, 1071).

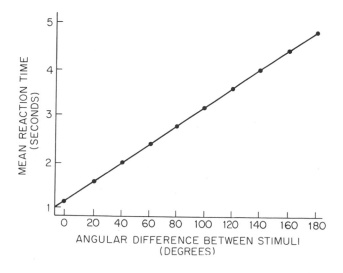

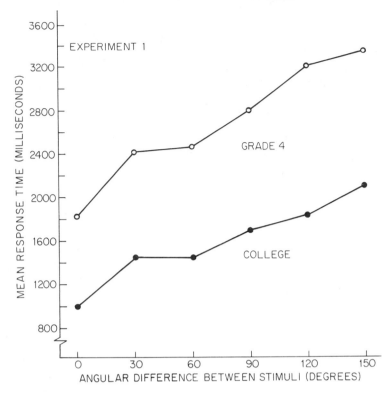

FIGURE 4-5C   Children's solution times at various angular differences between standard and comparison stimuli (from Kail, Pellegrino, & Carter, 1980).

esses, adults' absolute level was superior, but the pattern of performance was the same.

Chronometric methods are perhaps the most frequently used approaches for studying information processing. Chi and Klahr's (1975) work on subitizing, Sternberg and Rifkin's (1979) work on solving analogy problems, and Keating and Bobbitt's (1978) work on memory scanning are three examples of the approach from earlier chapters. The methods have a natural fit with flow-diagram and production-system representations that portray thinking as occurring in a step-by-step sequence, with each step taking time. Thus, it is not surprising that these investigators used flow-diagram and production-system languages as well as the chronometric methods.

Although chronometric methods are often useful, they are not useful in all situations. They require that the experimenter present a great many trials, that children pay close attention and respond quickly, and that the experimental procedure be carefully controlled. Further, they are not useful in obtaining all types of information. If, on an IQ test, we asked children what they would do if they went to the store to get a loaf of bread and the grocer didn't have any (an actual item on one well-known intelligence test), we would be less interested in how long they took to answer than in any errors they made on the problem. The errors would take on special interest if they conformed to a pattern that could be discerned on other questions as well. To discern these types of consistent patterns, information-processing researchers have devised specialized methods for analyzing errors.

Methods of Error Analysis

The analysis of error data is not new to the study of children's thinking. Piaget relied heavily on it, and Binet, who devised the first widely used IQ test, also used it (Tuddenham, 1962). Recently, however, the method has been extended so that patterns of correct answers and errors become ways of testing precise models of people's reasoning. I will illustrate this use with research I have done on the balance-scale task.

The error analysis technique that I devised, the *rule assessment approach*, is based on two assumptions. The first is that children try to solve problems by using rules, with the rules progressing from less to more sophisticated with age. The second assumption is that hypothesized rule progressions can be tested by creating problem sets in which children who use different rules produce distinct patterns of correct answers and errors.

An example may help illustrate how the rule-assessment approach works. Recall the flow-diagram and production-system representations of children's rules for solving balance-scale problems (p. 100). In Rule I, they based their judgments on the weights on each side. In Rule II, they also considered distance when the weights were equal. In Rule III, they always considered both weight and distance, but did not know how to resolve conflicts. In Rule IV, they computed torques when such computations were necessary to solve conflicts. But a question remained: How could we determine which of these rules, if any, individual children used?

One way was to design problems where children who used different rules would produce different patterns of correct answers and errors. Specifically, we could examine children's correct answers and errors on six types of problems (Table 4–5):

1. *Balance problems*, with the same configuration of weights on pegs on each side of the fulcrum;
2. *Weight problems*, with unequal amounts of weight equidistant from the fulcrum;
3. *Distance problems*, with equal amounts of weight different distances from the fulcrum;
4. *Conflict–weight problems*, with one side having more weight, the other side having its weight farther from the fulcrum, and the side with more weight going down;
5. *Conflict–distance problems*, with one side having more weight, the other side more distance, and the side with more distance going down;
6. *Conflict–balance problems*, with the usual conflict between weight and distance cues and the two sides balancing.

TABLE 4-5 Predicted Percentage of Correct Answers on Each Problem Type for Children Using Each Rule

Problem type	Rule			
	I	II	III	IV
Balance	100	100	100	100
Weight	100	100	100	100
Distance	0 (Should say "Balance")	100	100	100
Conflict – Weight	100	100	33 (Chance Responding)	100
Conflict – Distance	0 (Should say "Right Down")	0 (Should say "Right Down")	33 (Chance Responding)	100
Conflict – Balance	0 (Should say "Right Down")	0 (Should say "Right Down")	33 (Chance Responding)	100

As shown in Table 4–5, children who used different rules would produce different response patterns on these problems. Those using Rule I always would predict correctly on balance, weight, and conflict–weight problems and never would predict correctly on the other three problem types. Children using Rule II would behave similarly except they would solve distance problems. Those adopting Rule III invariably would be correct on all three nonconflict problem types and would perform at a chance level on the three types of conflict problems. Those using Rule IV would solve all problems.

One nonintuitive prediction of the rule models is that on certain balance scale problems, younger children will answer correctly more often than older ones. On conflict–weight problems, for example, younger children, who use Rules I and II, should answer consistently correctly. Since they only consider relative amounts of weight, and since the side with more weight always goes down on these problems, they will always be correct. In contrast, older children, using Rule III realize the complexity of one side having more weight and the other more distance, do not know how to resolve the conflict and therefore must "muddle through" and be correct only one-third of the time.

The rule models also predict which problems will elicit especially large developmental changes. On distance problems, performance should improve from below chance for children using Rule I to 100 percent correct for children using all three other rules. Children using Rule I see that the two sides have the same amount of weight and therefore expect the two sides to balance. In fact, the two sides never balance on these problems because the weights are different distances from the fulcrum. Children using Rule II, III, or IV consider both weight and distance on these problems, and therefore should always answer them correctly.

Another useful feature of the rule models is that they predict which particular error rule users will make on a given problem, as well as the fact that they will make some error. For example, both children using Rule II and children using Rule III often will err on conflict-balance problems, but the particular errors will differ. All of the Rule II children's errors should involve choosing the side with more weight, whereas the Rule III children's errors should be distributed evenly between the side with more weight and the side with more distance. The rule models' predictions of which error a rule user will make on each problem greatly reduces the number of rules that a child might be said to be using.

Siegler (1976; Experiment 1) examined 5-, 9-, 13-, and 17-year-olds' knowledge about balance scales. A stringent criterion was set for concluding that an individual child had used a particular rule. The child's response on at least 26 of the 30 balance-scale problems had to be the one predicted by that rule. In spite of this stringent criterion, the response patterns of 90% of children did fit one of the four rule models. Five-year-olds most often used Rule I, 9-year-olds most often used Rule II or III, and 13- and 17-year-olds most often used Rule III. Few children of any age used Rule IV.

The expected patterns of performance on the six problem types also emerged. For example, the percentage of correct answers declined between ages 5 and 17 on all six of the conflict-weight items but on none of the other 24 items on the test. Similarly, as the rule models suggested, the developmental increment on every distance problem was greater than on any other item. As can be seen in Figure 4–6, the performance of children who were said to use a given rule closely approximated the performance predicted by the relevant rule model.

I was curious whether children's verbal explanations of their reasoning would reveal the same knowledge as the rule assessments. Therefore, after children made their predictions, the experimenter asked them to explain

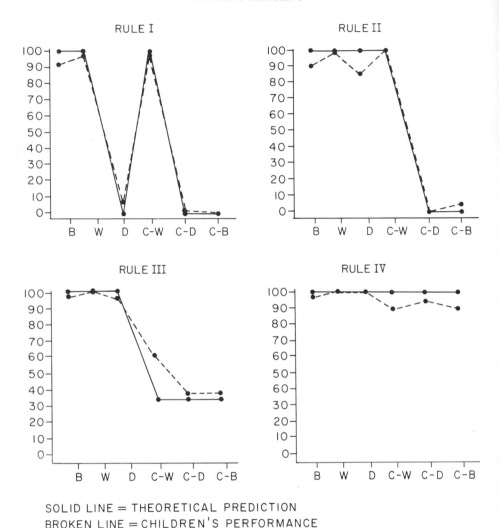

SOLID LINE = THEORETICAL PREDICTION
BROKEN LINE = CHILDREN'S PERFORMANCE

FIGURE 4-6   Children's adherence to rules on balance-scale task. Solid lines indicate percentage correct on each type of problem that children would produce if they adhered perfectly to that rule. Broken lines indicate percentage of correct answers on each type of problem actually produced by children classsified as using that rule. Note: B = Balance problems, W = Weight problems, D = Distance problems, C-W = Conflict-weight problems, C-D = Conflict-distance problems, C-B = Conflict-balance problems.

how they knew which side would go down. For 80% of children, the two indicators of knowledge agreed. The 20% of cases where they did not, however, demonstrated why nonverbal methods often are used to study children's thinking. Most of the 20% were cases where the children's predictions indicated that they used Rule II, but their explanations indicated that they used Rule III. That is, children *said* that they considered weight and distance in predicting which side would go down (a Rule III explanation), but their predictions revealed that the only times they chose the side with the greater distance was when the weights were equal on the two sides (a Rule II approach). Children probably were unaware of exactly when they considered each feature and thus could not give a detailed explanation of their strategy. Analyses of correct answers and errors, however, revealed their underlying reasoning.

Error analyses often are useful for revealing how children solve problems and how they understand concepts. However, they are less useful for revealing the moment-by-moment processes by which children perceive the world. Here, eye-movement analyses have proven to be especially helpful.

Analysis of Eye Movements

The idea of using eye movements to study thinking is an old one. They have been used to study visual information processing since the 19th century (e.g., Javal, 1878). Then, as now, the basic assumption was that the material on which the eye is focusing also is the material on which the mind is focusing; this view has been labeled the *eye-mind assumption*. Advances in the last decade in the quality of machines for measuring eye movements and in the precision of psychological theories of the mind's activities have allowed increasingly rigorous tests of the eye-mind assumption. The results indicate that there is much truth to it.

To understand analyses of eye movements, it is necessary to know a few facts about vision. Although people's impression of vision is of a continuous process, close observation of the way our eyes actually move indicates a two-stage cycle: brief *saccades* (eye movements), that take roughly 1/100 of a second, followed by stable *fixations* that range from 1/5 of a second to a few seconds. The purpose of the saccades is to bring the fovea of the eye, the point of highest acuity, to focus on the material that we desire as the next input. People use information in the periphery of the eye, as well as context and knowledge about the material, to guide the distance of saccades so that new fixations fall on important material. Little if any information about visual forms is obtained during saccades. Rather, this information is obtained during fixations. The durations of the fixations vary greatly depending on the difficulty of the material, its importance, and numerous other factors.

Now consider how a typical eye-tracking apparatus works. Suppose that a child is in an experiment on reading. The child sits in a chair and looks at a TV monitor about two feet away. The monitor displays a page from a book. The eye-tracking system sends a small beam of infrared light, invisible to the naked eye, onto one of the child's corneas. The reflection of this light indicates the point where the child's eye is fixating on the TV screen. Superimposing the material on the screen onto the corneal reflection reveals what material the child is looking at. An eye camera takes pictures of this corneal reflection once every few milliseconds, allowing rapid tracking of changes in eye position. When the session is over, the data are fed into another computer for analysis. Such automated scoring is crucial to analysis of eye movements; five minutes of average speed reading generate approximately 18,000 eye fixations.

Eye-movement analyses yield two types of data: data about the sequence of locations on which the eyes focus and data about the duration of attention at each location. These two types of data allow us to examine different aspects of thinking. Vurpillot's (1968) analysis of visual scanning illustrates the information that sequential data can yield. Just and Carpenter's (1980) analysis of reading illustrates the utility of duration data.

Vurpillot was interested in how children learn to scan scenes to extract all the information that is available. The experimenter showed 4- to 8-year-olds two houses, each house having six windows (Figure 4–7). The children needed to determine whether the houses were identical, and if not, where they differed. The implicit model of ideal performance was that children would scan a window in one house, then the corresponding window in the second house, then another window in the first house, then the corre-

FIGURE 4-7 Sample of stimuli by Vurpillot (1968). Children needed to find whether houses were different (as in the top pair) or identical (as in the bottom pair).

sponding window in the second house, and so on until they either found a difference or had examined all windows of the house. Vurpillot's optimal performance model also prescribed that scanning should proceed through a systematic sequence of locations. It would proceed from top to bottom of each column or across each row rather than haphazardly. Scanning systematically would minimize memory load for what had already been examined and what still needed to be examined.

Vurpillot's analysis indicated that with age, children's scanning became increasingly systematic and comprehensive. They more often looked back and forth between corresponding windows in the two houses and more often proceeded down a column or across a row within a house. They became more likely to scan all the windows before answering that the houses were identical and focused on a greater number of features in each window. Vurpillot could not have obtained the data on which these conclusions were based without information concerning the sequence of eye movements.

Now we can examine an approach that emphasized the duration of eye movements, Just and Carpenter's (1980) model of reading. Their model rested on two assumptions. The first was that when and only when people fixate on a word, they are processing it. Thus, the length of the fixation is a direct index of the attention given to the word. The second assumption was that readers interpret each word as they encounter it, rather than waiting for more information. This sometimes leads to inaccurate interpretations, but readers do it nonetheless.

Just and Carpenter's focus on the duration of eye fixations allowed them to discover where people spend their time and processing resources while reading. One factor that influenced processing was the nature of individual words. On average, people fixated more than three times as long on verbs as on connectives such as *or* and *and*. The familiarity of the word also influenced its processing. Although readers focused on virtually every word, they focused longer on unfamiliar words than on familiar ones, and much longer on very unfamiliar words than on relatively unfamiliar ones. Just and Carpenter hypothesized that readers use the extremely long fixations on very unfamiliar words to build new entries in long-term memory. These new entries would resemble the types of semantic networks used by Gentner (1975) to characterize understanding of possession verbs such as *give* and *sell*.

Features of sentences and paragraphs, as well as individual words, influence fixation times. In particular, readers spend extra time integrating new information with existing knowledge at predictable times in passages. Sentences that contain information especially crucial to the passage's meaning are processed for more time than other sentences. The last word in a sentence also receives extra time, relative to other words in the sentence. Since the end of a sentence signals the end of a thought, it is a good place for integration of previous and new information to occur. Consistent with this interpretation, the amount of time students spent looking at the last word in the sentence was longer for the last word in a generally difficult sentence than for the same word in less difficult sentences. Similar, extra-long fixations occur at the last word in a paragraph, another likely place for integrative processes to operate.

Just and Carpenter concluded that although reading may seem to be a smooth, even process, it in fact is far more eventful. The type of word, the word's place in the sentence, and the sentence's place in the paragraph all influence fixation times. The pattern of fixation times allowed insights into the reading process that would have been impossible without such data.

Eye-movement analyses frequently reveal which objects people are thinking about and what types of processing they are doing, but less often reveal exactly what they are thinking. When people focus on the last word of a sentence, we can infer that they are integrating new with previous material, but can only guess the precise thoughts that go into the integration. To find out what people are thinking, protocol analyses, based on people's verbal reports of their thought processes, often are useful.

Protocol Analysis

How to evaluate people's verbal reports about their thinking has long been, and still is, controversial. The first large groups of psychologists interested in cognition worked at the end of the 19th and beginning of the 20th century. They were known as *introspectionists* because they believed that people's insights into their own thought processes, and their subsequent verbal reports about the introspections, provided crucial evidence about how thought occurs. In the early part of the 20th century another group of psychologists, known as *behaviorists*, argued that introspections were misleading and that they should not be used in the scientific study of psychology. Still later, another group, the *Gestaltists*, contended that *verbal protocols* (verbal comments during the course of problem solving) were useful for generating hypotheses but not for testing them. The reports could suggest ideas but could not provide conclusive evidence.

Despite the controversy that has accompanied reliance on verbal protocols, they are used quite often. The main reason is that such protocols often reveal information that other methods cannot. In one illustrative study, Karmiloff-Smith and Inhelder (1977) presented children with wooden objects and asked them to balance each object on a balance scale. Some of the objects were symmetrical, with weight evenly distributed over the length of the object. Others were obviously asymmetrical, with one side of the object being larger (and heavier) than the other. Still others looked symmetrical but in fact contained a weight hidden inside one of the ends. Karmiloff-Smith and Inhelder paid careful attention to the children's verbal statements about what they were doing as well as to their actions.

The statements made by 6- and 7-year-olds indicated that at the beginning of the experiment they focused on spatial symmetry. They made such comments as "I'll try the middle first . . . halfway along" and "Things always balance in the middle." They also drew analogies to other more familiar situations, as in the comment, "It's like a seesaw, you put a block at each end." After experience with the apparatus, the children began to separate the influence of weight from that of spatial position, as reflected in the comment, "Oh, it's always just the opposite of what I expect . . . maybe it's this block glued to the end here." Somewhat older children, 8- and 9-year-olds, drew more sophisticated conclusions from their experience with the apparatus. They recognized the difference between appearance and reality, and began to balance the board on their finger to see if one side was heavier even though both sides looked the same.

The investigators concluded that as children gained experience with the objects, they increasingly viewed their observations as tests of their theories about how objects balance. They became less likely to view the outcomes as isolated successes or failures of their goal of balancing. Such a conclusion would be difficult to draw on the basis of chronometric, eye-movement, or error analyses. It was a contribution that only would emerge from analyzing children's statements about what they were thinking.

Researchers who use computer languages to represent thinking have relied especially heavily on verbal data. A record of ongoing comments, combined with observations of concurrent nonverbal behaviors, provides an extremely rich data base. Computer languages are flexible enough to express this richness, yet precise enough to indicate exactly what the statements might mean. Thus, they provide a good means for expressing theories about the thought processes underlying verbal statements.

Newell (1968) provided the following rules of thumb for how to formulate a computer simulation of the thinking that generated people's verbal comments while solving a problem. First, the experimenter presents a problem and asks the person in the experiment to say aloud whatever he or she thinks about while solving it. That person's statements are recorded and, along with a record of ongoing nonverbal behavior, become the raw data of the study. After repeated scrutiny of what transpired, the investigator formulates a flow diagram of the problem solver's solution process. Finally, the investigator writes a computer program, probably in the form of a production system, to characterize the crucial features of the flow diagram and of the original verbal and nonverbal data.

Newell described several steps in proceeding from the flow diagram to a production-system model. The first step is to formulate productions corresponding to the individual steps in the flow diagram. Each production must create the necessary symbols in short-term memory for its successor to fire. The next step is to restate as many productions as possible as variants on a few basic ones. This helps to organize the overall production system into a coherent and economical form, much as writing a subroutine does in other computer languages. The final step is to compare the simulation's behavior to the flow chart and to the original verbal and nonverbal data, and to revise the production system where it does not fit.

Note that in this approach, verbal data are treated exactly like chronometric, eye-movement, or error data: as a target behavior for a model to regenerate. This treatment avoids the historic impasse over whether verbal reports reflect the true contents of the mind. They, like errors, solution times, and eye movements, are assumed to reflect some of the mind's contents, though all the reflections are imperfect.

Despite the success of many analyses based on verbal data, objections to the use of such data have persisted. For example, Nisbett and Wilson (1977) argued that people cannot observe directly their cognitive processes and that they therefore often report them inaccurately. In response to these criticisms, Ericsson and Simon (1980) attempted to specify when verbal reports are and are not useful indices of cognitive processes. Their formulation does much to resolve this long-lived controversy.

Ericsson and Simon started with a few relatively uncontroversial assumptions. They divided memory into short- and long-term components. Short-term memory was where active symbol manipulations occurred. Long-term memory was where information was stored on an enduring basis. Symbols in short-term memory were produced only by relatively slow processes, those taking a second or more. Quicker processes such as recognition were thought not to produce symbols in short-term memory.

Ericsson and Simon's basic assumption about verbal reports was that if people report information when it enters short-term memory, the verbal report will be an accurate index of thought processes. This is because the symbols in short-term memory reflect those ongoing thought processes. However, if people retrieve information from long-term memory before reporting it, the verbal report will be a relatively inaccurate index of the cognitive processes it is supposed to reflect. People will draw inferences, both accurate and inaccurate, to fill in information that no longer is available directly. If asked to explain how you decided to live where you currently are living, you probably could generate an answer, but how confident would you be of your recollection?

Ericsson and Simon presented considerable evidence consistent with these views. When people report their thoughts while they are solving problems, and when the reports concern relatively slow processes, they usually correspond well to other measures of thought processes such as solution-time and eye-movement patterns. When the reports are made retrospectively or when they concern very rapid processes, people show little knowledge about their thought processes. Obtaining valid verbal reports requires careful planning, but the insights that can be obtained often make the care worthwhile.

SUMMARY

Choices of methods and languages are inherently related to each other, and both influence, and are influenced by, available theories. For example, theories that posit an ordered sequence of processing steps are most easily expressed in languages that imply step-by-step processing, and are most easily tested by methods that focus on the time course of processing. Methods and languages create conditions that favor development of particular types of theories, and the theories in turn stimulate development of methods and languages even better fitted to expressing and testing the theories.

Specialized languages and methods are essential for studying cognition. Natural languages often are too vague and imprecise to accurately describe children's thinking. With older children, who are more capable of active cooperation, precise languages and methods become especially important.

Flow diagrams are especially useful for describing the sequence of thought processes children go through. Comparing the flow-diagram models that characterize different levels of development also can reveal exactly what is changing in children's thinking. In addition, flow diagrams can suggest interesting predictions about the time course of information processing. For example, in the study of the balance scale, they suggested that people who know how to solve all balance-scale problems compute torques only when the problem cannot be solved in other ways. This implication proved to be accurate.

Production systems are most useful for indicating exactly how symbol manipulations lead to cognitive activity and behavior. Two distinctions are crucial in production systems. One is between the short-term memory and the production system proper. An immediate situation, represented by the symbols in short-term memory, leads a production in the production system to produce some action. Possible actions include adding symbols to or deleting actions from the short-term memory, and changing something in the physical environment. The other key distinction is between the condition and action side of each production. The situation described by the short-term memory symbols matches the condition side of the production. Then the action side of the production inserts new symbols into the short-term memory or effects a behavior in the external world. Production systems are especially useful for developing ideas about the exact symbol manipulations that go into cognitive activity and in demonstrating the sufficiency of hypothesized models to account for observed behavior.

Semantic networks are most useful for describing general knowledge about the world, knowledge that may be used in many contexts. The networks are composed of *propositions* that link subjects and predicates. Because all the propositions are interconnected, any part of the knowledge can be reached from any other part. Gentner (1975) demonstrated how semantic networks can be used to predict the order of acquisition of possession verbs, such as *give* and *take*. Her work also indicated that network analyses could distinguish between the aspects of acquisition order that are due to the inherent structure of the concepts and the aspects that are due to the relative amount of exposure children receive to them.

Scripts are used to capture knowledge of standardized sequences of actions. Nelson's research suggested that even preschoolers have scriptlike knowledge about situations they encounter often, such as eating in restaurants and at day care centers. These results were at odds with the view that 4- and 5-year-olds do not possess abstract symbolic knowledge.

Perhaps the essential characteristic of methods that have been developed to study information processing is their emphasis on the *pattern* of data. Four methods have been most widely used: chronometric, error, eye-movement, and verbal-protocol analyses. *Chronometric analyses* focus on the time course of information processing. One of the most widely used chronometric methods is the *subtractive technique.* In this approach, children perform tasks that require one, two, three, or more executions of a particular process. If the process is being executed *serially* (one execution after another), then each additional execution should demand the same additional time. This method has proved useful in analyzing mental rotation in both children and adults, as well as for analyzing performance on a number of other problems.

Error analyses involve examining patterns of answers to infer reasoning and problem-solving strategies. It has proved possible to postulate rules and to design problems that indicate the rule individual children are using. On tasks such as the balance scale, most children use stable rules; the rules become increasingly sophisticated with age; and the rules are related to children's explanations of their reasoning but not identical to them.

Eye-movement analyses reveal moment-to-moment changes in visual information processing. Both the sequence of locations at which people look and the length of time for which they examine each location are revealing. Such analyses have indicated that with age, children's visual scanning becomes more systematic and more exhaustive. They also have indicated that reading involves fixations of radically different lengths on different words. Readers fixate longer on unfamiliar words and on words at the ends of sentences and paragraphs than on other terms.

Protocol analyses can help us understand what people are thinking as they are thinking it. They can reveal the theories that guide people's behavior, as in Karmiloff–Smith and Inhelder's study of what children think makes objects balance. Protocol analyses seem most valid when they are made concurrently with the thoughts they describe and when they concern processes that last for a second or more rather than faster processes.

RECOMMENDED READINGS

Ericsson, K. A., & Simon, H. A. (1980). Verbal reports as data. *Psychological Review, 87,* 215–251. A fresh look at the longstanding question of when are people's introspections about their own thought processes valid.

Kail, R., Pellegrino, J., & Carter, P. (1980). Developmental changes in mental rotation. *Journal of Experimental Child Psychology, 29,* 102–116. A precise analysis of how children mentally-rotate objects, and a fine illustration of how chronometric methods can be used with children.

Klahr, D., & Siegler, R. S. (1978). The representation of children's knowledge. In H. Reese & L. P. Lipsitt (Eds.), *Advances in child development, Vol. 12.* New York: Academic Press. An explicit comparison of the virtues of flow diagram and production system analyses. Brings out the strengths and weaknesses of each approach.

Vurpillot, E. (1968). The development of scanning strategies and their relation to visual differentiation. *Journal of Experimental Child Psychology, 6,* 632–650. A study that was years ahead of its time; illustrates the usefulness of eye movement analyses for studying children's thinking.

5
PERCEPTUAL DEVELOPMENT

A 4-month-old girl is shown two movies, with their screens side by side. In one movie, a woman is playing peekaboo. She repeatedly hides her face with her hands, uncovers it, and says "Hello baby, peekaboo." In the other film, a hand holds a stick and rhythmically strikes a wood block. The experimenter plays either the one sound track, with the woman saying peekaboo, or the other, with the drum beat, but not both at the same time.

Somehow, the infant knows which sound track goes with which visual sequence. She demonstrates this knowledge by spending more time looking at the screen showing the pictures that accompany the sound track than at the screen showing the other movie.

Spelke (1976) found that almost all 4-month-olds do this. Of the 24 infants she tested, 23 looked for more time at the screen with the appropriate video accompaniment than at the alternative. Their performance was not simply due to their preferring one movie; they looked at the appropriate screen regardless of which sound track was playing.

This example is representative of current findings about perceptual development in a number of ways. The children in the study are less than 6 months old. The investigator used a simple experimental procedure yet asked a fundamental question about the nature of human beings: Do people innately know how to integrate sights with sounds? The results of the study show greater perceptual abilities in young infants than might have been expected.

Perceptual development is a complex topic, and it is easy to become bogged down in masses of details. It therefore may be worthwhile to note the central theme of this chapter before the details. This central theme is the remarkable rapidity with which perceptual functioning reaches adultlike or near-adultlike levels. In many aspects of perception, infants reach adultlike levels of functioning by age 6 months. To put this in perspective, consider the level of performance of 6-month-olds in other areas of cognitive development. Six-months-olds cannot ordinarily say even one word. They do not appear to understand anything that is said to them. They can solve few problems. They do not search for playthings that suddenly disappear from view. The advanced accomplishments in perception stand in marked contrast. Indeed, given the obvious value of skilled perception for remembering, solving problems, and learning language, perceptual development may function as a well-designed launching pad from which other aspects of cognitive development take off.

Perceptual development covers a huge variety of topics; no one chapter can include all of them. As a result, I made three decisions about what to include in the present chapter. First, all the studies will involve human subjects. A great deal about perceptual development has been learned in studies of nonhuman animals, but the studies of people seemed likely to be of the greatest interest. Second, the focus is on development during the first half year of infancy. This seems to be the period during which the most dramatic perceptual development occurs. In addition, the aspects of perceptual functioning that show the greatest changes beyond infancy are intextricably intertwined with the operations of memory and will later be easily discussed in that context (Chapter 7). Third, research on the development of vision is given the greatest emphasis; research on audition (hearing) and on the integration of vision and hearing is given the next greatest emphasis; and research on taste, smell, and touch is not discussed at all. This distribution of coverage roughly reflects the distribution of research in the field. Most of what is known about perceptual development is known about either vision or audition, and much more is known about vision than audition.

Regardless of which sensory system is involved, perceptual development can be viewed as a form of adaptation to the physical environment. Three functions—attending, identifying, and locating—seem especially crucial to the adaptive process, and the discussions of vision, audition, and intersensory integration are organized around them. *Attending* involves determining what in a situation is worthy of detailed processing. *Identifying* involves establishing what a perceptual pattern is by relating the pattern to entries already in memory. *Locating* involves determining how far away an object is, and in what direction.

An example may make more meaningful the distinctions among the three functions. If you are in an Asian jungle, and a tiger is charging, you need to orient your attention toward the tiger, to identify it as a tiger, and to locate how far away it is so that you can decide whether to climb a tree,

TABLE 5-1   Chapter Outline

shoot a gun, or pray. The example illustrates how attending, identifying, and locating are conceptually distinct, but it also illustrates how they are interrelated. A blur of motion in the periphery of the eye might stimulate the initial attention to the tiger. More careful and focused attending would presumably follow identifying the moving object as a tiger. Yet more careful attention would follow locating the tiger as nearby and rapidly approaching.

This set of decisions about what to include and what to emphasize leads to the organization of this chapter shown in Table 5-1. The chapter is divided into three main sections: vision, audition, and intersensory integration. Discussion of each of these systems is organized around the three functions described above: how children decide where to attend, how they identify objects, and how they locate where objects are. Much of the work chronicles infants' capacities at different ages and how they make transitions from less to more mature levels of functioning. Other aspects of the discussion focus on more applied concerns. For example, at the end of the chapter, the focus is on an exciting and useful extension of perceptual development research: sonar aids to help blind children move around their environments.

A brief homage to infancy researchers.   Before launching into these topics, a few introductory comments should be made about the joys and frustrations of doing research with infants. For the reasons described above, investigators of perceptual development spend much of their time working with extremely young infants. Although the infants are cute and appealing, the relation between the data we can obtain from them and the inferences we can draw often is dauntingly complex.

Consider some patterns that might arise in an experiment on shape perception, in which we present newborns and 3-month-olds with a square and a triangle that differ only in shape. The one straightforward case is where both newborns and 3-month-olds demonstrate the ability to discriminate between the shapes. In such a case, we can conclude that the ability is innate. Consider the possible interpretations, however, if newborns do not demonstrate such ability but 3-month-olds do.

1. Newborns do not perceive the difference between squares and triangles because they have not had sufficient experience with them. To see the difference, they must first manually explore square and triangular objects.

2. Infants do not perceive the difference between squares and triangles at birth, but the means for perceiving them is innate. Actually perceiving the differences requires the unfolding of a biologically programmed visual capability that becomes functional a few months after birth, regardless of whether infants handle triangles and squares.

3. Infants perceive the differences between some squares and triangles at birth, but their vision is not sufficiently acute for them to perceive the difference between the particular shapes they are shown in the experiment.

4. Infants perceive the difference between some square- and triangular-shaped surfaces at birth, but only when they are in complex natural environments in which the square- and triangular-shaped surfaces are moving relative to other parts of the environment.

5. Infants perceive the difference between squares and triangles at birth, but their limited control of their heads and eyes does not allow them to demonstrate this competence by looking where they would like.

Some of these interpretations can be tested. If newborns' limited acuity prevents them from making the discrimination, then large objects with high levels of contrast may allow them to succeed. If infants perceive square and triangular surfaces only when they are in natural settings and moving relative to other objects, movies with these properties can be made. However, if limited control of the eyes and head is the problem, conditions that demonstrate the infants' perceptual abilities will not be easy to design. Typically, investigators compromise between what they would like to do and what is practical: Their youngest age group is one older than newborns but still young enough that demonstrating competence is impressive. Even at 3 or 4 months, infants' immature physiology renders the demonstration of any perceptual competence a challenging enterprise.

Why should it matter so much if the infants in these experiments are a few days rather than a few years old? The reason is related to the venerable nature/nurture issue: How does people's biological inheritance contribute to development, how does their experience contribute to development, and above all, how do the two interact? The key consideration is the plausibility of various mechanisms leading to a perceptual capability. If the question is whether people are biologically programmed to divide wavelengths of light into qualitively distinct colors, 4-month-olds would seem to be as reasonable subjects as newborns. Envisioning any experience in the first four months that would communicate to infants how their society assigns color names to wavelengths is difficult. Other capacities, such as *depth perception*, pose a different case. It is easy to imagine how experience in seeing objects and then crawling to them might help infants realize the usefulness of visual cues for inferring how far away the objects are. The younger the infant who can be shown to appreciate depth cues, the less likely such experiential explanations become.

If learning about infants' early perception were not so essential, the enterprise almost surely would have been abandoned years ago. The first problem in performing experiments with infants lies in getting infants who will participate. Unlike older children, infants are not found in large numbers in convenient locations such as nursery and elementary schools. Even when researchers locate sufficient numbers of infants who will participate problems abound. The types of experiments that can be performed and the types of measures that can be used are severely limited. It is challenging to create a situation they understand. For most of the first year, infants do not understand enough language to follow even simple instructions. Then there are problems of interest and alertness. Infants have short attention spans. They often fall asleep in the middle of experiments. This leads to an extraordinarily high ratio of time spent trying to perform experiments to time spent actually collecting usable data. One student of infant perception wrote, "In my laboratory, we allow two hours to obtain a five minute video recording of one infant reaching" (Butterworth, 1978, p. 363).

Even when infants are in the experimental room and are interested and alert, there is the question of what to measure. Verbal protocols are out of the question, since infants cannot talk. Reaction-time measures also tend to be unprofitable, since infants' reaction times are influenced by a large number of factors unrelated to the experiment. Error patterns and eye movements are more revealing, but even here infants' performance is notably less systematic than that of older children, and therefore more difficult to interpret. Thus, great ingenuity has been required to devise measures that reveal how infants perceive the world.

The difficulties of doing research with infants have had several consequences. Many experimental findings in the area are based on smaller samples of subjects than would be ideal. Many intriguing issues remain unsolved because no adequate methods have been devised to address them. In light of these difficulties, it is unsurprising that until twenty-five years ago, almost nothing was known about perceptual development in infancy. It is surprising, however, and truly impressive, that researchers have learned as much as they have in the last twenty-five years.

VISION

As recently as 1960, many psychologists, pediatricians, and nurses believed that newborn infants were functionally blind (Lamb & Campos, 1982). A very different picture has emerged recently, however. The visual capabilities of newborns are not so great as they will be even six months later, but the newborns definitely can see many objects and events in the world.

Attending to Visual Patterns

From the day of birth, infants look at some objects and events more than others. These preferences may be crucial to development. Cognitive growth will presumably be more rapid if infants orient to informative parts of the environment rather than to uniformative ones. But how informative should informative be? Objects and events that are too far beyond infants' current knowledge of the world may be impossible for them to understand.

Researchers have proposed four main explanations for how infants decide where to attend: an orienting reflex, a set of rules for looking, a preference for moderate discrepancy, and the relative dominance of cortical and subcortical mechanisms. Each of these explanations will be discussed in this section.

The orienting reflex.　When people see a bright flash of light or hear a sudden loud noise, they orient their attention to it even before they can identify the source of the sight or sound. The Russian psychologist Pavlov explicitly noted that this phenomenon includes intense stimuli such as bright lights and loud noises, but is not unique to them. Rather, people orient toward any novel stimulus. The *orienting reflex*, as it has been labeled, seems to be present from the time of birth. It seems adaptive in two ways. It helps people react quickly to events that call for immediate action. It also helps us direct attention away from other objects that have been in the visual field for some time and that are now "old news."

Sokolov (1963) proposed a theory of how the orienting reflex works. When people see or hear a stimulus, they transmit a representation of it to the cortex of the brain. In the cortex, a very rapid matching process is performed in which the representation is compared to other recently encountered stimuli. If the new stimulus does not match previous ones, then an orienting reflex occurs. Orienting entails changes in brain wave patterns, slowing of heart rates, increases in skin conductance, and increased alertness.

In contrast, if the stimulus has been presented repeatedly in the recent past, *habituation* occurs. A person who habituates to a stimulus reacts to it less than the usual amount. The level of brain activity decreases, as does the sensitivity of the sense organs to the stimulus

Several investigators have tested Sokolov's theory of the orienting reflex by examining anencephalic infants (infants born without a cortex). If Sokolov's theory were correct, we would expect such infants not to habituate to familiar stimuli, because they would not have a cortex within which to compare previously encountered stimuli to new ones. An initial report (Brackbill, 1971) supported this prediction. A later report, however, obtained completely contradictory findings (Graham, Leavitt, Strock, & Brown, 1978). The anencephalic infant they studied showed an orienting response when novel stimuli were presented. The infant also habituated to familiar stimuli. That is, as shown in Figure 5–1, the infant's heart rate, which initially showed a large decrement five to seven seconds after a speech sound (a typical orienting response), showed very little change after six exposures to the sound. The finding conclusively demonstrated that cortical activity is not necessary for orienting or for habituating; subcortical mechanisms must be sufficient to produce both responses.

Especially intriguing, the pattern of orienting and habituating in Graham et al.'s 1-month-old anencephalic infant actually was precocious. It was typical of a 2-month-old intact infant. Graham et al. concluded that very early in development, cortical activity may hinder rather than facilitate orienting. Similar hypotheses of early cortical activity interfering with

FIGURE 5-1   Orienting response of an infant born without a cortex. The curves indicate changes in the infant's heartbeat rate after he heard someone talk. On the first trial, there was a large decrease in the infant's heartbeat rate five to seven seconds after the word was pronounced. This is a typical orienting-response pattern. By the sixth trial, there was little change in heartbeat rate. Thus, the infant habituated to the sound despite not having a cortex (adapted from Graham, Leavitt, Strock, & Brown, 1978).

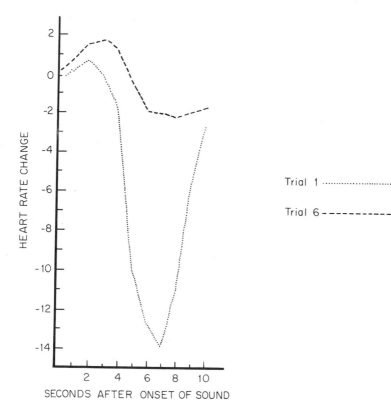

Trial 1 ·····················
Trial 6 ----------

relatively more mature subcortical functioning will appear in several contexts in this chapter.

Rules for scanning the environment. As implied by the discussion of orienting response, newborn infants enter the world with impressive abilities to look for and find informative parts of the environment. They are not passive recipients of whatever the environment presents; rather, they seek interesting objects to inspect. Haith (1979) suggested that newborns even possess rules for finding the interesting parts of their environments. In particular, he suggested that newborns use the following five rules to guide their looking:

1. If you are awake and alert, and the light is not too bright, then open your eyes.
2. If opening your eyes reveals darkness, then scan the environment intensively.
3. If opening your eyes reveals light, then scan the environment broadly.
4. If you find an edge, stop scanning broadly and continue scanning around the edge. Cross the edge and look at the other side if you can.
5. When you are scanning near an edge, reduce the range of fixations perpendicular to the edge if there are a lot of contours in the area.

These rules help infants attend to certain interesting aspects of their environments, but may result in their missing others. In particular, they may give rise to infants' scanning the edges of objects to the exclusion of their interiors. Salapatek (1975) presented infants with a display in which one shape was inside another. For example, a circle might be inside a triangle. Almost all of the newborns' eye fixations fell on the outer edges of the external figure. Not until 2 months of age did infants scan the interior as well as the exterior shape. As shown in Figure 5–2, the same pattern holds for the scanning of faces. One-month-olds scan the external contours of faces, but not until 2 months do they focus on the internal details (Haith, Bergman, & Moore, 1977).

Not surprisingly, infants' attentional patterns influence what they remember. This point has been made in several experiments using the *habituation paradigm*, the most frequently used research strategy for studying infant perception and memory. It is based on the observation, noted earlier, that as objects become increasingly familiar, people tend to pay less attention to them. The habituation procedure includes two phases. First is the familiarization phase, in which a picture or object is shown repeatedly. Then a new picture or object is introduced, either side-by-side with the familiar one or alone. If infants consistently attend more closely to the novel stimulus, they are presumed to recognize the difference between the two stimuli.

To study the effects of attentional patterns on what infants remember, Milewski (1976) presented 1- and 4-month-olds with an habituation procedure in which they first saw one geometric shape inside another. The

1-Month-Old   2-Month-Old

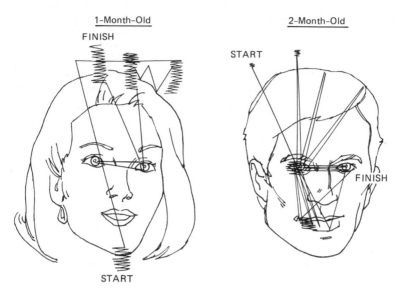

FIGURE 5-2   Visual scanning of a person's face by 1- and 2-month-olds. (after Salapatek, 1975). The concentration of horizontal lines on the chin and hairline of the face on the left indicates that the 1-month-old focused on the external contours. The concentration of horizontal lines on the mouth and eye of the face on the right indicates that the 2-month-old focused on internal features.

shapes would remain on the screen only if the infants sucked at a nipple at a sufficiently high rate. As the infants habituated, their rate of sucking decreased, and they saw the shapes less often. When the rate of sucking became low enough, either the inner figure, the outer figure, or both were changed.

The 4-month-olds responded with renewed interest to all of the changes. They increased their rate of sucking following any change in the inner or outer figure. The 1-month-olds dishabituated only when the outer shape or both shapes were changed. Changes in the inner shape alone did not influence their sucking rate. This lack of effect cannot be explained by the 1-month-olds being unable to clearly see the inner shape. When other 1-month-olds saw the inner shape alone, and were habituated to it, they then dishabituated to changes in it. Thus, very young infants' focusing of attention on the outermost contours of objects can limit what they remember.

Cohen (1972) drew a distinction that becomes especially relevant in the scanning patterns of slightly older infants. He contrasted *attention-drawing* and *attention-holding* properties of stimuli. The central idea is that gross physical characteristics of objects might attract an initial orientation, but the objects' meaningfulness, that is, which properties of the object the infant can represent, determines whether the initial orientation persists. Cohen suggested that the same attention-drawing properties continue to influence perception throughout life, but that attention-holding properties change greatly with age and experience. A loud noise or a flash of light grabs the attention of adults as well as infants, but infants and adults differ considerably in what they find interesting enough to continue looking at. Note the similarity of Cohen's ideas about attention-holding properties to the discussion of encoding in Chapter 3 (pp. 89–92); in both cases, as children's knowledge about certain objects increases, they represent them in increasingly sophisticated ways.

The moderate-discrepancy hypothesis. What qualities of objects hold an infant's attention beyond the initial attention-drawing event? Several researchers have hypothesized that infants are most interested in looking at objects that are moderately discrepant from their existing knowledge (e.g., Greenberg & O'Donnell, 1972; McCall, Kennedy, & Applebaum, 1977). These investigators view moderate discrepancy as important in two senses: in the sense of degree of difference from specific familiar objects, and in the sense of degree of difference from the general level of complexity the infant can represent. At the level of specific familiar objects, an infant might show unusual interest in his mother's sister if she looked quite a bit like his mother. At the level of overall complexity, an infant whose representations of concentric circle patterns was currently limited to three concentric circles might be more interested in looking at a new pattern with four circles than one with either three (already familiar) or five (too unfamiliar).

Several findings seem consistent with the moderate-discrepancy hypothesis. As infants grow older, they increasingly look at more rather than less complex stimuli. For example, in studies in which infants are shown checkerboards, 3-week-olds spend more time looking at 2-by-2 than at 8-by-8 boards; 14-week-olds show the opposite preference (Brennan, Ames, & Moore, 1966). This pattern of data is exactly what would be expected if infants always preferred looking at stimuli at the outer edge of their growing ability to comprehend complexity. The familiarity of the specific pattern also influences preferences. After repeated exposure to both 2-by-2 and 24-by-24 checkerboards, 4-month-olds showed greater preference for the more complex boards (DeLoache, Rissman & Cohen, 1978). Again, as the children's ability to deal with complexity increased, they preferred more complexity.

Part of the appeal of the moderate-discrepancy hypothesis is that it suggests a mechanism of great potential importance for all aspects of cognitive development. If people are programmed to orient toward material that is just beyond their current understanding, they will be continually pulled toward more sophisticated attainments. If there were 10 possible levels of understanding in an area, they would first attend to the material that could be grasped with the simplest level of understanding, then to the material that could be grasped with the next more complex understanding, and so on. They spontaneously would choose the optimal sequence of experiences for learning.

Regardless of the general validity of the moderate-discrepancy hypothesis, the degree to which the hypothesis accounts for infants' looking preferences is unclear. There is little doubt that with age and familiarity, infants prefer to look at increasingly complex stimuli. It is less obvious, though, that they prefer the stimuli *because* such stimuli are moderately discrepant from what they currently comprehend. In the absence of detailed assessment of what infants can comprehend, how can we tell whether a novel stimulus is moderately discrepant, very discrepant, or only slightly discrepant from their existing capabilities? As will be seen in the section on visual acuity, there are plausible alternative explanations for the developmental trend toward preference for greater complexity. Thus, at this time we simply do not know whether infants' preference for looking at increasingly complex stimuli reflects a preference for moderate discrepancy or whether it has another cause.

Cortical and subcortical attentional mechanisms. Bronson (1974) proposed a fourth explanation of developmental changes in infants' attentional patterns: that the changes are due to the relative rates of maturation of the visual cortex of the brain and of subcortical structures. He noted that visual scanning could be controlled either by the visual cortex or by subcortical structures involved in vision, such as the retina and the superior colliculus. He further argued that the subcortical structures were relatively more mature at birth than was the visual cortex and that they played a larger role in directing attention in the first months after birth than they would later. One effect of this early subcortical dominance was that attention-drawing properties of objects, which are especially salient subcortically, would dominate the deployment of attention early on. With greater influence of the visual cortex, attention-holding properties would become increasingly important later.

One source of evidence supporting this analysis was the anatomical immaturity of the visual cortex at birth. It is unclear that this part of a newborn's brain is sufficiently developed to direct choices of where to look. Another reason to think that subcortical rather than cortical functioning is largely responsible for directing infants' earliest looking was that infants in the first month of life behaved in many ways like animals with known lesions (damaged tissues) on the visual cortex that would render the cortex inoperative. A third source of evidence was that infants' scanning in the second and third months focuses increasingly on internal detail, which would have greater salience for the cortical than for the subcortical mechanisms.

Bronson's theory has not gone unchallenged. The most significant criticism is that the visual cortex may be more functional at birth than he recognized. Detailed physiological analyses have revealed that certain cells and synapses in the visual cortex are functional even before birth (Maurer & Lewis, 1979). Nonetheless, Bronson's views are consistent with a wide range of physiological and behavioral data. The trend toward increasing cortical involvement in the deployment of attention seems likely to exert a major influence on where infants look.

What, then, can we conclude about infants' deployment of visual attention? The orientation reflex and certain rules for scanning the environment appear to be present from birth. These procedures for orienting are helpful under most circumstances, but also may lead children to miss certain types of nonsalient relevant information. Attention-drawing properties seem quite constant throughout life, whereas attention-holding properties change considerably with age. Both physiological maturation of the visual cortex and changes in what constitutes moderate discrepancy offer attractive accounts of developmental changes in orientation of attention, though both explanations are open to challenge.

Next we turn from considering the determinants of infants' visual attention to considering how they identify objects and events that they see.

Identifying Objects and Events

This section first focuses on two capabilities that are useful in identifying. These are visual acuity and color perception. Then the discussion turns to how infants use these capabilities to identify objects such as faces, and events such as motion.

Visual acuity. The single capability that is most crucial for identifying objects is the ability to discriminate the objects from the ongoing flux of the visual field. This ability to discriminate stimuli—to see clearly their similarities and differences—is known as visual acuity. Typically, the Snellen chart, which for years has hung in virtually every optometrists's office, is used to measure visual acuity. The letters you can read from twenty feet away are used as the reference point. If you can just read at twenty feet the letters that a person with "normal" vision can read at 150 feet, your vision is said to be 20/150.

Large differences exist between the visual acuity of normal adults and of infants. At maximum levels of contrast, acuity improves from approximately 20/500 to 20/100 between birth and 6 months of age (Dobson & Teller, 1978).

Distance from an object is not the only variable that influences how well people can discriminate among objects. Two other influences are *spatial frequency* and *contrast*. These influences can be understood by referring to Figure 5–3. Spatial frequency refers to the number of dark bars per degree of visual angle. The spatial frequency becomes greater as we move from left to right in the picture. The importance of this variable can be appreciated by imagining seeing an American flag 50 feet away. The relatively low spatial frequency in the area of the stripes would make it possible to discriminate where one ended and the next began. The greater spatial frequency in the

FIGURE 5–3 Spatial frequency and contrast determine a person's contrast sensitivity function. In the above illustration, the spatial frequency increases from left to right and the contrast increases from top to bottom (from Banks & Salapatek, 1981, photo provided courtesy of Dr. Martin Banks).

area of the stars, however, would probably make such discriminations impossible there for anyone not blessed with the eyes of an eagle.

Figure 5–3 also illustrates the concept of contrast. Contrast refers to the difference between the intensity of the brightest part of the white space and the darkest part of the bars. Within each bar, contrast grows greater as we move from top to bottom. More intuitively, it is easier to read a book in a brightly lit room than in a dimly lit one because the contrast between black print and white background is greater under the brighter illumination.

Banks and Salapatek (1981) noted that the influences of spatial frequency and contrast can be integrated into a single measure, the *contrast-sensitivity function*. This measure provides an especially revealing picture of the similarities and differences between infants' and adults' acuity.

Figure 5–4A shows a typical adult contrast-sensitivity function. The curve plots the level of contrast needed for an adult to detect a pattern at a particular spatial frequency. It shows that a typical adult's visual acuity is greatest at a moderate spatial frequency of about 3 cycles/degree, that acuity falls off somewhat at very low spatial frequencies, and that it falls off sharply at spatial frequencies of over 10 cycles/degree.

Figure 5–4B illustrates the development of visual acuity between 1 and 3 months. The 1-month-old's vision is as sensitive as the 3-month-old's at the lowest frequency. However, the 3-month-old's acuity is considerably superior at higher spatial frequencies.

The 1-, 2-, and 3-month-olds' contrast sensitivity functions differ from that of the adult in two ways. They are much lower (compare the numbers on the vertical axes of the graphs), indicating that the infants' absolute visual acuity is less good. They also are shifted to the left, indicating that their vision is relatively good at low spatial frequencies and relatively bad at higher ones.

Banks and Salapatek used these findings to explain a number of aspects of infants' visual perception. Recall the finding discussed earlier, that young infants prefer simple checkerboard patterns and older infants more complex ones. This was interpreted to mean either that with age, infants prefer greater complexity, or that they always prefer moderate levels of complexity but that what constitutes moderate complexity changes.

Banks and Salapatek suggested an alternative: that the changing preference is due to improved visual acuity rather than to any more cognitive difference. They showed that the infants' most preferred check sizes could be predicted from the maximum contrast sensitivity of each age group. As the peak of infants' contrast-sensitivity curves shifted to higher spatial frequencies, they preferred to look at checkerboards with more and smaller checks—that is, at checks with higher spatial frequencies. Especially convincing, the absolute as well as the relative frequencies of the checkerboard patterns infants preferred at each age could be predicted from their contrast-sensitivity functions.

What might account for the development of visual acuity? Banks and Salapatek suggested that two neural factors might be important. One was the spacing of cones in the retina: The closer together the cones, the greater the visual acuity. Banks and Salapatek cited evidence that the spacing of cones decreases ten- to twenty-fold between birth and adulthood. The other factor was the size of individual neurons' *receptive fields* (the area of the retina whose firing influences the particular neuron). The smaller the receptive field, the finer the acuity. The size of the receptive field of several types of neurons involved in vision decreases after birth in kittens and monkeys; human visual development probably follows a similar pattern.

Banks and Salapatek's research elegantly illustrates how changes in such basic perceptual capacities as visual acuity may underlie changes in

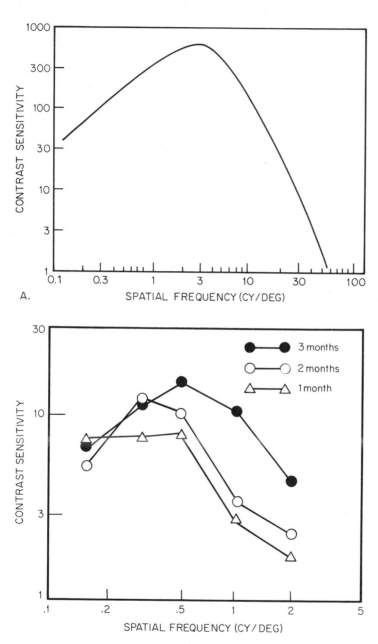

FIGURE 5-4 Typical contrast-sensitivity functions of an adult and of 1-, 2-, and 3-month-olds. The adult's contrast sensitivity is greatest at middle spatial frequencies (around 3 cycles/degree). The infants' contrast sensitivity is greatest at lower frequencies (around .5 cycles/degree), though their sensitivity to middle frequencies increases greatly by age 3 months (from Banks & Salapatek, 1981).

more cognitive aspects of perception, such as preferential looking, in the first half year of life. The research also has an interesting relation to Piaget's construct of functional assimilation (Chapter 2). As described, functional assimilation refers to people's tendency to exercise the most advanced capabilities they possess, even without any external reward. Infants' preference for looking at the most complex pattern they currently can perceive clearly exemplifies this tendency and shows that it extends to perception as well as to other aspects of cognition.

A clinical application of visual acuity research. Above and beyond what they have revealed about normal development, methods developed to study visual acuity are proving useful for diagnosing infants suspected of having abnormal vision. One technique, developed by Dobson (1983), involves showing infants cards divided into two halves. One half is an undifferentiated gray field; the other is a striped area with alternating black and white columns, like that on page 146. When shown such cards, infants strongly prefer looking at the striped area *if their visual acuity is sufficiently good so that they do not see the striped area as just another gray field.* Presenting such cards to infants with known or suspected visual difficulties provides a means of assessing whether the infants' vision is sufficiently impaired to warrant corrective surgery.

Dobson (1983) described several case histories in which ophthalmologists referred to her infants with suspected visual problems. In one case, a 2-month-old boy, born 4 weeks prematurely, was suspected of being blind. In pediatric examinations, he seemed neither to fixate on stable objects nor to follow moving ones. Dobson's preferential looking procedure revealed that the boy's vision was well within normal limits; he consistently looked toward the striped area rather than the gray field even when this required quite good acuity. By 4 months of age, the boy also was showing everyday evidence of appropriate looking. In this case, the technique saved the boy's parents several months of unnecessary worrying, and saved the boy from unnecessarily being treated as a blind child.

The preferential looking technique also has proved valuable for diagnosing whether children with a variety of problems need surgery. Among these are cataracts, muscular weakness in the eyelids, and cross-eyedness. Even when infants have these problems, their visual acuity may still be sufficiently good that there is no need for surgery; in other cases, surgery is required. Given the inherently conflicting needs to correct many visual impairments as early as possible, while at the same time avoiding surgery wherever possible, any technique that allows early accurate diagnosis of what an infant actually can see is welcome news to both physicians and parents.

Size and shape constancy. When scientists and philosophers in the 17th century began to understand optics, they quickly appreciated how remarkable it is that we see objects as having constant shapes and sizes. Viewed from a long distance, even a large object casts a small retinal image. Viewed from an indirect angle, a square casts a trapezoidal retinal pattern. Yet despite the variability in the images on our retinas, we effortlessly identify a friend as having the same height and build regardless of whether he is close or far, to the side or straight ahead. The ability to see an object as having the same size, regardless of its distance, is known as *size constancy*. The ability to see an object as having the same shape, regardless of the angle at which it is seen, is known as *shape constancy*.

Bower (1965) noted that these constancies raise a fundamental issue about perceptual development. How do people learn that the sizes and shapes of objects do not change when their position does? Do they eventually realize from handling rigid objects that their shapes and sizes are constant whatever their perceptual appearance? Or does the visual system correct for the seemingly misleading retinal images even without motoric experience?

Day and McKenzie (1981) demonstrated that infants as young as 4 months perceive sizes as constant despite changes in retinal images. In the habituation procedure that they used, the infants saw a cube moving back and forth in front of them. When they had habituated to this situation, they were presented either a different size object moving back and forth along one of the paths they had seen or the same object moving along one of the paths. For both the different-size and the familiar object, the retinal images that were cast were among the ones they had seen before. Despite both sets of retinal images being familiar, the infants dishabituated significantly more to the novel object than to the familiar one. Thus, 4-month-olds can perceive objects' constant physical size despite continuous changes in the retinal image produced by the object.

Even younger infants can perceive shape constancy. To "desensitize" infants to changes in the orientation of a square, 3-month-olds were repeatedly shown a particular square on a particular trapezoid at a variety of orientations (Caron, Caron, & Carlson, 1979). Once they habituated to these changing orientations (and changing retinal patterns), infants were presented the shape they had not seen earlier at a novel orientation or the shape they had seen earlier in the same novel orientation. The infants dishabituated more to the unfamiliar shape than to the familiar one, thus indicating that they possessed shape constancy by at least this age.

Color vision.   Why have so many animals evolved to see the world in color? Bornstein (1978) suggested that one reason is that color vision enhances ability to identify objects and events. It does this by heightening contrasts, by making constancies easier to detect, and by increasing visibility.

Adults can see wavelengths of light ranging from roughly 400 to 700 nanometers (nm). They see particular wavelengths as particular colors. For example, they perceive the wavelengths 450–480 nm as clearly blue,

510–540 nm as clearly green, 570–590 nm as yellow, and 615–650 as red. Although adults perceive some wavelengths as mixtures, (for example, 500 nm is perceived as bluishgreen), they see most as unambiguously one color or another.

The key issue in research on infants' color vision has been whether they, like adults, perceive colors as qualitatively distinct entities. The methodological difficulties in investigating this problem prevented it from being investigated for many years. Although researchers were interested in the issue, they had no means to investigate it.

Finally, Bornstein (1976a; b) broke the impasse by applying a version of the habituation paradigm to the problem. First he habituated groups of 3-and 4-month-olds to a light that adults saw as being a particular color (for example, green). Then he presented two new lights that differed from the original stimulus by the same absolute wavelength. However, the two new lights differed in their psychological relation to the original one. One new light was within the same color category as the original; that is, adults saw it as being a slightly different shade of green. The other wavelength was across a color boundary; despite its being no farther away from the original in terms of its wavelength, adults perceived it as blue. Presumably, if infants perceive colors in the same categorical manner as adults, and saw different colors as more distinct than different shades of the same color, they would dishabituate to the wavelength that was across the color boundary to a greater extent than to the one that was on the same side of the boundary.

The infants followed exactly this pattern. They dishabituated to a greater extent when the novel stimulus lay across the color boundary. As shown in Figure 5–5, this finding has been obtained for each of the three major color boundaries. The finding has recently been supplemented by a demonstration that children less than 1 *week* old also discriminate red and yellow from gray (Adams & Maurer, 1984). These results, together with the fact that people all over the world classify the same wavelengths as constituting prototypic colors, suggest strongly that color vision is an inherent property of the human nervous system.

Next we turn to how infants use their basic capacities, such as visual acuity and color vision, to identify objects such as faces and events such as motion.

Identification of faces.   Attention to the faces of mothers, fathers, and other people has been hypothesized to play a unique role in early infant development. Having an infant son or daughter attend closely to your face is a gratifying experience for a parent, and having them show that they recognize you is even more so. From an evolutionary perspective, these responses seem adaptive in increasing the likelihood that the parent will care for the infant.

Some researchers have argued that infants are born with a predisposition to look at faces. Others have argued that infants learn to associate faces

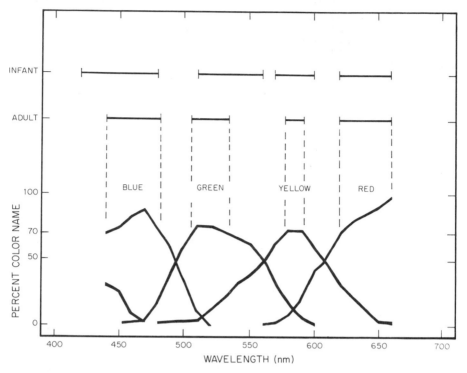

FIGURE 5-5 The similarity of 4-month-olds' and adults' perception of colors. The graphs near the bottom show the percentage of adults who label a given wavelength by the particular color name. The horizontal lines at the top show the range of wavelengths over which infants and adults do not seem to discriminate. Note that the breaks in the horizontal lines, indicating wavelengths between which infants and adults do discriminate, correspond closely to the transition points from one color to another in the adults' verbal descriptions of the same wavelengths (from Lamb & Campos, 1982).

with food and comfort and that these associations account for infants' interest in faces. Yet others have argued that faces are no more appealing to infants than are many other stimuli.

Fantz (e.g., 1958; 1961) conducted some of the earliest and most important studies on face perception. He presented infants ranging in age from 4 days to 6 months with three patterns: a standard face, the same face but with features in scrambled positions, and a bull's-eye pattern. At almost all of the ages he examined, Fantz reported a small but consistent preference for looking at the real face rather than the scrambled one, and a strong preference for both faces over the bull's-eye pattern.

Fantz's studies stimulated others to examine larger groups of infants under more carefully controlled conditions. These studies have supported and extended his conclusions about 6-month-olds. It is now apparent that by this age, infants prefer actual faces to pictures of faces, talking and moving faces to silent and immobile ones, and familiar to unfamiliar ones, as well as unscrambled to scrambled ones (Sherrod, 1979).

Many of these preferences do not appear in the first few months, however, and it is unclear that visual acuity at this time is sufficient to allow infants to see clearly many of the stimuli that have been used. Even at ages where infants clearly discriminate among the presented forms, the basis on which they do so often is unclear. For example, actual faces differ from pictures of faces in brightness, depth, texture, movement, and many other qualities. Infants' preference for the live faces could be based on any or all of these.

This leaves us with the basic question; Are faces special for infants? The answer seems to be, "Compared to what?" As yet, there is little reason to believe that the particular configuration of the human face is more attractive for infants younger than 4 months than its component parts would indicate. On the other hand, many aspects of the human face attract infants' attention: It moves, is bright, has curves, has high contrasts, is symmetrical, and is associated with sounds. Whether or not the human face is special to young infants, it certainly interests them.

Identification of biological motion.   Faces are not the only biologically important stimuli that interest infants. Infants as young as 4 months can identify the coordinated rhythmic patterns of movement characteristic of people and other animals and are interested in looking at them (Bertenthal & Proffitt, 1982; Fox & McDaniel, 1982). When a small number of luminescent dots are attached to the torso and limbs of a person, and only the dots are visible, the dots' pattern of movement conveys that of the person. Even when the dots are presented alone, moving as they would if attached to a person, 4-month-olds look at them more often than randomly arranged moving dots or arrangements identical to the original biological movement except for being rotated 180 degrees (placed upside down). Thus, they prefer biologically natural motion to motion patterns than do not have that characteristic.

In summary, we can see both extensive early visual identification capacities and extensive development of these capacities in the first six months. Newborns seem to enter the world with a certain amount of visual acuity, especially at low frequency ranges. They are far from being blind, as was once thought, though their acuity undergoes great improvement over the first half year and considerable further improvement beyond that period. They see at least the outlines of objects quite clearly, as well as some high-contrast interior detail. They also see the world in color, and seem to divide the world into essentially the same qualitatively distinct colors as adults do. By 3 or 4 months, if not earlier, infants possess size and shape constancy. Both faces and biological motion possess many qualities that attract infants' attention in the first six months. It is not clear that infants perceive faces as special, but there is little doubt concerning the faces' attractiveness for them.

In the next section we examine how infants determine where objects are relative to themselves.

Locating Objects

Locating objects poses infants with a series of problems. How can they infer how far away objects are? How can they use locational information to avoid falling off uneven surfaces? How can they use information from memory to infer distance? Finally, how can they retain information about locations even when they move around and the directions of objects relative to themselves change?

The fact that people of any age can solve these problems is remarkable. The display of light on the retina at any given time only seems to specify height and breadth, not depth; how can a three-dimensional world be represented in a two-dimensional retinal image? Similarly, knowing the direction of objects from ourselves is difficult because we cannot always see the objects and because we move around. To illustrate this latter problem, try to point straight in the direction from where you are at the moment to your best friend's house. Below, we consider in turn infants' perception of depth, their ability to avoid falling off uneven surfaces, their use of information from memory to infer distance, and their ability to retain directional information.

Monocular cues to depth.   Although a retinal display at any one moment does not specify the distance of objects, people's movements and adjustments to those movements provide rich information about depth. Some of the most useful information comes from monocular cues, that is, information available to each eye independently. This can be seen in the role of *accommodation*. Accommodation refers to changes in the shape of the lens of the eyeball that are made to create the sharpest possible focus for an object at a given distance. The degree of tension in the muscles that control accommodation differs at different distances, and thus provides information about distance.

Research on accommodation illustrates the way in which the interconnectedness of perceptual skills creates complexities in drawing conclusions about the degree to which infants possess any one of them. Haynes, White, & Held (1965) presented a checkerboard to infants and concluded that in the first few months after birth, the infants did not accommodate to the object. When shown the checkerboard, infants below 4 months maintained a constant focus that was appropriate if the object was 19 centimeters away, but that would be out of focus at other distances. By the time infants were 4 months old, however, they showed high levels of accommodation.

Banks (1980) noted that the results may have had little to do with accommodation per se, however. Because the same checkerboard was used at all distances, infants would have needed increasingly fine acuity to detect that it was out of focus as it was moved farther away. Therefore, limited acuity, rather than inability to accommodate, may have underlain Haynes et al.'s findings.

To test this interpretation, Banks presented 1- and 2-month-olds with checkerboards as had been done in previous studies. Unlike in previous studies, however, the infants saw larger checkerboards at the farther distances, so that the degree of acuity needed remained constant. Under these conditions, 1-month-olds showed some accommodation and 2-month-olds showed quite good accommodation. Banks attributed the changes in the first two months to decreases in *depth of focus*, (the range of distances from a fixation point within which there is no difference in blurriness). These results suggested an alternative to the conclusion by Haynes et al. that infants do not accommodate to differing distances of objects. They do accommodate, if they can see the object clearly enough, but their limited acuity reduces the range of objects that lead them to use this ability.

Banks also proposed an interesting account of how accommodation develops. The key element of the account is a mutually beneficial interaction between two capabilities: accommodation and acuity. Within Banks's account, neurologically based improvements in acuity create a shorter depth of focus, which allows infants to detect greater blurriness at points other than the optimal focal point. This greater difference between the clearest point and others stimulates infants to accommodate in order to maximize the clarity of the focus. Clearer focus, in turn, stimulates development of elements at the retinal and cortical levels that allow still greater acuity.

This type of interactive process, which Banks labeled *reciprocal dependency*, may be a quite common developmental phenomenon. For example, a number of investigators have hypothesized that learning to segment spoken language into separate sounds facilitates the development of reading, and that learning to read in turn facilitates the ability to segment speech into component sounds (Perfetti, 1984).

Less is known about several monocular cues other than accommodation that infants may use to infer depth. One of the most important of these is *motion parallax*. When a person moves his head, closer objects appear to move faster than objects that are farther away. Another monocular cue to depth is *occlusion;* when two objects overlap, the one that is closer obscures the one that is farther. *Texture* is a monocular cue to depth in that an object seems rougher closer to the viewing point (because more details can be seen). A final monocular cue is *visual expansion*, which refers to objects filling an increasing portion of our visual field as we approach them or they approach us. Infants can use all four of these by the time they are 7 months old, though they may not use them in the first months of life (Yonas & Granrud, in press).

Binocular cues to depth.   Because people's eyes are several centimeters apart, the pattern of stimulation that impinges on the two retinas almost always differs. This retinal disparity is valuable for estimating the distance of objects from oneself. The value can be illustrated by going to an unfamiliar location, closing one eye, and trying to estimate how far away objects are. Most people estimate considerably more accurately with two eyes open than with only one.

Aslin and Dumais (1980) noted that three hierarchically-related abilities are necessary for adults to perceive depth binocularly. The first is *bifoveal fixation*, the focusing of the foveas of both eyes on the same point. Without bifoveal fixation, there is no common object being focused on by the parts of the eye with the greatest acuity, and therefore few or no binocular depth cues. The second level of binocular depth perception is *fusion*, the integrating of the two retinal images into a single perceived object. The presence of bifoveal fixation and the absence of fusion results in what is commonly called double vision. The third level is *stereopsis*, the perception of depth based on retinal disparity. The abilities are hierarchical in the sense that to perceive depth based on retinal disparity (stereopsis), it is necessary to fuse the discrepant retinal images into a single perception; and to fuse the images into a single perception, it is necessary for both eyes to fixate at the same place.

Aslin (1977) assessed 1-, 2-, and 3-month-olds' bifoveal fixation. To do this, he moved a cross back and forth at different speeds and examined the infants' eye movements. Even the 1-month-olds' eyes converged and diverged in the appropriate direction, given a change in the position of the cross. However, only the 2- and 3-month-olds changed their eye positions sufficiently for frequent bifoveal fixation. Aslin concluded that much of early visual experience involves misaligned images. By 3 months, however, bifoveal fixation seems to predominate.

Fusion is an especially difficult ability to study, since it inherently involves the subjective experience of the two retinal images forming a single perceived object. Aslin used a clever procedure for studying infants' ability to fuse the retinal images. After the infants fixated both foveas on an object, the experimenter placed a distorting wedge-shaped prism in front of one eye. Adults report that doing this makes them see a double image, and they move their eyes to try to recreate a single perception. Six-month-olds also react to the prisms with eye movements, but 3- and 4-month-olds do not, suggesting that fusion develops between these ages.

Stereopsis, the appreciation of relative distance based on retinal disparity, has been studied using *random-dot stereograms*. In these stereograms, dots are positioned so that if they are viewed by just one eye, they seem to form a random pattern. When the patterns of dots available to the two eyes are fused into a single image, however, a three-dimensional object emerges.

Fox, Aslin, Shea, and Dumais (1980) presented such a stereogram to 2-to 5-month-olds. The experimenters moved the dot displays in such a way that the apparent shape would move to the right or left side of a screen. Four-and 5-month-olds consistently looked toward the side where the apparent object would be perceived by someone who possessed stereopsis. The 2-month-olds failed to do this. Their behavior was not attributable to their not following moving shapes with their eyes, since all of them had consistently followed a standard object when it was presented earlier. Thus, stereoscopic depth perception seems to be present by age 4 months, though it may not be present before then. Because fusion is necessary for stereopsis, the results imply that fusion too must be present by 4 months of age.

The role of experience in perceptual development has not been discussed in any detail in this chapter. The reason is that little is known about it. Interesting data has been collected, however, about the role of visual experience in the development of binocularly based depth perception. Banks, Aslin, and Letson (1975) tested binocular functioning in children and adults who, due to being cross-eyed, did not focus bifoveally until the condition was corrected by surgery. After surgery, all the children and adults aligned their eyes correctly. However, only those whose vision was corrected before age 3 years had normal binocular depth perception. The two eyes not focusing on the same object does not seem to have any detrimental effects until roughly age 4 months, the time at which bifoveal fixation ordinarily becomes the rule. The degree of harm resulting from continued binocular deprivation grows until about 3 years, at which time, unfortunately, the damage seems to have been done.

Thus, in addition to the normal developmental period for binocular depth perception, birth to 4 months, there seems to be a sensitive period within which the ability must develop if it is ever to do so. This sensitive period seems to last for the first 3 years of life. The existence of such critical periods makes all the more valuable the development of techniques for diagnosing suspected visual abnormalities during infancy (p. 149).

Using depth cues to avoid falling.   Although studies of the visual cliff are among the best known of all psychology experiments, few people know what motivated their originators to conduct them in the first place. A psychologist, Richard Walk, was at Fort Benning, Georgia, watching paratrooper trainees practice jumping from a tower. The tower was 34 feet above the ground. The goal was for the trainees to learn to jump without becoming tangled in parachute strings and for them to relax before jumping. Strong straps would break their descent after eight to ten feet, and the device had an excellent safety record. As Walk described, however,

> The device is perfectly safe but perceptually it is like a jump off a 34-foot cliff. Strong individuals stride up the tower, walk to the open door with confidence, look down, blanch, tremble, and refuse to go farther. Others have the same physiological reactions, but they go forward; and in exiting, their knees collapse under them, and they fall out the door like limp sacks of wheat (1979, p. 84).

Walk and Gibson (e.g., 1961) conducted a large number of studies of a visual cliff apparatus like that shown in Figure 5–6. A chick or a kid (goat)

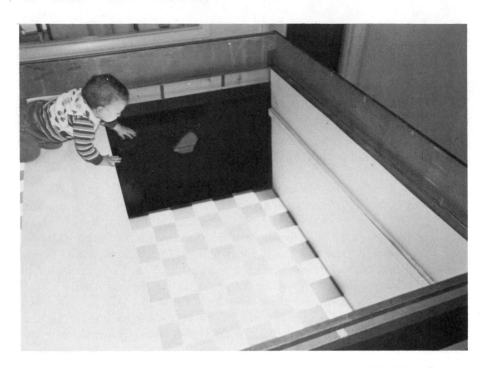

FIGURE 5-6   An infant approaches the visual cliff (photo provided courtesy of Dr. Joseph Campos).

would be placed on a board. It could move toward either of two glass surfaces. One surface had a pattern only a small distance below the glass. The other had the pattern considerably farther below. Thus, the one side looked like a small drop and the other like a cliff. Kids, chicks, and other animals avoided the deep side consistently. Human newborns could not be tested, since they cannot move around independently. However, 6-month-olds, who can crawl, avoided the deep side just as the newborn animals had (e.g., Walk & Gibson, 1961). The findings gave rise to speculation that depth perception was an inherent quality of newborn mammals.

Other observations have shed doubt on whether this interpretation applies to human infants. In particular, human infants younger than 6 months, who cannot crawl but who have learned to use a walker, go to the deep side of a visual cliff without any apparent fear (Campos, Hiatt, Ramsay, Henderson, & Svejda, 1978). Rader, Bausano, and Richards (1980) suggested one possible interpretation. Perhaps an innate visuo-motor program that leads other mammals to avoid cliffs from birth does not take effect in humans until roughly 6 months of age. With animals that can locomote at birth, like chicks and goats, ability to perceive sharp drop-offs is critical from day one. For human infants, the need is less urgent.

Using memory to infer the distance of objects.   The directness or indirectness of perception has been a basic point of contention between two schools of thought within perceptual development. *Perceptual invariance theorists*, such as J. J. and Eleanor Gibson, believe that all perception is direct. By this they mean that memory for previous events has no role in perception; only currently visible stimuli are influential. *Constructivists*, such as Hebb (1949), take an opposing position. They believe that memory for previous experiences is a fundamental part of perception. These positions have not proved easy to test. However, a recent study by Granrud, Haake, and Yonas (in press) provides an exemplary model of how such comparisons can be done.

Granrud et al. tested whether memories of the sizes of objects influenced 7-month-olds' perception of how far away the objects were. Their experiment was based on the simple observation that all else being equal, infants reach for objects they perceive to be closer. The experiment included two phases. In the first, infants were given experience playing with two objects, one big and the other small, so they could learn the objects' sizes (Figure 5–7). In the second, the experimenter placed two similar objects a moderate distance from the infants. The only difference between these objects and the ones the infants had played with earlier was that the smaller object had been replaced by a larger version of the same object (Figure 5–7C).

Constructivist and perceptual invariance theories make directly opposing predictions about what should happen under these conditions. Constructivists would expect infants to reach more often for the form that previously had been smaller. The infants' reasoning would be that if the object occupied as large an area on their retinas, it must be closer, because a smaller object would otherwise occupy a smaller area on the retina. Invariance theorists, on the other hand, would predict that since memory has no role in perception, and since the immediate stimuli are of apparently equal distance, infants should reach for the two equally often.

In fact, the 7-month-olds more frequently reached for the object that originally had been smaller. This indicated that they used their memory of its previous size to guide their perception of its present distance. Thus, infants can use their memories of objects to guide their perceptions.

Adjusting to changes in spatial position.   Piaget (1971) suggested that before infants are 1 year old, they exhibit a kind of sensorimotor egocentrism. Recall from Chapter 2 that egocentrism refers to young children's tendency to view the world solely from their own perspective. Piaget claimed that in infancy the egocentrism is quite literal, and that infants represent locations of objects only in relation to themselves. For example, they might continue to represent an object as being a right turn away from themselves even after they moved to the opposite side of the object, resulting in it being on their left. Piaget's hypothesis was supported by the findings of Acredolo (1978). She found that 6- and 11-month-olds frequently failed to compensate for changes in their own spatial position. They continued to turn in the direction that previously had led them toward an object but that no longer did so.

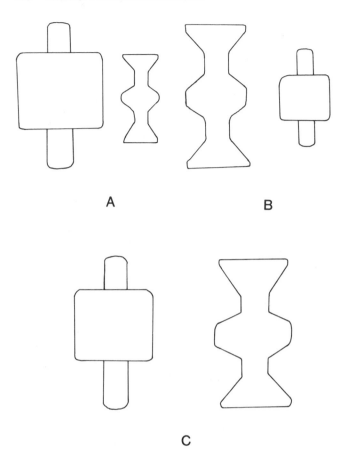

FIGURE 5-7   Stimuli used by Granrud, Haake, and Yonas (in press). In the habituation phase, some infants played with stimulus pair A, whereas others played with stimulus pair B. All were shown stimulus pair C in the dishabituation phase. The key prediction was that infants in both groups would usually reach for the object that previously was smaller if they used their memory of the objects' sizes to infer which one now was closer (photo provided courtesy of Dr. Carl Granrud).

This difficulty in adjusting to changes in spatial position can be mitigated if either distinctive landmarks or gravity provide cues to the object's location (Rieser, 1979). Under such conditions, 6-month-olds usually turn in the appropriate direction, even when it differs from the direction that previously led to finding the object. Adjusting to changes in position also seems to be less of a problem when testing is done in the infant's home than when it is done in an unfamiliar environment. Thus, Piaget's suggestion that infants less than 1 year old perceive space egocentrically seems to have considerable validity, but the limitation does not seem absolute.

To summarize, infants use a variety of monocular and binocular cues to locate how far away objects are. The monocular cues include accommodation, motion parallax, texture, visual expansion, and occlusion. Accommodation undergoes a particularly interesting developmental path, in which improvements in acuity seem to trigger improvements in accommodatory ability, which in turn seem to stimulate further improvements in acuity. Binocular-depth cues can be considered hierarchically: In adults at least, bifoveal fixation is essential for fusion, and both are essential for stereopsis, the inference of depth from purely binocular cues. By age 4 months, all three of the capabilities seem to be present. Infants' perception of depth seems to be influenced by inferences based on previous memories, as well as the stimuli in the immediate environment. Finally, infants below 1 year have difficulty finding objects' locations when their own position relative to the object has changed. The difficulty is lessened, however, if distinctive landmarks provide clues to the object's location or if the experiment is conducted in the infant's home.

These varying developmental paths should not obscure the fundamental fact of just how skilled early visual perception is. This skill can be seen when infants' visual perception is compared with efforts to program computers to perceive the world. Early in the history of artificial intelligence research, investigators wrote programs that skillfully performed supposedly complex tasks such as playing chess and proving logic theorems. In contrast, no program yet written has visual capabilities approaching those of a 4-month-old. Research on infants' visual skills is one of those areas that reveal just how remarkable people really are.

HEARING

Investigators have conducted fewer studies on auditory than on visual perception. Nonetheless, they have learned a considerable amount, in large part because results of the studies have been very consistent. The studies converge on the conclusion that from the first few months of life, infants have impressive abilities to attend to sounds, to identify what they are, and to localize where they are.

Attending to Sounds

Even before birth, infants demonstrate surprising auditory abilities. When babies in the uterus are exposed to intense (loud) sounds, they move around more and their hearts beat faster. By 1 week of age, infants hear and respond to a wide range of sounds. Their responses are both familiar and dramatic. When presented with loud noises, they look startled, blink their eyes rapidly if they are open or squeeze them tightly shut if they are already closed, and jerk their limbs erratically. Quieter sounds elicit less dramatic reactions. Although development of the ear is not complete until the end of the first year, the newborns' auditory system is functional from the first days.

One focus of research on infants' auditory perception has been on their intensity thresholds, the volume needed for them to hear that some sound is being made. Although newborns do not have as low intensity thresholds as adults, the differences are not huge. In addition, individual differences are quite marked in infant auditory perception. Some newborn infants show hearing approaching that of most adults, whereas others' hearing appears considerably less good (Acredolo & Hake, 1982).

Infants are more attentive to some sounds than to others. They appear especially attentive to speechlike sounds. Several general characteristics of their hearing predispose them in this direction. They react most noticeably to sounds in the frequency range of 1,000 to 3,000 Hz, the range in which most speech occurs. They also react more to sounds that, like speech, include a range of frequencies, than to pure tones, in which all sound is at a single frequency.

The infants' heightened reactions to sounds in the frequency range of speech could be due either to greater ability to hear sounds in that frequency range or to greater interest in sounds in that range. For many years researchers assumed that infants could hear sounds more clearly in that range. Recently, however, Schneider, Trehub, and Bull (1979) provided compelling evidence that the difference is in what sounds infants find interesting. Sounds at certain frequencies may be heard but may not elicit responses from the orienting system, just as Sokolov (1963) hypothesized that familiar visual stimuli might not.

Schneider et al. first rewarded 6-, 12-, and 18-month-olds whenever they turned their heads in the direction of a tone. The purpose of doing this was to condition the infants to turn in the direction of any sound they could hear, even if they did not find it inherently interesting. When the infants learned to do this, the experimenter began to vary the intensity of the tones and their frequency. The goal was to determine the least-intense sound infants could hear at each frequency.

Infants of all ages proved to be as able or better able to detect frequencies higher than those typical of speech than frequencies in the speech range. In addition, at the highest frequencies, the infants' auditory acuity approached that of adults'. It was much poorer at lower frequencies. The results indicated that most auditory development beyond infancy occurs in the low-frequency ranges. It also indicated the need to distinguish between the sounds infants find sufficiently interesting to attend to and the sounds that they can detect.

Identifying Sounds

Infants show remarkably adultlike ability to identify and discriminate between sounds that differ only subtly. Many of the most impressive demonstrations of this ability concern speech perception. However, infants' ability to identify and discriminate among other sounds, such as musical tones, also is keen.

First consider speech perception. Two-month-olds discriminate between such similar sounds as *ba* and *pa*, *ma* and *na*, and *s* and *z*. Their perception of the differences between these sounds seems to be categorical, just as their perception of the differences between colors is.

Eimas, Siqueland, Jusczyk, and Vigorito (1971) first demonstrated categorical speech perception. The logic of their experiment was closely akin to that which motivated the Bornstein color-vision experiment (p. 150). One of the dimensions along which speech sounds differ is in voice onset time (VOT). To make some sounds, such as *ba*, people begin to vibrate their vocal cords almost as soon as they start making the sound. *Ba* thus has a short VOT, since the onset of voicing (vibration of the vocal cords) begins early in the sound. In making other sounds, such as *pa*, people do not begin vibrating their vocal cords until a longer time after the onset of the sound. *Pa* thus has a longer VOT. Despite the physical dimension underlying this difference being continuous (amount of time before vibration of the vocal cords begins), adults hear sounds with VOTs less than a certain value as qualitatively distinct from sounds with VOTs greater than that level. A sound is either a *ba* or a *pa*, never something in between.

In the first experiment to demonstrate categorical perception in infants, Eimas et al. habituated infants as young as 1 month with a sound that adults perceive as being a *pa*. Then the infants were presented one of two sounds identical to the initial one except in their VOTs. The VOTs of the two new sounds were equally distant from that of the original sound to which the infants had habituated. However, one of these sounds was perceived by adults also to be a *pa*, whereas the other was perceived as a *ba*. If infants perceived the sounds categorically, they too would dishabituate more dramatically to the sound that adults heard as a *ba*. On the other hand, if they responded to the absolute difference in VOT between the old and new sounds, they would dishabituate equally to the two new sounds.

Apparently the infants heard the sounds as qualitatively distinct. They dishabituated to a greater extent to the *ba* than to the *pa*, despite the equal physical distance between the original and the two new stimuli. The finding is not unique to these two sounds. Infants have shown similar abilities to discriminate syllables on the basis of the role of the lips (*ba* versus *ga*), tongue height and placement (*a* versus *i*), and numerous other features of speech (Morse, 1972; Trehub, 1973). They also are sensitive to features that occur over a more extended chain of speech, such as rising or falling intonation and accenting of a particular syllable (Morse, 1972; Aslin, Pisoni, & Jusczyk, 1983).

Might these discriminations be due to the particular language infants hear around them? A study with Guatemalan infants between 4 and 6 months suggests a negative answer. The Guatemalan infants were of interest because the Spanish they heard placed the VOT boundary between *ba* and *pa* at a different place than English and most other languages. In spite of this linguistic experience, the infants dishabituated in a way that indicated that they placed the VOT boundary between *ba* and *pa* where English does (Lasky, Syrdal-Lasky, & Klein, 1975). Thus, infants may enter the world with sensitivities attuned to particular boundaries.

These predispositions do not persist forever. Although infants are sensitive to many contrasts not used in the languages they hear, they later lose sensitivity to these features. Werker, Gilbert, Humphrey, and Tees (1981) demonstrated this phenomenon with English- and Hindi-speaking adults and 7-month-olds brought up in North America. The task was one in which two sounds differed only on a contrast that differentiates words in Hindi but not in English. After repeatedly presenting one sound, the experimenter abruptly switched to the other. To get a reward, subjects needed to turn their head to one side when the sound changed. Among the infants, eleven of twelve accurately perceived the change, as did all of the Hindi-speaking adults. However, only 1 of 10 English-speaking adults accurately perceived it. As the authors concluded, "There may be a decrease in speech perceptual abilities with either age or linguistic experience" (p. 354).

Some researchers have interpreted these findings of innate sensitivity to certain speech boundaries as helping to explain why only humans, of all species, developed speech. Kuhl and Miller (1975), however, demonstrated the same sensitivity to these contrasts in chinchillas. Subsequent investigators have demonstrated similar sensitivity in rhesus macaque monkeys. The phenomenon may be similar to that in face perception: Infants may not be uniquely attuned to speech sounds, but they have a variety of sensitivities that prepare them to identify and discriminate among them.

Speech perception involves more than the ability to discriminate among sounds. Another vital ability is identifying the voices of different speakers. Infants as young as 3 days old not only seem able to identify their mothers' voices, but also seem to prefer them. DeCasper and Fifer (1980) established a situation in which the infant's sucking was followed either by presentation of the mother's voice or by the voice of a female stranger. They found that the 3-day-olds sucked at a higher rate when the reward was the mother's voice.

In DeCasper and Fifer's experiment, none of the infants had spent more than 12 postnatal hours with their mother. Although this experience may explain the preference for the mother's voice, another possibility is that the preference was based on familiarity with the voice obtained before birth. Evidence supporting this possibility was found in a study in which expectant mothers were asked to recite a prose passage a number of times over a several-week period prior to birth. After the babies were born, an experimenter played a tape recording of the mother reading that passage or an unfamiliar passage. The babies sucked at a higher rate in response to the familiar passage (Spence & DeCasper, 1982).

When adults talk to infants and young children, they often speak in a style known as *motherese*. This style is characterized by high pitch and exaggerated intonations. In a study of German mothers, Stern, Spieker, and MacKain (1982) found that 77% of the mothers' utterances to infants between birth and 6 months of age fell into the motherese category. Almost none of the statements that these mothers addressed to adults did. The likely reason is that infants prefer such intonations and pitches. Fernald (1981) found that 4-month-olds who were presented statements in motherese and standard conversational styles turned their heads more often toward the ones in motherese.

In sum, infants are able to discriminate speech sounds, voices, and intonation patterns from each other. They also have clear preferences concerning where boundaries in speech dimensions should be and which voices, material, and intonations they wish to listen to.

Now consider perception of music. Infants perceive the distinctions between some types of musical sounds categorically, just as they perceive speech sounds. In listening to the types of sounds made on a violin, adults perceive some as plucks and others as bows. The differences between plucks and bows can be reduced to a single dimension known as *rise time*. Two-month-olds discriminate between plucks and bows, but not between stimuli equally discrepant in rise time that adults hear as two types of plucks or two types of bows (Jusczyk, Rosner, Cutting, Foard, & Smith, 1977).

Although both speech and musical sounds are processed categorically, it appears that different parts of the brain predominate in processing them. The left hemisphere of the brain predominates in speech perception, whereas the right hemisphere dominates in perception of complex nonspeech sounds such as music. This pattern of hemispheric dominance has been discovered by studying *auditory evoked responses*. The experimenter places electrodes at specific points on the left and right sides of the head, presents a stimulus simultaneously to the two ears, and records the amount of electrical activity on each side of the brain. When the stimulus involves speech, the left hemisphere shows greater brain activity—that is, a greater auditory evoked response. When the stimulus involves music, the pattern is reversed, with the right hemisphere showing greater activity.

Some *lateralization*—that is, specialization of different parts of the brain for processing different types of stimuli—may be present even before most babies are born. Newborns born 4 to 6 weeks prematurely show greater left-hemisphere responding to speech sounds, just as adults do (Molfese & Molfese, 1979). By age 2 months, infants show both differential hemispheric processing and some amount of memory for musical sounds. In one experiment (Best, Hoffman, & Glanville, 1982), infants heard a musical note or a speech sound presented to both ears until they had habituated to it. On the tenth trial, the alternative type of stimulus was presented to one of the ears. The 2-month-olds dishabituated to the musical sound to a greater extent when it was presented to the left ear, which transfers information to the right hemisphere. The finding demonstrated early specialization of the right hemisphere for processing complex nonspeech sounds such as musical tones and also sufficient memory for both the speech sounds and the tones so that infants could recognize new stimuli as different. Thus, the beginnings of lateralization may be among the reasons that very young infants can identify both speech and musical sounds.

Auditory Localization

After his daughter was born, an unusually dedicated psychologist named Wertheimer entered the delivery room. Rather than simply admiring the child, Wertheimer brought a clicker and sounded it first on one side of the room and then on the other. From the first sounding of the clicker, the baby turned her head in the direction of the sound. Thus, at least a crude sense of *auditory localization* (the ability to locate sounds in space), seems to exist from birth (Wertheimer, 1961).

Surprisingly, newborns seem better able to localize sounds than 2- and 3-month-olds, though not better than 4-month-olds. This pattern of data, which will appear in a number of contexts throughout the book, has been labeled a *U-shaped curve*. At first, performance is at a high level, then it drops, then it returns to a high level. The U-shaped pattern is of special interest because it often indicates that different mechanisms are responsible for the same behavior at different points in development. This seems to be the case in auditory localization.

Muir, Abraham, Forbes, and Harris (1979) conducted a longitudinal study in which they repeatedly examined four infants over the first 4 months of the infants' lives. They found that three of them showed a U-shaped pattern of auditory localization. As shown in Figure 5–8, the infants first showed high levels of head turning toward the side from which the sound came, then showed reduced levels, and then, by about 4 months, returned to the prior high levels. The decline in the middle was not due to lack of interest in the sounds. Even when an infant's mother or father called the child's name in the middle of a group of rattle sounds, the pattern of head turning did not change.

Muir et al. proposed an explanation much like that which Bronson (1974) proposed for infants' visual behavior. They suggested that auditory localization in the first month after birth reflects subcortical functioning. In the second and third months, cortical activity increases and it replaces subcortical activity as the dominant influence on infants' auditory localization. However, at this point, the cortical activity is not sufficiently developed to produce accurate localization. Only in the fourth month does the cortical activity become sufficiently developed to reinstate accurate localization.

To summarize, infants enter the world with substantial auditory capabilities, and the capabilities develop further in the first few months. The

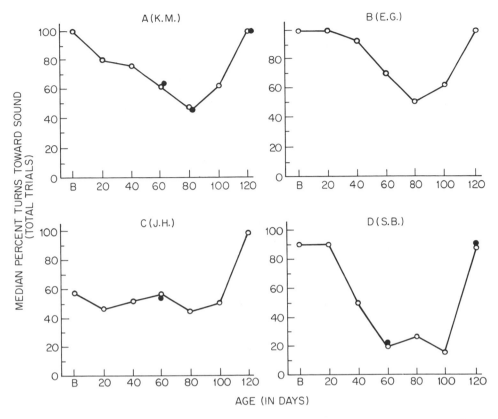

FIGURE 5-8 Percentage of trials on which four infants turned toward sounds. Infants were tested every 20 days from birth to 120 days (from Muir, Abraham, Forbes, & Harris, 1979).

capabilities are evident in which sounds attract infants' attention, in their ability to identify sounds, and in their ability to localize where sounds originate. Sounds with frequencies and other characteristics that resemble speech are especially likely to attract infants' attention. This seems to be due more to the sounds interesting them than to the sounds being especially easy for them to detect. When identifying either speech or musical tones, infants, like adults, appear to process the sounds categorically. Also like adults, the infants' left hemispheres seem to be most involved in processing speech sounds, and the right hemispheres in processing musical tones. The ability to localize sounds shows a U-shaped pattern between birth and 4 months. It is best at the two extremes, and is less good in between. A plausible explanation is that subcortical mechanisms produce the early high level of skill, whereas cortical mechanisms produce similarly good localization beyond age 4 months.

INTERSENSORY INTEGRATION

How do infants integrate the information they receive from different sensory systems into a single coherent experience? One plausible developmental path would be that they first develop each system separately and then, when each has reached some level of competence, integrate the separate sources. Piaget (1971) proposed just such a theory. Recent investigations of infants' intersensory integration suggest a quite different picture, however. It now appears that sights and sounds are integrated from birth.

Demonstrations of intersensory integration have been presented under other headings throughout this chapter. These studies have shown that intersensory integration influences all three of the functions that have been examined: attending, identifying, and locating.

Sokolov's (1963) discussion of the orienting reflex exemplifies how intersensory integration influences infants' attention. One of Sokolov's observations was that a loud noise causes infants to attend to the source of the sound. The way Sokolov knew that the infants were attending to the source of the sound was that they looked at it. That is, they used auditory information to guide visual attention.

Both sights and sounds are also used to identify objects and events. Recall Spelke's study in which 4-month-olds looked more often at the movie whose visual images were in keeping with the sounds they were hearing (the mother playing peek-a-boo or the drum beat). If the infants were not trying to integrate visual and auditory information to understand the events, they would have had no reason to act in this way.

The Sokolov observation just cited also provides evidence for coordination of vision and audition in locating objects. In fact, all the studies of auditory localization that were discussed used head turns toward the source of the sound as the primary measure of localization. Head turning would not be a useful measure if infants did not look toward the sources of sounds, presumably in an effort to supplement their auditory perceptions with visual information.

Many additional findings about how infants use information from different senses to attend, identify, and locate have also been obtained.

Attending

Newborns seem to possess rules for looking in the presence of sounds, much like the ones described earlier that they follow when looking in the absence of sounds. Mendelson and Haith (1976) showed newborn infants lines in an otherwise blank field, and presented sounds when the infants looked at particular parts of the display. One rule that the infants' looking followed was directly implied in the above paragraphs: When you hear a sound, and you are looking somewhere else, look toward the source of the sound. Another rule concerned what to do when you already are looking at the apparent source of a sound. Under this condition, you should center attention closely on that source and shorten the length of your eye movements. The rules seem likely to promote attention to animate objects, such as people and other animals, since most animals make noise. Consistent with this view, Haith, Bergman, and Moore (1977) reported that introduction of a voice intensified 5- to 7-week-olds' scanning of a face, particularly their scanning of the eyes.

Identifying

Spelke's experiment demonstrated use of both auditory and visual information in identifying the events in the movie. Slightly older infants also integrate visual with tactile (touch) information to identify objects. Ruff and Kohler (1978) presented blindfolded 6-month-olds with either a ball or a cube to explore with their hands. When later presented both objects, the infants spent more time looking at the object that they had earlier handled. Apparently, the information infants obtained manually influenced the information they later sought visually.

Locating

To obtain objects for their use, infants must locate the objects in space. Von Hofsten (1982) reported a number of intriguing experiments demonstrating that newborns use visual information about locations to guide their reaching. He presented them with an appealing object that slowly moved back and forth in front of them. The infants moved their hands toward the objects in all three dimensions. On their best-aimed movements, their hands slowed down as they approached the objects, just as older children's and adults' would. This coordination could not be a learned response, since the newborns would have had no experience with grasping and actively manipulating objects.

A surprising finding of von Hofsten's research is that infants reach skillfully for moving objects as soon as they are able to reach accurately for stationary ones. Von Hofsten found that infants just becoming able to reach accurately for stationary objects also anticipated the paths of moving objects. That is, they reached toward where the object would be by the time their hand intersected its path, rather than reaching toward its position at the moment when they started reaching. The degree of coordination between vision and reaching improves slowly over a prolonged period of infancy and childhood, but the basic coordination seems to be present from early infancy.

Sonar aids for blind children.   Earlier we discussed how research on visual acuity had proved useful for diagnosing infants suspected of having defective vision. The recent development of sonar aids for blind children indicates that knowledge of perceptual development may be useful for devising innovative treatments as well as diagnostic procedures. These sonar aids can be viewed as a kind of intersensory compensation, since they allow blind children to use their hearing to locate obstacles in their paths and thus allow them to move around freely in their environments.

A scientist from New Zealand, Leslie Kay, invented the sonar aid in the early 1960s. The device provides people with the same types of information used by dolphins and bats to locate objects in their environments. It sends out and receives back ultrasonic waves, and then transduces the reflected waves to frequencies that people can hear through earphones. The earphones are lightweight and comfortable. Figure 5–9 shows a child wearing a sonar aid. (See Humphrey & Humphrey, in press, for a more extensive description of the machine's physical characteristics, as well as its usefulness for blind children).

The sonar aid works by providing information about the distances, directions, and textures of objects. The frequency of the signal indicates the distance of the object. The closer the blind child approaches to an object, the lower the tone that is reflected. The child can adjust the absolute frequencies depending on the type of distances of interest in a particular situation. If a girl wanted information about objects that were close by, as she might if playing indoors, the range could be set so that objects six feet away would make the highest sounds and closer objects proportionally lower sounds. If the girl were going to play with friends outside, she might set the sonar aid so that objects twenty feet away made the highest sounds.

The direction of objects is reflected in information much like that which people use to auditorially determine the location of objects. That is, an object on the right side produces a louder signal to the right ear than to the left. The degree of the discrepancy indicates just how far from the forward position the object is. The child's head turns are also useful in determining the direction of the object. By turning her head until the loudness of the right and left ear signals are equal, the child could determine the object's direction.

Information about an object's texture is provided by the purity of the

FIGURE 5–9   A blind child wearing a sonic guide reaches for an object (photo provided courtesy of Dr. G. Keith Humphrey).

tone. The waves reflected from smooth surfaces such as glass and metal approach pure tones.Rougher surfaces, such as bushes and trees, reflect more complex tones. In addition, a rough surface will give rise to characteristic patterns that can help in identifying what object is present.

If sonar aids can provide useful information to blind people, what would be the optimal age for children to begin to wear them? Alternative theories of perceptual development suggest different answers. Researchers who, like the Gibsons, emphasize the perceptual capabilities that are present from early in infancy might be expected to advocate early use of the aids, because they can build on early-existing capabilities. Some researchers in this tradition, in particular Bower (1979), have suggested that it is crucial to begin use of the sonar aids early in infancy, because blind infants otherwise may lose the ability to use them effectively. Constructivists such as Hebb might also advocate early use of the sonar aids, on the logic that learning can occur from early in infancy and the more opportunities for learning, the better. On the other hand, Piaget might argue that children do not possess a clear figurative notion of space until age 3 or 4 years, and therefore might only become confused by the sonar aid's information before then.

To evaluate the optimal age for providing blind children with the aids, some information about the typical development of blind individuals is essential. Much of the developmental course is like that of sighted children, including the ages at which children raise their heads and chests, sit, roll over, and stand. Walking, however, is considerably slower to develop in blind children. Fraiberg (1977) suggested that the sight of attractive objects provides a "lure" for walking, and that the absence of this lure among blind children was responsible for the delay. She also suggested that until blind children reach for objects that they hear making sounds, they do not learn to walk; and that the desire to make contact with objects that make sounds is a crucial motivator of walking in blind children. By this logic, the sonar aid's assignments of sounds to ordinarily silent objects might motivate blind children to begin walking earlier. Ability to walk earlier could, in turn, aid blind children in learning about their environments. The argument suggests that the sonar aid might best be introduced at the time when children begin walking or shortly before, that is, at 9 to 15 months.

Aitken and Bower (1982) examined four blind children in an effort to determine the optimal age for starting them with the sonar aid. The children began to wear the aid at 6, 8, 13, and 14 months. The youngest infant developed at an unusually rapid rate for a blind person. She began reaching for objects with both hands at 7 months and began walking independently at 16 months. The infant who started using the device at age 8 months also developed fairly rapidly. At 8 months he began reaching for objects with both hands, at 15 months used the aid to avoid objects when he was walking in a walker, and at age 20 months walked independently. The two older infants, however, did not learn to use the aid effectively.

Humphrey and Humphrey (in press) found that older children also can learn to use the sonar aid effectively. The two children they studied began using the device at 19 and 31 months respectively. The 31-month-old, Eddy, has made especially impressive progress with the aid. When the aid was on, Eddy's exploration of a new environment was described as "smilingly confident." He both avoided obstacles and skillfully sought objects to climb on. When the aid was removed, Eddy's steps became "slower, smaller, and more hesitant." He became unwilling to explore further following repeated collisions with chairs and tables. The skill in using the device has extended to outdoor activities. Eddy has been seen running down his driveway, turning onto the sidewalk, moving onto the street just before the sidewalk ends and a grassy area begins, and avoiding poles, trees, and walls in his path.

Lee, the younger child, also has made progress in using the sonar aid, but his progress has not been as rapid as Eddy's. In particular, he has learned to reach for and grasp objects, but has not yet learned how to walk. Children who start using the device at yet older ages also show substantial benefits. Strelow, Kay, and Kay (1978) reported that introducing it to a 6½-year-old girl allowed her to walk independently for the first time.

It thus seems clear that both infants and older children can benefit from the sonar aid. It allows them to reach for objects more accurately, to walk at earlier ages than they might otherwise, to anticipate objects in their path, and generally to explore their environments. Children introduced to the aid early in infancy may learn to use it more quickly, but there is no critical period beyond which the aid is not helpful. Indeed, given the greater complexity of the tasks that older children can accomplish using the sonar device, it seems equally plausible that they learn most rapidly from it.

Perhaps the most eloquent testimony for the value of the sonar aid comes from an individual introduced to the device as an adult.

> In the first few months the Sonicguide functions primarily as an obstacle detector. Slowly but surely one starts putting things together and over a period of time begins using it as an environmental sensor. I can't tell you enough how gratifying it is to be able to recognize the sound of a tree, a person, a picket fence, etc. With the glasses there is information which may help in not only mobility, but in providing a sense of what's "going on in the world around me."
>
> After using the Sonicguide 5–10 hours a week for the past three years, I am at the point that I react very naturally to its signals. I no longer have to think about what each signal could mean, rather I react instinctively. I go around someone on the sidewalk without even realizing I've done it: that's how much a part of you it becomes. (Lepofsky, 1980)

A chronological summary. We have considered infants' perceptual development from the perspective of how each sensory system develops. Also considering what perceptual capacities infants possess at different ages in the first year may help in forming a larger picture of development in this period. Table 5–2 lists a number of the perceptual capabilities that we can be confi-

TABLE 5-2 Perceptual Abilities Infants Clearly Have at Different Ages

AGE	CAPABILITY		
	VISION	HEARING	INTERSENSORY INTEGRATION
Birth	Orienting reflex. Looking rules. Color vision.	Orienting reflex. Almost adultlike volume thresholds in medium-and high-frequency ranges. Prefer mother's voice.	Look toward source of sounds. Looking rules for responding to sounds. Visually guided reaching.
1 month	Scan external contours of object.	Hear speech sounds as qualitatively distinct.	
2 months	Scan interiors of objects. Good accommodation.	Categorical perception of musical sounds.	
3 months	Consistent bifoveal fixation on objects. Shape constancy.		
4 months	Prefer organized "biological" motion patterns. Binocular depth perception (stereopsis). Size constancy.		Integrates sights and sounds with similar rhythms.
5 months			Use time when sounds reach ears to infer where sounds come from. Turn in proper direction to find objects when landmarks are present. Integrate visual and tactile information.
6 months	Avoid visual cliffs.		
7 months	Several monocular depth cues are used: occlusion, texture, etc. Use memory to infer distance.		Blind infants can benefit from sonar aids.

173

dent infants have developed by the ages listed. The estimates are deliberately conservative; infants may well possess some of these abilities earlier than is apparent in the table. Indeed, only a few days before writing this paragraph, I had to lower the age of attainment of color vision from 4 months to the first month of life, because I became aware of the Adams and Maurer (1984) study.

This table reveals an interesting pattern: Hearing seems to develop considerably more rapidly than vision or intersensory integration. All the basic developments in hearing that are listed are achieved by age 3 months. This is not the whole story, of course. Infants' hearing is still improving quantitatively. For example, they are becoming able to hear softer sounds, especially in the lower frequencies. They also will later lose the ability to perceive some speech contrasts, as their hearing becomes increasingly attuned to their own language. And it also is possible that further research on infants' hearing will reveal some auditory abilities they do not possess at all until after they are 3 months old, or that further research will reveal that all the visual and intersensory capabilities also develop by equally young ages. For the present, though, it is striking just how advanced hearing is in early infancy. The level of development seems even more impressive when we realize that we are viewing it against the backdrop of all these other extraordinarily early-developing capabilities.

SUMMARY

Perceptual functioning reaches adultlike or near-adultlike levels remarkably rapidly. At birth infants have considerable ability to see, hear, and integrate information from different sensory systems. These abilities develop considerably further in the next 6 months. The abilities are evident in how infants attend to, identify, and locate objects and events.

Researchers have suggested four main explanations for where infants deploy their visual attention. One hypothesis is that they have an orienting reflex which leads them to attend to loud noises and bright lights and also to unfamiliar rather than familiar objects. Another is that their looking is guided by a set of rules, such as that they should focus their scanning on the area around an edge when they find one. A third is that they attend most to objects that are moderately discrepant from their existing knowledge. The fourth is that in the first few months, subcortical mechanisms dominate infants' visual attention, whereas beyond 4 or 5 months of age, cortical mechanisms play a larger role. All four processes may be part of how infants determine where to look and how their looking patterns change with age and experience.

A number of abilities related to visual identification of objects and events show marked growth in the first 6 months. Visual acuity improves from roughly 20/500 to 20/100. The improvement is especially marked at moderate spatial frequencies. Underlying the improved acuity may be increased density of cones in the retina and smaller receptive fields of neurons. Color vision seems adultlike from the first days of life. Infants see colors as qualitatively discrete entities and divide the wavelength spectrum at about the same points as adults. Both faces and biological motion have attributes that attract infants' attention, and infants can discriminate them from other types of objects and motions.

Locating objects demands being able to identify how far away and in what direction objects are. Infants use both monocular and binocular cues to locate the distance of objects from themselves. Among the most important monocular cues are accommodation, motion parallax, occlusion, texture, and visual expansion. Binocular depth cues fall into three hierarchically ordered categories. To use purely binocular cues to depth requires fusion of separate retinal images into a single percept, and such fusion requires fixation of both foveas on the same target. Stereopsis, the binocular perception of depth, seems to be present by about 4 months of age. In addition to infants being able to perceive the depth of objects from cues in the immediate display, they can also use their memories of the true size of objects to infer how far away the objects must be.

The levels of auditory perception shown by young infants are at least as impressive as their achievements in visual perception. Infants are especially attentive to speechlike sounds. This appears to be due to their being interested in the sounds, rather than to their being able to detect them more easily than other sounds. The frequency range typical of speech and the fact that speech consists of a range of frequencies rather than pure tones are two of the factors that attract infants' attention.

Infants' identification of both speech and musical tones is categorical, much like their color perception. The categorical perception is not due to the particular language infants hear; infants may set categorical boundaries at points different from those that appear in their native language. In addition to being able to discriminate between specific sounds, newborns also are able to identify more general speech characteristics. For example, they can discriminate their mothers' voices from those of other women. They also show a preference for motherese, a form of speech characterized by high-pitched sounds and exaggerated intonations.

Auditory localization shows a U-shaped function. At birth and after 4 months of age, localization is quite accurate. During the interim, the ability is less acute. The pattern, like infants' pattern of visual attention, may reflect a shift from subcortical to cortical dominance.

Intersensory integration might be expected to develop only after vision, hearing, and other senses had reached high levels of functioning. In fact, it seems to be present from the earliest days. Vision, audition, and reaching are used together to attend to, identify, and to locate objects and events.

Perceptual development research has yielded practically-important discoveries useful for diagnosing and treating infants. Research on visual acuity has led to techniques for diagnosing whether infants with suspected visual abnormalities can see well enough to avoid corrective surgery. On the treatment side, sonar aids show great potential for helping blind children navigate around their environments. These devices substitute sounds for the sights that blind people cannot experience. The sonar aids provide information about the distance of objects, their direction, and the type of object involved. Some researchers have hypothesized that the aids should be introduced during the first year, but they seem to be effective even when introduced considerably later.

RECOMMENDED READINGS

Aslin, R. N., & Dumais, S. T. (1980). Binocular vision in infants: A review and a theoretical framework. In H. W. Reese & L. P. Lipsitt (Eds.), *Advances in child development and behavior.* New York: Academic Press. Describes the development of binocular perception in such clear terms that even those unfamiliar with the area can understand the growth of this complex system.

Banks, M. S., & Salapatek, P. (1981). Infant pattern vision: A new approach based on the contrast sensitivity function. *Journal of Experimental Child Psychology, 31,* 1–45. An elegant and persuasive analysis of why infants look at some things more than others.

Bornstein, M. H. (1978). Chromatic vision in infancy. In H. W. Reese & L. P. Lipsitt (Eds.), *Advances in child development and behavior.* New York: Academic Press. A classic description of infants' surprising color vision abilities in the first few months of life.

Granrud, C. E., Haake, R. J., & Yonas, A. (in press). Infants' sensitivity to familiar size: The effect of memory on spatial perception. *Perception and Psychophysics.* Provocative demonstration of infants' ability to integrate knowledge about the sizes of objects to perceive how far away they are.

Haith, M. M. (1980). *Rules that babies look by.* Hillsdale, NJ: Erlbaum. Appealing description of how infants choose where to look, and how their visual scanning patterns change.

Humphrey, G. K. & Humphrey, D. E. (in press). The use of binaural sensory aids by blind infants and children: Theoretical and applied issues. In F. Morrison & C. Lord (Eds.), *Applied Developmental Psychology, Vol. 2.* New York: Academic Press. Heartening description of blind children's use of sonar aids to maneuver around their environments.

6
LANGUAGE DEVELOPMENT

The Egyptians, before the reign of Psammetichus, used to think that of all the races in the world they were the most ancient. Psammetichus, however, when he came to the throne, took it into his head to settle this question of priority, and ever since his time the Egyptians have believed that the Phrygians surpass them in antiquity and that they themselves come second. Psammetichus, finding that mere inquiry failed to reveal which was the original race of mankind, devised an ingenious method of determining the matter. He took at random, from an ordinary family, two newly born infants and gave them to a shepherd to be brought up among his flocks, under strict orders that no one should utter a word in their presence. All these arrangements were made by Psammetichus because he wished to find out what word the children would first utter, once they had grown out of their meaningless baby-talk. The plan succeeded; two years later the shepherd, who during that time had done everything he had been told to do, happened one day to open the door of the cottage and go in, when both children running up to him with hands outstretched, pronounced the word "becos." Psammetichus ordered the children to be brought to him, and when he himself heard them say "becos" he determined to find out to what language the word belonged. His inquiries revealed that it was the Phrygian word for "bread," and in consideration of this the Egyptians yielded their claims and admitted the superior antiquity of the Phrygians (Herodotus, about 450 B.C., cited in Bickerton, 1983, pp. 102–103).

Psammetichus's research is exemplary neither for the quality of its experimental design nor for its ethical sensitivity. However, it does illustrate the central role that language development has long occupied in ideas about human nature. People often distinguish themselves from other animals on the grounds that they alone use language. Some investigators also view language as special in another sense: that it is fundamentally different from other mental abilities. Most children need prolonged instruction in order to read and write, yet almost all children speak skillfully by the time they are 3 or 4 years old. Cognitive development shows a surprising face when we realize that perhaps the most profound ability anyone acquires is one that everyone acquires to a high degree of skill by the time they are 3 or 4.

Using language presents many of the same challenges that accompany other cognitive tasks. Children are born with limited information-processing capacities. Language constitutes a task environment that severely taxes these capacities. The demands are present on several levels simultaneously. Speaking effectively requires enunciating clearly, ordering words within sentences grammatically, and organizing sentences in ways that communicate coherent thoughts.

In response to these demands, children engage in a variety of cognitive activities that enable them to communicate. Their well-developed auditory perception system, described in the last chapter, allows them to hear clearly what other people say. This accurate perception helps them learn to pronounce words correctly. They pay attention to and remember the order of words that they hear in particular phrases, while also searching for generally applicable grammatical rules.

Above all, they attend to meanings, both the meanings other people are trying to get across and the meanings they wish to convey. Emphasizing meanings is an intelligent approach to language acquisition. After all, language is a tool for adapting to the social world. Sentences that express intended meanings will further that adaptation, even given serious shortcomings in pronunciation and grammar. Sentences that do not express intended meanings will not be adaptive, even if grammar and pronunciation are perfect.

The fundamental issue raised by this analysis, the issue that is at the very heart of this chapter, is how children learn language so rapidly. Perhaps children are born with a special ability to learn language above and beyond their more general learning abilities. Alternatively, given children's massive exposure to language, maybe they could learn almost any skill by age 3 or 4 if they were given comparably intense experience.

The question boils down to which *mechanisms* enable children to learn language. Are the mechanisms specifically designed for language learning (e.g., a specific *language acquisition device*) or are they the same mechanisms that lead to other types of learning (e.g., a general ability to induce rules)? My personal suspicion is that widely applicable learning mechanisms produce most forms of language learning. Quite a few of the investigators whose work is reviewed in the chapter take the opposite position, though. They are convinced that language learning is so unlike the other cognitive achievements of very young children that it must be produced by special mechanisms.

The issue of language-specific versus general learning mechanisms is not a new one. It was at the heart of a famous argument between two giants of modern intellectual life: B. F. Skinner and Noam Chomsky. Chomsky's (1959) review of Skinner's (1957) book *Verbal Behavior* sparked the debate. The core of the argument concerned how children learn grammar. Skinner argued that children learn grammar in the same way they learn everything else: through modeling and reinforcement. In his view, they start the learning process by imitating sentences of adults and older children. If their statements are comprehensible, parents do what the child wants, thus reinforcing the statements. If they are inaccurate or incomprehensible, the parent does not do what the child wants, thus not reinforcing them. Skinner also presumed that parents play a large role in their children's language development. The parents would shape their children's language by translating understandable but ungrammatical statements into correct grammatical form.

Chomsky strongly contested this view. He based his case on the indisputable fact that even 3-year-olds create thousands of statements that they never have heard anyone else say. Illustratively, I recently heard a 3-year-old boy say, "What is that truck doing, washing the street for?" Neither adults nor other children would have been likely to produce this exact statement in the child's presence, due to the rarity of the event and the awkwardness of the grammatical form. Thus, the boy almost certainly did not learn the statement through simple imitation. Nor would he have been likely to learn it through reinforcement. If he had never produced the sentence before, he could not have been reinforced for it. However, the comprehensibility of the sentence, and the fact that children produce many sentences similar to it, suggest that it is not simply a random mistake. Rather it seems to reflect a grammar the child has constructed that differs from adult grammars.

Rather than learning specific responses, Chomsky argued, children learn grammatical rules. Data on children's learning of past tense forms strikingly supported this position. Many of the most common verbs have irregular past tense forms: *came, went, put, broke,* and *hit,* to name a few. Once children learn the standard rule for producing past tense forms (verb + *ed*), however, they try to apply the rule to these irregular verbs as well as to the regular ones. They wind up producing such terms as *goed, eated,* and *thinked* (Brown, 1973), as well as such double past tense forms as *wented, ated,* and *thoughted* (Kuczaj, 1981). These errors indicate that language is at least partially rule governed, rather than being a simple collection of reinforced responses.

Further, reinforcement and rote imitation of sentences do not appear to be necessary for children to learn to speak grammatically. Although some children repeat many sentences that they hear verbatim, other children seem never to do so; both groups of children learn to speak grammatically (Marat-sos, 1983). Further, parents reward accurate rather than grammatically correct sentences. A true but ungrammatical statement will generally be accepted; a false statement phrased in a grammatically impeccable form will often be corrected (Brown, 1973).

These and related observations of what children actually say and parents actually do, together with Chomsky's theoretical criticisms, provided a devastating counterargument to Skinner's view that language development is produced totally by imitation and reinforcement. If we focus entirely on this issue, we would conclude that Chomsky unequivocally won the debate. At least two other issues that underlay the disagreement between the theorists remain controversial, however.

One is the issue of language-specific versus general learning mechanisms that was raised earlier. The fact that reinforcement and imitation alone cannot account for language learning does not mean that children must possess a special language-acquisition device. Children learn complex rules for forming concepts, solving problems, playing games, and engaging in diverse activities other than speaking grammatically. Recall the discussion of children's rules for solving balance-scale problems (Chapter 3) and infants' rules for looking for and finding the informative parts of the environment (Chapter 5). Thus, children's acquisiton of language rules can be viewed as simply one manifestation of a basic human rule-learning ability, no different from any of the others except for the massive amount of opportunities the world affords for practice and learning through observing.

A counterargument to this position is that languages logically could use such a vast variety of grammars that if children had no biologically given "hunches" about the forms of grammar that might be used, they would never become grammatically competent. From this point of view, language learning involves a vast collection of potential dead ends; trying to induce the rules without any prior ideas about them seems like the proverbial search for the needle in a haystack. The counter-counterargument is that quite general biases about which rules are most likely (e.g., try all simple rules first to see if one of them works), of the type that help children form rules in other areas, may also be sufficient for language development. And so the argument continues.

A second issue raised by the debate involves whether the structural or the functional aspects of language are most worthy of investigation. Skinner emphasized that the central function of language was communication. He was less interested in the rules underlying pronunciation and ordering of words within sentences than in the ways people communicated meanings. Researchers interested in communication have emphasized how infants elicit speech from caretakers, how beginning speakers choose their one-word utterances to be maximally meaningful, and how children adjust their language so that it can be comprehended by someone who is ignorant about a topic.

Others, like Chomsky, have been more interested in how children learn grammar and other formal characteristics of languages. From this perspective, grammar is an important part of language, even though it is not strictly necessary for communication; parents seem to understand ungrammatical statements such as "Why you want go home?" as well as equivalent sentences stated grammatically. Grammar is also of interest because children seem to be intrinsically interested in it (they willingly learn to speak grammatically despite not being reinforced for doing so). In sum, many of the issues raised in the Skinner/Chomsky debate have endured well beyond the debate itself.

The discussion of language development in this chapter is organized into two main sections. The first of these describes the typical course of language development. Here we consider children's production of sounds before they know any words, their first words, and how they combine words into larger units. In the second main section, we focus on more theoretical issues. The initial focus is on what language is, which aspects of language are unique to human beings, and how languages might be invented. Next we examine the relation of language to thought, and especially the light shed on this issue by deaf children's learning of sign language. Finally, we consider mechanisms that may be involved in language development. The topics are outlined in Table 6–1.

THE COURSE OF LANGUAGE DEVELOPMENT

Language can be divided into four parts: *phonology, grammar, meaning, and communication.* Phonology concerns the ways in which people produce meaningful sounds, such as pronouncing words correctly. Grammar involves the ways in which they order words and denote tense and number within sentences. Meaning involves correspondences between particular words and phrases on the one hand and particular objects, properties, and events on the other. The fourth part, communication, involves the way the rest of language is used to convey messages that may not be present in the literal meaning of words (for example, if I ask, "Do you know what time it is?" I am not looking for a "yes" or "no" answer, even though that is what would be called for according to the literal meaning of the sentence).

These four parts of language first assume prominent roles at different points in development. By most standards, phonology is the first to become important. Before babies can speak intelligibly, they need to control their sound-making capabilities sufficiently well to say what they want to say. Issues of word meaning become prominent soon after. As soon as children can pronounce words, the issue arises of which ones they use first, and what

TABLE 6-1   Chapter Outline

they mean by them. Roughly a half year after children begin saying single words, they begin to string together phrases of two or more words, and grammar becomes an issue. Do children order their words in a consistent way, and if so, what conceptual framework do they use to order them? Finally, linguistic communication is complexly interconnected with all the other aspects of language and could reasonably be placed at any point in the ordering. The aspects of communication that are of greatest interest in the present context, however, develop after the earliest grammatical competence. Therefore, the focus of the discussion will move from pronunciation to word meaning to grammar to communication.

The Earliest Sounds

As noted in the last chapter, infants have impressive ability to discriminate among a wide variety of sounds. They also are able to produce all the sounds that appear in any known language. However, an important limit on their early language-making capacity is their difficulty in producing a specific sound when they want to say it. Development comes in increasing ability to produce sounds at will and increasing ability to combine them with other sounds to produce words.

When people are not talking, air passes freely through the windpipe, nose, and mouth. We speak by impeding the airflow in various ways. The two fundamental classes of impediments correspond to the two fundamental classes of speech sounds: vowels and consonants. With vowels, the only impediment to the airflow comes in the vocal cords. There is no further blocking by the tongue, teeth, or lips. Consonants, on the other hand, include impediments by the tongue, teeth, and lips as well as the vocal cords. The difference can be seen in pronouncing a vowel such as *a* or *i* and then pronouncing a *b* or *p* sound. In the former case, we do not use our lips; in the latter case, we do. This distinction between vowels and consonants exists in all languages.

Different vowels are distinguished primarily by the placement of the tongue. Tongue placement differs along both vertical and horizontal dimensions. As shown in Table 6–2, the vowel sound in *meet* is produced with the tongue relatively far forward in the mouth and with its tip near the irregular surface just above the top teeth, the *alveolar ridge*. In making the vowel sound in *mat*, however, the tongue is much lower. (Because people have little conscious awareness of the tongue's location within the mouth, it will be helpful to use your fingers to determine your tongue's location when making these sounds).

The main distinction among consonants is whether the flow of air is entirely halted by the placement of the tongue (*stops*) or whether the flow of air is largely but not entirely impeded (*fricatives*). The typical *t* sound is an example of a stop; the typical *s* sound is a fricative. Another major distinction among consonants is whether they are *voiced*. Voiced sounds are those where a strong vibration is evident when you place your finger on your Adam's apple. The voicing feature can be seen by contrasting pairs of sounds that are identical except for being voiced or unvoiced. For example, the *zh* sound (as in *leisure*) is voiced but the *sh* sound is not. Whether a sound is voiced or unvoiced, whether it is a stop or a fricative, and a handful of other features determine the exact sound that is made.

How does the ability to make these sounds develop? Kaplan and Kaplan (1971) suggested that development involves four stages:

1. *Crying.* Infants' first sounds are cries. Many parents believe they can infer the meaning of these cries sheerly on the basis of their sounds. It turns out, however, that parents cannot tell why their infants are crying (hunger, boredom, rashes) from hearing tape recordings of the cries (Muller, Hollien, and Murray, 1974). The finding suggests that parents infer from the context why their infants are crying, rather than relying solely on the sounds the infants make.

2. *Cooing.* By the end of the first month, infants make sounds other than crying. In particular, they make cooing sounds by placing their tongues near the backs of their mouths and rounding their lips. These coos are much like the *uh* sound that older individuals make in pronouncing the word *fun*.

3. *Babbling.* By 6 months of age, infants produce a wider variety of sounds. These include consonants as well as vowels. For the first time, infants also combine vowels and consonants, and thus produce their first syllables. The intonations of the babbling increasingly resemble those of speech.

TABLE 6–2   Location in Mouth Where Tongue is Placed for English Vowel Pronunciations

	FRONT OF MOUTH	MIDDLE OF MOUTH	BACK OF MOUTH
High in Mouth	meet		cooed
	mitt		could
Middle of Mouth	mate	glasses	code
	met		cawed
Low in Mouth	mat	mutt	cod

4. *Patterned speech.* Near the end of the first year, the variety of sounds that infants make *decreases*. Infants more frequently make sounds that occur in their language and less and less frequently make sounds that do not.

This stage sequence helps to explain an otherwise surprising phenomenon. Even in languages that have nothing else in common, infants' first words are similar. These initial words resemble the syllables that infants most often babble spontaneously. They start with consonants, end with vowels, and often involve repetition of the same sounds. Thus, it is no accident that throughout the world, words such as *dada*, *mama*, and *papa* are names for parents and are among the first words that children learn (Table 6–3).

In Table 6–3, the consonants *m* and *n* are associated with the meaning *mother*, but not *father*. This pattern is no fluke; across 1,072 terms for mother and father drawn from the world's languages, 55% of the terms for mother included nasal sounds such as *m* and *n*, but only 15% of the terms for father did (Jakobson, 1971). Jakobson proposed an intriguing explanation for the difference. The only phonemes that can be produced when the lips are pressed to the breast and the mouth is full are the nasal sounds, such as *m* and *n*. Later, infants may reproduce these sounds at the mere sight of food, to express a desire to eat, or to ask for any ungranted wish. Thus, terms including *m* and *n* would be especially convenient ways of naming the person who most often provides food and fulfills desires, the baby's mother. More generally, the use of these easy-to-make sounds to indicate these important meanings is a particularly nice example of cultures adapting to children's natures in a way gratifying to parent and child alike.

The Earliest Words

The similarity between children's babbling and the first words they learn makes it difficult to identify just when babies start to use words. Parents often discern words interspersed in their children's babbling months

TABLE 6-3   Early Words for Mother and Father in Ten Languages

	MOTHER	FATHER
English	mama	dada
German	mama	papa
Hebrew	eema	aba
Hungarian	anya	apa
Navajo	ama	ataa
Northern Chinese	mama	baba
Russian	mama	papa
Spanish	mama	papa
Southern Chinese	umma	baba
Taiwanese	amma	aba

before even sympathetic friends and relatives believe that the syllables really are words. Most dispassionate observers place the typical age of children's first words between 10 and 13 months, though deviations in both directions are common.

By the age of 18 months, most children can say between 3 and 100 words. These words seem to many observers to have a characteristically childlike flavor. One-year-olds use words such as *ball*, *doggie*, and the special favorite *more* but almost never words such as *chair* or *animal*. Specifying the distinction between the types of meanings children express in this early period and the ones they do not has proved difficult, though.

When children begin to talk, they speak in single words. Presumably they do this because correctly combining the sounds needed to form a word demands all their limited cognitive resources. Toddlers' frequent long pauses between the syllables of a single word contrast sharply with older children's fluent expression of whole sentences; clearly the process of automatization of this skill (Chapter 3, p. 70) has just begun. The children effectively compensate for this limited capacity, however, by choosing single words that convey larger meanings. These single words are often called *holophrases* because they express the meaning of a whole phrase. When 1-year-olds say *ball*, the word seems to imply an entire thought, such as "Give me the ball," "That is a ball," or "You took the ball away" (Elliot, 1981). Parents and older children can interpret these single-word statements through the toddlers' intonations and the physical and social context.

Toddlers' choices of single words suggest that they have considerable insight into the meanings adults might read into their statements. Greenfield and Smith (1976) found that in naturally arising situations, children in the one-word stage who want a banana say *banana* rather than *want*. Because of the many things the child could want, and the relatively few aspects of bananas about which the child could be commenting, *banana* is the more informative term. However, when offered a banana they did not want, children say *no* rather than *banana*, presumably because saying *banana* would be misinterpreted. The early word choices are an appealing example of the kind of intelligent strategy construction emphasized in Sternberg's (1985) theory (Chapter 3, pp. 75–80).

Children throughout the world express similar meanings in their earliest words. They talk about people: "dada," "papa," "mama." They talk about vehicles: "car," "truck," "train." They also talk about food, clothing, and household implements, such as keys and clocks. Interestingly, as Clark (1983) noted, children in the earliest language development studies, more than 50 years ago, talked about the same topics as modern children.

The fact that young children use a word does not guarantee that they mean the same thing by it that older individuals do. Deviations from standard meanings are most frequent from the time children begin speaking to approximately age 2½. As children's vocabularies increase, the percentage of deviations decreases. This decrease is particularly evident in *overextensions*, terms that include not only the standard meaning but others as well ("dog-gie" is used to refer to cats as well as dogs). Rescorla (1976) reported that the percentage of overextensions decreased from 45% of all words toddlers used when their vocabularies included between one and 25 words, to 35% when their vocabularies numbered between 26 and 50 words, to 20% when they included between 51 and 75 words.

Why might beginning language learners make overextension errors? Clark (1973) suggested one appealing explanation: the *semantic feature hypothesis*. This hypothesis can be illustrated in the context of how children learn the names of animals. At first they might use a rule that depended on only one feature, such as, "If it has four legs, call it a doggie." This rule would lead to overextensions; cats as well as dogs would qualify as doggies. Later, children would add features to their naming rules that would eliminate the overextensions. For example, they might form the rule, "If it has four legs *and it barks*, then call it a doggie." Thus, overextension errors reflect a point in development at which too few features are attached to words.

This account raises a further question: Why would beginning language learners define words in terms of too few features? Proponents of the semantic feature hypothesis suggested a reasonable explanation. If children must err in their word meanings, they are better off erring by having too few rather than too many features attached to words. Initially defining words in terms of a single feature does produce overgeneralizations, but it also helps children convey meanings. Beginning language users cannot possibly know words for everything that they would like to name. If a child sees a cat and says "doggie," other people will usually figure out what the child means. On the other hand, consider what would happen if a child would use a term on-ly if it matched all features of the object or objects to which it had previously been applied. If the first dog the child saw looked like Lassie, the child might develop the definition "If an object has four legs, moves, barks, has long hair, has a long nose, and likes children, then call it doggie." This definition would eliminate overextensions, but would lead to underextensions. For ex-ample, Rin-Tin-Tin would not qualify as a doggie because his hair was short. Children who applied such conservative definitions would be able to talk about very few objects, which would seriously limit their ability to con-vey meanings. Thus, given the difficulty children face in learning word meanings, overgeneralizations seem a relatively small price to pay for limited knowledge.

The semantic feature hypothesis makes understandable some impor-tant characteristics of children's early use of language, but it also is somewhat misleading. Differences between children's comprehension and production of language are revealing here. The same child who refers to several different types of animals as "doggies" will consistently choose the toy dog if asked to choose the doggie from among several different toy

TABLE 6-4 Words Most Commonly Appearing in the First 50 Words Children Learn (After Nelson, 1973)

CATEGORY AND WORD[a]	FREQUENCY[b]	CATEGORY AND WORD[a]	FREQUENCY[b]
FOOD AND DRINK:		VEHICLES:	
Juice	12	Car	13
Milk	10	Boat	6
Cookie	10	Truck	6
Water	8		
Toast	7	FURNITURE AND HOUSEHOLD ITEMS:	
Apple	5	Clock	7
Cake	5	Light	6
Banana	3	Blanket	4
Drink	3	Chair	3
		Door	3
ANIMALS:			
Dog (variants)	16	PERSONAL ITEMS:	
Cat (variants)	14	Key	6
Duck	8	Book	5
Horse	5	Watch	3
Bear	4		
Bird	4	EATING AND DRINKING UTENSILS:	
Cow (variants)	4	Bottle	8
		Cup	4
CLOTHES:			
Shoes	11	OUTDOOR OBJECTS:	
Hat	7	Snow	4
Socks	4		
		PLACES:	
TOYS AND PLAY EQUIPMENT:		Pool	3
Ball	13		
Blocks	7		
Doll	4		

[a] Adult form of word used. Many words had several variant forms, in particular the animal words.
[b] Number of children (of 18) who used the word in the 50-word acquisition sequence.

animals (Clark, 1983). If asked to choose the cat from among the toy animals, many children who have referred to cats as "doggies" comprehend what is meant and choose the right animal (Clark, 1983). Thus, some, perhaps many, of the children's overextensions may be due to their having difficulty recalling the correct term rather than to their not knowing any features that distinguish the different objects. Again, from the standpoint of communication, the children are acting sensibly; if they refer to cats as "doggies," most people will know what they mean.

Although children's first words have a characteristic flavor, it is difficult to characterize just what types of words they are. One approach is that children's earliest words are terms with important *functions*. Researchers who believe this also tend to believe that children's emphasis on functions comes out in another way; the meanings they associate with their earliest words overemphasize the importance of functions at the expense of other aspects of meaning, such as shape and size.

Nelson (1973) has been the strongest advocate of the view that children first use words that describe important functions. She examined the first 50 words acquired by eighteen children (Table 6–4). Consider her findings about children's allusions to furniture. They often referred to clocks, blankets, and keys, but rarely to stoves, tables, and chairs. Nelson characterized the difference as being that the objects children named either moved by themselves or could be moved by the children. Thus, she argued, children named these objects because of their function, what they could do or what they allowed children to do. (Note, though, that this is not the only possible interpretation of Nelson's data. It might equally well have been argued that stoves, which children rarely mentioned, have important functions for children and that clocks, which children frequently mentioned, do not).

Other investigators have argued that children's earliest words are those with perceptually salient appearances, and that children overemphasize perceptual appearance in their assignment of meaning to words. Clark (1973), the best-known advocate of this position, based her argument largely on children's overextension errors. Children throughout the world call round things, such as walnuts, stones, and oranges, *balls*. These objects share no function with balls, but do share a similar appearance. Many children also label pet cats, lions, and leopards as *kitty-cats*, despite the different functions of these animals. Even Nelson's data on the importance of motion could be reinterpreted as supporting Clark's position, since movement is a perceptually salient quality.

Clearly, the two positions are not incompatible. Both appearance and function could influence early word meanings. Indeed, Bowerman (1980) provided convincing data that this is exactly what happens. Bowerman carefully observed her daughters, Eve and Christie, over a period of several years. She recorded not only what they said but the context within which they said it. Both children overextended many of their early words. Typically, their overextensions were consistent with the particular instance from which they first learned the term. Eve and Christie's overextensions emphasized a variety of notable aspects of the objects and actions they named, though perceptual appearance and function (in that order) were the most common.

Two examples from Bowerman's children are shown in Table 6–5. The first example is especially instructive. Eve learned the term *kick* in the context of kicking a ball. She later overextended the term in ways that resembled this original use, even though many of the events she referred to are not ordinarily labeled *kicks* in English. *Kick* was used to refer to sudden sharp contact between a part of the body and an object, to an object being propelled, and to the waving of a limb. Each of these was part of the context in which Eve first learned *kick*. Bowerman concluded that a critical task for children learning language is to determine which particular features of an object or event referred to by a particular word are relevant to the word's meaning.

This argument seems to me quite convincing. When children hear an unfamiliar word, they cannot be sure which aspect of the situation it labels. Some words refer mostly to functions (e.g., *helps*), others to surface attributes (e.g., *red*), others to actions (e.g., *hits*). Interesting appearances and important functions both increase the likelihood of children being sufficiently interested in something to learn its name early on. Thus, both will characterize many of the first words children learn and will be prominent in the meanings they assign to those words.

The Two-Word Phase and the Beginning of Grammar

When children are about 1½ years old, they begin to speak in two-word phrases. This is the true beginning of grammar, because it represents the first occasion where words need to be ordered. From the earliest two-word phrases, children appear to use rules to order the words in their statements. But what type of rules do they invent?

Analysis of the language children hear suggests two main types of rules they might induce: those based on formal grammatical considerations and those based on meaning. Within a grammatical analysis, most English sentences follow the order subject-verb-object. For example, in the sentence "John hit the ball," *John* is the subject, *hit* is the verb, and *the ball* is the object. In terms of its grammatical structure, the sentence "The ball was hit by John" follows the same subject-verb-object order. Here, *ball* is the subject and *John* is the object. Thus, children could form a rule for two-word phrases such as, "Either say the subject first and the verb second, or say the verb first and the object second."

The language children hear also presents a second type of regularity: regularity in the order in which meanings are expressed. In most cases, the

TABLE 6-5   Some Early Words and Their Referents (from Bowerman, 1982, p. 284)

1. Eva, kick.

   Prototype: kicking a ball with the foot so that it is propelled forward.

   Features: (a) waving limb; (b) sudden sharp contact (especially between body parts and other object); (c) an object propelled.

   Selected samples. Eighteenth month: (first use) as kicks a floor fan (Features a, b); looking at picture of kitten with ball near its paw (all features, in anticipated event?); watching moth fluttering on a table (a), watching row of cartoon turtles on television doing can-can (a). Nineteenth mo.: just before throwing something (a, c); "kick bottle," after pushing bottle with her feet, making it roll (all features). Twenty-first mo.: as makes ball roll by bumping it with front wheel of kiddicar (b, c) pushing teddy bear's stomach against Christy's chest (b), pushing her stomach against a mirror (b); pushing her chest against a sink (b), etc.

2. Christy, night night.

   Prototype: person (or doll) lying down on bed or crib.

   Features: (a) crib, bed; (b) blanket; (c) nonnormative horizontal position of object (animate or inanimate).

   Selected examples. Sixteenth month: (first use) pushing a doll over in her crib; from this time on, frequent for putting dolls to bed, covering and kissing them (Features a, b, c). Seventeenth mo.: laying her bottle on its side (c). Eighteenth mo.: watching Christmas tree being pulled away on its side (c); after puts piano stool legs in box, one lying horizontally (c); after putting a piece of cucumber flat in her dish and pushing it into a corner (c). Nineteenth mo.: as M flattens out cartons, laying them in pile on floor (c); often while looking at pictures of empty beds or cribs or wanting a toy bed given to her (a, sometimes b); laying kiddicar on its side (c). Twentieth mo.: "awant night night," (request for M to hand her blanket); she then drapes it over shoulders as rides on toy horse (b), etc.

---

person who does something (the agent) is mentioned first in a sentence, the behavior he engages in (the action) is mentioned second, and the recipient of the action (the patient) is third. Children in the two-word phase thus might form a rule, "Either name the actor who did something first, and the action second, or name the action first and the patient second." This approach would have the advantage of treating sentences that meant the same thing in the same way. Both "John hit the ball" and "The ball was hit by John" would be described either by "John hit" or "hit ball." The grammatical analysis, in contrast, would summarize the first sentence as "John hit" or "hit ball," but would summarize "The ball was hit by John" as "ball hit" or "hit John."

Some investigators have explained children's two-word phrases in grammatical terms, while others have emphasized meaning. Braine (1963) proposed the best-known grammatical account, the *pivot–open approach.* He suggested that beginning language users do not use grammatical classes as abstract as subject, verb, and object, but that they substitute a different type of grammatical category system based on the positions of words within sentences. Within this system, young children always use certain frequent words in the first position, always use other frequent words in the second position, and place less-frequent words in either position. The fixed-position terms would not be combined with each other, but rather only with the words that could be in either position. Braine labeled the fixed position words as *pivots* and the variable-position words as *open*. To illustrate why Braine proposed this pivot-open view, consider some of the statements made by Andrew, a young child Braine observed:

> more cereal, more cookie, more high, more hot, more sing;
> no bed, no name, no plug, no down, no home;
> boot off, shirt off, water off, light off.

It is not difficult to imagine from these observations why Braine hypothesized the pivot-open system. "More," "no," and "off" are either always first in the phrase or always second. Less-frequent words are placed in the remaining position.

Nonetheless, two serious challenges soon arose. First, many children did combine pivots with each other, contrary to the predictions of the model. Kendall, a child studied by Bowerman (1973), produced the following statements: "Kendall sit, Kendall read, Mommy read, Mommy walk, Daddy walk, horse walk, horse run." All these words seemed to be pivots, yet Kendall combined them.

The second challenge was that analyses that emphasized meaning proved to more accurately describe the types of two-word statements children made. In a great many languages that have been studied, children's two-word utterances emphasize the same meaningful relations: agent-action ("Mommy hit"), possessor-possessed object ("Adam checker"), located object-location ("shoe bed"), attribute-object ("big car"), recurrence ("more juice"), and disappearance ("juice allgone") (Bloom, 1970, Schlesinger, 1971). Within each relation, words are ordered in a regular fashion. For example, when describing an object that disappeared, a child always might say "juice allgone" and never "allgone juice." However, the regularity is specific to the meaning being expressed.

These observations have led to the insight that much of grammatical development is closely tied to the acquisition of meanings. Even adults have difficulty learning artificial grammars where the grammatical regularities have no relation to the meanings being expressed (Maratsos, 1983). In addition, children's learning of meanings seems to play a large role in enabling them to learn grammar (Braine, in press). These observations support the general perspective that the goal of language is communication. Children learn some purely grammatical relations, but for the most part, expression and understanding of meaning is primary.

Development Beyond the Two-Word Phase

After the two-word phase, language development explodes in all directions. The precision with which speech sounds are made; the variety, complexity, and length of sentences; and the variety and complexity of word meanings all skyrocket. Table 6–6 may provide a feel for the rapidity of language development in early childhood. The absolute numbers in this estimate of vocabulary size, like all estimates of vocabulary, are influenced by a number of assumptions about what counts as a separate word (e.g., if children know the words, *like, likeable, likely,* and *likelihood,* how many words should we say they know?). The estimates in Table 6–6 are quite conservative and probably understate the number of words children know at all ages. Nonetheless, the rate of increase is striking. Until about 18 months children's vocabularies grow slowly. In the next three months, however, they more than double. In the three months after that, they again more than double. By 3 years, the size has more than tripled that at 2 years, and the rapid growth continues for several years thereafter.

Vocabulary size is not the only aspect of language that shows spectacular growth in the period after the two-word stage. Similar dramatic growth is evident in phonology, grammar, and word meanings. Below, these developments are discussed in turn.

Phonological development beyond the two-word stage.   Earlier we discussed infants' ability to discriminate among sounds. Although such discriminations are necessary for learning language, they are not sufficient. Children must remember the sounds long enough and precisely enough to identify words and phrases. Development in the precision and durability of these discriminations appears to continue well beyond the first few months of infancy.

Garnica (1973) performed an experiment that raised questions about how well 1-year-olds remember the subtle discriminations between sounds they can make. Children were given two toy figures and were told the name

TABLE 6-6 Size of Vocabulary at Various Ages (After M. E. Smith, 1926)

	AGE	NUMBER OF WORDS	GAIN
YEARS	MONTHS		
	8	0	
	10	1	1
1	0	3	2
1	3	19	16
1	6	22	3
1	9	118	96
2	0	272	154
2	6	446	174
3	0	896	450
4	0	1540	318
5	0	2072	202

of each figure. The two names differed only in a single phoneme, for example, "Pab" and "Bab." Then the children needed to make one of the figures perform an action. This task required them to maintain in memory the "Pab"-versus-"Bab" discrimination for a few seconds, long enough to execute the action. The 1-year-olds proved adept at maintaining some discriminations, such as *m* versus *l*. Maintaining others, however—for example, *p* versus *b*, proved difficult.

Later studies (Barton, 1978) showed that 1-year-olds possess some abilities to remember phonological distinctions that were not apparent in the Garnica study. Barton used the same task as Garnica, with one large exception. Rather than needing to remember meaningless syllables, the toddlers needed to remember the distinction between familiar terms that differed only in these same phonemes (e.g., "pig" and "big"). The 1-year-olds proved quite adept at doing so. The general point is one that applies to many areas of cognitive development. Children display many abilities in dealing with familiar stimuli that they do not show in less-familiar situations.

Toddlers experience some difficulty in discriminating among sounds, but they experience much more difficulty in pronouncing the sounds appropriately. Some of the problem stems from their not being able to produce the sound they want when they want it. Thus, their pronunciation is inconsistent; they sometimes mispronounce words that at other times they pronounce correctly. Another part of the problem stems from certain sounds simply being difficult for them to make. Almost none of children's early words include complex consonant clusters such as the *str* in *stripe*. This phenomenon probably has two causes. First, children may avoid saying words that they cannot pronounce intelligibly. Second, languages may accommodate children by not using difficult-to-pronounce words for objects toddlers want to talk about (people, animals, vehicles), just as they do by using words such as *mama* to refer to mothers. Most children do not overcome these pronunciation difficulties quickly. Well into the elementary school period, producing such sounds as *sh*, *th*, *s*, and *r* remains difficult.

Many children are quite conscious of their pronunciation difficulties. Their knowledge is an early example of *metalinguistic awareness*, awareness of what you know, and don't know, about language. As an example of this metalinguistic awareness, consider the following conversation between a psycholinguist and his 2½-year-old son:

FATHER:	Say "jump."
SON:	Dup.
FATHER:	No, "jump."
SON:	Dup.
FATHER:	No. "Jummmp."
SON:	Only Daddy can say "dup!" (Smith, 1973; p. 10).

Grammatical development beyond the two-word stage. Following the two-word stage, children begin to acquire many of the grammatical conventions used in adult language. For example, English-speaking children learn to indicate that an event happened in the past by appending *ed* to the verb. They learn to indicate that more than one individual was involved in an event by appending *s* or *es* to the noun. These acquisitions make children's language sound much less childish.

One of the most challenging tasks in this period is learning to ask *wh* questions: questions starting with *who, what, when, where,* and *why.* Bellugi (1965) documented three stages in the development of such forms. At first, children not only fail to produce *wh* questions, they do not even understand them. Consider the following example (from Dale, 1976):

MOTHER	CHILD
What did you hit?	Hit.
What did you do?	Head.
What are you writing?	Arm.

Later, children begin to answer *wh* questions appropriately. They also ask such questions, but only in the sense of adding the *wh* term and the appropriate pronoun to the beginning of a simple statement. For example, when an adult said, "You bent that game," a child answered, "Why me bent that game?" (Brown, Cazden, & Bellugi, 1969). Children at this level of understanding do not use auxiliary verbs (e.g., *has, was, did*), which are crucial in many English questions. They thus ask questions such as, "Why not he eat?" and "Why he smiling?" which lack the usual terms *does* and *is.*

Still later, children begin to use auxiliary verbs, but not necessarily correctly. This is unsurprising, considering the number of processing steps necessary to transform a simple statement into a *wh* question. Consider what a child needs to do to transform "He thinks *x*" into "Why does he think *x*?"

1. Adopt a questioning intonation.
   Result: "He thinks *x*?"
2. Add the *wh* term to the beginning of the sentence.
   Result: "Why he thinks *x*?"
3. Realize that *does* must be added after the *wh* term.
   Result: "Why does he thinks *x*?"
4. Delete the *s* from *thinks.*
   Result: "Why does he think *x*?"

In light of the number and complexity of these transformations, it should not be surprising that children continue to err when asking *wh* questions for several years beyond the time they first attempt them. By age 5, though, most children have mastered *wh* questions and a variety of other grammatical forms.

What change mechanisms lead to such rapid progress in grammar during the preschool period? One possibility is that the structure of the brain changes in this period to a way that influences the process of grammatical acquisition. Lenneberg (1967) proposed perhaps the best-known theory of the relation between brain development and the growth of grammar. His central claim was that there exists a critical period, between 18 months and puberty, during which the brain is more prepared to learn grammatical transformations than it has been earlier or will be later.

As noted in the chapter on perceptual development, the brain consists of two major structures, the left and right hemispheres. Lenneberg claimed that at birth, either hemisphere could be used for language production and comprehension, but that by 18 months, the left hemisphere ordinarily dominates language processing. He also contended that if a child did not learn language by puberty, the left hemisphere would assume other functions and that learning grammar would become difficult or impossible. Finally, he claimed that people past puberty have more difficulty learning foreign grammars than younger individuals, because they are past the critical period during which learning grammars is easiest.

Lenneberg's account has been questioned on several grounds. As noted in the discussion of auditory perception, hemispheric specialization begins before the hypothesized critical period. At the other end of the proposed critical period, learning of foreign grammars does not actually appear to be easier for young children than for adults. Snow and Hoefnagel-Hohle (1978) tested knowledge of Dutch among 3- and 4-year-old and adult immigrants to Holland. Both the children and the adults were spending their first year in the country. The adults in fact learned grammar much more completely than the 3- and 4-year-olds. Earlier reports of immigrant children learning new languages faster than their parents appear to be due to the children's superior mastery of new phonologies rather than to any superior grammatical competence.

Recently, an entirely different type of argument has been advanced to support the position that the brain includes language-specific learning mechanisms that are crucial for grammatical acquisition. Wexler (1962) has attempted to prove through formal logic that unless people were born with strong and accurate intuitions about the forms grammars could take, grammars (or at least Chomsky's transformational grammar) would be unlearnable. This form of argument is potentially powerful. If transformational grammar could not be learned unless the brain included certain built-in mechanisms, and if children learn transformational grammar, then the brain must include these mechanisms.

The validity of the argument, however, depends on the validity of the assumption that children are learning transformational grammar. If they in fact are learning a different grammatical system (i.e., a grammatical system in which meaning plays a large role), the formal logical arguments about learnability become of uncertain relevance. It seems that meaning in fact does play a large role in the grammars children learn. Thus, the formal logical argument may not be as compelling as it at first appears.

There is an important and general moral in all this. It is difficult, perhaps impossible, to evaluate the roles of learning mechanisms without having a detailed understanding of what is learned. Until we know more about what grammars children actually acquire, we will be limited in our ability to evaluate the plausibility of hypothesized acquisition mechanisms. Lenneberg's and Wexler's position that learning of grammar depends on the brain including language-specific learning mechanisms may yet be shown to be correct. Demonstrating the point, however, will require evidence about what grammars children learn and what activities specific parts of the brain promote. This evidence has not yet been obtained.

Development of meaning beyond the two-word stage.   How do children acquire so many word meanings in the few years of the preschool period? Their problem in learning word meanings is not simple. Even if a parent points to a dog and says, "That's a dog," the lesson is unclear. From the child's perspective, the parent might mean that the object is an animal, a collie, a mammal, a furry object, or any other number of possibilities. That people are able to make accurate inferences under such problematic circumstances has been called "the riddle of induction" (Quine, 1960).

Language provides a number of clues to word meanings that, if appreciated, greatly reduce the range of possible meanings. Even 2- and 3-year-olds seem to understand that if the word is introduced without any modifier ("This is Baff"), it probably is a proper noun such as a name; if it is introduced as "some baff," it probably is a mass noun such as a liquid or other undifferentiated mass; and if it is introduced as "a baff" or "the baff," it is probably a count noun such as an animal, vehicle, or tool (Macnamara, 1982). They also seem to expect that most of the individual words that appear in language and that are introduced by "a" or "the" refer to classifications (e.g., animals or dogs) rather than relations (e.g., a dog eating a bone) (Markman & Hutchinson, 1984). These expectations may account for the rapid acquisition of count nouns by young children.

Although children's acquisition of word meanings is generally rapid and painless, the exceptions are enlightening, because they point to concepts that children find especially confusing. One class of words whose meaning children find difficult is *relative adjectives.* These are terms such as *big* and *little, tall* and *short, more* and *less,* and *deep* and *shallow.* Children first understand *big* and *little,* then *tall* and *short,* and finally *deep* and *shallow* (Donaldson & Wales, 1970).

Why would children master the words in this order? Analysis of the number of meanings expressed by the words suggests an answer. *Big* and *little* apply to any comparison involving size. *Tall* and *short* apply only to those instances in which size is involved *and* the type of size is vertical. *Deep* and *shallow* apply only when sizes are involved, the types of size are vertical, and the vertical size extends downward from some reference point (such as the surface of a body of water). Again, children first learn words that apply most broadly, and only later learn terms whose applicability is more restricted.

Consistent differences also appear in when children master the two words within each pair of relative adjectives. In each pair, one term is considered *marked*, the other *unmarked*. The unmarked term is called unmarked because it is used to refer to the dimension when the value of the dimension is unknown. Illustratively, asking "How tall is she?" has no implication concerning the person's height; she could either be tall or short. In contrast, asking "How short is she?" implies that we already know that she is fairly short. Thus, *big, tall, more,* and *deep* are unmarked, whereas *little, short, less,* and *shallow* are marked.

Children consistently learn the unmarked terms earlier. In addition, 3- and 4-year-olds often use the meaning of the unmarked term to refer both to itself and to the marked term. For example, Donaldson and Balfour (1968) found that many 3½-year-olds consistently reacted to instructions to choose the set with less by choosing the one with more. Palermo (1973) found that under certain circumstances, even 7-year-olds interpreted *less* as meaning *more*.

The reason for this ordering is not well understood, but two explanations, both involving frequency, seem plausible. One involves the relative frequency with which children hear the terms. Because unmarked terms are used in neutral contexts as well as ones in which a positive value is anticipated, children may hear these terms more than the marked ones and thus have more opportunity to learn them. The other explanation involves the frequency of children wanting to use the terms. Children often ask for more food, play, or affection, and enjoy commenting on how big they and their toys are. When they want less, however, they typically withdraw from the situation rather than talking about it, or just say "no." They take little pride in discussing how small they and their toys are. In sum, both how often children hear marked and unmarked terms and how often they wish to express the meanings specified by them may contribute to their learning unmarked terms first.

Even when children do not understand exactly what a word means, they often successfully disguise their lack of understanding through clever nonlinguistic strategies for inferring what must be meant. This has become evident in studies of the meanings of prepositions that indicate location: *in, on, under, on top of, over, above,* and so on. Clark (1973) described two ways in which children use the physical context to discriminate between the meanings of such statements as "Put object 1 *in* object 2" and "Put object 1 *on* object 2."

1. If object 2 is a container with an open side up, put object 1 into it.
2. If object 2 is a container with a closed side up, put object 1 on top of it.

Clark found that children below 3 years followed these rules when they heard *in* and *on*. They seemed to know that both words referred to locations, but not to know the distinction between them. Note that in most situations, children's understanding of *in* and *on* would have appeared perfect from an early age. Ordinarily, when we say to a child "Put 1 *on* 2," 2 is a surface. When we say "Put 1 *in* 2," 2 usually includes an opening on the top. Thus, children's context-based strategies serve them in good stead as far as behaving appropriately, even when they do not understand precisely what they are being asked to do.

What of more complex learning? Do children ever reorganize their knowledge of word meanings to reflect a more mature general level of thinking, as might be suggested by a Piagetian analysis of cognitive development?

Apparently they do. Bowerman (1982) provided several compelling examples of children reanalyzing their knowledge about word meanings and discovering heretofore unrealized regularities. One of her examples involved the way in which 2- to 6-year-olds learn about verbs of causation. Some verbs, such as *drop* and *kill*, imply that an agent caused the event to happen. Other verbs, such as *fall* and *die*, express similar meanings except that no causal agent is implied. By the nature of the terms, *killing* implies a killer, though *dying* does not imply a cause of death.

Bowerman found that children quickly learned some causal terms, that they later incorrectly substituted noncausal terms with otherwise similar meanings (as in the phrase "Fall it"), and that only later did they restrict *fall* to noncausal contexts and *drop* to causal ones. This sequence resembles the one described by Brown and his colleagues (1969) in accounting for overgeneralization of past tense and plural forms. First, children learned correct forms individually by rote, then they noted a similarity among terms and began to apply a general rule that causal and noncausal terms could be used interchangeably, and finally they grasped both similarities and differences in word meanings.

Children progress similarly in learning the verbs to which the prefix *un* can be attached. At first glance, these words, such as *uncover*, *undress*, *unlock*, and *unstaple*, would not seem to have anything in common that distinguishes them from illegal words such as *unbreak* and *unspill*. As in the cases of the grammatical morphemes and the size-related adjectives cited earlier, careful analysis of the language input suggests an explanation. It turns out that in English, *un* can often be attached to verbs that involve either contact between objects (*unlock* and *unstaple*) or the functions of covering or enclosing (*undress* and *uncover*). In contrast, *un* almost never can be attached to other verbs.

Bowerman (1982) found that her children's first use of verb forms that started with *un* involved correct rote repetition of terms such as *unbuckled* and *untangled*. Later, the children began to attach the prefix in new and often incorrect ways. For example, one of her children said "I hate you! And

I'll never unhate you or nothing!" Such early errors were soon supplanted by errors suggesting that the child grasped the rule. The same child who vowed never to unhate her mother recited a ghost story eight months later and said "He tippitoed to the graveyard and unburied her." Although *unburied* does not happen to be a word in English, it does conform to the rule that *un* can be attached to terms involving containment. Like the findings with causal verbs, these data indicate that both rote learning and generalization influence how children acquire word meanings.

Children face many situations where they lack a particular word to express a meaning. How should they solve this problem? One solution that they use quite frequently is to make up words. Clark (1981) cited such examples as *fire-man* (someone who burns things), *hitter man* (someone who hits things), *hugging machine* (thing for hugging people), and *eating thing* (thing for eating with). As these examples suggest, children's innovative uses of language are far from random. They seem to reflect rules such as combining words that are words in their own right, using component terms that can be applied widely (*thing, machine*), and using component words that have a single meaning. These simple rules lend children's speech some of its colorful character.

Another base of the colorful character of children's language is their use of metaphors and related nonliteral expressions. At roughly two years of age, they begin to produce metaphors, for example by calling a piece of string "my tail" (Winner, McCarthy, & Gardner, 1980). Most of these early metaphors are based on perceptual similarity, as in the tail example. More abstract metaphors take much longer to master. Consider the metaphorical expression "The prison guard had become a *hard rock*". At around age 6 or 7 years, most children interpret this sentence to mean "A witch turned the guard into a rock" (Winner, Rosensteil, & Gardner, 1976). Later, at around age 9, they deny the meaningfulness of the sentence entirely, by saying, "A person can't be a rock." Still later, at around age 10 or 11, they interpret the sentence metaphorically, and modify their usual interpretation of the one phrase so that it makes sense in the context of the other.

At first glance, the early magical interpretation about the witch having turned the guard into a rock would seem either to stand in the way of a correct interpretation or to be simply a wrong turn. The process that leads to the early and later interpretations may be quite similar, though. Children may as a matter of course first try to interpret statements literally. If the literal interpretation does not make sense, they may then search for an interpretation that is sensible. One resolution that is almost always applicable, but that usually is not especially compelling, is to take the statement as literally given, but to assume that it applies to a magical world where the usual constraints of reality are suspended. Another, more sophisticated, strategy is to identify any clear relations that exist between the features of the two terms that are being compared. Focusing on the qualities of rocks and some prison guards as cold, unfeeling, and unresponsive exemplifies this strategy. With metaphors where the relevant qualities needed to interpret the sentence sensibly are easily accessible, such as many perceptual metaphors, even first graders correctly interpret the sentences more often than chance would suggest. With metaphors where the relevant qualities are obscure, even adults sometimes resort to magical explanations (Reyna, 1985). Thus, magical and metaphorical interpretations emerge as two strategies that can be used when literal interpretations fail; development seems likely to be due to increased knowledge of attributes of the entities being compared, and to increased ability to keep in mind multiple features of the entities long enough to identify the points of similarity.

The Development of Communication Skills

The ultimate purpose of language is communication. At first impression, communication might simply seem to be an aspect of meaning. In a sense it is, but the types of meaning included under the heading often depend on cultural convention as well as on literal definitions of words. For example, if I ask my daughter's teacher, "Is she doing well in school?" I am not looking for a "yes" or "no" answer, even though such an answer would be consistent with the meanings of the individual words and of the phrase as a whole. Even preschoolers respond to the intent of questions, rather than to their literal meaning, which shows they have mastered some of the communicative conventions of their language (Shatz, 1978).

Communication is at its heart an interactive process between individuals. In keeping with this fact, it is worthwhile to go back and forth from how infants motivate adults to talk to them to how adults motivate infants to listen to them, to the communicative strategies of somewhat older children to the communicative devices of adults in talking with these somewhat older children.

No one knows exactly when in life the first communication skills originate. Some such skills seem to be present even in the first half year. One that may be particularly important for infants is motivating older people to talk to them. Although 3- and 4-month-olds cannot respond to conversation with relevant statements, hearing people speak helps them learn to talk. Infants act in several ways that motivate adults to talk to them. In particular, they move in rhythm with adults' intonations and make sounds at points where the adult is about to stop talking (Condon and Sanders, 1974). Such behaviors roughly resemble the give and take of typical conversations. They encourage adults to talk more with the infants than if the infants remained motionless or behaved in ways uncorrelated with what the adult was saying.

Adults, in turn, speak to infants in ways that encourage them to listen. As noted in the last chapter, they use the form of speech known as motherese. They use short, simple sentences (for example, "See the doggie"), speak in high registers, exaggerate intonations, and elongate vowels (as when saying "Wheeee"). The style of speech is sufficiently distinctive that preschoolers abstract its form and use it in speaking to yet younger children (Shatz, 1983).

Why do older individuals use motherese to talk to infants? Investigators disagree whether the short, simple sentences are useful for inducing the grammatical structure of language. Wexler (1982) argued that such sentences would provide a hopelessly poor base from which to learn if children were not born with strong, accurate intuitions about the forms that grammars take. In his view, motherese actually increases the difficulty of inducing grammar.

Others, such as Clancy (1984), contend that the simplified input is useful in learning the meaning-based grammars that young children first acquire. Her argument resembles the moderate-discrepancy hypothesis discussed in Chapter 5. If children learn most efficiently from input just beyond their current level of understanding, then the short, simple sentences may be the ideal learning experience. While there may be disagreement about whether motherese makes learning grammar easier or harder, however, everyone agrees that it is useful for maintaining infants' attention to intended communications (as discussed in the previous chapter on pp. 165). Thus, improving communication, rather than facilitating learning of grammatical structure, may be the true function of this style of speech.

As children begin to speak, they supplement in many ways the attention-holding strategies with which they began. Some of the new strategies seem to be unique to beginning language users. Several investigators and countless parents have noted some toddlers' tendencies to repeat entire phrases with only minimal grammatical alterations (Billman & Shatz, 1981; Keenan, 1977). When I once asked my then 2-year-old son, "Are you a great big boy?" he responded, "I are a great big boy." The early responses to *wh* questions that were described above provide another example of such imitations. The imitations often are considerably longer than the child's typical sentences at that time. They may provide a stepping-stone for constructing longer and grammatically more complex sentences than the child has previously generated.

Young children also are surprisingly adept at understanding the unspoken conversational rules of their language communities. Bloom, Rocissano, and Hood (1976) described some of the knowledge of children around 2 years of age. The children seemed to know that they should speak immediately after their conversational partner stopped talking. One manifestation was that they spoke more often after being spoken to than when they would have needed to initiate the conversation. They also responded appropriately to questions. Their replies were more closely related to the topic of the question than were their responses to other statements. This follows the conversational convention that questions demand a relevant answer, whereas simple statements can be followed by the introduction of new topics.

Young children's knowledge of conversational rules also extends to differences among types of questions. Crosby (1976) and Rodgon (1979) found that 2-year-olds were more likely to respond "yes" or "no" to questions that began with "Did you" than to questions that began with "What" or "Where." This does not mean that the children perfectly understood the content of the questions. Their answers to "Did you" questions, though conforming to the demand to say "yes" or "no," often were factually incorrect. Similarly, Ervin-Tripp (1970) found that young children often begin their answers to "Why" questions with "because" even when that is the only appropriate part of their answer. Thus, 2-year-olds appear to follow a set of rules for answering questions that are based on the particular words at the beginning of the question: "If you hear a question beginning with 'Did you,' begin your answer with 'yes' or 'no'; if you hear a question beginning with 'Why,' begin your answer with 'because' " and so on. The strategy resembles the one by which children responded to the terms *in* and *on*, even when they did not completely understand them.

Although 2-year-olds know they should answer questions, their parents' active intervention is necessary to keep conversations going beyond a single question-answer sequence. One way in which they accomplish this goal is by building new questions into their responses to their children's statements (Kaye & Charney, 1980). Another strategy that parents adopt is to ask "What?" not only when they have difficulty understanding the words in their children's statements, but also when they do not understand their meaning. Gallagher (1981) indicated that even children under 2 at times respond to such statements by revising their earlier statements. In sum, the combination of children's and parents' strategies for communicating are quite successful in overcoming the children's limited early capacity for processing language.

Although even babies and toddlers are effective communicators, skill in communications continues to develop for many years thereafter. The need to progress beyond egocentric communications is one area where development occurs well into middle childhood. Recall the referential communications problem, described in Chapter 2 (p. 57), where children needed to describe which one of a set of squiggles they were thinking about. The purpose of the communication was to allow other children looking at the same squiggles to know which was being described. In addition to having difficulty producing unambiguous descriptions, 4- and 5-year-olds have difficulty knowing whether the communication is ambiguous or whether they simply did not listen properly to it. There are several separable skills here: communicating clearly, listening carefully, and evaluating objectively whether the fault for missed communications lies in unclear messages or inadequate listening.

Sonnenschein and Whitehurst (1984) found that being able to evaluate objectively the quality of the communication is the key skill. Five-year-olds who were taught how to evaluate the quality of communications when they were not part of the conversation later transferred their learning both to producing accurate communications and to knowing when the person talking had given them an ambiguous message. They did not show comparable transfer when trained either to produce clear messages themselves or when trained to identify when instructions they needed to follow were unclear. What the most successful training seems to have done was to allow the 5-year-olds to see the message through the eyes of both communicator and listener. That is, it allowed them to take a nonegocentric perspective.

THEORETICAL ISSUES IN LANGUAGE DEVELOPMENT

So far, we have focused on how typical children exposed to typical language input learn phonology, grammar, meaning, and communications skills. In the remainder of the chapter, we will examine more theoretical questions. Is language unique to humans? How were languages invented? What mechanisms make language learning possible? Much of the evidence that bears on these questions involves the language learning of atypical populations who receive atypical language inputs: animals, deaf children, and people born into communities with no dominant language. Below, this evidence is discussed.

Is Language Unique to Humans?

People have long prided themselves on being the only species that could use language. The French philosopher René Descartes (the same man who penned the phrase "I think, therefore I am") wrote

> . . . it is a very remarkable fact that there are none so depraved and stupid, without even excepting idiots, that they cannot arrange different words together, forming of them a statement by which they make known their thoughts; while, on the other hand, there is no other animal, however perfect and fortunately circumstanced it may be, which can do the same.

More recently, Chomsky (1968) commented

> Even at low levels of intelligence, at pathological levels, we find a command of language that is totally unattainable by an ape that may, in other respects, surpass a human imbecile in problem-solving ability and other adaptive behavior. (p. 9)

Psycholinguists have been greatly interested in testing this view. The earliest efforts to determine whether other species could learn language involved efforts to raise a chimpanzee in one's own home. The goal was to see how much language chimpanzees would learn in a rich linguistic environment. Kellogg and Kellogg (1933) raised a chimp, Gua, in their home, along with their own child, Donald. Gua learned to understand about 70 phrases (about the number that intelligent dogs learn), but never spoke. Hayes (1951) raised Vicki, another chimp, in her home and made heroic efforts to teach her to speak. Vicki mastered four wordlike sounds, but did not progress further.

At least part of Gua's and Vicki's problem was that chimpanzees' vocal cords are unsuited to speaking. For this reason, more recent investigators have tried to teach chimps nonverbal forms of language. Several have demonstrated fairly extensive language learning. Premack (1976) taught a chimp named Sarah to accurately answer questions expressed by plastic chips of different colors and shapes. Many chips referred to concrete objects, such as bananas and pails, and to properties of concrete objects, such as color and size. Others referred to relations, such as *the same as, put into,* and *give.* Sarah learned both meanings and some aspects of grammar. She discriminated between sentences that differed only in the order of words ("Randy give apple Sarah" versus "Sarah give apple Randy"). Unlike human children, however, Sarah did not use the chips to initiate conversation, and did not form statements that differed greatly from what she had heard before.

Chimps are not the only nonhuman species that can learn aspects of language. Dolphins also appear to have this capability. Herman, Richards, and Wolz (1983) taught two bottle-nosed dolphins, Phoenix and Akeakamai, both a spoken and a gesture-based language. The language consisted of 30 words that could be combined into over 450 two- to five-word commands. The language included a grammar so that the order was crucial to inferring their meaning. The dolphins not only learned the terms and grammar they were taught, but also successfully carried out instructions they were given for the first time. Thus, they, like the chimpanzees, demonstrated some of the linguistic creativity thought by Chomsky to be the essence of language.

The fact that dolphins and chimpanzees can learn some aspects of language demands modification of the view that all of language is a uniquely human capability. Nonetheless, as has been pointed out by several critics (Seidenberg & Petitto, 1979; Terrace, Petitto, Sanders & Bever, 1979), the results do not indicate that the linguistic capabilities of human and nonhuman species are identical. Even the most capable animals do not approach the richness of expression and understanding of 2½-year-old children. The chimpanzees' expressions are not concise and to the point like toddlers' telegraphic speech, but rather include many redundancies. Perhaps the most basic difference is that the languages are not invented by nonhuman species. Ancient people seem to have invented many languages at many times in the earth's history. As far as we know, no nonhuman species ever invented such a complex, flexible language.

How Do People Invent Languages?

This question might seem impossible to answer, since the world's languages were invented so long ago. However, Bickerton's (1983) work on creole and pidgin languages provides relevant data. Bickerton studied a contemporary version of Psammetichus's experiment (p. 177). In the past few centuries, laborers frequently have been imported to harvest crops on isolated islands with few or no native inhabitants. In a number of these situations, the imported laborers were not exposed to the language of the colonial landlords, who were a small minority of the population in any case. Since the laborers were imported from diverse countries, they did not share a common language with each other. Under such conditions, the workers improvised simple makeshift languages for communicating essential information among themselves. These are called *pidgin* languages.

The children of the laborers grew up with the pidgin being the only common language of the community. In spite of this impoverished linguistic background, they developed much richer languages called *creoles*. The creole languages that children developed in different parts of the world show surprising similarity to each other, despite the fact that the children who invented them had no contact with children in other creole communities. This similarity, together with the similarity of creoles to young children's statements in other language communities, led Bickerton to suggest that creoles reflect natural language-learning tendencies in young children. (Table 6–7).

The pidgin languages of the parent generation and the creoles of the child generation differ in a number of ways. Pidgins lack many features of standard languages. Such common parts of speech as articles (e.g., *a, the*), prepositions (e.g., *in, on*), and auxiliary verbs (e.g., *was, will*) may not exist in them. Expressing unusual or complex meanings often is difficult in pidgin languages, in part because of the absence of these terms. Creole languages,

TABLE 6-7 Comparison of English-Speaking Children's Sentences and Correct Creole Forms

CHILD LANGUAGE	CREOLES
Where I can put it?	Where I can put om? (Hawaii)
Daddy throw the nother rock.	Daddy t'row one neda rock'tone. (Jamaica)
I go full Angela bucket.	I go full Angela bucket. (Guyana)
Lookit a boy play ball.	Luku one boy a play ball. (Jamaica)
Nobody don't like me.	Nobody no like me. (Guyana)
I no like do that.	I no like do that. (Hawaii)
Johnny big more than me.	Johnny big more than me. (Jamaica)
Let Daddy get pen write it.	Make Daddy get pen write am. (Guyana)
I more better than Johnny.	I more better than Johnny. (Hawaii)

HUMAN

 SMALL ANIMAL

 VEHICLE

 AIRPLANE

 UNATTACHED MASS

 TREE

FIGURE 6-1   Some signs used in American Sign Language (from Newport, 1982).

in contrast, include articles, prepositions, and auxiliary verbs. Typically, they borrow vocabulary from the language of the landlords, but develop grammars that have unique features.

Bickerton's theory that creole languages reflect children's innate language-learning tendencies has been criticized on a number of grounds. Some linguists believe that the grammars of the creole languages are more like those of languages to which the children were exposed than Bickerton recognizes. Others wonder why many of the world's languages would evolve away from the creole form if it were more natural than the others. Even admitting the possible validity of such criticisms, the work on creole languages is thought provoking. At minimum, children from diverse language communities show the ability to meld together different forms into a coherent, shared, easily learnable language that allows them to express complex meanings. The speed with which they accomplish this also is noteworthy.

Is Language Inherently Verbal: Deaf Children's Sign Language

Theories of language acquisition usually focus on how hearing children learn to talk. Not all children learn to communicate through speaking, though. In particular, deaf children frequently learn to communicate through gestures. Their development offers an opportunity to determine which aspects of language learning are inherent parts of the way people acquire any language, and which are due to the specifically verbal nature of the languages most people learn.

Deaf children's language development illustrates that the motivation for language is basic to humans and does not depend on their being able to hear. Goldin–Meadow (1979) described the language development of six deaf children, all of whom had hearing parents who did not know sign language. Despite this unpromising-sounding language environment, all of the children invented signing systems to express themselves. The children developed simple grammars that helped communicate the relations among the terms. For example, in a situation involving a transfer of an object to a person, they consistently named the object of the transfer before the recipient ("Coke Johnny").

Further analyses indicated similarities between the meanings expressed in these first gestures and the meanings expressed in hearing children's first words (Goldin–Meadow & Morford, in press). The gestures and words both referred to toys, animals, clothing, vehicles, and people. Both also seemed to reflect the same goals: to note the existence of objects and to comment on or request some action the objects could perform. Older deaf children, like hearing children, use considerable non-literal languages such as metaphor, simile, and invented words such as "little-eyed people" who in one deaf child's fantasy story were said to inhabit the center of the earth (Marschack & West, 1985). It appears, then, that many features of language development are due to children's biologically given language-learning capabilities and to the demands of using language, rather than to the specifically verbal nature of ordinary language.

Many deaf children also learn formal gestural systems, such as American Sign Language (ASL). Stokoe (1960) described three dimensions that determine meaning within ASL. One is the location at which a sign is made. The most common locations, in order of frequency, are the area in front of the body where the hands ordinarily move, the chin, the trunk, the cheek, the elbow, and the forehead. These also are the locations at which young children find it easiest to produce signs, one more instance of languages having evolved to facilitate learning by young children (Bonvillian, Orlansky, & Novack, 1983). A second dimension that distinguishes signs is hand shape. Several common hand shapes are shown in Figure 6-1. The third dimension along which signs vary is hand movement. For example, in the "vehicle wandering upward" sign, the active hand moves upward in a winding pattern.

Is ASL fundamentally similar to other languages, or is it a more limited form of expression? Two qualities of natural languages that are often thought to be crucial are that they are categorical and that they use grammatical markings. We can examine ASL on each of these dimensions.

As noted in the perceptual development chapter, spoken languages are categorical at the level of individual sounds. We hear a sound as a *pa* or *ba*, but not as a little of each. They also are categorical at the level of word meanings. People are said to walk, jog, skip, or run; languages do not provide single words for characterizing the hundreds of fine gradations in the ways that people move. Instead, words represent distinct concepts.

ASL gestures are not categorical in the sense that speech perception is. If asked to identify gestures as literally identical or different, ASL users can do so. However, the signs are categorical in the sense that word meanings are. Supalla (1982) illustrated this in discussing how motion and location are depicted by skilled ASL users. Motion presents a case where continuous depiction would seem advantageous. Finer differences than can be described orally can be depicted by having one's hands follow the precise path that is being followed. Like other natural languages, however, ASL depicts motion categorically. It divides motions into seven categories. Intermediate cases are not generated by compromising between signs: For example, a slight amount of contact is not depicted by a less intense version of the objects-coming-into-contact sign. Instead, a modifier is added to the basic contact term.

The version of ASL described by Supalla is not used by every ASL user. Newport (1982) distinguished between two variants of ASL. Her distinction closely resembles that between pidgin and creole languages. The large majority of deaf people in the United States are born to hearing parents. In such homes, children and adults often invent simple signing languages for communication before they are exposed to any more formal gestural language. Such "home sign" languages typically lack grammatical markings. Even when they later learn ASL, these children of hearing parents often fail to learn much of its grammar.

The people who most frequently acquire the more elaborate ASL system, involving a sophisticated grammar and flexible means of expression, are deaf children born to deaf parents. These individuals are exposed to a formal sign language from infancy onward. Interestingly, though, the sign language that they usually see their parents using is the relatively simple form used by first-generation deaf people. It would be extremely valuable to understand the reasoning processes by which children induce the sophisticated language from the simpler one, but at present these processes are poorly understood.

Mechanisms of Language Development

The mechanisms through which children learn language already have received considerable attention. Skinner's ideas about external reinforcement and imitation, Chomsky's postulated language-acquisition device, Bickerton's hypothesized language-learning tendencies that allow children to progress from pidgins to creoles, and numerous investigators' descriptions of children's strategies for inferring meaning and communicating have been discussed. The issue is of sufficient importance, however, that it seemed worthwhile to save some of the best-specified and most provocative ideas for this final section of the chapter. Among these are ideas concerning the roles of generalization, rote imitation, analogizing, and comparison of linguistic input to children's expectations about how that input should be organized.

Rote imitation and analogy.   MacWhinney (1978) illustrated the roles of rote imitation and analogy in his model of children's acquisition of *morphophonology*. Morphophonology involves the production and comprehension of words and parts of words that serve grammatical purposes, such as *s*'s that indicate plurals and *ed*'s that indicate past tenses. The model is quite broad in scope, yet also is precise and well specified. It describes how children learn not only English but also several other languages: German, Hungarian, and Finnish among them.

MacWhinney emphasized two basic mechanisms that he believed govern how children learn morphophonology: *rote imitation* and *analogy*. The role of rote imitation can be seen in the correct irregular forms that children produce. As noted earlier in the chapter, among children's early words are correct plural and past tense terms, both regular *(jumped)* and irregular *(ran)*. They produce these terms long before they know rules for generating typical past tense and plural forms. The most straightforward explanation is that they imitate the words as whole units.

Analogy is a more complex learning process. Berko (1958) illustrated its working in an experiment in which children needed to name imaginary animals. First the experimenter showed children a drawing of an imaginary animal and said "Here is a *wug*." Then the experimenter showed two such animals and said "Here are two ——." The children consistently filled in the term "wugs." MacWhinney proposed four information-processing steps through which children could produce this answer through analogy.

1. Forming a goal of generating the plural of *wug*.
2. Locating *bug* (or *rug* or *jug*) as the form most analogous phonologically and grammatically to *wug*.
3. Comparing *bug* to *bugs* to identify the difference between singular and plural forms.

4. Placing the sound that differentiates *bug* from *bugs* at the end of *wug* to form *wugs*.

This process would allow children to generate correct grammatical forms in the absence of any opportunity to imitate.

MacWhinney also discussed how rote imitation and analogy relate to each other. Basically, if children know a rote form, they use it; if they do not, they attempt to analogize to another term. Support for this view is found in comparing those terms where children frequently overgeneralize with those terms where they rarely do. At some points in development, a child will use both correct irregular verb forms (e.g., *ran*) and overregularized forms (e.g., *standed*). Close examination of the terms that children produce during these periods indicates that with frequent verbs such as *run*, they usually produce the correct irregular form. With less frequent verbs such as *stand*, they usually overgeneralize (Cazden, 1968). Presumably, children more often use rote imitation with words they have more opportunities to imitate and more often analogize to grammatically regular terms with less-often-heard terms.

Regularity detection. Maratsos (1982) emphasized the role of regularity detection in children's learning of German grammar. In German, nouns are divided into masculine, feminine, and neuter, and different articles are applied to each. When speakers wish to say *the*, they use *der* with masculine nouns, *die* with feminine nouns, and *das* with neuter nouns. Similarly, to label inanimate objects *it*, German speakers say *er* with masculine nouns, *sie* with feminine nouns, and *es* with neuter nouns.

How do German speakers know which form to use with which term? Meaning is not as useful a guide as might be expected. For example, *spoon* is a masculine term, *fork* is feminine, and *knife* is neuter. Nor is phonology a consistent guide, though it is often helpful.

Maratsos instead proposed a two-stage learning process. First, children learn arbitrary associations between a noun and some sex-linked term such as *der* or *das*. Then they induce rules from these initial associations. If children knew that *sie* is used with *fork*, they could induce that *die* also will be, since terms modified by *sie* consistently are also modified by *die*. The several other aspects of German that depend on whether the term is masculine, feminine, or neuter could be induced through the same process. Thus, according to Maratsos, children notice consistent linguistic patterns, abstract the rule underlying them, and then apply the rules to new cases. The similarity of these ideas to Klahr and Wallace's regularity detection mechanism (Chapter 3, p. 86) should be apparent.

Basic child grammar. Imitating, analogizing, and applying rules are general learning mechanisms that children use in many domains other than language. Language-specific mechanisms also have been proposed. One of the most appealing of these is Slobin's (1983) hypothesis that there exists a *basic child grammar* that children impose on whatever language input they receive.

Slobin suggested that children expect grammar to assume certain forms and adjust their expectations only when the language they learn directly contradicts their expectations. They expect that certain meanings but not others are sufficiently important that they should be reflected in grammar, and also that particular meanings should be expressed in particular places within phrases. When meanings children believe are important are marked by the grammar of the language, and when they are marked in the place children believe they should be, children learn the grammatical forms quickly. When the markings are in different places, or when children do not expect the meaning to be important at all, they learn slowly and make many errors.

One general principle that Slobin suggested children use is, "An operator that affects a whole phrase or clause should not be placed within that phrase or clause, nor should it require changing of elements within that phrase or clause" (p. 6). Illustratively, negatives affect the meaning of the entire clause they modify. When we say, "He didn't run to the store," the negative "didn't" modifies the meaning of the entire clause "run to the store." Children's errors indicate that they try to keep the negation outside of the clause even when the language they hear places it inside. In Turkish, the correct order is to indicate the verb, then to indicate whether the meaning is negative, and then to complete the verb phrase (as in "He run didn't to the store"). Children often err, however, by moving "didn't" outside the verb phrase, as is done in English. Thus, the children's expectations can for a time override the language to which they are exposed, leading to grammatical errors.

Children's expectations about what is important do not always conform to those of adults. For example, Polish toddlers find it easy to learn a difference that to most American adults seems very subtle: the difference between *perfective* and *imperfective* tenses. Perfective forms indicate that an action was executed once and completed; imperfective forms indicate that an action was executed repeatedly. In English, we might say "He opened the door" either in the perfective sense ("He opened the door once") or the imperfective ("The doorman opened the door again and again"). In Polish, the verb would need to have a particular ending to indicate which of the two meanings was intended. Slobin reported that in languages such as Polish, in which this difference is explicitly noted as part of the verb, children quickly and easily learn the distinction. On the other hand, in languages where verbs take different endings when used with male nouns than with female ones, children have difficulty learning the endings. Slobin suggests that since maleness or femaleness is more reasonably a property of the noun, children are surprised to find it reflected in the verb's ending and therefore have difficulty learning it.

Several general lessons emerge from Slobin's work. First, children initially order their statements according to the meanings of the words, rather than according to the formal grammar of their language. Second, certain meanings are more important than others to children. They learn these meanings first, and their errors often involve treating differently classes that vary in meaning but not in their grammatical use. Third, young language learners possess certain expectations about where in sentences particular meanings should be expressed. Some meanings are inherently related to the verb and should be expressed there; other meanings are inherently part of the subject and should be marked there; other meanings affect the whole clause and should be marked outside of it. As in other cognitive domains, then, children's language learning emerges as closely related to their existing knowledge and expectations.

SUMMARY

The acquisition of language in the first few years of life is one of children's greatest achievements. They become skilled in phonology, grammar, meaning, and communication. Phonology refers to the way in which people produce and hear sounds. Grammar involves the ordering of words within statements, as well as the specification of tense and number. Meaning refers to relations between words and the objects and events they describe. Communication is the way phonology, grammar, and meaning are used to express desires and intentions, elicit reactions, and provide information.

Phonological development proceeds in a regular sequence. First infants cry, then they coo, then they babble, and finally they produce syllables and words. Languages throughout the world take advantage of the types of first syllables that babies produce by making these names of caretakers: *mama*, *papa*, *dada*, and so on. Later phonological development occurs in ability to remember distinctions long enough to use them to learn new words and in the clarity of pronunciation.

Children's initial statements involve only one word. They are often called *holophrases*, because the single word expresses a larger unit of meaning. Somewhat later, children produce two-word phrases. This marks the true beginning of grammatical development, because it is the first time children need to order words in their statements. At first they base their ordering of words on the words' meanings. The orders follow standard meaningful patterns such as agent-action and possessor-possessed object. After the two-word period, children learn how to form *wh* questions, as well as other complex grammatical constructions.

The first words of children throughout the world are quite similar. They refer to people, animals, toys, and vehicles. Some investigators have thought that children's early word meanings excessively emphasized functions. Others have hypothesized that the first words overemphasized perceptual appearances. The most reasonable resolution seems to be that children's early word meanings may overemphasize appearance, function, or any other aspect of the context in which they learn the words. Later development of word meanings proceeds rapidly and for the most part correctly, but some difficulties remain, as in distinguishing the meaning of relative adjectives such as *more* and *less*.

Development of communication skills begins early in life. Infants motivate older people to talk to them by moving in synchrony with the speech intonations and making sounds when the adults stop talking. Adults and older children motivate infants to listen by adopting the conversational style known as motherese. By age 2 or 3, children know that they should answer "Did you" questions with "yes" or "no" and that they should answer "Why" questions with "because," even when they do not understand the meaning of the remainder of the sentence.

Research on language development has made possible more informed answers to several long-standing philosophical questions. Chimpanzees and dolphins have proved capable of learning some aspects of language, thus disproving the view that all of language was a uniquely human ability. The language that they have learned is far less elaborate than that of normal 2- and 3-year-old human children, though, and is more redundant. Research on deaf children who learn sign language has illustrated many parallels to the way that hearing children learn language. They express similar kinds of meanings and, like hearing children, invent certain kinds of grammars. This finding indicates that these aspects of language learning are due to the way humans learn language rather than to the specifically verbal nature of the language most people learn.

The final section of the chapter examined mechanisms of language acquisition. Children appear to approach language acquisition with certain expectations about the form the language will take: What meanings will be deemed important enough to mark grammatically and where these meanings should be marked. They use processes such as rote imitation, analogy, and rule induction to proceed beyond these initial expectations to learn the particulars of their native language.

RECOMMENDED READINGS

Bowerman, M. (1982). **Starting to talk worse: Clues to language acquisition from children's late speech errors.** In S. Strauss (Ed.), *U-Shaped behavioral growth.* New York: Academic Press. Presents several intriguing cases in which children, after using a set of words correctly for several years, start to use them incorrectly. Bowerman makes a compelling case that these "late errors" actually reflect cognitive growth in the children's understanding of the words' meanings.

Goldin-Meadow, S. & Morford, M. (in press). **Gesture in early child language: Studies of deaf** and hearing children. *Merrill-Palmer Quarterly.* Charming description of how deaf children invent signs to express themselves.

MacWhinney, B. (1978). **Processing a first language: The acquisition of morphophonology.** *Monographs of the Society for Research in Child Development, 43,* Whole No. 174. One of the clearest descriptions of the mechanisms through which language learning seems to take place.

Maratsos, M. P. (1983). **Some current issues in the study of the acquisition of grammar.** In P. H. Mussen (Ed.), *Manual of child psychology: Cognitive development, Volume III* (J. H. Flavell and E. M. Markman (Eds.)). New York: Wiley. A comprehensive and well-written summary of what has been learned about how children learn grammar. Makes a persuasive case that learning of grammar is at least partially separate from learning of meaning.

Slobin, D. I. (1983). **Crosslinguistic evidence for basic child grammar. Paper presented at the Biennial Meeting of The Society for Research in Child Development, Detroit, April.** Describes apparent predispositions of children to learn certain forms of language rather than others. The predispositions that go along with the structure of English seem entirely natural; the predispositions that diverge from the structure of English seem almost incredible, at least to this basically monolingual reader.

7
MEMORY DEVELOPMENT

"Memory is the mother of all wisdom." (Aeschylus, 5th century B.C.)
"Memory is the treasury and guardian of all things." (Cicero, 1st century B.C.)

Ancient playwrights and orators are not the only ones who have noted the centrality of memory in human civilization. The many movies and television shows that focus on amnesiacs reflect popular recognition of how our very identities depend on our memories: Lose your memory, lose your identity. People's fascination with mnemonists, individuals who perform prodigious memory feats, attests to a similar recognition. But how does memory operate, and how does it develop?

Four areas of potential memory development have received the greatest attention: *basic capacities*, *strategies*, *metamemory*, and *content knowledge*. The organization of most of this chapter will center on these four proposed sources of memory development. Before launching into this detailed discussion, however, it seems worthwhile to get a quick feel for some of the main phenomena of human memory. Therefore, the chapter is divided into two main parts. The first is devoted to three experiments that reveal a number of basic characteristics of memory. The second is organized around the four areas in which memory development may occur. Table 7–1 displays the organization of the chapter.

TABLE 7-1   Chapter Outline

THREE EXPERIMENTS ON MEMORY

A surprising number of the most basic findings about memory emerge from a few classic experiments. One of the main lessons of these experiments is the effectiveness of strategies in aiding memory. Another is the influence of prior knowledge on what and how people remember. A third is the fact that people typically remember the gist of material they encounter, rather than its literal form.

To obtain the maximum benefit from the three experiments, assume the role of a subject in them. Write down your answers on a sheet of paper, for reference in the discussion after the experiments. Also, be sure to follow the instructions carefully.

Experiment 1

Read the following 12 words, proceeding from the top to the bottom of one column and then from the top to the bottom of the other. Do this twice. Then cover the words and write them in any order:

ball	bird
chair	cord
hammer	comb
cup	tree
typewriter	ghost
book	meat

Now do the same thing with the following list:

couch	orange
table	banana
lamp	dog
rug	rat
pear	horse
pineapple	sheep

Experiment 2

Read the following group of numbers once, cover them, wait for 15 seconds, and write them in order:

3428670159

Now do the same thing with the following list:

212 467 9032

Experiment 3

Read the following story.

The War of the Ghosts

One night two young men from Egulac went down to the river to hunt seals, and while they were there it became foggy and calm. Then they heard war-cries, and they thought: "Maybe this is a war-party." They escaped to the shore, and hid behind a log. Now canoes came up, and they heard the noise of paddles, and saw one canoe coming up to them. There were five men in the canoe, and they said:

"What do you think? We wish to take you along. We are going up the river to make war on the people." One of the young men said: "I have no arrows." "Arrows are in the canoe," they said. "I will not go along. I might be killed. My relatives do not know where I have gone. But you," he said, turning to the other, "may go with them."

So one of the young men went, but the other returned home.

And the warriors went on up the river to a town on the other side of Kalama. The people came down to the water, and they began to fight, and many were killed. But presently the young man heard one of the warriors say: "Quick, let us go home: that Indian has been hit." Now he thought: "Oh, they are ghosts." He did not feel sick, but they said he had been shot.

So the canoes went back to Egulac, and the young man went ashore to his house, and made a fire. And he told everybody and said: "Behold I accompanied the ghosts, and we went to fight. Many of our fellows were killed, and many of those who attacked us were killed. They said I was hit, and I did not feel sick."

He told it all, and then he became quiet. When the sun rose he fell down. Something black came out of his mouth. His face became contorted. The people jumped up and cried.

He was dead. (Bartlett, 1932/1967, p. 65)

Now cover the page, and try to write out as much of the story as you can remember.

Many of the lessons of these experiments probably are clear simply from having participated in them. On the following page, the lessons are discussed.

Lessons of the Experiments

Experiment 1.   In Experiment 1, almost all people remember more words from the second list than from the first. They typically divide the 12 words in the second list into three categories—furniture, fruit, and animals. Then, when they attempt to recall the words, they use the category names to help them remember. They might say to themselves, "Furniture, let's see, did I see carpet, no, did I see table, yes, OK, 'table,' did I see lamp, yes, 'lamp,' " and so on.

In contrast, when they try to remember the first list, there are no simple categories to help them. After they recall a word, the next is a new problem. People are flexible and often take advantage of whatever opportunities a task affords. Thus, in the first list, they might note that *typewriter* is followed by *book*, and might link the two by thinking to themselves, "Typewriters can be used to write books." They also might link *bird* and *tree*, or *cup* and *meat*. Such insights typically aid memory for the first list, but not enough to overcome the advantage of the more easily categorized second list.

The fact that people can organize to-be-remembered material into categories is no guarantee that they will do so. Young children might not notice that couch, table, lamp, and rug are all furniture. If they did not, they might not benefit from the categorical structure. The ability to recognize potentially useful organizations may be a potent source of memory development.

Memory in this situation and others depends on two broad classes of processes: *encoding* and *retrieval*. As discussed in Chapter 3 (p. 89), encoding refers to the cognitive activities used to represent information on a particular occasion. One of these activities might be to note that the first four words in the second list are furniture, that the next four are fruits, and so on. Retrieval refers to the cognitive activities that the memorizer performs when later trying to remember the material that was presented. A person trying to retrieve a list might use category names as *retrieval cues* and think, "Let's see. There were three categories. What were they? Oh yeah, one was furniture. . ."

How can we tell whether people use organizational strategies to memorize material? One of the most powerful pieces of evidence is *clustering*, the consecutive recitation of the words within a category. If you remembered any of the pieces of furniture, you probably remembered and named them consecutively. This cannot in general be attributed to people tending to remember items in order. In the first list, *cord*, *comb*, *tree*, and *ghost* were presented consecutively, but few people recite them together. Another source of evidence for the use of organizational strategies comes from *intrusion errors*. It is much more likely that in recalling List 2 in Experiment 1, you mistakenly inserted categorically consistent terms, such as other fruits, tools, and pieces of furniture than that you inserted unrelated terms.

Experiment 2. In the second experiment, you were asked to recall in order two lists of numbers. You probably remembered more from the second than from the first list. The key difference was that you could draw an analogy between the second list and a long-distance phone number. The familiar phone number form increases the efficiency of the rehearsal process most people use to retain the numbers.

The influence of knowledge on memory is obvious in the phone number example. However, even in situations in which people lack knowledge directly relevant to the material they are trying to remember, they often find indirect links. Ericsson, Chase, and Faloon's (1980) case history of S. F. vividly illustrates this point.

Before the experiment began, S. F. was a seemingly unremarkable college sophomore. His grades were average, and he did not appear to be of unusual intelligence. One fact about him was unusual, however, and this proved to be important: He was an accomplished cross-country runner.

S. F. participated in a forward digit-span experiment. The task is similar to the one you performed on List 1 of Experiment 2. The experimenter presents a randomly ordered list of numbers at a rate of one word per second; the participant needs to repeat the numbers in order. A frequent assumption in interpreting performance on digit-span tests is that recall of each digit requires one unit of memory capacity. Thus, the number of digits recalled is interpreted as indicating the capacity of short-term memory.

Previous research indicated that college students can correctly repeat lists of seven or eight digits, but not much longer ones (Brener, 1940). A person who correctly repeated the 10 digits in the first list in Experiment 2 would be unusual, and would be thought to have an exceptional memory capacity of 10 units. S. F. was not exceptional in this regard. He could recall only seven digits when the experiment started. Yet by the end, he could recall more than 75 digits, a length that compares favorably with the achievements of professional mnemonists who perform on late-night television.

S. F. was not given special instructions in how to be a memory expert. He was, however, given extensive practice. For one hour per day, three to five days per week, for more than 1½ years, he was asked to recall lists of randomly ordered digits. If he correctly recalled all the digits in a list, his next list was one digit longer. If he failed to recall all of them, his next list was one digit shorter. Under these unexceptional conditions, his digit span improved from 7 to 79 digits.

How did he do it? S.F.'s verbal reports were revealing. He said that he drew on his familiarity with cross-country racing to encode groups of three or four numbers as running times. For example, he encoded 3492 as "3 minutes 49.2 seconds, near world-record time (for the mile)." On those numeric combinations that he could not code as running times, he employed supplementary strategies such as viewing the numbers as ages (e.g., 893 was encoded as 89.3, "a very old man").

These strategies were useful but alone could not account for S. F.'s improvement. Even if he held seven 4-digit running times in memory, rather than seven single-digit numbers, he only would recall 28 numbers. S. F. solved the problem by adopting the clever strategy of organizing the individual running times into super groups. Each of these super groups contained a pair of four- digit times followed by a pair of three-digit ones. Transcending his previous ability to recall seven 4-digit numbers, he became able to recall three or four of the new 14-digit numbers. Eventually, he constructed super-supergroups in the same way.

Since S. F.'s remarkable achievement, Chase, Ericsson, and their colleagues have extended the research in several ways. First they taught D. D., another cross-country runner, S. F.'s memory strategies, thus demonstrating that ability to learn the strategies was not unique to S. F. Second, as shown in Figure 7–1, the new student has surpassed S. F.'s previous level. He now can recall more than 100 digits. Thus, the previous record of 79 digits recalled was not an absolute limit on memory. Third, the research has been extended to a new task, mental multiplication. Here too, college students who

FIGURE 7–1   Mean digit span for S. F. and D. D. as a function of practice. By the end of training, S. F., the first memory-span expert, could remember more than 75 digits. D. D., who was taught S. F.'s strategies, eventually was able to remember more than 100 digits (data provided courtesy of James Staszewski).

MEAN DIGIT–SPAN FOR SF AND DD AS A FUNCTION OF PRACTICE

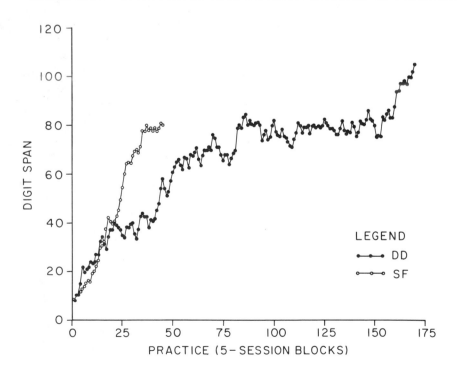

have been given a great deal of practice have reached heights equal to or exceeding those of famous memory experts.

Aside from testifying to what people can accomplish with sufficient practice and determination, S. F.'s case history also illustrates several notable characteristics of memory. First, it demonstrates the pervasive influence of strategies and of prior knowledge of the content being remembered. Memory span traditionally has been thought of as a straightforward measure of memory capacity. Even there, S. F. demonstrated that strategies and content knowledge enter in.

Second, S. F.'s case indicates the importance of knowing what strategy people are using to perform tasks. Without knowing about S. F.'s running-time strategies, it would have been impossible to anticipate which number sequences would be easy and which difficult. Yet because Chase, Ericsson, and Faloon knew what he was doing, they could design long number sequences that he could remember perfectly and others that were much shorter that he could not recall.

Third, the case illustrates the specificity of memory skills. Despite S. F.'s proficiency at recalling long strings of numbers, his memory capacity had not changed. When, after three months of practice, he was asked to recall letters rather than digits, his span for the alphabetic materials was a very average six consonants.

In summary, S. F.'s case exemplifies the capabilities that people can develop with practice. As Figure 7–1 indicates, at no time during the 1½ years of the experiment did S. F.'s improvement cease. As Ericsson, Chase, and Faloon (1980) concluded, "there is seemingly no limit to improvement in memory skill with practice" (p. 1182).

Experiment 3. The role of meaning is implicit in S. F.'s memory heroics. He chose to encode numbers as running times and ages because these were meaningful to him. Experiment 3, involving *The War of the Ghosts*, illustrates the effects of meaning in a different way. The meaning of this story is difficult to grasp. As a result, when people retell it, they usually omit many details, insert statements not present in the original, and distort the entire episode in a way that makes it more consistent with typical stories. The following is what one of Bartlett's (1932) subjects recalled a week after he heard the original:

> Two young men from Edulac went fishing. While thus engaged they heard a noise in the distance. "That sounds like a war-cry," said one, "there is going to be some fighting." Presently there appeared some warriors who invited them to join an expedition up the river.
> One of the young men excused himself on the ground of family ties. "I cannot come," he said, "as I might get killed." So he returned home. The other man, however, joined the party, and they proceeded on canoes up the river. While landing on the banks the enemy appeared and were running down to meet them. Soon someone was wounded, and the party discovered that they were

fighting against ghosts. The young man and his companion returned to the boats, and went back to their homes.

The next morning at dawn he was describing his adventures to his friends, who had gathered round him. Suddenly something black issued from his mouth, and he fell down uttering a cry. His friends closed around him, but found that he was dead.

This rendition is both shorter and more coherent than the original. There is no mention of the ambiguous statement "Behold, I accompanied the ghosts and we went to fight." Arbitrary details that do not affect the rest of the story also have been changed: for example, the substitution of "Edulac" for "Egulac."

Results such as these point to several further properties of memory. First, memory focuses on gist rather than on literal statements. Words may be inserted, omitted, or transformed, but basic themes are retained. Second, people's memory reorganizes information so as to make logically inconsistent events coherent. The difficulty of finding a coherent organization is what makes the *War of the Ghosts* such an elusive story. Third, emphasis on gist and efforts to make logically anomalous events sensible increase over time. Bartlett's subjects adhered more closely to the original story when they retold it a few minutes after hearing it than when they retold it a week later. Finally, people often recall unusual but colorful details along with the gist of the story. Few people forget that "something black came out of his mouth" when they recall the story.

The phenomena illustrated in these three experiments create a basis for understanding a crucial question about children's memory:

WHAT DEVELOPS IN MEMORY DEVELOPMENT?

Given an older child, a younger child, and a situation that both are seeing for the first time, the older child almost always will remember more. This is the central fact of memory development. Brown and DeLoache (1978) noted that the difference can be explained in four ways.

One possibility is that older children have superior basic capacities. Translated into terms of a computer analogy, this view suggests that what develops is the hardware of memory—its absolute capacity or its speed of operation—rather than the software—the particular procedures used to memorize material. A second possibility is that what develops is memory strategies. Older children know a greater number of memory strategies and use them more often, more effectively, and more flexibly than younger children. A third possibility is that metamemory is a main source of memory development. Older children may have superior knowledge about their own memories and may use this knowledge to regulate more effectively their memory procedures. Finally, the fourth possibility is that older children have greater prior knowledge of the content they need to remember and that this greater content knowledge helps them remember new situations involving related material. If a 12-year-old English boy and an American boy of the same age both watched a cricket match, the English child would remember more; if they both watched a baseball game, the American child would. Of course, these four approaches to the question "What develops?" are not mutually exclusive; all of them, or any combination of them, could contribute to the superiority of older children's memory.

Below we consider what is known about the contributions to memory development of changes in basic capacities, strategies, metamemory, and content knowledge. Just to preview what will emerge, it appears that some of the sources of development contribute more than others, and that some sources play large roles in certain periods of childhood but not others. It may be worthwhile to apply your intuitions about memory development, what you have learned about children's thinking generally, and what you learned from the three experiments at the beginning of this chapter to predicting which of the four potential sources of memory development will be most influential in infancy and early childhood, in middle childhood, and in late childhood and adolescence.

The Role of Basic Capacities

Basic capacities are frequently used, rapidly executed memory processes such as recognition, association, and retrieval. They are the building blocks of cognitive activity, in the sense that all more-complex cognitive activities are built up by combining them in different ways. Because they are so frequently used, developmental differences in them could account for an enormous number of other developmental differences in memory performance. Atkinson and Shiffrin's (1968) division of memory into sensory, short-term, and long-term stores provides a useful framework for considering basic capacities and how they develop.

Sensory memory.   Sights and sounds enter the memory system through the sensory store. If young children were unable to simultaneously take in as many sights and sounds as older children, their ability to learn and remember might be seriously impaired. Young children could be limited either in the number of objects they can simultaneously represent in the sensory store, in the speed with which they can represent the objects, or both.

The first possible limit does not seem to be a serious problem. The absolute capacity of the sensory store is constant over a wide age range; 5-year-olds can represent as many objects at a sensory level as adults (as discussed in Chapter 3, p. 67). It remains possible that the capacity of the sensory store increases between birth and age 5, but there is no particular reason to believe that it does.

On the other hand, the speed with which sensory representations are formed does increase during childhood. As noted in the discussion of methods for studying thinking (Chapter 4), one of the central features of people's processing is that it takes time. This is true even for basic perceptual and memory functions. For example, presenting a stimulus does not immediately result in a fully developed representation of the stimulus in the brain. Instead, the process takes between 1/10 and 1/3 of a second, depending on viewing conditions and the complexity of the stimulus (Ganz, 1975). The process is analogous to the development of a photographic print, in which the image becomes sharper and sharper while it is developing.

Children take longer to form such sensory representations than do adults. Under near-optimal viewing conditions, adults can represent objects at a sensory level in 1/10 of a second; under the same conditions, 7-year-olds require 1/7 of a second to do so (Hoving, Spencer, Robb, & Schulte, 1978). The differences in time are small, but when multiplied by the huge amount of sensory-level processing that people do each day, the differences might have broad effects.

Short-term-memory processes.   Development of short-term memory, like development of sensory memory, could involve changes in the number of objects that can be represented, the speed with which they can be represented, or both. Pascual–Leone (1970) explored the first possibility. He hypothesized that 5-year-olds could simultaneously hold two symbols in short-term memory, that 7-year-olds could keep three, 9-year-olds four, and 11-year-olds five.

To test this hypothesis, Case (1972) orally presented children with sets of numbers in which all the numbers until the last were in ascending order. The task was to insert the last number in its correct position in the series. For example, children might be presented the series 5, 14, 23, 8; they would need to answer "5, 8, 14, 23." The objective was to find the longest series on which children of different ages could perform consistently correctly. This length would be their short-term memory capacity. Case found that 6-year-olds dealt competently with ascending sequences as long as two numbers, that 8-year-olds could cope with three-number sequences, and that 10-year-olds could manage four-number sequences. These data were consistent with the predictions of Pascual–Leone's model of the number of symbols children could simultaneously hold in memory at different ages.

Consider other possible interpretations, though. Older children know more about numbers. This greater familiarity could help them to remember the numbers, as the case of S. F. suggested. Older children also are better able to use strategies, such as rehearsal, that allow them to circumvent their capacity limitations. Pascual–Leone and others have made admirably persistent attempts to overcome these methodological complexities and to convince skeptics that short-term memory capacity does increase. However, the multiple possible interpretations of why children might perform better on such tests has led to considerable doubt about their conclusions. My guess is that most researchers would not bet large sums of money that short-term memory capacity increases. Then again, they probably also would not bet large sums against the possibility.

What about the speed of operation of short-term memory? Relevant evidence comes from Keating and Bobbitt's (1978) study of intellectually gifted and intellectually average children's speed of short-term memory scanning (Chapter 1, p. 16). The rate with which average children could scan their short-term memories increased substantially between ages 9 and 17; the rate of gifted children's scanning was already high at age 9 and did not increase further. Thus, it appears that the rate at which most children can examine the contents of their short-term memories increases during late childhood and adolescence, but that gifted children reach mature scanning rates at earlier ages.

Long-term memory processes. There is no reason to think that changes in the capacity of children's long-term memory are a source of development. At all ages, the capacity of long-term memory is for all practical purposes unlimited. When we learn new facts, there is no danger of old ones being evicted.

Information in long-term memory also is surprisingly durable. When people were asked 35 years after graduation to recognize which pictures had been taken of people in their high school class and which were people from another local high school, they correctly recognized 90% of the pictures (Bahrick, Bahrick, & Wittlinger, 1975). The name *long-term memory* thus is a fitting one.

As with sensory and short-term memory, although the capacity of long-term memory seems to be constant across childhood and adolescence, the speed of execution of long-term memory processes appears to increase. Keating and Bobbitt (1978) supplemented their study of short-term memory scanning by examining 9-, 13-, and 17-year-olds' rate of retrieval of information from long-term memory. Their procedure involved two tasks that differed only in that one demanded retrieval of certain information from long-term memory and the other did not. Thus, the added time needed to perform the task that required the retrieval from long-term memory would reflect the time required for the retrieval. If older children retrieve information from long-term memory more rapidly, then the *difference* in the time required to perform the two tasks (the time needed for the extra retrieval) should decrease with age.

Keating and Bobbitt found exactly this pattern. Summed over a number of trials, the 9-year-olds took 7 seconds longer to perform the task that required retrieval of the extra information, the 13-year-olds took 5.5 seconds longer, and the 17-year-olds took 4 seconds longer (Figure 7–2). Thus, the speed of retrieval from long-term memory increases with age.

Two of the most crucial long-term memory processes, recognition and

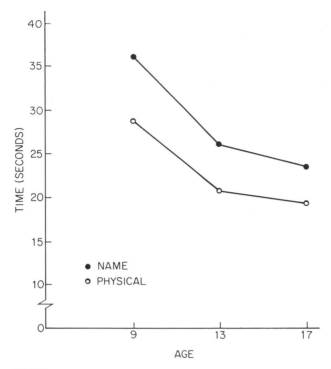

FIGURE 7-2 Times required by 9-, 13-, and 17-year-olds to perform physical-match and name-match tasks. The difference between the times needed to perform the two tasks indicates the amount of time needed to retrieve information from long-term memory. Thus, the smaller difference between the two times for the older children indicates that they needed less time than younger children to retrieve information from long-term memory (data from Keating & Bobbitt, 1978).

association, do not fit very well under either the "absolute capacity" or the "speed of processing" headings. Although their importance remains great throughout life, these processes seem to play especially critical roles in early development. Infants do not possess memory strategies, lack knowledge about the world, and are ignorant of the workings of their own memory. Still, they manage to learn and remember a great deal. Their well-developed abilities to recognize and to associate stimuli with each other may explain much of this early learning.

Recognition. It is difficult even to imagine cognitive development taking place without the ability to recognize. Indeed, recognition is strikingly accurate from early in life. Perlmutter and Lange (1978) noted that 2½-year-olds typically recognize pictures more accurately than adults recall them. People in underdeveloped as well as developed societies recognize proficiently (Cole & Scribner, 1974).

How early are children able to recognize objects as familiar? The visual habituation paradigm can help answer the question. This paradigm, which was introduced in the chapter on perceptual development, is based on the observation that as a picture is shown repeatedly, infants look less and less at it. However, the infants show renewed interest when pictures they recognize as different are shown.

This method has revealed that infants possess some recognitory ability from the day they are born. Even newborn *preterm* infants retain information well enough to prefer a new picture (Werner & Siqueland, 1978). Infants' ability to recognize familiar objects also is surprisingly durable. Even two weeks after they are habituated to a particular form, 2-month-olds continue to prefer a different form (Fantz, Fagan, & Miranda, 1975).

Although all normal infants seem to be born with some ability to recognize objects as familiar, infants differ considerably in how rapidly they show this recognition. These individual differences in rate of recognition may be due to processes similar to those measured on later intelligence tests and may be indicative of early intelligence. How many trials 7-month-olds require to habituate to stimuli is surprisingly closely related to how well the same children will perform on intelligence tests when they are 7-years-old (Fagan & Singer, 1983). Rate of habituation actually seems to better predict later intelligence than do tests specifically designed to measure infant intelligence (Fagan, 1984). Infants who quickly recognize objects would presumably have more time and energy to learn about other aspects of the world. Given the huge number of recognitions that people make every day, even small differences in recognition time could have large effects on learning.

On what basis do infants recognize objects as familiar? To answer this question, Strauss and Cohen (1978) habituated 5-month-olds to an object with a particular form, orientation, size, and color. An example might be a large, black, right-side-up arrow. Later, the infants were shown the original object plus another one that varied in any or all of the attributes. The alternative object could be a white, large, right-side-up arrow. In this example, for the infants to prefer the new object, they would need to remember the color of the original, for this is the only dimension that differentiates the new from the old object.

Immediately after 5-month-olds were shown the original stimulus, they remembered all four attributes. Fifteen minutes later, they remembered only form and color. Twenty-four hours later, they remembered only form. Thus, even though 5-month-olds might remember an object at two different times, they remember it on the basis of fewer and fewer attributes.

Infants demonstrate impressive recognitory abilities, but those of preschoolers are almost incredible. Brown and Scott (1971) presented 4-year-olds with a series of pictures and occasionally stopped and asked whether the child had already seen that one. With intervals as great as 25 pictures, the 4-year-olds correctly recognized 100% of the pictures. These pictures were designed to be as different as possible, thus allowing children to remember on many different bases. In a follow-up experiment, Brown and

Campione (1972) presented preschoolers with a recognition task where the differences between original and novel pictures were more subtle. The two differed only in the pose of the object—for example, a dog running or a dog eating. The recognition test was also delayed further in time—by two hours. Preschoolers still selected the correct pose on 95% of trials.

Young children's recognition abilities are so impressive that they often seem to be equivalent to those of older children and adults. Olson (1976) commented, "A variety of studies have shown either no developmental changes at all or very small ones very early in development. . . . Such experiments argue for viewing picture recognition performance as a basal, developmentally invariant aspect of the memory system" (p. 248).

When the recognition task is made sufficiently difficult, however, older children are better at recognizing than younger ones. Sophian and Stigler (1981) presented preschoolers and adults with artifically constructed faces that differed in one attribute or three. As can be seen in Figure 7–3, the differences between the faces were quite subtle; thus, the recognition task was more difficult than most. Adults recognized 93% of the pictures, preschoolers only 59%. Thus, if the recognition task is sufficiently difficult, age differences in recognition do appear. The lengths that experimenters need to go to reveal such differences, however, attest to the high quality of recognition at all ages.

Association.   The ability to associate stimuli and responses also seems to be present from birth. Siqueland and Lipsitt (1966) set newborns a simple task. If, on hearing the tone, the newborns turned their heads to the right, they received a sweet solution. They received the same soothing liquid if, when a buzzer sounded, they turned their heads to the left. The infants learned to respond correctly very quickly.

Infants also possess the ability to learn in situations where the reinforcement is less tangible than food. Rovee and Fagen (1976) placed a mobile above 3-month-olds' cribs and attached a string from one of their ankles to the mobile. If the infants kicked their legs, the mobile would move in interesting ways.

The infants' rate of kicking quickly increased when they learned that the kicking would make the mobile move. In a later study, 3-month-olds remembered what they had learned for as much as eight days after the initial experience (Sullivan, Rovee-Collier, & Tynes, 1979). When a novel mobile was substituted for the familiar one, the infants at first did not transfer their learning to it. They soon learned to do so, however. The infants seemed to recognize the connection between their kicking and the movement of the new mobile quite suddenly, often dramatically increasing their kicking at some point in the experiment. The apparent suddenness of the change suggested that infants, like adults, may from time to time have insights.

Learning in early infancy does not seem to be limited to literal situa-

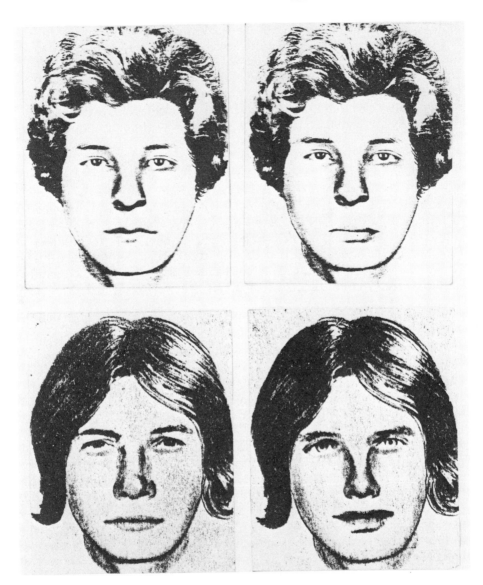

FIGURE 7-3 Examples of pairs of faces differing on one feature (top pair) or three features (bottom pair) (from Sophian and Stigler, 1981. Photo provided courtesy of Dr. Catherine Sophian).

tions; infants can generalize. Rovee and Fagen (1976) found that when they introduced a new mobile, between one and three days after infants learned to kick to move the initial one, the infants kicked less often. In contrast, infants who were not exposed to the new mobile until four days after seeing the original one kicked as much as they had initially. The investigators interpreted this as meaning that in the first few days after exposure to the original mobile, infants remembered both its details and its general characteristics. Noticing the differences between the new mobile and the old one, and being unsure how the new mobile worked, they kicked less often. After four days, however, they forgot the specifics of the previous mobile but remembered its general appearance and function. This led them to respond to the new mobile as they had to the earlier one. Infants, like older children and adults, may rapidly forget details, but their memory for the gist of situations is quite durable.

Infantile amnesia.   If infants can recognize, associate, and learn, why are adults almost never able to remember specific events that happened to them during infancy? We all have many childhood memories, but memories of infancy are extremely rare. Even when people claim to remember early occurrences, for example when under hypnosis, checks on the accuracy of their statements often reveal that they are recalling stories they heard later rather than the actual event. The phenomenon is not limited to human beings; rats also show little recall of events that occurred in their infancy (Spear, 1984).

How might this inability to recall the earliest experiences be explained? The sheer passage of time does not explain it; recall from page 225 people's excellent recognition of pictures of classmates from high school 35 years earlier. Another seemingly plausible explanation, that infants simply do not form enduring memories at this point in development, also is incorrect. Nelson and Ross (1980) demonstrated that 2-year-olds remember for at least a year certain events that happened only once. Nor does Freud's (1905/1953) explanation that infantile amnesia reflects repression of sexually-charged episodes seem likely. While such repression may well occur, people cannot remember any other events from infancy either.

Two other explanations seem more promising. One involves the possibility that a fundamental reorganization of the central nervous system leads to memories formed before the reorganization becoming inaccessible after the reorganization. This view leads to the expectation that animals whose central nervous systems are quite mature at birth, and that therefore would not need to be reorganized, should not show infantile amnesia. In at least one instance, this prediction has proven accurate. Guinea pigs, whose nervous systems are quite mature at birth, remember experiences in the first 2 or 3 days of life as accurately as adult experiences (Kail, 1984). Whether people's central nervous systems undergo any reorganization after birth is unknown, however.

The other likely explanation for infantile amnesia involves the relation between the ways in which infants encode information and the ways in which older children and adults try to retrieve it. Whether people can remember depends critically on the fit between the way in which they earlier encoded the information and the way in which they later attempt to retrieve it. The more of the context that is identical at the times of encoding and retrieval, and the better able the person is to reconstruct the perspective from which he encoded the original material, the more likely it is that recall will be successful (Tulving, 1983).

A variety of factors work against older children's and adult's retrieval efforts closely matching infants' and toddlers' encoding. The spatial perspective of a person who is usually standing up and whose head is five or six feet above the ground is very different from that of a person who is usually lying on the ground and who is only two feet tall even when standing. Older children and adults often try to retrieve the names of things they saw, but infants would not have encoded the information verbally. Time of the day and season of the year are meaningful retrieval cues for adults ("I remember it happened on a warm summer afternoon"), but again are unlikely to closely match the way in which they encoded their experiences when they were infants. These incompatibilities between early encoding and later retrieval efforts are very likely to be at least part of the explanation for infantile amnesia. Whether they are the whole story remains to be seen, though.

Evaluation.   Evaluating the contribution of basic processes to memory development is not a simple task. Depending on the perspective taken, it can legitimately be argued that basic processes contribute to memory development (1) in large and direct ways; (2) little, if at all; or (3) indirectly, but importantly. Below, each perspective is laid out.

First consider the perspective from which basic processes are large and direct contributors to memory development. From the initial days out of the womb, infants can recognize, associate, generalize, and perform other basic processes. These capacities allow them to learn and remember a tremendous amount before they possess strategies, knowledge about their memories, or content knowledge. Without the basic capacities, all other memory activities would have no effect. For example, rehearsing a phone number would be useless if we could not associate the phone number with the person whose number it was. In sum, understanding how basic processes operate is essential to understanding how children's memories work at all ages.

Now consider the perspective from which basic processes appear to contribute little if at all to memory development. The amount of material that children can represent in sensory, short-term, and long-term memory does not appear to change much with age. Thus, *improvements* with age in children's ability to remember cannot be attributed to improvements in the capacity of their memory. Similarly, because recognition is so skillful at early ages, improvements in overall memory functioning cannot be attributed to it. The speed with which children's memory operates does increase with age. The effects of these changes on overall memory proficiency are not as large as might be expected, however. Individual differences in how rapidly people execute basic memory processes have not in general correlated highly with how much they remember (Cooper & Regan, 1982).

That is, children whose basic memory skills operate the most quickly are not necessarily the ones who remember the most. From this perspective, basic processes may be important for memory in general, but contribute little to the development of memory.

Finally, consider a third perspective in which basic processes exert a large but indirect effect on memory development. From this perspective, the main contributions of basic processes to developmental improvements in memory reside in the basic processes allowing children to acquire useful strategies and content knowledge. Within this view, the improved strategies and content knowledge are the direct causes of children's improving memory. Without the basic processes, though, the strategies and content knowledge would never have been learned. Thus, the contribution of basic processes to developmental improvements in memory is seen as absolutely essential but indirect.

Fortunately, there is no need to choose among these three perspectives. Each one holds a considerable amount of truth, and a full appreciation of the contribution of basic processes to memory development requires all three.

The Role of Strategies

Strategies play a large role in memory development. One researcher went so far as to write, "The major reviews of the literature in this area are in essential agreement that differences in memory abilities can so far be ascribed entirely to differences in strategies" (Baron, 1978, pp. 411–412).

One fundamental question concerns exactly what memory strategies are. Naus and Ornstein (1983) defined them as "cognitive or behavioral activities that are under the deliberate control of the subject and are employed so as to enhance memory performance" (p. 12). The crucial aspects of this definition are that strategies involve mental or physical activities, that these activities occur in between presentation of the material that is to be remembered and the act of remembering, that the activities are voluntary, and that they are intended to improve memory for the material. Children use strategies in all phases of memorization: when they encode material, when they store it, and when they retrieve it.

Children's acquisition of these strategies varies with the particular strategy, but, as Waters and Andreasson (1983) noted, certain characteristics are common to the development of all strategies. When children first acquire a memory strategy, they use it in only some of the situations where it is applicable. They limit it to materials where the strategy is easy to use and to situations that are relatively undemanding. They also are quite rigid in applying the strategy and often fail to adapt to changing task demands. All of this changes with development. Older children and children more experienced in using a strategy more actively initiate it; use it in more diverse situations, including ones that make the strategy difficult to execute; use higher-quality versions of the strategy; and become more flexible in tailoring the version of the strategy they use to the particulars of the situation. Below we consider when and how these changes occur for several broadly applicable memory strategies.

Rehearsal. Atkinson and Shiffrin's (1968) emphasis on rehearsal (Chapter 3) suggested that the acquisition of this skill might be crucial for memory development. Consistent with this view, the quantity and quality of rehearsal change greatly during childhood. Children younger than age 6 or 7 years rarely rehearse, whereas children 8 years and older often do.

Rehearsing can be of great use to children. Consider the following incident:

> "A nine-year-old boy memorized the license plate number on a getaway car following an armed robbery, a court was told Monday. . . The boy and his friend . . . looked in the drug store window and saw a man grab a 14-year-old cashier's neck . . . After the robbery, the boys mentally repeated the license number until they gave it to the police."

(*Edmonton Journal*, January 13, 1981, cited in Kail, 1984). Without rehearsing the license number, the boys almost certainly would have forgotten it before they could tell the police.

Why don't children below age 6 or 7 use memory strategies such as rehearsal? An early hypothesis, based on the ideas of Reese (1962), was that the children's not rehearsing represented a *mediational deficiency.* In this view, young children do not rehearse because they cannot effectively regulate their behavior through internal processes like rehearsal. The main alternative, proposed by Flavell (1970), was that children's not rehearsing was due to their simply not knowing how or when to do so (*production deficiency*). The main difference between the positions lay in their predictions as to what would happen if young children somehow could be induced to rehearse. The mediation-deficiency view suggested that it would not help them remember; the production-deficiency view suggested that it would.

In one sense, the controversy was settled early in favor of the production-deficiency position. Five-year-olds could learn to rehearse. When they did so, their recall improved. On the other hand, even when 5-year-olds rehearse, their recall rarely reaches the level of older children's. Their rehearsal also seems to be of lower quality than older children's. Thus, in keeping with the mediation-deficiency position, rehearsal does not do the same thing for them that it does for older children.

Consider some of the evidence for these conclusions. Flavell, Beach, & Chinksy (1966) presented 5- and 10-year-olds with seven pictures and pointed to three of them. Children knew they would need to point to the same pictures in the same order, but had to wait 15 seconds before doing so. Only 10% of the 5-year-olds but 85% of the 10-year-olds moved their lips or repeated the pictures' names aloud in the 15 seconds between when the pictures were presented and when the children were asked to name them. Children who rehearsed recalled more objects than those who did not. When original nonrehearsers were taught to rehearse the words, their recall also improved. Differences between learning-disabled and normal children's recall show a parallel pattern. The learning-disabled children rehearse less often and recall less material, and training them to rehearse leads to improved recall (Torgeson & Goldman, 1977).

The quality of rehearsal continues to improve well beyond the age at which children first rehearse. When presented with a list of words to remember and asked to rehearse aloud, 8-year-olds typically rehearsed each new item in isolation. After hearing the new word *cat*, they would say "cat, cat, cat" (Ornstein, Naus, & Liberty, 1975). Most 13-year-olds, by contrast, combined the past few words with the newly presented one. After hearing *cat*, they said "desk, lawn, sky, shirt, cat." This latter approach led to considerably better later recall.

Young children's rehearsal often continues to be less useful than that of older children, even when both groups receive instructions concerning how to rehearse effectively. To improve the quality of young children's rehearsal, Naus, Ornstein, and Aivano (1977) instructed both 8- and 11-year-olds to use three different items in their rehearsal sets. This reduced but did not eliminate age differences in recall. On closer examination, Naus et al. found that the 11-year-olds continually changed the items they rehearsed, whereas the 8-year-olds regularly included the first two items from the entire set along with the most recently presented item. The younger children's procedure led to excellent recall of the first two members of the set, but not to generally superior recall.

The Flavell et al. (1966) study demonstrated that 5-year-olds could be taught to rehearse, and that when they were their recall improved. Other studies have provided even more dramatic evidence of the potential effectiveness of instruction in rehearsal. For example, providing retarded children with extensive training and practice in rehearsal leads to their recall being as accurate as that of adults with average IQs who have not been trained (Belmont and Butterfield, 1977).

These successes are only half the story, however. Getting young children to generalize their training to new situations has proved much more difficult than getting them to rehearse in the original situation. This is true even if the strategy proved effective in the first case. Keeney, Cannizzo, and Flavell (1967) taught children to rehearse, but the children failed to employ the strategy later when they were not explicitly instructed to use it. Hagen, Hargrove, and Ross (1973) found that when the experimenter stopped prompting children to rehearse, their recall declined to the level of children who never had been taught the strategy.

It is possible to produce some transfer of strategies to new situations, particularly when the new situation is close in time, the same experimenter is present on both occasions, and the experimenter notes improvement in the child's performance and indicates approval of the rehearsal (Kennedy & Miller, 1976). Explicitly telling children when the strategy is useful also helps to produce transfer (Pressley, Forest-Pressley, Elliott-Faust, & Miller, 1985). The difficulty of producing such transfer is notable, however. In sum, young children can learn to rehearse effectively and, if given very careful instruction, will maintain the strategy over time. However, the quality of their strategies is not as high as that of older children, and only the most carefully-planned instruction leads them to use the strategies in new situations.

Organization.   Developmental changes in children's organization of material parallel developmental changes in rehearsal. As with rehearsal, 5-and 6-year-olds use the strategy considerably less often than do 9- and 10-year olds. Also as with rehearsal, the quality of older and younger children's organizations differ. Younger children divide lists into a greater number of categories, each having fewer members. Their categories are less stable, with considerable reorganization often occurring from one trial to the next (Moely, 1977). Again as with rehearsal, normal children use organizational strategies more often than learning-disabled children, and teaching the strategies to the learning-disabled children greatly aids their recall (Dallago & Moely, 1980; Rabinowitz & Chi, 1985).

A final parallel involves learning new strategies. Children as young as 4 or 5 years can learn organizational strategies (Moely, Olson, Halwes, & Flavell, 1969). On the other hand, they often do not transfer the learning to new situations, often fail to use them later even in similar situations, and often organize less effectively than do older children (Williams & Goulet, 1975). Thus, leading children to organize material is not the same as leading them to organize it consistently and effectively.

Children's organization of material raises an issue that goes to the very heart of the question "What is a strategy?" This issue concerns whether procedures that produce organization are always voluntary. Consider two types of behavior that look like identical examples of organization, but that differ in their reason for occurring. One conforms closely to the definition of strategies that was provided earlier in the chapter: a behavioral activity that is "under the deliberate control" of the child. A girl trying to recall a list of words that included hammer, nail, and screw might think, "OK, there were some tools. Was 'hammer' one of them? Yes. What are some other tools? Chisels and nails and screws are tools. Was 'chisel' on the list? No. Was 'nail' on it? Yes. Was 'screw' on it? Yes." The girl's clustering of the tools in recall would be a major source of evidence for the organization that she in fact imposed on the terms.

Now consider a second sequence of behavior, in which only involuntary associations between different members of a category are operating.

Suppose the same girl needed to remember the same list. If she first thought of "hammer," she might next say "nail," because hammers reminded her of nails. Having said "nail," she might next recall "screw" because she associated nails with screws. This use of associations between items does not meet the usual definition of a strategy, because it is not under the child's deliberate control. Behaviorally, however, the clustering in children's recall is identical to that which would be produced if the child had used a strategy.

The confusion of these two similar-looking behavioral patterns is more than a logical possibility. Much of the clustering that young children show seems due to associations between different members of a category rather than to intentional organization. Lange (1973, 1978) was the first to discuss this problem. He noted that young children mainly show clustering in situations in which the words they are memorizing are highly associated with each other. They often only recall category members directly associated with each other. For example, in the category "birds," they might recall robins, blue jays, and sparrows, but rarely ostriches, chickens, and other birds not closely associated with the first birds that come to mind. This pattern is less evident when people proceed from the general category down to the individual category members. Thinking of robins does not usually remind us of ostriches; thinking of birds more often does.

Bjorklund and Zeman (1982) provided a different type of evidence for the same position. On standard recall tasks, 10-year-olds showed greater clustering and greater total recall than 6-year-olds. When asked to remember the names of classmates, however, the 6-year-olds clustered as much and recalled as accurately as the 10-year-olds. Presumably, the interitem associations among the children's representations of their classmates allowed the younger children to cluster their names in recall, even when they did not use a deliberate organizational strategy.

It seems, then, that organization in recall can come about through either involuntary associative mechanisms or voluntary strategic ones. Actually, the situation is probably even more complex than this dichotomy suggests. The very fact that terms are highly associated may make it easier for young children to use voluntary strategies to remember them. Hearing "dog, cat, and lion" may more readily bring to mind the fact that all are animals than hearing "opossum, worm, and fly." High associations among terms, and high associations between individual terms and the category, may make organization in the voluntary strategic sense more likely. The challenging task for the future is to devise new measures of organization that indicate when each process is operating and to explain how automatic and voluntary processes interact.

Elaboration. Elaboration is closely related to organization, but can be used even where no categorical relation exists between the items being remembered. It refers to activities that create connections among two or more items through placing them in a shared activity, relation, or episode. A girl who needed to remember her schoolbook, her lunch, and her arithmetic assignment might form an image of two pieces of bread sandwiching the book, with the book's pages holding the assignment. Such elaborative imagery facilitates recall in a variety of circumstances (Pressley, 1982).

Elaborative images are not the only useful elaborations; elaborative verbal phrases also can be memorable. In my sophomore year in high school, my English teacher told the class to remember what *alliteration* meant by thinking of the phrase "apt alliteration's artful aid." The phrase must have been an effective memory aid for me to have remembered both it and the meaning of *alliteration* for this long.

Elaboration is a relative latecomer among the strategies children use spontaneously; it appears to develop well into adolescence. In one study, 47% of 10-year-olds said they had used elaboration, whereas 94% of 14-year-olds said that they had (Pressley & Levin, 1977). The children and adolescents who said that they had elaborated remembered consistently more than the ones who said they had not.

The quality of older and younger children's uses of elaborative strategies differs in a number of ways. Older children's elaborations are more likely to involve active interactions. Elaborations involving such active elaborations (e.g., "The *lady* flew on a *broom* on Halloween") generally help children more than elaborations involving passive relations ("The *lady* had a *broom*") (Buckhalt, Mahoney, & Paris, 1976; Reese, 1977). Older children also are better at retrieving the elaborations they generate. For example, when 6- and 11-year-olds were taught to elaborate, the 11-year-olds benefited even without being told to think back to the images they earlier had generated, whereas the 6-year-olds needed to be told to recall them (Pressley & Levin, 1980). Finally, older and younger children are differentially influenced by self-generated and experimenter-generated elaborations. Older children benefit more from elaborations that they make up themselves (Reese, 1977); younger ones benefit more from those of the experimenter (Turnure, Buium, & Thurlow, 1976). This may be due to differences in the quality of the elaborations. Older children seem to elaborate in ways particularly meaningful to them, thus leading to superior recall. Younger children often elaborate in obscure or unmemorable ways, thus producing inferior recall.

Despite spontaneous elaboration continuing to increase into the adolescent years, even very young children can benefit from instruction in how to elaborate. Here, however, it is important to distinguish between instruction in verbal elaborations and elaborative images. Children as young as 4 years can connect two terms by a verb or preposition, and they remember more when they do so. However, they do not consistently benefit from instructions to form images depicting similar interactions until roughly age 11 (Pressley, 1982). Pressley attributed the difference to the children needing greater information-processing capacity to represent the images than the verbal phrases, and attaining the required capacity by age 11.

Deployment of cognitive resources.   In the chapter on infants' perceptual development (Chapter 5), a good part of the discussion focused on the determinants of what infants attend to. As noted in that chapter, much of infants' attention has an elicited, involuntary feel to it. Older children's attention, by contrast, has a more planful, selective flavor. With age and experience, children become increasingly able to ignore irrelevant aspects of the environment, to focus clearly on comparatively subtle aspects of problems that happen to be relevant in the particular situation, and to allocate their learning time efficiently.

Hagen and Hale (e.g., 1973) have provided numerous demonstrations of children's developing ability to ignore irrelevant material so that they can more effectively attend to relevant information. In their experiments, children typically are presented with a series of cards, each with two pictures. The experimenter says that one picture on each card is the important one. At the end of the series, the experimenter surprises the children by asking them to recall all of the items, those previously labeled irrelevant as well as those labeled relevant.

It should not be surprising that 14- and 15-year-olds remember more items than 5- and 6-year-olds among those items that the experimenter earlier said were important. It may be more surprising, though, that the older children often remember no more of the items that were said to be unimportant. In some experiments, the older children actually remembered fewer of the "irrelevant" items than the younger children. It seems that a large part of the reason older children remember more of the "important" items is that they focus their attention more completely on them.

Older children are also less at the mercy of the *salience* (perceptual strikingness) of the particular stimuli they are shown. They do what the task calls for, even if the particular context does not make it easy to do so. In one experiment, Odom (1978) presented 4- and 6-year-olds with a version of Piaget's matrix classification task (p. 48). As in the Piagetian task, the matrix included three rows and three columns. Eight of the places were filled in; children needed to infer the contents of the ninth. Some children were presented matrices that differed on two salient dimensions, such as size and color. Other children were presented matrices whose stimuli differed on two less-salient dimensions, such as texture and orientation. When the stimuli differed on dimensions of low salience, the 4-year-olds performed much less well than the older children. However, when the dimensions were highly salient, the 4-year-olds performed nearly as well. The finding was especially striking given the difficulty 4-year-olds usually have on the matrix task. The 4-year-olds' ability to solve these matrix tasks, but not more typical ones, suggests that their frequent failures on other matrix tasks stem from difficulty in focusing on nonsalient dimensions, rather than from inability to simultaneously consider two dimensions, as Piaget had suggested (Chapter 2, p. 36).

Perhaps the most frequent use children make of memory strategies is in deciding what and how much to study. Not surprisingly, children deploy their cognitive resources in studying increasingly effectively with age and experience in school. Flavell, Friedrichs, and Hoyt (1970) asked 4- to 10-year-olds to memorize the pictures that appeared in each of 10 windows. In order to see the picture in a given window, the child needed to press a button that would uncover it for as long as the button was held down. The duration of the button press provided an index of the time each child spent studying each picture. In general, older children spent more time studying than younger ones. They engaged in a greater variety of strategies, such as naming pictures, rehearsing the names, and testing themselves. Each of these activities was associated with greater recall.

Allocating study time is a tricky business. Consider just the dilemma posed in studying for later examinations after receiving the results of earlier ones. Is the best strategy to concentrate primarily on the topics that caused the most errors earlier, or is it better to distribute study time over other topics as well? Focusing on the material that you didn't remember should help performance there, but might lead to worse performance than previously on the material you were able to recall. On the other hand, spending time reviewing the material you already remembered might be a waste of time.

Not surprisingly, children who are just learning to study have difficulty making these choices. In one study where children were given a chance to study after performing partially correctly on an initial memory test (Masur, McIntrye, & Flavell, 1973), 7- and 9-year-olds took different paths. The 9-year-olds focused on the items they had not remembered; the 7-year-olds distributed their attention more widely. The 9-year-olds' strategy sounds more sophisticated, but in fact it did not help them. Those children who focused on the previously missed items did no better on a later test than those who reviewed a broader range of items. Apparently the items they forgot between the first and second testings canceled out the items that they previously had not remembered but later learned.

How do children learn to deploy cognitive resources effectively? It seems that a large part of the answer is that parents lead them through tasks by at first doing the most difficult parts of the task for the children and gradually passing responsibility on to them. Parents seem quite sensitive to what children do and do not understand. They try to have children execute some components of the task that they already can do and others that they are just on the edge of acquiring (Rogoff, Ellis, & Gardner, 1984). They model correct procedures. They also encourage children to verbalize what they are doing; this practice helps the parents keep track of their children's understanding and helps the children remember how to execute the procedure themselves (Price, 1984). Facility in these instructional activities itself seems to grow with age and experience; adults are considerably superior to 9-year-olds, for example, in teaching 7-year-olds to remember new problem-solving strategies (Ellis & Rogoff, 1982). Thus, through a combination of modeling effective procedures, direct verbal instruction, focusing the child's attention on tasks that are a moderate distance beyond their current competence, and encouraging children to verbalize what they are doing, parents help children to deploy cognitive resources effectively.

Evaluation. Age-related improvements in both how often strategies are used and in their quality seem to be quite important in helping children remember. Older children use memory strategies more frequently than younger ones, with the greatest changes occurring between ages 5 and 10. Use of the strategies has a large beneficial effect on children's ability to remember in many situations. Children younger than those who generally use strategies spontaneously can learn them, though such learning often fails to generalize over time and to new tasks. Finally, we understand some of the ways in which strategies contribute to memory development. Part of the improvement resides in children using more effective versions of the strategies (e.g., rehearsing more different items). An additional part resides in children's execution of the procedures becoming automatized and thus allowing them to adjust more finely their strategies to meeting task demands. Yet another part may arise through older children's greater content knowledge making it easier for them to use strategies in more contexts.

All of this evidence suggests that heightened use of memory strategies plays an important role in memory development. This role probably is largest for improvements beyond age 5. Memory improvements before age 5 must have other origins, since preschoolers rarely use memory strategies.

One of the more intriguing findings about memory strategies was that training children to use such strategies was no guarantee of their continued use. This raises the question, "How do they decide which strategy to use?" Children are often quite sensible about these decisions. For example, when the previously presented items remain visible, 8- to 11-year-olds use high quality versions of rehearsal in which they rehearse many different items. When the previous items are not visible, they adopt the lower quality but easier-to-execute strategy of rehearsing one item at a time (Guttentag & Ornstein, 1985). One possibility is that children use their understanding of their own memory processes—their metamemory—to make these decisions. This possibility is examined in the next section.

The Role of Metamemory

A good reader proceeds smoothly and quickly as long as his understanding of the material is complete. But as soon as he senses that he has missed an idea, that the track has been lost, he brings smooth progress to a grinding halt. Advancing more slowly, he seeks clarification in the subsequent material, examining it for the light it can throw on the earlier trouble spot. If still dissatisfied with his grasp, he returns to the point where the difficulty began and rereads the section more carefully. (Whimbey, 1975, p. 91)

This is what skilled readers do. Young and poor readers proceed differently. In one study, 9- to 15-year-olds read passages and later needed to recall information from them, much as would happen in a classroom. Older children were significantly more likely than younger ones to reread the passage when they could not recall the information needed to answer the question (Garner & Reis, 1981). Further, at each particular age, children who generally were good comprehenders were significantly more likely than those who generally were poor comprehenders to look back to help them remember.

The type of knowledge involved in the decision to look up material that cannot be recalled is known as *metamemory*. Metamemory is defined as knowledge about memory—knowledge about its fallibility, about strategies for overcoming its limits, about the effects of the passage of time, about when you are not understanding, and about how to construct new strategies when existing ones prove inadequate, among other things. The main questions about each of these are what children know at various ages and how what they know influences their overall memory functioning.

Brown, Bransford, Ferrara, and Campione (1983) noted that children have two basic types of knowledge about memory. They have explicit, conscious, factual knowledge about it: For example, they are consciously aware that short lists of words are easier to remember than long lists. They also have implicit knowledge, which they may not even know they have, about how to monitor and regulate memory. This implicit knowledge is like the counting principles discussed in Chapter 1, in that the knowledge guides children's performance without them being aware of it. For example, the good reader in the above quotation could have been completely unaware of his reducing his reading rate when he did not understand. Still, the fact that he slowed down reveals implicit knowledge that slowing down is a good way to improve comprehension when material is difficult. Below we examine both children's explicit knowledge of facts about memory and their implicit knowledge, revealed when they effectively regulate their memory activity.

Factual knowledge about memory. Kreutzer, Leonard, and Flavell (1975) posed children perhaps the most basic question concerning factual knowledge about memorial limitations: "Do you forget?" Almost all children beyond first grade indicated that they at times did forget. However, a substantial minority of 5-year-olds (30%) denied that they ever did.

With age, children also become more realistic about how much they are likely to remember. When 4-year-olds were asked how many of ten pictures they could remember, more than half of them thought they could remember all ten (Flavell, Friedrichs, & Hoyt, 1970). In fact, none could remember this many. Other studies also have found that young children consistently overestimate their memory capacity (Cavanaugh & Perlmutter, 1982). In this respect, young children resemble adults who are beginners in an area. Adults who are novices at chess greatly overestimate their memory for positions of chess pieces, just as young children often do in situations that are unfamiliar to them (Chi, 1978).

Wellman (1983) suggested that children's factual knowledge about memory is more than a collection of individual beliefs about which tasks are most difficult, which strategies are most effective, and which people are the best at remembering. Even in the preschool period, when children do not have a great deal of factual knowledge about memory, they organize their individual ideas into theories of how memory, and in particular their memory, operates. One way in which these theories are apparent is in children's beliefs about the nature of the mind and the brain. Five-year-olds are aware that the brain is involved in thinking, knowing, remembering, and being smart (Johnson & Wellman, 1982). They are less convinced that it is involved in specific cognitive activities such as writing, spelling, and talking, though they are more likely to believe it is involved in each of these than in simple motor or perceptual acts. The majority of 8-year-olds know that the brain is involved in all of these activities.

Johnson and Wellman also found that children gradually differentiate between the mind and the brain. At age 6 or 7, they think that the mind and the brain are very similar; whatever activities the one is involved in, so is the other. By early adolescence, they view the brain as being involved in almost all behaviors, including simple motor and perceptual activities, but view the mind as only being involved in intellectual ones. This differentiation probably reflects a realization that thinking stems from the same biological base as many other human capabilities (thus the increasingly adequate descriptions of what the brain does), but also that our culture sets apart intellectual activities and categorizes them under the heading of "the mind."

Regulation and monitoring of cognitive activities.   The very frequency with which we are aware that we don't understand testifies to the fact that we often monitor our ongoing understanding. Yet, as anyone who ever has tried to assemble model airplanes or to learn new games from the instructions can attest, it is often hard to know whether we are understanding or not. Markman (1979) demonstrated this experimentally. Children between ages 8 and 11 heard passages containing self-contradictory information, such as the following description of how to make Baked Alaska:

> To make it they put the ice cream in a very hot oven. The ice cream in Baked Alaska melts when it gets that hot. Then they take the ice cream out of the oven and serve it right away. When they make Baked Alaska, the ice cream stays firm and does not melt. (p. 656)

Almost half of the 8- to 11-year-olds who listened to the story did not note the contradictions about the ice cream's melting and not melting, even when asked, "Did everything make sense?" Even when warned in advance that there were problems with the story, many 8-year-olds did not detect the contradictions. This was not due to the children not remembering the story. They could repeat it quite accurately. Markman explained the findings by suggesting that children often concentrate on the reasonableness of each statement, rather than on whether they make sense as a group.

Although 10- and 11-year-olds do not always adequately monitor their comprehension and their memory, even young preschoolers show some skill at monitoring. Recall the feeling-of-knowing experiments described in Chapter 3 (p. 69). Adults could predict whether they knew a word that fit a particular definition, even if they could not remember the word itself (e.g., *sextant*). Cultice, Somerville, and Wellman (1983) showed that preschoolers have similar abilities. Shown photographs of adults, 4- and 5-year-olds could predict whether they later would recognize the name of the person in the photograph even if they could not recall it at the time.

Children's monitoring of their cognitive states does not respect any boundary between memory, language, and perception. Their ability to monitor their perceptual impressions and to compare them with prior information stored in long-term memory is evident in their ability to distinguish between appearance and reality. Flavell, Flavell, and Green (1983) presented 4- and 5-year-olds with certain imitation objects, such as a spongelike object that looked just like a rock. The children were encouraged to play with the objects so that they knew the objects were not what they appeared to be. Then they were asked questions aimed at seeing whether they distinguished between what the objects looked like and what they "really, really were." The children were asked similar questions about the objects' color and size. Here, they viewed the objects through a blue plastic sheet or through a magnifying glass.

The majority of 4- and 5-year-olds could distinguish between what the object currently looked like and what its identity, color, and size really were. The children's errors also showed an interesting pattern. When they erred on the object's identity, they usually made the mistake of thinking that it didn't look like what it was (they would say that the toy rock did not look like a real rock, though it did). When they erred on the color and size of the objects, their most common mistake was to think that the color and size were what they seemed to be when viewed through the colored plastic and magnifying glass (they thought the rock really was blue). Children in China make the same types of errors (Flavell, Zhang, Zou, Dong, & Qi, 1983). Flavell and his colleagues explained the differing errors by pointing to the nature of children's experiences with qualities of objects and with the objects' identities. Qualities of objects, such as size and color, often change; given the way in which light and color are perceived, the children's view that the rock really is blue is not entirely off base. On the other hand, aside from magic shows and television, children have no experience with one object becoming another. It may be difficult for them to suppress what they know about an object's identity to consider objectively what it looks like.

Other evidence of young children's ability to monitor their cognitive functioning comes from their use of language. From age 2 onward, children spontaneously correct their pronunciation, their grammar, and the names they attach to objects. They also comment on their own and others' use of language, and adjust their language to the listener's knowledge and general cognitive level. Clark (1978) reviewed numerous experimental demonstrations of such competence. To these, I can add several anecdotes about my then 2-½-year-old daughter. One night she told me, "You're a 'he,' Todd's a 'he,' and girls are 'she's.'" Two weeks later, she encountered difficulty pronouncing the word *hippopotamus* and explained, "I can't say it because I can't make my mouth move the right way." Thus, despite the difficulty that even 11-year-olds encounter monitoring some of their understandings, even 2-year-olds are able to monitor others.

Why some children are skilled in choosing procedures for remembering and others are not is of fundamental importance for understanding memory development. One appealing possibility is that children's increasing knowledge about memory and about the general cognitive system leads them to think and remember more and more effectively. Evidence for this intuitively reasonable position has been surprisingly long in coming. Early investigations revealed little support for it. In some studies, children's knowledge about their memories were only weakly related to their memory performance. In others, there was some relation, but only a weak one (Markman, 1973; Moynahan, 1973; Salatas & Flavell, 1976).

Several factors might contribute to these weak relations between factual knowledge about memory and memory performance. Consider just one aspect of the problem—why children who knew that a strategy was useful might not use it in a particular situation. They might know that the strategy was useful but think that some other strategy was superior in the particular situation. They might know that the strategy was useful but judge the task sufficiently simple to perform without it. They might know abstractly that the strategy was useful but not be very good at executing it. Under such circumstances, they might not even try to use it. Finally, they might know that the strategy was useful, recognize its utility for the situation, and be skilled in using it, but simply decide that it wasn't worth the bother. Flavell and Wellman (1977) termed this the "original sin" hypothesis.

More detailed assessment of children's knowledge about memory, including their beliefs about what strategies cause them to remember better, may be the key to finding connections between metamemory and strategy use. This was the implication of a recent study by Fabricius and Hagen (1984). They created a situation in which 6- and 7-year-olds sometimes would use an organizational strategy to help them remember and sometimes would not do so. The nature of the materials the children were memorizing was such that the organizational strategies would almost always improve their recall. Although all children had the opportunity to make this observation, only some of them saw it this way. Others attributed their success not to the organizational strategies but instead to their looking longer, using their brain, slowing down, and so on. The children's attributions accurately predicted whether they used an organizational strategy a week later when they were in a different situation with a different experimenter. Fully 90% of the children who earlier attributed their success to use of the organizational strategy used the strategy on the second occasion. Only 32% of children who thought other factors responsible for their earlier success used the organizational strategy in the later session.

Evaluation.   Children's understanding of their own memories is at the same time both an intriguing topic and a frustrating one. Some of its appeal lies in the interesting aspects of children's thinking that it leads us to consider—children's understanding of the difference between appearance and reality, for example. An additional part lies in the plausibility of its central premise—that what children know about their memories influences how they attempt to remember. Yet another part lies in the potential benefits of teaching children metamnemonic skills and thereby improving their performance in school. A number of promising attempts to improve the educational performance of retarded children and low achievers, particularly in the area of reading, emphasize the importance of the children acquiring metamnemonic skills (Baker & Brown, 1984; Borkowski, 1980; Kendall, Borkowski, & Cavanaugh, 1980; Palincsar & Brown, 1984; Paris & Myers, 1981; Pressley, Borkowski, & O'Sullivan, in press).

The frustrating part becomes apparent when we try to determine whether children's metamemory actually does play a large role in the typical course of memory development. Their knowledge about memory definitely improves with age, particularly in the period after the preschool years. The relation of the knowledge to their memory performance has proved far from straightforward, however. As Wellman (1983) noted, "There is no question but that some sorts of knowledge about memory figure strongly into some sorts of memory performances, and that this changes with age. Exactly how, where, and when metamemory does and does not play what role is relatively uncharted territory" (p. 49). As this statement suggests, both the conditions under which children's metamemory influences their memory performance and the mechanisms by which it does so remain unclear.

A large part of the difficulty goes back to the lack of a precise definition of what *metamemory* is. Knowledge about memory, the standard definition of the term, can include a huge range of types of knowledge. The clearest cases involve statable, conscious facts about memory and planfully undertaken memory strategies. For example, knowing that writing down phone numbers is useful in remembering them, and thinking, "I'll forget this number if I don't write it down; I'd better get a piece of paper and a pen" easily falls within the metamemory category. Many activities classified under the heading "metamemory" are quite different from this example, though. Even brief expressions of puzzlement on the face of a 5-year-old hearing confusing instructions can be taken as evidence of metamemory operating, despite the 5-year-old later saying the instructions were entirely clear (Flavell, Speer, Green, & August, 1981). Note that such expressions of puzzlement are almost certainly not planful, statable, or conscious. Nor do they directly involve either facts about memory or strategies. The point is not that the expressions of puzzlement do not reflect metacognitive knowledge—in important senses they do—but that the mechanisms that produce them may be quite different from the ones that produce children's view that writing down phone numbers is a good way to remember them. Thus, the lack of a firm definition of what metamemory is may account for the difficulty in saying how it works and when it influences children's attempts to remember.

What can be done about this problem? Brown, Bransford, Ferrara, and Campione (1983) suggested one attractive solution. Simply accept that statable, factual, conscious knowledge of memory may be unrelated to monitoring and regulation of memory activities, and then think about them separately. This possibility seems interesting not only because of the differences in the natures of these two types of knowledge, but also because they may contribute most to memory development at very different times in childhood. Monitoring and regulation of memory may contribute from early in development, whereas factual knowledge may contribute primarily in late childhood and adolescence. Some of the largest general differences between children and adolescents seem to be in their ability to make realistic estimates of their abilities, in their seeing clearly what new problems demand of them, and in their general planfulness. Perhaps children do not use their factual knowledge of memory much when they first acquire it, but rather wait until these more general qualities arise in them, during late childhood and early adolescence, to use it. Although relations between adolescents' metamnemonic knowledge and their memory performance have not received much attention, they may provide the key to understanding where metamemory fits into memory development.

Whatever the eventual distinctions that researchers make, children's knowledge of their memories seems not only interesting but practically important as well. In the discussion of children's reading in Chapter 9, we will encounter a remarkably successful training program initiated by Palincsar and Brown (1984) to teach poor readers to understand better what they are reading. The program teaches them to effectively monitor their comprehension while reading. Anything that works as well as this program does is well worth learning more about.

The Role of Content Knowledge

Almost everyone has noted at one time or another how much easier it is to remember new information when we already possess related information.

Since older children know more than younger ones about almost everything, they might be expected to be better at remembering from this greater knowledge alone, even if they did not differ in any other way relevant to memory. Prior knowledge of related content affects memory in several ways. First, it influences how much children recall. Second, it influences *what* they recall. Third, age-related differences in measures of basic capacities and strategies may be attributable to changes in content knowledge. Fourth, under some circumstances, differences in content knowledge outweigh all other age-related differences. Fifth, formation of networks of associations and improved encoding may be two mechanisms through which content knowledge influences children's memory for new material. Evidence concerning each of these contentions is discussed below.

Effects of content knowledge on how much and what children recall. The fact that older children regularly recall more than younger ones may in large part be due to the older children knowing more about the material they are trying to remember. When younger children are as familiar as older ones with what they are trying to recall (names of school teachers and television characters), they at times remember just as much (Lindberg, 1980).

If content knowledge influences memory, then detailed analyses of what people already know should help us anticipate what form their memories will take. Spilich, Vesonder, Chiesi, and Voss (1979) addressed this issue by studying people's memory for baseball games. First they considered what a person knowledgeable about baseball might know. As shown in Table 7–2, their analysis stressed *setting events*, which define the immediate situation, and *goals*, ranging from the top level of winning the game to the bottom level of avoiding strikes and accumulating balls. More knowledgeable people were hypothesized to differ from less knowledgeable ones primarily in their understanding of these setting events and goals.

Spilich et al. compared what college students high and low in baseball knowledge remembered about a game. As expected, the knowledgeable students recalled more information, especially the most important information. They were most likely to recall events relevant to goals at the top of the hierarchy and least likely to recall information at the lowest levels. In contrast, the less knowledgeable students recalled unimportant information as often as important information. They actually recalled a greater number of actions that were irrelevant to the progress of the game than did their more knowledgeable peers.

The two groups also erred in different ways. Unknowledgeable students often recalled sequences inconsistent with the rules of baseball, such as the first batter of an inning hitting into a double play. Those knowledgeable about baseball never made such errors. Instead, they tended to substitute one plausible detail for another. It is not hard to imagine why knowledgeable people's memory for new material takes the shape it does. Existing knowledge provides a framework for organizing new information,

TABLE 7-2 Baseball Knowledge Structure (from Spilich, Vesonder, Chiesi, & Voss, 1979)

SETTING

General:	Teams playing, team at bat, team in field, inning, miscellaneous conditions
Specific:	Relevant: teams' records as related to goal structure, players' records as related to goal structure Irrelevant: team attributes, player attributes
Enabling:	Batter at bat and pitcher ready to pitch

GOAL STRUCTURE

LEVEL	TEAM AT BAT	VARIABLES	VALUES	TEAM IN FIELD
1	Winning game	Game outcome	Win—lose	Winning game
2	Scoring runs	Score	Domain of game scores	Preventing runs from scoring
3	Getting runners on base and advancing runners	Pattern of base runners	Eight possible patterns	Preventing runners from getting on base or advancing by making outs
		Outs	0, 1, 2, 3	
4	Having "Balls,"	"Balls"	0, 1, 2, 3, 4	Getting "Strikes,"
	Avoiding "Strikes"	"Strikes"	0, 1, 2, 3	Avoiding "Balls"

NONGAME ACTIONS

Relevant nongame actions

Irrelevant nongame actions

serves as a base against which to check the plausibility of recalled sequences, and facilitates inferences about future events.

Like the adults who were knowledgeable about baseball, children regularly draw inferences that go beyond the information they are given. For example, when young children heard a story about a helpless creature with a broken wing, they had no trouble identifying the creature as a bird, despite this information never having been stated literally in the story (Paris, 1975). With age and increased knowledge, children draw a greater number and variety of inferences (Paris & Lindauer, 1977), but the basic inference-drawing capability is almost certainly an innate part of children's thinking. Note that drawing inferences is closely related to memory focusing on the gist of events rather than the details. Inferences are formed to fill in gaps and to make events coherent—that is, so there will be a gist to remember.

In perhaps the most controversial experiment that has ever been performed on memory development, Piaget and Inhelder (1973) reported that with appropriate changes in children's knowledge, their memory for a previous event can become more accurate, rather than less accurate, with the passage of time. Five- to 8-year-olds saw a row of sticks, ordered from shortest to longest, and tried to remember the row in preparation for a later recall test. A week later, the children were asked to draw the row of sticks they had seen. Six to eight months later, the test was repeated.

Surprisingly, children's reproductions actually were more accurate on the second testing than on the first. That is, they were more likely to draw a correctly ordered row half a year after they saw the original row than a week after they saw it.

Liben (1975) suggested that the improvement might be due to children better understanding the idea of ordering rather than to their better remembering the initial configuration of sticks. To test this hypothesis, she asked children to imagine and draw ten sticks standing up straight in a row, without their having seen any row previously. Older children's drawings were ordered according to size much more often than those of younger children. 5-year-olds drew ordered rows on 19% of trials, while 8-year-olds did so on 82%. Thus, the improvement that Piaget and Inhelder observed over the six-month period between their two tests may not have stemmed from improved memory for the original situation, but rather from better understanding of the idea of ordering.

The children's performance is most interesting for the questions it raises about the nature of memory. By most definitions of memory, it is logically impossible for an internal representation of an event to improve over time. If children do not store information in memory initially, they cannot retrieve it later. From this viewpoint, children in the Piaget and Inhelder experiment may simply have been inferring what the row probably looked like rather than remembering. it. On the other hand, Piaget and Inhelder distinguished between two types of memory. One was memory in the strict sense, which they defined as memory for the attributes of stimuli shown in the particular situation. The other was memory in the wider sense, defined as the operation of intelligence and knowledge on new and old information. They argued that memory in the wider sense inevitably influences memory in the strict sense; all remembering that we do involves both memory for literal details and also inferences and abstractions. Given the inherent importance of inferences and of memory for gist in people's remembering, Inhelder and Piaget's position becomes increasingly plausible the longer it is considered (see Liben, 1977, for a more extensive analysis that reaches a similar conclusion).

Content knowledge as an explanation for other memory changes.
Changes in basic capacities and strategies often are used to explain age-related improvements in children's ability to acquire specific content knowledge. This equation can be reversed, however. Increasing knowledge of specific content may contaminate supposedly pure measures of memory capacity, thus creating a false impression that the basic capacity has changed. In addition, increasing content knowledge may make possible the acquisition of more advanced strategies by freeing processing resources.

Huttenlocher and Burke (1976) suggested that apparent increases in basic capacities, such as the absolute capacity of short-term memory, may actually come from changing content knowledge. Their argument was based on two assumptions. First, they assumed that both children and adults have limited attentional resources, which determine the capacity of their short-term memory. Second, they assumed that the more people know about an item, the less attention they require to keep that item in short-term memory. Given these two assumptions, whenever young children know less than older ones about the material they are trying to remember, they would be expected to remember less well. Even if their total attentional resources were as great, they would need to expend more attention on each item, which would not allow the attention to be distibuted over as many items, which would lead to lower apparent memory capacity.

Greater content knowledge also may help older children learn and use new memory strategies. Chi (1981) provided relevant evidence. She examined a 5-year-old's learning of an alphabetic retrieval strategy for her classmates' names (first think if any names start with *A*; then think if any names start with *B*; etc.). Although the strategy was novel, the girl learned it and applied it to recalling her classmates' names rather easily. However, the same girl could not apply the alphabetic strategy to remembering a set of names of people she had never met.

These results may hold an important implication for how children learn to use new strategies. Early in the acquisition process, they may be able to employ strategies effectively only on familiar content. Practice using the strategies with the familiar content may lead to execution of the strategies becoming automatized and making fewer demands on the children's processing resources. This automatization, in turn, could allow children to apply the strategies to more demanding, unfamiliar contents. Thus, the familiar contents may serve as a kind of practice field upon which children can exercise emerging cognitive skills such as new memory strategies.

Age versus knowledge.   Chi (1978) provided the most dramatic demonstration to date of how greatly content knowledge can influence children's memory proficiency. Both in its drama and in its basic message, the study closely resembles the study of S. F., the cross-country runner who could remember 75 unrelated numbers. Chi's study involved a comparison of the memory abilities of two groups: 10-year-olds and adults. Both groups were tested on two tasks. One was a standard digit-span task; the other was a chess reproduction task, which involved seeing an arrangement of pieces on a board (a position from an actual game between two good players) and then needing to reproduce the arrangement from memory. By now you may have guessed that the 10-year-olds were not a random sample of children; they all belonged to a chess club and were very good players.

The findings were simple but striking; the 10-year-olds reproduced the chess configurations more accurately than the adults did. These findings were not attributable to the children being generally smarter or possessing better memories. On the digit-span task, the adults, as usual, were superior. The point is that differences in content knowledge can outweigh all other memorial differences between children and adults.

How does content knowledge aid memory?   Content knowledge clearly influences what and how much children remember, but how does it do so? Two mechanisms seem likely to be of major importance. One involves formation of networks of associations that link different entities and qualities to each other. The other involves encoding of distinctive features.

We already have discussed the role of associations in several contexts in this chapter. They emerged as important in producing strategic-looking behavior in situations where children do not seem to be using strategies under voluntary control (Bjorklund & Zeman, 1982; Lange, 1973). They also were important in allowing younger children to remember as much as older ones in situations where the younger children possessed equal numbers of associations for the items they were trying to remember (Richman, Nida, & Pittman, 1976).

Chi and Koeske (1983) provided additional evidence in an especially interesting context. They studied a 5-year-old budding dinosaur expert. Many young children are fascinated by dinosaurs, but this particular boy knew more than most. He could name 40 types of dinosaurs and owned nine books about them, with which he was intimately familiar. His mother spent an average of three hours per week reading him these books.

How would it be possible to get inside the boy's head to find out how his knowledge of dinosaurs was organized? Chi and Koeske used two procedures to do so. First, on six separate occasions, the boy was asked to name all the dinosaurs he knew. The dinosaurs the boy consistently clustered together in recall were viewed as being organized into a group in his memory. Second, the boy played a game with the experimenter, in which she named two or three traits of a dinosaur, and he guessed which dinosaur it was.

Based on what they learned about the boy's knowledge of dinosaurs, the investigators developed a semantic network model of what he knew (recall the discussion of semantic networks in Chapter 4). Part of this model is shown in Figure 7-4. One main part of the representation is the particular dinosaurs. As can be seen in the figure, Chi and Koeske hypothesized that the child divided these dinosaurs into two main categories: armored dinosaurs (the group on the bottom left part of the figure) and giant plant eaters (the group at the top right). Links between a pair of dinosaurs indicate that the child recalled the pair in order on at least one of the six occasions; the more links, the more times the child showed that ordering.

Another main part of the representation is the qualities of the dinosaurs. The qualities named in Figure 7-4 are the clues that were effective in the second game in helping the boy figure out which dinosaur the experimenter had in mind. These qualities are indicated in small letters. The *di* in the middle of the figure is particularly interesting. It indicates that a number of dinosaurs shared a particular diet and that this diet was a useful cue to all of their identities. Thus, this diet seems to be a key part of the boy's representation of this subset of dinosaurs.

Chi and Koeske hypothesized that the boy would be most adept at remembering dinosaurs that were associated strongly with other dinosaurs and their properties. The boy's recall of dinosaurs from a list that the experimenter presented supported this prediction. He remembered more of the dinosaurs on the list that had many links to other dinosaurs than of the dinosaurs that had few such links.

Thus, the boy's existing knowledge made understandable not only how many dinosaurs he remembered but which specific ones he recalled. It also suggested a plausible learning mechanism. If he encountered a new dinosaur in his reading, he could relate it to the dinosaurs he already knew about, could infer many of its properties from his knowledge of theirs, and could contrast its unique features to theirs. He also could later remember the new dinosaur by first recalling the better-known ones associated with it. These processes would make it easier for the boy to learn about new dinosaurs than it would be for a child who had less existing knowledge about them.

In addition to linking related entities to each other, children must learn to distinguish between similar but separate entities. Learning the most efficient basis for making such distinctions helps children remember, because

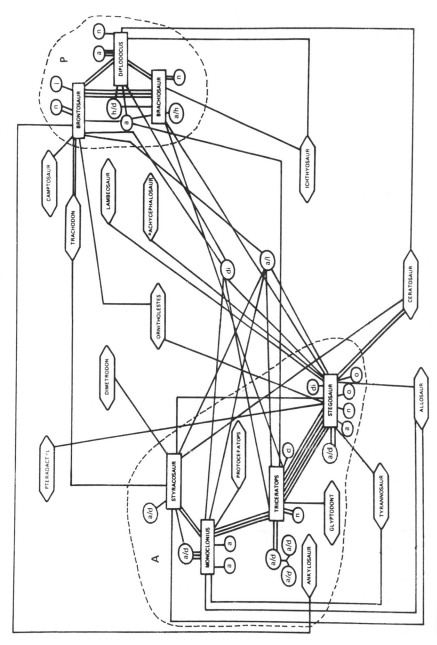

FIGURE 7-4 Semantic network representation of a 5-year-old's knowledge about dinosaurs. Those in the *A* group are armored. Those in the *P* group are giant plant eaters. Multiple lines between dinosaurs indicate especially close connections. Small letters connected to dinosaur names indicate known traits: *a* = appearance, *d* = defense mechanism, *di* = diet, *n* = nickname, *h* = habitat, *l* = locomotion (from Chi & Koeske, 1983).

they do not need to represent as much information and because the information they do represent will be useful for retrieving the material. Perhaps the prototypic case for thinking about how children identify such distinctive features arises in reading. Letters of the alphabet closely resemble each other. When seen on a standard page of a book, all are black, stationary, close together, and about the same height and width. To imagine the situation from the young child's perspective, visualize how hieroglyphics look when you see them in a museum.

Letters of the Standard (Roman) alphabet can be distinguished from each other by the presence or absence of a small number of critical features. Three examples of these features are whether the letter includes a vertical segment, whether it includes a curve, and whether it is symmetrical. Illustratively, *H* differs from *F* in that *H* is symmetrical around both horizontal and vertical axes, while *F* is not symmetrical around either. In addition, *F* has two horizontal lines while *H* has two vertical ones. (Note the similarity of this featural analysis to the one applied to the terms *big, small, tall, short, deep,* and *shallow* in the language development chapter.)

Do children use these critical features to distinguish among the letters? Gibson, Schapiro, & Yonas (1968) found evidence that they do. The investigators presented 7-year-olds with pairs of letters on a screen. The children needed to indicate as quickly as possible whether the letters were identical or different. Gibson et al. reasoned that if the children used the critical features, they would more quickly judge as dissimilar the pairs of letters that differed on many of them. Letters were chosen from among the set *CGPTROMNW*.

The distinctive-feature prediction was accurate. Letters that differed on many features, such as *G* and *W* or *W* and *T*, were judged different more rapidly than seemingly similar letters, such as *P* and *R* or *O* and *Q*.

Gibson and her colleagues used a statistical technique known as hierarchical cluster analysis to determine which features the 7-year-olds used to discriminate among letters. As shown in Figure 7–5, the first division that children made, reflected in the top division in the tree diagram, was whether the letter included a curved segment. They quickly distinguished all letters that included curved segments from all letters that lacked such segments.

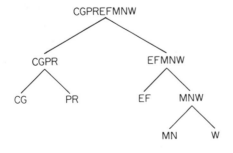

FIGURE 7–5 Letters 7-year-olds most easily discriminate from each other. Divisions closer to the top of the tree indicate easier discriminations (data from Gibson, Schapiro, & Yonas, 1968).

Within the set of letters that had curves, children distinguished those letters that also had a straight line from those that did not. Within the set of letters that lacked a curve, children discriminated those letters that included a diagonal line from those that did not. Finally, within the set of letters that lacked a curve but included a diagonal line, children discriminated those that included vertical lines from those that did not.

Sometimes the physical appearances of objects lead children to hone in quickly on the distinctive features, even if they do not know anything about the objects. In other cases, learning is necessary before they discover the distinctive features. The alphabet seems to fall into the latter category. Nodine and Steurle (1973) examined the eye movements of 5-year-olds who did not know how to read and of 6-year-olds who did. They found that the 6-year-olds focused more often on the distinctive features of letters. This focusing helped them to memorize sequences of letters more rapidly. Thus, encoding of distinctive features, as well as formation of networks of associations, can aid memory.

Evaluation. Increased content knowledge seems to explain a great deal about why older children remember more effectively than younger ones. It meets several basic standards for a good explanation of memory development: It clearly increases with age and is clearly related to how well children remember, as was evident in the studies of memory for chess and for dinosaurs. Improved content knowledge also suggests several plausible mechanisms that would lead to older children's superior memory. It provides a network within which they can place new information, serves as a check on the plausibility of their memories for particular events, facilitates their drawing of inferences, and helps them encode distinctive features. The growth of content knowledge also may partially account for the development of other competencies that have been proposed as explanations of memory development such as basic capacities and memory strategies. Much remains to be learned about how content knowledge helps children remember, but it seems more than likely that such knowledge is a major source of memory development.

What develops when in memory development? Early in this chapter I suggested that different aspects of memory might not only contribute different amounts to memory development but also might make their greatest contributions at different times. Table 7–3 summarizes the types of contributions to memory growth that basic capacities, strategies, metamemory, and content knowledge appear to make during three periods of development: birth through age 5, ages 5 through 10, and ages 10 through 15.

Many basic capacities, such as the ability to recognize familiar objects and to associate objects with each other, are present at birth. These capacities are crucial in enabling children to learn and remember from the

TABLE 7-3 Contributions of Four Aspects of Memory During Several Periods of Development

SOURCE OF DEVELOPMENT	0-5	AGE 5-10	10-ADULTHOOD
Basic Capacities	Many capacities present: association, generalization, recognition, etc. By age 5, if not earlier, absolute capacity of the sensory store and of short-term memory at adultlike levels.	Speed of processing increases.	Speed of processing continues to increase.
Strategies	Little evidence of strategy use.	Acquisition of many strategies: rehearsal, organization, etc.	Increasing use of elaboration. Continuing improvement in quality of all strategies.
Metamemory	Little factual knowledge about memory. Some monitoring of ongoing performance.	Increasing factual knowledge about memory. Improved monitoring of onging performance.	Continued improvements in factual knowledge, monitoring, and regulation of memory. Factual knowledge may exert increasing effects on memory procedures.
Content Knowledge	Steadily increasing content knowledge helps memory in areas where the knowledge exists.	Steadily increasing content knowledge helps memory in areas where the knowledge exists. Also helps in learning of new strategies.	Continuing improvements as in the 5-to 10-year period.

first days of life. The absolute capacities of the sensory store and of short-term memory may be constant from birth, or may develop in the period from birth to age 5, but good reasons exist to believe they are constant from age 5 onward. Beyond age 5, development seems to be limited to improvements in the speed with which the basic processes operate.

Memory strategies begin to contribute to memory development somewhat later than basic capacities. Rehearsal, organization, and several other strategies seem to first emerge around age 6 or 7. The frequency of use, the quality of the strategies, and the flexibility with which they are tailored to the demands of specific situations continue to develop well into later childhood and adolescence.

Two types of metamemory skills, factual knowledge about memory and monitoring and regulation of ongoing behavior, seem to have different developmental courses. Even before age 5, children monitor their ongoing comprehension in some situations, though the range of situations in which they do so continues to grow for many years thereafter. The monitoring seems to influence memory procedures throughout childhood. In contrast, factual knowledge about memory appears to develop primarily between ages 5 and 15, perhaps in response to attending school. The factual knowledge may exert most of its effects on memory procedures some years after it is first acquired, that is, in late childhood and adolescence.

Content knowledge contributes to memory development from early in life. It helps children draw proper inferences, directs their attention to the most informative aspects of objects and events, and provides a network within which they can place new information. It may also help them acquire new strategies by allowing them to exercise emerging skills in familiar contexts and to retain more information in short-term memory by reducing the amount of attention that must be paid to each item. Together, basic capacities, strategies, metamemory, and content knowledge account for the two essential features of memory development: first, that even infants in the first weeks of life have the ability to remember, and second, that the efficiency and effectiveness of memory continue to improve through childhood and adolescence.

SUMMARY

Memory development can be explained in four ways: changes in basic capacities, in strategies, in metamemory, and in knowledge of content related to the material being memorized. Some of these factors seem to exercise larger effects than others. Some seem to contribute significantly in certain age periods but not in others.

Even infants and young children possess basic memory capacities. Newborns can form associations and recognize objects as familiar. By age 3 months, infants possess a wide range of memory skills. They generalize, remember gist rather than detail, and even show insight. By the preschool period, if not earlier, numerous basic processes and capacities are at high levels. Among these are skill at recognition; adultlike absolute capacity of sensory and short-term memory; and high, though less than adultlike, speed of operation of sensory and short-term memory.

The use of broadly applicable strategies such as rehearsal, organization, and elaboration changes greatly with age. This change is particularly marked in the period between 5 years and adolescence. Children who use such strategies typically remember more than those who do not. Changes in the quality of strategies and the range of situations in which they are used continue well beyond the time at which they are first adopted. As strategies become better adapted to the demands of particular tasks, their effectiveness also increases. Young children can learn to rehearse, organize, and elaborate. However, these children often fail to use the strategies in later situations, and use them less effectively than do older children. In sum, learning of broadly applicable strategies seems to account for an important part of the improvement in memory that we see, particularly in middle childhood and beyond.

Interest in metamemory was motivated initially by the question of how children decide what memory activities to perform. Metamemory includes two distinct types of knowledge: factual knowledge about memory, and monitoring and regulation of memory activities. In the preschool years, children already monitor their thinking and behavior and use what they learn to correct speech errors, to predict when they will later be able to recognize something they cannot recall now, and to distinguish between appearance and reality. They also have some, though not a great deal, of factual knowledge about memory, and even have preliminary theories about the functions of the mind and the brain. Development of both factual knowledge and comprehension skills continues throughout life. At present, exactly how knowledge about memory influences memory activities is not well understood. Whatever the theoretical difficulties, though, children's understandings of their own memories seem to have important ramifications for their educational achievements, particularly their reading comprehension.

Knowledge of the content being memorized seems to greatly affect children's memory. Content knowledge guides children's memory for specific events, influences their ability to learn strategies, and helps them make plausible inferences. Under some circumstances, content knowledge can more than balance the influence of all other changes in memory that come with age and experience. Children who are experts on chess or dinosaurs can exhibit truly impressive memory in their area of expertise. Formation of networks of related associations and encoding of distinctive features appear to be two of the mechanisms that allow knowledge to influence memory for new material.

RECOMMENDED READINGS

Brown, A. L., & DeLoache, J. S. (1978). Skills, plans, and self-regulation. In R. S. Siegler (Ed.), *Children's thinking: What develops?* Hillsdale, NJ: Erlbaum. A nice summary of the basic interpretations of memory development, with a strong emphasis on the role of metamemory.

Cavanaugh, J. C., & Perlmutter, M. (1982). Metamemory: A critical examination. *Child Development, 53,* 11–28. Brown and DeLoache positively evaluated the potential of metamemory research; this review critically evaluates what actually has been learned from studies of metamemory.

Chi, M. T., & Koeske, R. D. (1983). Network representation of a child's dinosaur knowledge. *Developmental Psychology, 19,* 29–39. Charming in-depth analysis of a young boy's expert knowledge about dinosaurs.

Lange, G. (1978). Organization-related processes in children's recall. In P. A. Ornstein (Ed.), *Memory development in children.* Hillsdale, NJ: Erlbaum. An article that questions whether children's seemingly strategic behavior is in fact strategic. Raises fundamental questions about what we mean when we say that children use strategies.

Naus, M. J., & Ornstein, P. A. (1983). Development of memory strategies: Analysis, questions, and issues. In M. T. Chi (Ed.), *Trends in memory development research.* New York: Karger. The development of memory strategies does not stop when children first begin to use a strategy. This study documents the many small improvements that children make to maximize the effectiveness of their strategies.

8
CONCEPTUAL DEVELOPMENT

Consider for example the proceedings that we call "games." I mean board games, card games, ball games, Olympic games, and so on. What is common to them all? If you look at them, you will not see something that is common to *all*, but similarities, relationships, and a whole series of them at that . . . . In ball games there is winning and losing; but when a child throws his ball at the wall and catches it again, this feature has disappeared. Look at the parts played by skill and luck; and at the difference between skill in chess and skill in tennis. Think now of the game of ring-a-ring-a-roses; here is the element of amusement, but how many other characteristic features have disappeared! And we can go through the many, many other groups of games in the same way; can see how similarities crop up and disappear (Wittgenstein, 1970, pp. 31–32).

Wittgenstein's observations raise a fundamental question: What exactly is a concept? Before addressing this question, it may be worthwhile to consider a prior question: Why should people interested in children's thinking care what a concept is? The reason is that our beliefs about the nature of concepts greatly influence our beliefs about the nature of development. If we believe that people understand concepts in terms of concrete examples, as some philosophers do, we will focus on what makes an example especially compelling for a child. If we believe that concepts are understood as complex relations, as other philosophers do, we will pay the greatest attention to how children abstract the relations. Different views of the nature of concepts lead to different expectations about the order in which children will learn particular concepts, to different explanations of why some concepts are difficult for them to learn, and to different implications about how children should be taught new concepts.

What, then, are concepts? At a general level, concepts can be viewed as objects, events, qualities, and ideas that people group together as similar. This general definition leaves considerable room for refinement, however. One issue concerns the nature of the similarity of the instances that are grouped together. At least since Aristotle, the prevailing view of concepts has been that all instances have in common one or more *defining features*. Within this view, the presence of the defining features is both necessary and sufficient for an instance to be included in a concept. For example, the features *adult, male,* and *unmarried* define the concept *bachelor*. All people who are unmarried male adults, and no others, are bachelors.

Wittgenstein approached concepts differently. He argued that while some concepts, such as *bachelor*, may have defining features, most, like *games*, do not. He viewed this latter group of concepts as being loose amalgams of more-or-less similar instances. *Games*, for example, are united only by tendencies to have certain qualities, such as competition and a mix of skill and luck.

Accompanying the question "What are concepts?" is the question "What examples should be included under the heading 'concepts'?" The first examples that most people think of are those that refer to concrete objects: terriers, dogs, and animals; oranges, fruits, and foods; and so on. These object concepts are of special interest because they can be organized into hierarchies: terriers are a subclass of dogs, which in turn are a subclass of animals, for example. Organizing information into hierarchies greatly facilitates information processing in a variety of situations (Simon, 1981).

Object concepts are not the only concepts, however. Among other important groups are action concepts, such as jumping, running, and hugging; relational concepts, such as bigger, smoother, and brighter; and abstract concepts, such as space, time, and number. As will be seen in this chapter, the optimal way of thinking about children's conceptual understanding depends heavily on the type of concept being considered.

Another general issue concerns why children form concepts. Why group together objects and events that differ in their particulars? Concepts are important to children's thinking because they allow them to draw inferences beyond their experience with specific objects and events. If told that malamutes are dogs, a child immediately knows a variety of other facts about them: that they have four legs, a tail, fur; that they are animals; that they probably are friendly to people; and so on. Thus, concepts allow children to go beyond the information given.

The organization of this chapter. Conceptual development can be approached from two perspectives. One is to emphasize the *form of conceptual representations*. The other is to emphasize the *content of the representa-*

tions. The two approaches have different strengths and weaknesses, and seem best suited to studying different types of concepts. As shown in Table 8–1, the distinction between form-oriented and content-oriented approaches to conceptual understanding is at the heart of this chapter's organization.

Approaches that emphasize the forms of representations are attempts to identify the way people represent concepts independent of the particular concepts involved. Within this view, the nature of people's minds leads them to organize their knowledge of the world in a particular way; the details of the concepts are secondary. This approach has been especially common in studying object concepts, such as animals, tools, and furniture.

Three forms that children might use to represent concepts are *defining-features representations, probabilistic representations,* and *exemplar-based representations* (Smith & Medin, 1981). Defining-features representations are like those that appear in dictionaries. They are attempts to define concepts in terms of a few necessary and sufficient properties. From the time of Aristotle until quite recently, they have been viewed as being the primary form in which concepts are represented. Probabilistic representations are more like the articles in encyclopedias. Rather than just representing a few features that must always be present, children may represent concepts in terms of a large number of properties that are related to the concept and relevant to it. Finally, exemplar-based representations would be like a photograph album. Such representations would include detailed memories of particular instances of concepts. For example, children may represent *games* by all the particular games they knew about. Examples of each of the three forms of conceptual representation are shown in Figure 8–1.

Logically, children could represent concepts in all these forms; their knowledge of a single concept could include information about defining features, probabilistically related features, and prominent examples. In practice, however, many investigators have devoted their energies to arguing that children could only use one of the forms, that they could not use one of the forms, or that their natural tendency was toward one of them (Farah & Kosslyn, 1982). These positions have collectively been grouped under the heading of the *representational development hypothesis*—that young children's conceptual representations differ fundamentally from those of

TABLE 8–1   Chapter Outline

I.   Research Emphasizing Conceptual Form
A.   Defining-Features Representations
B.   Probabilistic Representations
C.   Exemplar-based Representations
II. Research Emphasizing Conceptual Content
A.   Children's Numerical Understandings
B.   Some Important Relational Concepts
III. Summary

A. DEFINING-FEATURES REPRESENTATION

Superhero =
— Imaginary
— Living being
— Has great powers

B. PROBABILISTIC REPRESENTATION

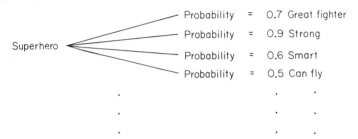

Superhero
— Probability = 0.7 Great fighter
— Probability = 0.9 Strong
— Probability = 0.6 Smart
— Probability = 0.5 Can fly

C. EXAMPLE-ORIENTED REPRESENTATION

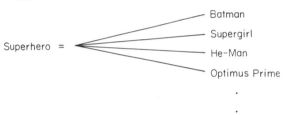

Superhero =
— Batman
— Supergirl
— He-Man
— Optimus Prime

FIGURE 8-1 Defining-features, probabilistic, and example-oriented representations a child might use for the concept *superhero.*

older people. This hypothesis has stimulated much attention to the form of children's representations.

An alternative to emphasizing the form of children's conceptual representations is to emphasize the content. Here the basic assumption is that children's minds are sufficiently flexible that they will represent concepts in all of the above-described ways. The question of central interest is what children know about particular concepts, rather than the general form of their conceptual representations. Thus, content-oriented approaches to conceptual development are closely related to the knowledge-oriented explanations of memory development discussed in Chapter 7. They also resemble the Piagetian approach in the types of relational and abstract concepts that receive the greatest attention: cause and effect, number, time, and space, for example.

The relation between approaches that emphasize form and those that emphasize content parallels a relation that was discussed in Chapter 3—that between Atkinson and Shiffrin's and Newell and Simon's theories. Approaches that emphasize the form of representations are like Atkinson and Shiffrin's theory in their search for general properties of the mind that hold across all situations. Approaches that emphasize the contents of representations resemble Newell and Simon's theory in emphasizing the adaptability of the information-processing system and in viewing the content of the particular concept (the task environment) as the crucial determinant of its representation.

Below we consider these two perspectives on children's conceptual representations.

RESEARCH EMPHASIZING CONCEPTUAL FORM

Defining-Features Representations

What would it mean for children to represent concepts in terms of defining features? First, children would know a set of features that are necessary and sufficient for an object to be an example of the concept. Second, they would view all examples of the concept as being equally good examples of it. There would be no such thing as one object being a better example of the concept than another. Third, they would organize different concepts hierarchically. The features of the most general concept would be included within the features of the next most general concept in the hierarchy, which in turn would be included within the features at the next most general level. For example, a boy would represent the concept *animals* in terms of three features: growth, metabolism, and reproduction. He would represent the concept *mammals* as having these three features and also the features of giving birth to live young and being warm-blooded. He would represent *lions* as having all five of these features and also the feature of being meat eaters, being a kind of cat, and so on. Thus, the most general category in the hierarchy (animals) has the smallest number of necessary and sufficient features, and the most specific category (lions) has the greatest number.

The representational development hypothesis.   The representational development hypothesis postulates that young children's concepts are not organized around necessary and sufficient features, whereas older children's and adults' concepts are. An especially influential research effort based on this view of concepts was that of the Russian psychologist Vygotsky, the same researcher whose work on the relation between language and thought was discussed in Chapter 4. Vygotsky (1934/1962) used a simple but compelling sorting task for studying children's concepts. He presented children a number of blocks that differed in size, color, and shape, and asked them to group together those that went together. Children 6 years and older who were given this sorting task typically chose a single quality as necessary and sufficient. For example, they might choose color as the necessary and sufficient quality and put all the red blocks together, all the green blocks together, and so on. Preschoolers, however, seemed to form what Vygotsky called *chain concepts*. These were concepts in which the basis of classification changed from example to example. The following type of evidence led Vygotsky to hypothesize that preschoolers used chain concepts:

> The child might pick out a few triangular blocks until his attention is caught by, let us say, the blue color of a block he has just added; he switches to selecting blue blocks of any shape—angular, circular, semicircular. This in turn is sufficient to change the criterion again; oblivious of color, the child begins to choose rounded blocks. . . . The chain formation strikingly demonstrates the perceptually concrete, factual nature of complex thinking. An object included because of one of its attributes enters the complex, not just as the carrier of that one trait, but as an individual, with *all* its attributes. (p. 64)

Preschoolers behave similarly in other situations as well. When they are asked to group objects together that belong together, they often construct *thematically* rather than *taxonomically* related groups. Instead of putting animals together, pieces of furniture together, and toys together, a preschooler might put together a dog and a Frisbee (because dogs like to chase Frisbees), a cat and a chair (because cats like to sit on chairs), and a game and a shelf (because the game belonged on a shelf) (Bruner, Oliver, & Greenfield, 1966; Inhelder & Piaget, 1964).

These types of observations led Vygotsky to hypothesize that children pass through three stages of conceptual development. Initially, they form thematic concepts, stressing relations between particular pairs of objects. Later, they form chain concepts, following abstract dimensions such as roundness, but often switching the basis of categorization, as in the above quotation. Still later, during the elementary school period, they form concepts based on stable necessary and sufficient features.

Additional support for the representational development hypothesis. Preschoolers' ways of solving *discrimination shift problems* give further credence to the representational development hypothesis. In a typical discrimination shift item, such as that shown in Figure 8-2, four stimuli differ along two dimensions: form and color in the example shown. The form could be either circular or triangular, and the color could be light or dark. Initially, children would be presented two objects and reinforced for choosing a particular value of a particular dimension. Illustratively, they might be reinforced for choosing the dark object in each pair. After they learned to choose these objects consistently, the reinforcement contingency was shifted in one of two ways, *intradimensionally* or *extradimensionally*. On intradimensional shifts, children were reinforced for choosing the opposite value within the same dimension. In Figure 8-2, color would remain the relevant dimension after the shift, but now choices of light objects rather than dark ones would be

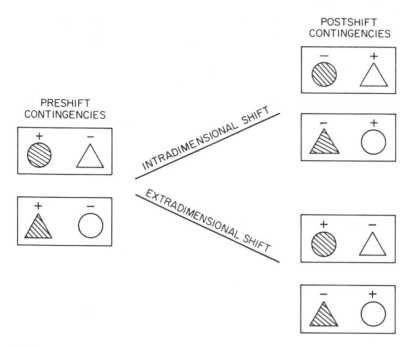

FIGURE 8-2   A discrimination shift problem. Shapes below " + " are reinforced. Shapes below " − " are not reinforced. Before the shift, children were reinforced for choosing the dark objects. After the shift, those in the intradimensional shift condition were reinforced for choosing the light objects (same dimension, different value); those in the extradimensional shift condition were reinforced for choosing the circular objects (different dimension but two particular objects are reinforced or not reinforced as before).

reinforced. On extradimensional shifts, the dimension as well as the value would be shifted. Now, choices of circular objects (form dimension) rather than dark objects (color dimension) would be reinforced.

Would intradimensional or extradimensional shifts be easier? Kendler and Kendler (1962) argued that this depends on the types of concepts children form most readily. If they most readily form concepts with necessary and sufficient features, the intradimensional shift should be easier. When the shift in reinforcement contingencies occurs, they already should know that color is the relevant dimension and only would need to learn that choice of light colors is now desired. On the extradimensional shift problems, the shift would demand that they learn both that a new dimension is relevant (form) and that a certain value of it would be reinforced (circular objects). Thus, these extradimensional shift problems would be harder.

The prediction would differ, however, if children formed concepts on an example-by-example basis. In this case, the extradimensional shifts would be easier. With an intradimensional shift, they would need to change their view of all four objects. However, with an extradimensional shift, their initial view would continue to be right for two of the four examples. Dark circles would continue to be reinforced and light triangles would continue not to be reinforced (Figure 8–2).

The difficulty of the problems turned out to be different at different ages. Children beyond age 7, like adults, learned the intradimensional shifts more rapidly. On the other hand, 5-year-olds made the two shifts at the same rate. Examination of the data indicated that 5-year-olds who were faster learners on other tasks learned the intradimensional shifts more rapidly, whereas 5-year-olds who were slower learners learned the extradimensional shifts more rapidly. The Kendlers concluded that the slower-learning 5-year-olds formed concepts in an example-by-example fashion, whereas the faster-learning 5-year-olds and older children abstracted dimensions and used them as the defining characteristic of their concepts.

A further consequence of this point of view is that preschoolers should learn the two items on which the reinforcement contingency is the same before and after the shift (the dark circle and the light triangle in Figure 8–2), more rapidly than the two where it changes (the light circle and dark triangle). On the first two items, but not the last two, the child's example-by-example approach will produce correct answers from the first trial after the shift. Tighe, Glick, and Cole (1971) found that this was the case. On the items that maintained the contingency, 4-year-olds answered consistently correctly almost from the beginning. On the items where the contingency changed, they learned slowly. In contrast, 10-year-olds learned equally quickly on the two sets of items. The conclusion again was that preschoolers form concepts on an example-by-example basis, whereas older children rely on necessary and sufficient features.

An evaluation. The defining-features view of concepts has led to a number of interesting discoveries about preschoolers' conceptual understanding. Among these are the discoveries that young children have difficulty sorting objects along a single consistent dimension, that they tend to sort objects into groups based on how the objects can interact rather than on their categorical relations to each other, and that they learn intradimensional shifts faster than extradimensional ones. These reflect important changes in which concepts children use most readily.

Should we believe the broader theoretical claim that young children's concepts differ fundamentally from those of older children and adults? I don't believe so, for four main reasons. First, if young children's concepts were fundamentally different from adults', it would be much more difficult to communicate with them than it is. Second, children's performance on relatively unstructured tasks, such as sorting, may reflect what they find interesting rather than what they know. Third, when using natural rather than artificial concepts, young children do form concepts that have necessary and sufficient features. Fourth, even older children and adults may not represent most concepts in terms of necessary and sufficient features. Below, these arguments are spelled out in greater detail.

First, as Fodor (1972) noted, it is not clear how adults could communicate with children if their concepts were fundamentally different from ours. Suppose we took literally the results of the sorting studies described above and concluded from children's thematic sortings that their concepts of dogs included dogs, leashes, dog houses, feeding dishes, and other dog-oriented paraphernalia. If an adult said "Dogs have wet noses," childen presumably would need to infer that feeding dishes and leashes, as well as dogs, have this property. Fortunately, children do not do this (see Carey, in press, for a more detailed discussion of this point).

The second cause for skepticism about the representational development hypothesis is that much of the performance interpreted as indicative of children's poorly formed concepts may reflect their interests rather than their knowledge. They may put dogs and bones together, rather than dogs and cows, because they find the relation between dogs and bones more interesting. Supporting this interpretation, Smiley and Brown (1979) found that preschoolers who sorted objects in thematic ways could explain perfectly the way in which categorically related objects were connected. Cole and Scribner (1974) reported similar findings with primitive people in Africa. Experimenters could elicit the ostensibly more sophisticated categorical sortings from the tribespeople only by asking, "How would a stupid man do it?"

A third consideration is that in more natural situations, young children do form concepts with necessary and sufficient features. Recall the research using the rule-assessment approach that was discussed in Chapter 3. On balance-scale problems, 5-year-olds consistently predicted that the side with more weight would go down. This quality alone was necessary and sufficient for predicting which side would dip. On problems involving the concept of distance, 5-year-olds consistently judged that the train that stopped farther down the track went for the longer time. On problems involving the concept of living things, they consistently indicated either that animals were alive or that animals and plants were alive.

The final argument against the view that children progress toward sole reliance on necessary and sufficient features is that human beings generally may not represent concepts in this way. If people represented concepts only in terms of necessary and sufficient features, all examples of the concept should be equally representative of it. Either an object would be a member of a concept or it would not. Both children and adults, however, view some objects as being better examples of concepts than others. They view apples as better examples of fruits than pineapples, tables as better examples of furniture than rugs, roses as better examples of flowers than crocuses, and so on (Mervis & Rosch, 1981). The defining-features approach does not predict this phenomenon, nor does it easily explain why it would be so.

For all these reasons, it seems unlikely that children progress from representations fundamentally different from those of adults to representations fundamentally similar to theirs. More likely, even young children form representations with defining features in some situations and even adults do not always use these representations.

Probabilistic Representations

Knowing that an object has four legs, can be sat on, and is made of wood makes it likely that the object is a chair but does not guarantee it (it could be a church pew). This type of example, like Wittgenstein's example of games, points to the possibility that children may represent concepts in terms of probabilistic relations between the concept and various features.

How would children form probabilistic concepts? Eleanor Rosch, Carolyn Mervis, and their associates developed one appealing theory. This theory was built around four powerful ideas for analyzing conceptual development: cue validities, basic level categories, nonrandom distributions of features in natural concepts, and prototypic examples.

Cue validities. How might children decide whether objects are examples of one concept or another? Rosch and Mervis (1975) suggested that they do so by comparing *cue validities.* The basic insight is that the presence of a feature makes it more likely that an object is a member of a concept in proportion to the frequency with which that feature occurs with that concept, and in proportion to the infrequency with which the feature occurs with other concepts. That is, the feature of flying makes it more likely that an object is a bird in proportion to the frequency with which flying is found in birds and in proportion to the infrequency with which flying is found in other animals.

The idea of cue validities helps the probabilistic approach to explain a phenomenon that proved troublesome for the necessary features approach: that some objects seem like better examples of a concept than others. The probabilistic approach suggests that the objects perceived as better examples are ones whose features have higher cue validities for that concept. Thus, people view apples as more representative fruits than pineapples because the size, shape, and texture of apples have higher validities for the fruit category. More generally, the probabilistic approach envisions people considering a large number of features of a newly encountered object, summing the cue validities of the features of that object for different concepts, and viewing the object as a member of whichever concept achieves the highest sum.

Basic-level categories. The notion of cue validities is closely connected to that of basic-level categories. Rosch, Mervis, Gray, Johnson, and Boyes-Braem (1976) noted that many object concepts are hierarchical: All instances of one concept are necessarily members of another. Thus, all robins are birds and all birds are animals. Rosch et al. proposed that in each hierarchy there is a single level, the basic level, at which the cue validities are maximized. For example, they suggested that *chair* is a basic-level category, whereas *furniture* and *kitchen chair* are not. The reasoning was that certain features would have very high cue validities for chairs—has legs, a seat, a back, and arms. More general concepts, such as furniture, would not have features with comparably high cue validities. Some pieces of furniture are hard and some are soft; some have backs and some do not; and so on. Less general concepts, such as kitchen chairs, would share all the features of the basic-level category, but would lack features that clearly discriminated them from other instances of the basic level category. What features clearly discriminate kitchen chairs from chairs in general, for example? Rosch et al. concluded that basic-level concepts such as chair are more fundamental ways of viewing the world than are superordinate concepts, such as furniture, or subordinate concepts, such as kitchen chair. Other examples of superordinate, subordinate, and basic-level concepts are shown in Table 8-2.

The idea of basic-level categories has several important developmental implications. One of the senses in which basic-level concepts are basic is that children learn them first. Rosch et al. (1976) presented 3-year-olds *oddity problems* involving three toys. Children needed to identify which two toys were similar. Sometimes the two similar toys were from the same basic category (two airplanes). Other times they were from the same superordinate category (an airplane and a car). The third object in either case would be from an entirely different category—for example, a toy dog. When two objects came from the same basic level category, the 3-year-olds consistently put them together; they did so on 99% of their choices. By contrast, when the two most similar choices had in common only a superordinate category, the 3-year-olds chose them only 55% of the time.

Language development shows a similar pattern. Children learn the words that name basic-level concepts before the words that name superordinate or subordinate ones (Anglin, 1977). Both hearing speakers of oral languages and deaf speakers of American Sign Language show this ordering (Rosch et al., 1976). Parents seem sensitive to the priority of basic-level categories in their children's development and base their introductions of

TABLE 8-2   Examples of Superordinate, Basic, and Subordinate Category Members

SUPERORDINATE LEVEL	BASIC LEVEL	SUBORDINATE LEVEL
Furniture	Table	End table
Animal	Bird	Canary
Food	Vegetable	Asparagus
Tool	Hammer	Tack hammer
Vehicle	Car	Fiero

new superordinate terms on known basic-level terms. For example, when they introduce the term "mammal," they will point to foxes, sheep, raccoons, and other animals and say "these are mammals." Use of such multiple basic-level examples seems to help children learn superordinate terms (Callanan, 1985).

Correlations among features of natural concepts. Conceptual understanding involves detecting more than the cue validities of individual features. Relations among features also are essential. One of Rosch et al.'s main arguments about the nature of concepts is that features of natural objects are not randomly distributed, but rather tend to cluster together. Things that bark also tend to have four legs, a tail, a wet nose, sharp teeth, and fur. Fortunately, even babies less than 1 year old are adept at noting correlations among features. They also seem to use these correlations to form new concepts.

Younger and Cohen (1983) used the habituation paradigm to demonstrate this point. They showed 10-month-olds pictures of four fanciful beasts, one by one (Figure 8–3). The values of the body and tail in each picture were correlated in the sense that if a beast had a certain type of body, it also had a particular type of tail. Thus, if you knew what type of body the beast had, you also could predict its type of tail.

Following these four exposures, the dishabituation trial was presented. On it, the 10-month-old saw an animal whose body and tail were not those that previously had appeared together, though each had been seen earlier with a different body or tail. Presumably, babies would find such a combination surprising if they had detected the earlier body-tail pairings, but not if they only attended to the body and tail as separate parts. Babies showed renewed attention to this new body-tail combination (Figure 8–3B). Thus, even infants consider relations among features in forming concepts.

Prototypes. A fourth concept introduced by Rosch and her colleagues was that of *prototypes*. Prototypes are the most representative instances of concepts—that is, the examples that have the highest cue validities. Lassie would be a prototypic dog not only because she was familiar but because she had qualities (e.g., size, shape, type of bark) representative of dogs in general.

A surprising aspect of prototypes is that they sometimes do not correspond to any particular example that has been encountered. Illustratively, children might see three examples: a large black dog, a small black cat, and a large white cat. Since in these three examples, large was the most frequent size, black the most frequent color, and cat the most frequent animal, the prototypic animal would be a large black cat.

Surprisingly, when shown a large number of pictures, both children and adults are more confident that they have seen such prototypic objects,

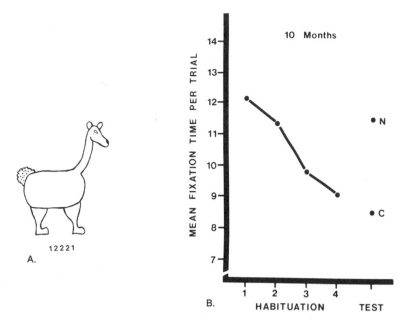

FIGURE 8-3 A. Example of stimuli presented to infants by Younger and Cohen (1983). B. Times spent looking at fanciful beasts during the habituation and dishabituation phases of the experiment. Note the recovery in looking time for the novel stimulus group (*N*) in which the body-tail relation was reversed. Note also the lack of recovery in the control group (*C*) in which the body-tail relation was maintained (from Younger & Cohen, 1983).

that in fact they have never encountered, rather than non-prototypic objects that they actually have seen earlier (Bransford, 1979). The role of prototypes in concept formation is reminiscent of people's excellent memory for the gist of material that was discussed in the last chapter; prototypes may be thought of as the gist of a single concept.

Evaluation. Saying that children's representations are probabilistic has much to recommend it. Some levels of conceptual representation do seem more basic than others, some instances seem more prototypic than others. Children are sensitive to relations among features from the first year of life, and use these relations to form new concepts. However, children may not represent all concepts in terms of probabilistic connections between various features and the concept. As suggested earlier, defining features may also play a role.

Consider an experiment in which 9-year-olds heard two stories describing a particular object, and then were asked whether that object could be an example of the concept (Keil & Batterman, 1984). As shown in Table 8–3, one story indicated that the object included many features people associate with the concept, but also indicated that it lacked the defining feature. The other story indicated that the object included the defining feature for the concept, but also indicated that it lacked many features people typically associate with the concept.

The 9-year-olds consistently realized that the defining feature was the only critical one for making the judgment. They more often judged the object with the single defining feature to be an instance of the concept than the object with the large number of typical features. The finding is difficult to interpret within a purely probabilistic view of concepts, where no distinction is made between different classes of features.

A different type of difficulty with the probabilistic view is a lack of definition of what constitutes a feature. Consider the concept "a beautiful face." What features define this concept? Certainly such features are more complex than a nose of a certain size, eyes of a certain color, or a mouth of a certain shape. What constitutes the feature "beautiful eyes": the color of the iris, the size of the iris and pupil, the contrast between the iris and pupil, the length of the eyelashes, or any of the myriad possible relations of these qualities to each other? Are the eyes a separate feature at all when we view faces, or rather a part of the face as a whole? The lack of clear definition of what constitutes a feature is shared by the defining-features approach, but this does not alleviate the slipperiness of the problem.

A final limitation of the probabilistic approach, related to the previous point, concerns its plausibility as a model of children's initial formation of concepts. Simply put, the approach does not specify how children first establish which features of unfamiliar objects and events they should encode. It assumes that children are already encoding the relevant features so they can learn their cue validities. Yet, as discussed in the section on encoding in the Chapter 3 discussion of the balance scale, establishing which features to encode is often quite difficult.

Bowerman's hypothesis about how children learn word meanings (re-

TABLE 8-3 Stories from Keil and Batterman (1984)

CHARACTERISTIC FEATURES BUT NOT DEFINING FEATURES

Your next-door neighbor painted his car yellow with black and white checks around the edges. The car even has a white bump on top. He likes to put on his cap and uniform and drive all over town every day. He never gives strangers rides, though, because he thinks it's too dangerous. Could that be a taxi?

DEFINING FEATURES BUT NOT CHARACTERISTIC FEATURES

This purple car with three wheels and rainbows painted on the tires is driven around by a woman in a nightgown and a football helmet. Whenever you want to go somewhere, you wave to her and she takes you wherever you want to go as long as you pay her. Could this be a taxi?

call the discussion of her daughter's acquisition of the work *kick* in the language development chapter) suggests a way out of this dilemma. When children are first learning a word or concept, they may assume that all the properties of the examples they encounter are relevant. Their concept at that point, and perhaps for some time after, may be closely tied to their knowledge of particular examples of the concept. The role of examples in children's conceptual representations is explored in more detail in the next section.

Exemplar-based Representations

In some ways it seems unlikely that examples could play a prominent role in conceptual representations. Even a 2-year-old has encountered so many particular examples of objects and events in his life that representing them all would seem impossible. It would seem to require a vast amount of memory space. It would also seem to require an ability to zoom through the many stored examples to find the particular one of immediate interest.

Farah and Kosslyn (1982) argued that these difficulties may be less serious than they initially appear, though. Space for storing examples may not be a problem because, as discussed in the last chapter, the long-term memory capacity of the human brain is for all practical purposes unlimited. Searching through large numbers of examples also seems to be less of a problem than might first be assumed. Standing, Conezio, and Haber (1970) found that college students could recognize as familiar or unfamiliar 2500 photographs they had seen for only 1 second each. The students were both quick and extremely accurate in searching through their memories of the many pictures they had seen.

Medin and Schaffer (1978) proposed a model of how exemplar-based representations might operate. Memories of specific examples were a prominent part of people's representations of concepts. People would evaluate whether a newly encountered object was an example of a concept by comparing it to specific examples they had encountered or to prototypes they had formed from the specific examples.

Assuming that conceptual representations include specific examples explains at least one finding that is not simply explained by defining-features or probabilistic models. Suppose a new example has features that resemble, to an equal extent, the overall distribution of features of objects in two known concepts. Suppose, further, that one concept already includes one particular example very similar to the new example, and that the other does not. Assuming that people retain information about specific examples suggests that they will classify the new object as an instance of the concept that already includes the similar case, because they will compare it to the case and note the high similarity. This is, in fact, what happens.

Carey (1978) suggested several theoretical reasons why children would find representing examples especially useful for constructing new concepts.

Consider the concept *tall*. The first three statements in which a child heard this term might refer to a tall building, a tall lady, and a tall drink. The three absolute sizes would be wildly discrepant. Further, children probably would not realize quickly that even among objects that are the same height, *tall* is more likely to be applied to thin ones. If concepts in general are this complex (and *tall* does not seem like an unusually complicated notion), retaining detailed information about the first few examples encountered would seem essential for inferring the abstract properties of the concept. This is the same logic that led Klahr and Wallace to postulate the time line as a detailed record of processing (Chapter 3).

What empirical evidence exists that young children's conceptual representations emphasize examples? Kossan (1981) reported one study supporting this position. She found that 7-year-olds learned more effectively under conditions that promoted careful attention to particular examples than under conditions that promoted learning of a rule for classifying new instances. In contrast, 10-year-olds learned equally well under the conditions that promoted learning of the rule. Kossan concluded that the 7-year-olds were more accurate in the example-based condition because it was closer to the style in which they habitually learn concepts. Both the finding and the conclusion are reminiscent of those obtained with the reversal-shift task described earlier in the chapter. There as well as here, young children seemed to represent the task in terms of separate examples and to learn in an example-by-example fashion.

Evaluation.   Exemplar-based approaches are newer than defining features or probabilistic views, and less is known about them. A few properties seem clear, though. Examples are unlikely to be the sole content of conceptual representations. The reason is evident when we consider what children need to do to decide whether a new object is an example of a concept. How do they compare the new object with known exemplars? Since the new object will almost never be identical to the old one, they must have some basis of comparison beyond a simple "matches/doesn't match." The only obvious way of performing such comparisons is to note similarities and differences between particular features of the overall examples. This analysis implies that the conceptual representation must include a description of typical and/or necessary features as well as the example as a whole.

A second difficulty with exemplar-based approaches is lack of specificity about what constitutes an example. When people see a honeybee buzzing around their backyard, do they remember the particular honeybee, do they remember just that it was a honeybee, or do they remember just that it was a bee? The simplest assumption for an example-oriented approach, that the individual bee is represented, seems unlikely. Recall that the objects people are most sure they have seen (the prototype) are sometimes objects they have never actually encountered. This finding seems difficult to explain if people remember specific examples but not more abstract characterizations.

What can we conclude, then, about the form of children's conceptual representations? It seems likely that children use all three forms of representation—defining features, probabilistically related features, and examples—from early in development. The relative frequency with which they use them may change, however. In particular, it seems that the use of defining features is more prominent in older children's representations.

More speculatively, development of many concepts may undergo the following pattern of change. At first, when the important features of the concept are poorly understood, children's representations may be built around examples. Once children accurately encode the relevant features of the concept, they can work on computing the probabilities that link features to particular concepts. Finally, children may distinguish between two types of features that always seem to accompany the concept: those that define it and those that are incidental to it.

At any given time, children will understand different concepts at different levels. Therefore, their representations of some concepts will emphasize defining features; their representations of other concepts will emphasize probabilistic information; and their representations of yet other concepts that they are just beginning to learn will emphasize examples. Further, information from previous representations will not be discarded. Older children's representations will include information of all three forms.

This view is consistent with numerous types of evidence. The way in which it accounts for the Keil and Batterman (1984) findings is instructive. Recall that 9-year-olds emphasized defining features over characteristic features when the two conflicted (as in the story about the taxicab). The performance of 5-year-olds was in some ways similar and in other ways different. The 5-year-olds did not emphasize defining features to as great an extent as did the 9-year-olds. However, on some relatively familiar concepts, the younger children did emphasize the defining features, and on other relatively unfamiliar concepts, the older children did not do so. This is exactly what we would expect if younger as well as older children are capable of representing concepts in terms of defining features, but if examples and probabilistic connections play relatively larger roles in their conceptual representations.

RESEARCH EMPHASIZING CONCEPTUAL CONTENT

An alternative approach to conceptual understanding is to emphasize how people adapt the content of their representations to the structure of the underlying concepts. Consider the concept of number. For me at least, the most interesting questions about children's understandings of numbers are not whether they represent numbers in terms of defining features, probabilistic relations, or specific examples. Rather, the most intriguing questions concern the specific content of their knowledge and what they do with this content: how they represent numbers, and what processes they apply to these representations to count, add, multiply, and perform other activities involving numbers. As the example suggests, approaches that emphasize content explore individual concepts in depth rather than attempting to draw conclusions about concepts in general.

Exploring concepts in such depth is worthwhile only if the concepts are very important. They must be concepts that are applied in many situations and that are basic to the way people experience the world. Some concepts that meet these criteria are the types of abstract ideas studied by Piaget: number, space, and time, for example. Others that meet them are concepts that specify fundamental relations among other concepts. Some of the most important relational concepts are causality, hierarchical classification, and transitivity. Below, research on one of the abstract ideas, number, is discussed in considerable detail. The reason for the detail is to communicate the kinds of characterizations that grow out of content-oriented approaches as well as to communicate the specific findings about the number concept. Following this, research on three relational concepts—causality, hierarchical classification, and transitivity—is discussed at a more general level.

Children's Numerical Understandings

Researchers frequently divide understanding of numbers into two parts: understanding of *cardinality* and understanding of *ordinality*. Cardinality refers to the property of absolute numerical size. A common property of people's arms, legs, eyes, and feet is that there are two of them. The cardinal property of two-ness is what these sets share. Ordinality refers to relational properties of numbers. The facts that someone is the third prettiest girl in the class and that five is the fifth number of the counting string reflect ordinal properties.

Cardinal properties of numbers.   Understanding of cardinal aspects of numbers begins surprisingly early in infancy. Infants less than 1 year old can discriminate one object from two, and two objects from three (Antell & Keating, 1983; Starkey & Cooper, 1980; Strauss & Curtis, 1981). All of these researchers have used the habituation paradigm. Infants see sets with a specific number of objects (e.g., two objects). Once they have habituated to displays having this number of objects, they are shown a set with a different number. The renewed looking that infants display attests to their having abstracted the numerical similarity of the previous displays.

How early does this capability for abstracting numerical quantities begin? Antell and Keating's study makes the most dramatic claim: In their experiment, infants between 1 and 7 *days* old dishabituated when shown a different size set. The claim that infants this young discriminate among numbers remains controversial, however, because the newborns in this study may have responded to differences in brightness rather than number (Strauss & Curtis, 1984). Even if this proves to be the case, though, there is little doubt that by 4 months of age infants discriminate among small numbers of objects.

Discriminating among larger numbers of objects poses greater difficulty for infants. Infants below 1 year do not appear to discriminate four objects from five or six objects (Starkey & Cooper, 1983; Strauss & Curtis, 1981). This finding suggests that infants identify cardinalities through *subitizing*, a perceptual process that people can apply only to small sets of objects.

Chi and Klahr (1975) demonstrated that 5-year-olds and adults also subitize to identify the number of objects in small sets. Their experiment used the subtractive technique described in Chapter 4 (p. 116). Recall that the central assumption of this method is that each successive application of a process takes a constant amount of time. In Chi and Klahr's experiment, participants were shown a number of randomly arranged dots and needed to determine how many dots there were. The hypothesis was that as long as people subitized, the time to identify the number of objects would increase by a constant amount for each additional object in the set, and as long as they used counting, the time also would increase by a constant amount. At the point at which they switched from the rapid subitizing process to the slower counting process, however, the size of the increments would increase, since each increment made by counting would take a longer time than each increment made by subitizing.

This prediction proved accurate. As shown in Figure 8–4, the amount of time it took 5-year-olds to determine the number of objects rose only slightly from one to three objects, with the difference between one and two similar to that between two and three. In contrast, the amount of time rose sharply as the size of the set increased beyond three. The difference between three and four objects was similar to that between four and five, five and six, and so on. The data also revealed the absolute amount of time required by the two processes, a rare and desirable feature of this study. As shown in Figure 8–4, the 5-year-olds required 200 milliseconds to subitize each additional object; they took a full second to count each object beyond their subitizing range. The finding suggested that older children, like infants, establish the cardinality of small sets through subitizing.

Counting.   By age 4 years, children master another fundamental numerical skill, counting. They become skillful both in reciting the counting string and in assigning one and only one number to each object being counted.

First we can consider how children learn the counting string, the ordered set of positive integers starting with one. Learning in this domain

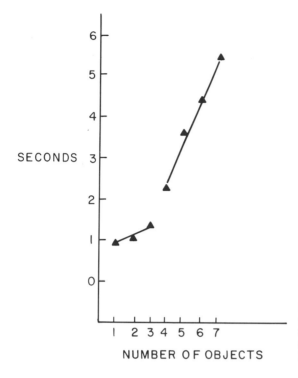

SECONDS

6

5

4

3

2

1

0

1 2 3 4 5 6 7

NUMBER OF OBJECTS

FIGURE 8-4 Number of seconds required by 5-year-olds to determine how many objects there were in different-size sets (data from Chi & Klahr, 1975).

presents an especially clear example of children's representations progressively adapting to the inherent organization of the task environment (see the discussion of Newell and Simon's theory in Chapter 3).

The early part of the counting string is essentially arbitrary. Children need to learn the first twenty number words more or less by rote. As Ginsburg (1977) noted, it would be logically possible for children to figure out the order of the numbers 13–19 on the basis of analogies with earlier numbers (if 6 is followed by 7, 16 should be followed by 17). Available data, however, indicate that they do not use this analogy in learning to count (Siegler & Robinson, 1982).

After the number 20, the situation changes. Rather than memorizing each number word separately, children can generate the numbers 21–29 by successively appending the first nine integers to the decade name. If they remember that 30 follows 29, they can then repeat the process by successively appending the 9 digits to 30, and so on.

Children who counted beyond 20, a level reached by most 4-year-olds, understood both the arbitrary and the rule-governed part of the counting string (Siegler & Robinson, 1982). Their mastery of the arbitrary segment was evident in their correct or nearly correct recitation of the first 20 numbers. Their mastery of the rule was evident in ways other than correct performance. As shown in Figure 8–5, a disproportionate number of children stopped at a number ending in 9: 29, 39, 49, and so on. This is the

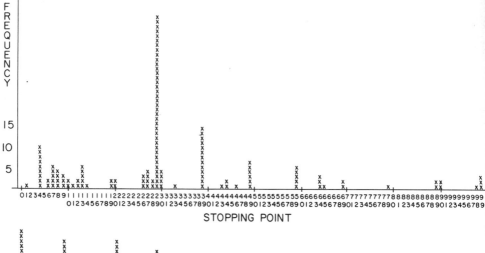

STOPPING POINT

FIGURE 8-5 Points at which 3-, 4-, and 5-year-olds stopped counting. Children who counted beyond 20 most often stopped at a 9 number. Children who stopped below 20 did not show this distribution of stopping points (from Siegler & Robinson, 1982).

pattern that would be expected if children knew the rule for appending the digits to the decade name, but did not always know the name of the next decade name. The children's pattern of omissions also was revealing. A high proportion of omissions were of the form "27, 28, 29, 50, 51, 52." Children would skip from a number ending in a 9 to a higher decade name. The pattern of repetitions was similar. Children produced such patterns as "37, 38, 39, 20, 21, 22 . . ." Also revealing were the nonstandard numbers that children produced. These generally involved appending a number not among the first 9 integers to a decade name. The most common sequence was "29, 20-10 . . ."

Children who did not count as high as 20 showed a different pattern. They did not stop counting especially often with 9 numbers, did not produce omissions or repetitions from a 9 number to a decade name, and did not produce nonstandard numbers of the type described above. Thus, the pattern of data produced by children who counted beyond 20 was not an inherent part of counting. Rather, it seemed to be a product of the same knowledge that enabled them to count beyond that point.

What procedure might produce performance like that of the children who counted beyond 20? A model of one such procedure is shown in Figure 8-6. The model includes two parts: a representation of the information that

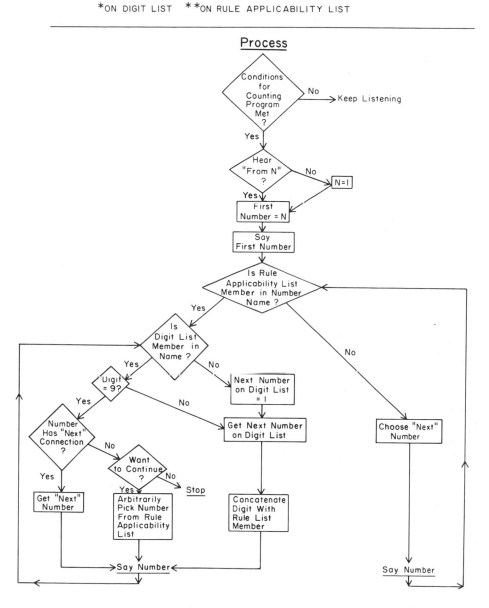

FIGURE 8-6 A model of how 4-year-olds count. Procedure used to generate numbers through 20 depicted in lower-right part of diagram. Procedure used to generate numbers beyond 20 depicted in lower-left part of diagram (from Siegler & Robinson, 1982).

children have about numbers, and a process that operates on the representation to produce behavior. The representation involves labeling numbers as being members of two special lists. One is the *digit list*, the numbers from 1 to 9 that can be appended to decade names. The second is the *rule applicability list*, the decade names from 20 to 90 to which digit list members can be appended. One other type of information is also included in the representation: "next" connections linking each number below 20 to the next higher number and linking higher 9 numbers, such as 29, to rule applicability list members, such as 30.

The process operates on this representation as follows. Children start counting by saying "1." Since they do not encounter a rule applicability list member in this or in any other early number name, they repeatedly execute Steps 6–8 to generate the numbers 1 through 20. Finally, they reach the number 20, a rule applicability list member. Performance then proceeds in the way indicated in Steps 9–19. As shown in Step 10, since no digit list member is in the name 20, children retrieve a 1 and append it to 20, creating 21. From 21 to 29, there is always a digit list member in the number name. Children simply retrieve the next digit list member and append it to 20 until they reach 29. As indicated in Step 15, if 29 has a "next" connection (presumably to 30), children say the next number and repeat the cycle. If it does not, they need to decide whether to stop or to arbitrarily pick some other number that is on their rule applicability list, such as 50 or 20. Eventually they reach some 9 number that does not have a "next" connection and decide to stop.

This model accounts for all four types of counting data described above. The critical choice point occurs when children reach a 9 number for which they do not have a "next" connection (Step 17). If they decide to stop, they will have stopped at a 9 number. If they decide to continue, they may choose a rule applicability list member that is too far advanced (resulting in patterns of omissions such as "27, 28, 29, 50") or one that is not far enough advanced (resulting in patterns of repetitions such as "37, 38, 39, 20"). Finally, if they are unsure where the digit repetition list ends, and guess that it ends later than it does, they will produce nonstandard numbers such as "20-10." All that remains for the children's representation to correspond to the inherent structure of the counting string is for them to learn the remaining "next" connections between "9" numbers and the succeeding decade names.

Counting of objects.   Between 2 and 4 years of age, children also become proficient in counting objects. As briefly discussed in Chapter 1, Gelman and Gallistel (1978) hypothesized that from early in the preschool period, children's learning of counting is guided by knowledge of principles. In particular, children were believed to understand the following five principles:

1. *The one-one principle:* Assign one and only one number word to each object.
2. *The stable order principle:* Always assign the numbers in the same order.
3. *The cardinal principle:* The last number assigned indicates the number of objects in the set.
4. *The abstraction principle:* The other principles apply to any set of objects.
5. *The order irrelevance principle:* The order in which objects is counted is irrelevant.

Several types of evidence persuaded Gelman and Gallistel that children understood all of these principles by age 5 and most of them by age 3 or 4. Even when children erred in their counting, they showed knowledge of the one-one principle, since they assigned exactly one number word to most of the objects. For instance, they might count all but one object once, either skipping or counting twice the single miscounted object. These errors seemed to be ones of execution rather than misguided intent. Children demonstrated knowledge of the stable order principle by almost always saying the number words in a constant order. Usually this was the conventional order, but occasionally it was an idiosyncratic order such as "1, 3, 6." The important phenomenon was that even when children used an idiosyncratic order, they used the same idiosyncratic order on each count. The 2- to 4-year-olds demonstrated knowledge of the cardinal principle by saying the last number with special emphasis. They showed understanding of the abstraction principle by not hesitating to count sets that included different types of objects. Finally, the order irrelevance principle seemed to be the most difficult, but even here 5-year-olds evidenced understanding. Many of them recognized that counting could start in the middle of a row of objects, as long as each object was eventually counted. Although few of the children could state the principles, their counting suggested that they understood and used them.

Number conservation.   As described in Chapter 2, Piaget's number-conservation task begins with two rows that have equal numbers of objects, at least six objects per row. One of the rows is lengthened or shortened. Finally, the child is asked whether the two rows still contain the same number of objects.

This number-conservation task can be placed in a broader context. As Klahr and Wallace (1976) and Halford (1982) noted, a sophisticated understanding of conservation implies understanding of three transformations, not one. Not only should the child understand that certain transformations do not influence quantity, but also that transformations involving addition increase number and transformations involving subtraction decrease it. Further, early understanding of conservation might apply to small sets of objects but not large sets (Bryant, 1974; Gelman, 1972; Winer, 1974). In sum, understanding of conservation involves understanding of the effects of at least three transformations on both small and large sets of objects.

Children acquire understanding of these different conservation problems at different points in development, but they acquire the understandings in a consistent order. The earliest understandings involve the effects of addition and subtraction on small sets. Children as young as 4 years know that adding an object to a row with only a few objects results in more objects and that subtracting an object from such a set results in fewer objects. However, if the number of objects in the two rows is large, or if the only transformation is to elongate or compress a row, 4-year-olds judge the longer row to have more objects.

Gradually, children extend their knowledge to additional transformations and larger sets. First they learn that merely spreading or compressing a row with a few objects leaves the number of objects unchanged. Next they learn that adding an object to a set with many objects increases its number and that subtracting an object decreases it. Finally they learn that simply spreading out or contracting a large set leaves its number unchanged. Interestingly, this last type of problem to be mastered was the very one used by Piaget in his number-conservation task.

At this point, which most children reach at around age 6 or 7, they can solve all number-conservation problems. Development of the concept is not yet complete, though. At first, children solve the problems by counting the number of objects in each row after the transformation and comparing the numbers, or by placing the objects in the rows in one-to-one correspondence and seeing if either row has anything left over. Later, however, they learn how to solve the problems without counting or pairing. Instead, they rely on the type of transformation that was performed. If one row had an object added, it necessarily has more; if one row had an object subtracted, it necessarily has less; and if nothing was added or subtracted, the two rows continue to have the same amount.

This last discovery is important because it allows children to transfer knowledge from number conservation to other types of conservation problems. Counting and pairing are useful for solving number-conservation problems, but cannot be applied to other conservation tasks. For example, how could counting be used to solve a conservation of liquid quantity problem? On the other hand, relying on the type of transformation allows children to solve all conservation problems. Adding material always results in more, subtracting always results in less, and the lack of addition or subtraction always results in the same amount. Given this analysis, it was not surprising that children who solved number-conservation problems by counting or creating one-to-one correspondences rarely solved liquid quantity or solid quantity conservation problems. By contrast, children who solved number-conservation problems by relying on the type of transformation could apply this reasoning to solving liquid and solid quantity conservation problems as well. (Siegler, 1981).

An interesting general implication of this sequence is that ability to solve all problems correctly does not always mark the end point of development. At times, more generalizable or more efficient ways of solving problems may exist. Under these circumstances, conceptual understanding may continue to develop even after children can solve all problems in a domain.

Understanding of Ordinal Properties of Numbers.   Ordinal properties of numbers refer to relations among the numbers. A number may be first or second in an order or it may be greater than or less than another number. Mastery of ordinal properties of numbers, like mastery of cardinal properties, begins in infancy. However, understanding of ordinal properties seems to begin later, between 12 and 18 months.

Among the most basic ordinal concepts are *more* and *less*. Strauss and Curtis (1984) and Cooper (1984) demonstrated knowledge of "more than" relations in infants. Strauss and Curtis repeatedly presented 16-to-18-month-olds with two squares, one containing one dot, the other containing two dots. They reinforced the babies for selecting the square with two dots. Then they presented two new squares (e.g., squares with four dots and three dots). The babies more often chose the set of dots that maintained the "larger" relation, thus indicating understanding of this ordinal property. Whether babies of this age understand "less than" relations, however, is unclear at present (Cooper, 1984; Strauss & Curtis, 1984).

Understanding of numerical magnitudes.   In the preschool period, children learn to compare numbers apart from the objects they represent. That is, they learn to solve such problems as "Which is bigger, six or three?" To study the process by which they do so, Siegler and Robinson (1982) asked 4-year-olds to compare the magnitudes of all 36 of the possible pairs of numbers 1 through 9. The children's patterns of errors resembled older children's and adults' patterns of solution times. In all cases, the easiest magnitude comparisons were those involving small numbers (e.g., 2 versus 1) and those involving large numerical differences (e.g., 9 versus 3).

The reason for these results was suggested by analyses using a powerful mathematical technique: *multidimensional scaling.* This technique is used to depict the similarity of stimuli to each other. The less people differentiate between two stimuli, the closer they will be in the spatial diagrams that depict the results of the scaling analyses. When people internally represent a set of stimuli as differing along only one dimension, the spatial diagrams that emerge from multidimensional scaling depict the stimuli as points along a single line. When people internally represent stimuli as differing along two or three dimensions, a two- or three-dimensional representation of the stimuli emerges.

Intuitively, we might expect children's judgments of the relative sizes of numbers to fall onto a single dimension, corresponding to the size of the numbers. The larger the difference in the sizes of two numbers, the easier it would be to know which was larger. In fact, the results of the multi-dimensional scaling analyses indicated that preschoolers represent numbers in a different form. As shown in Figure 8–7, they grouped the numbers into four clusters. One cluster was formed by the "big" numbers, six, seven, eight, and nine. A second was formed by the medium-size numbers, four and five. A third cluster was formed by the small numbers, two and three. The number one seemed to form a smallest-number category in and of itself. The clustering scheme is reminiscent of the differentiations that other 4-year-olds made in the number-conservation experiments between small and large number sets. Moreover, Miller and Gelman (1983) obtained similar clusters of numbers in an experiment in which they asked 5-year-olds, "Here are three numbers: which two are most similar?" Thus, young children seem to divide numbers into groups and to use the divisions to solve different types of problems.

A model that produces magnitude comparison performance in keeping with these data is shown in Figure 8–8. The representation of numbers involves probabilistic links between each number and the four categories of smallest, small, medium, and big numbers. For example, the probability that the number two would be labeled "small" was .72. These probabilities were obtained by asking children directly whether each number was small, medium, or big. Thus, the .72 reflects the percentage of children who said that two was small.

The process operating on this representation is shown in Figure 8–8B. Children retrieve labels for each number being compared with the probabilities shown in Figure 8–8A. For example, if two was being compared to another number, the probability that a child would retrieve the label "small" for two would be .72. If the labels that the child retrieves differ, the number associated with the larger label is chosen as being greater. If the

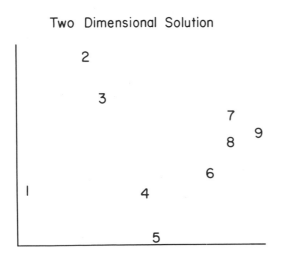

Two Dimensional Solution

2

3

7

8   9

6

1   4

5

FIGURE 8-7 Multidimensional scaling solution for magnitude comparison data. The numbers seem to cluster into four groups rather than being ordered along a single dimension of increasing magnitude (from Siegler & Robinson, 1982).

Representation

Category		1	2	3	4	5	6	7	8	9
					Number					
Smallest		.7								
Small		.2	.72	.61	.22	.06			.06	
Medium		.1	.28	.33	.67	.72	.67	.56	.27	.44
Big				.06	.11	.22	.33	.44	.67	.56

Process

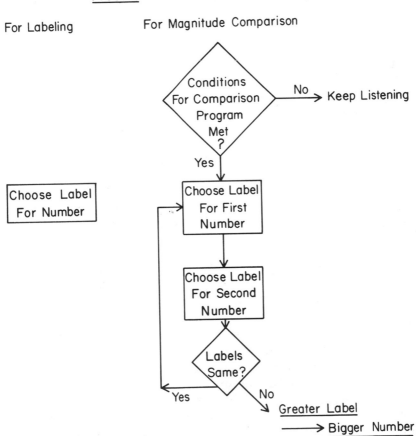

FIGURE 8-8 Model of how 4-year-olds decide whether one number is larger than another. The numbers in the matrix at the top are the probabilities with which 4-year-olds labeled each number as *smallest, small, medium,* or *big* (from Siegler & Robinson, 1982).

labels are the same, the child again chooses labels with the probabilities shown in the representation and again compares the labels. The cycle continues until the two labels differ.

This model explains why children have an easier time judging which number is bigger when the numbers are far apart. Such numbers are unlikely to share a common label; the bigger number almost always will be associated with the bigger label. It also explains why comparisons involving two small numbers are easier than comparisons involving two big numbers. Smaller numbers are grouped in categories with fewer members than are bigger numbers. For example, one is a category by itself, and two and three form a category by themselves, but six, seven, eight, and nine are all grouped together. This grouping is likely due to children having more experience with smaller numbers, and therefore differentiating among them to greater degrees than larger numbers.

Why might children group numbers into categories? The adage "Divide and conquer" provides a hint. Learning the relative magnitudes of the many numbers they encounter would pose a daunting task for young children. For the numbers 1 through 9 alone, there are 36 pairs to memorize. On the other hand, if children divided the numbers into the four groups suggested by Figure 8-7 and always answered that the number with the bigger label was larger, they would answer correctly on almost 90% of problems. As a strategy for rapidly learning new material, dividing material into categories has much to recommend it.

A summing-up: preschoolers' knowledge of numbers. Even preschoolers know quite a bit about numbers. Their knowledge extends to counting, number conservation, numerical magnitudes, and as will be discussed in the next chapter, addition and subtraction. How do children integrate these particular understandings into a general concept of number?

Siegler and Robinson (1982) formulated the model shown in Figure 8-9 to represent preschoolers' knowledge of numbers. The representation is organized hierarchically: numbers as a class are at the top, then categories of numbers (e.g., small numbers), and then individual numbers (e.g., six).

First consider the top level of the hierarchy, numbers as a class. Preschoolers seem to understand that all numbers can be operated on by the same processes. They can be used to count, their magnitudes can be compared, they can be added, and so on.

At the next lower level of the hierarchy are categories of numbers. On a variety of tasks, preschoolers seem to treat numbers within a category similarly, but treat differently numbers in separate categories. In number-conservation experiments, they divide numbers into some categories where they count or pair the objects in the set, and other categories where they choose the longer row as having more objects without bothering to count. In comparing the sizes of numbers, they divide numbers into categories and

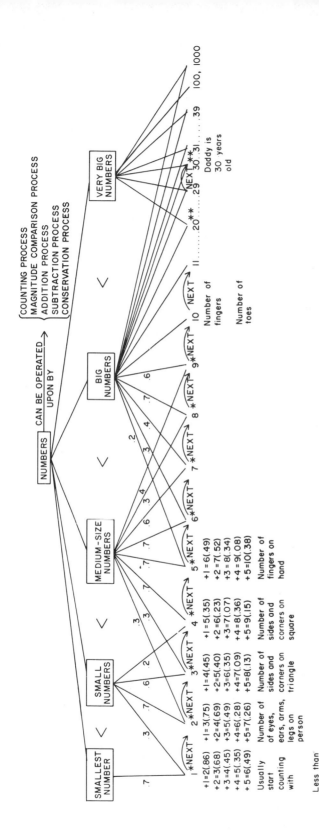

FIGURE 8-9 Model of 4-year-olds' representations of numbers. Model includes knowledge about number conservation, counting, numerical magnitudes, and addition (from Siegler & Robinson, 1982).

289

judge numbers in bigger categories to be larger than numbers in smaller categories. In judging the similarity of numbers, they rely on comparable categories. Thus, preschoolers seem to represent numbers in a variety of contexts, in terms of categories.

The lowest level of the hierarchy involves individual numbers. Even young children know a considerable amount about individual numbers. For example, they often know that one is the number with which you start counting. It is the number of heads, bodies, noses, and mouths on a person. It is the smallest number. Preschoolers also have information about groups of individual numbers. They tie the numbers one to nine, and perhaps other numbers as well, to category labels on a probabilistic basis. Illustratively, nine is labeled as "medium size" with probability .4 and as "big" with probability .6.

What is gained by hypothesizing this type of shared representation? One advantage is in cognitive economy. Certain information may be used across multiple tasks. A shared representation avoids the need for children to represent the same information multiple times.

A second potential advantage involves learning. Children may better see relations among concepts when a single representation includes all of the information. For example, children may more easily realize the relations among number conservation, counting, and magnitude comparison when information about all three is contained in a common representation.

A third potential benefit involves generalization. In learning any one aspect of a concept, children have difficulty separating characteristics unique to that aspect from characteristics that apply to all aspects of it. This was evident in the difficulty that the 5-year-olds in Keil and Batterman (1984) had in separating characteristic from defining features of concepts. By comparing many different aspects of a concept children can arrive at valid generalizations about that concept. For example, by integrating their knowledge about different aspects of numbers, children would eventually realize that operations that can be applied to one set of numbers can generally be applied to all numbers. In sum, it seems well worthwhile for children to integrate their understanding of different aspects of a concept, and for us to try to understand how they do so.

Some Important Relational Concepts

Certain concepts inherently entail relations among other concepts. Three of the most important of these are causality, hierarchical classification, and transitivity. Causality involves the specification of cause–effect relations—that is, the specification of how one event generates another. Hierarchical classification centers on the formation of set/subset relations. Transitivity involves the way in which knowledge of some ordinal relations within a set of objects is used to deduce other ordinal relations within the set.

Piaget studied each of these relational concepts and concluded that children did not understand any of them until the concrete-operations period. It now appears, though, that even young preschoolers know a considerable amount about such relations. These early strengths that children show are as important to an overall understanding of development as are the limitations Piaget documented.

Causal inferences.   As noted in Chapter 2, Piaget found that in response to such questions as "What causes the wind?" young children give nonphysically based answers such as "The wind blows because it wants to." Piaget attributed such answers to the children reasoning animistically (attributing human qualities to inanimate objects) and magically. However, Piaget may have mistaken the children's lack of knowledge of particular physical causes for a general misunderstanding of causation. That is, they may have produced such answers not because they were convinced of their correctness, but rather because they simply had no idea what a good answer would be. (What does cause the wind to blow?)

The British philosopher David Hume (1739–1740/1911) described three features that seemed to him necessary for inferring that two events are causally connected. The cause must precede the effect. The cause must be close to the effect in space and time. The effect must regularly accompany the cause. Do young children grasp these three principles: precedence, contiguity, and regularity?

Both children's language use and their problem-solving activity indicate that from early in the preschool period, they understand that causes must precede effects. First consider evidence from their language use. Hood and Bloom (1979) found that 2- and 3-year-olds choose causal terms appropriately. Most of their spontaneous causal statements refer to social and motivational causes such as, "I hit you because you made my angry." Somewhat older children appropriately discuss physical causes as well. Corrigan (1975) found that 4- and 5-year-olds understood 90% of the causal expressions they heard, and used the term "because" correctly in 80% of situations

Preschoolers show understanding of the importance of precedence in solving causality problems. In several experiments, 3- and 4-year-olds have been shown three events in the order A-B-C and then have been asked, "What made B happen?" The children have consistently chosen event A, which preceded event B, rather than event C, which followed it (Bullock & Gelman, 1979; Kun, 1978).

Preschoolers also grasp the importance of temporal and spatial contiguity. In fact, as Piaget (1969) argued, they may assign too much importance to it. Mendelson and Shultz (1976) found that 8-year-olds considered both contiguity and regularity in drawing causal inferences. In contrast, 5-year-olds considered only temporal contiguity. If one event sometimes followed immediately after another, and sometimes did not follow it at all, 5-year-olds but not 8-year-olds judged the relation to be causal. Thus, preschoolers may not fully appreciate the importance of regularity in inferring causation.

Children's understanding of causation extends beyond Hume's three principles in at least one very important respect: They understand the significance of generative mechanisms. Shultz (1982) provided a particularly clever demonstration to support this contention. He presented 3-year-olds with a yellow and a green lamp, both of which could produce a spot of light on the wall. Before turning on either lamp, however, the experimenter placed a mirror between the green lamp and the wall. Then the experimenter turned on the green lamp, which, because of the placement of the mirror, did not produce any light on the wall. After five seconds, the experimenter simultaneously slid the mirror in front of the yellow lamp and turned that lamp on. Now a light appeared on the wall, since there was no barrier between it and the green lamp.

The experimenter asked the children which lamp made the spot on the wall. Temporal contiguity would seem to favor the yellow lamp, since it had been turned on at the same time the light appeared. However, the 3-year-olds usually chose the green light as the cause. Shultz argued that they did this because they understood how lamps produce impressions on walls and how barriers can prevent lights from producing an impression. This knowledge was sufficiently powerful to more than balance the fact that the yellow light was turned on at the same time that the light appeared on the wall (see Bullock, Gelman & Baillargeon, 1982, for additional evidence supporting this conclusion).

Thus, children seem to understand a good deal about causation before they enter the concrete-operations stage. They understand the roles of precedence, contiguity, and generative mechanisms. They also use causal terms correctly in speech. Their causal reasoning is limited in at least one respect, however: They frequently overemphasize contiguity at the expense of regular but delayed relations.

Hierarchical classification.   Hierarchical classification involves the realization that all members of one set are necessarily members of another set. It also entails understanding of the asymmetry of the relation. Just because all members of one set necessarily are members of another does not imply that all members of the second set are members of the first. The fact that all grapes are fruit does not imply that all fruits are grapes.

We already have encountered one test of understanding of hierarchical classification: Inhelder and Piaget's (1964) class-inclusion task. Recall from Chapter 2 that this task involves presenting children with a number of objects that can either be viewed as members of a single set or of two subsets. For example, children might be presented four bears and six lions, a total of ten animals. Then they would be asked if there were more of the larger subset or more of the set (more lions or more animals). Children below age 8 usually answer that the subset contains more animals—that is, that there are more lions than animals. They compare the two subsets (lions and bears) rather than the set and the superset (lions and animals). Inhelder and Piaget believed that children did this because they could not simultaneously view an object as both a lion and an animal. This weakness would prevent them from relating concepts hierarchically, that is, simultaneously viewing objects as members of both broader and narrower sets.

It now appears, though, that many characteristics other than ability to view objects as simultaneously belonging to multiple sets conspire to make this class inclusion task difficult (Winer, 1980). Trabasso, Isen, Dolecki, McLanahan, Riley, and Tucker (1978) listed the difficulty of executing the following processes as contributing to young children's poor performance: the wording of the question, the quantification of the number of objects in the subsets and the set, the comparison of the sizes of the larger subset and the set, and the complexity of the appropriate decision rule. Thus, in response to the question "What develops in class inclusion?" Trabasso et al. answered, only partly in jest, "Everything" (p. 178).

Markman (1973) demonstrated in an especially compelling fashion how variables once thought to be irrelevant, because they have little to do with the logic of set-subset relations, can influence children's class-inclusion performance. She contrasted questions involving *class* nouns with questions involving *collection* nouns. A simple way of distinguishing between class and collection nouns involves the terms that can be used to refer to subsets and supersets. In class nouns, (such as *trees* and *cats*) both subset and superset can be referred to by the superset term. Both oak trees and trees in general can be labeled *trees;* both Persian cats and cats in general can be called *cats.* In collection nouns, such as *forest* and *gang,* this is not the case. An oak tree can be a member of a forest, but it cannot be called a forest. A child can be a member of a gang but cannot be called a gang. Both collection and class nouns can enter into hierarchical relations, though. Both the oak/forest and the oak/tree relations are hierarchical.

Markman presented 5- and 6-year-olds with class-inclusion questions that were identical except for the use of class nouns or collection nouns. Some children heard questions similar to Inhelder and Piaget's, in which class nouns were used. Illustratively, they saw five baby frogs, a mommy frog, and a daddy frog, and were asked "Here are some frogs . . . . Who would own more, someone who owned the baby frogs or someone who owned the frogs?" Other children were asked about the same array of objects, but heard a collection noun used to describe them: "Here is a family of frogs . . . . Who would own more, someone who owned the baby frogs or someone who owned the family?"

The 5- and 6-year-olds who received the class nouns (baby frogs versus frogs) rarely answered correctly; this replicated Inhelder and Piaget's findings. However, the 5- and 6-year-olds who received the collection nouns (baby frogs versus frog family) answered consistently correctly. Collection nouns may focus children's attention on hierarchical relations since terms such as family and forest always involve a part-whole relation, and therefore make the problem easier (Markman & Callanan, 1983).

From another perspective, even when children solve the standard class-inclusion problem, they may not do so through purely logical means. Children of ages 7 to 9 usually solve class-inclusion problems by comparing the number of objects in the particular subset they were asked about to the number of objects in the whole set, and choosing the one with the larger number (Markman, 1978). Not until age 10 or 11 do they consistently solve class-inclusion problems by using the purely logical relations. That is, not until then do they seem to realize that the subset is inherently smaller than the set regardless of the particular numbers of objects involved. The pattern with class inclusion thus closely resembles that found with number conservation. In both problems, children initially can solve some problems from the domain but not the traditional Piagetian problem. Later, they can solve the traditional problem as well as simpler versions, but do so through counting and comparing the number of objects in the two sets. Only several years later do children shift from solving the problem by relying on empirical relations to solving it by relying on purely logical ones.

Transitive inference. Transitive inference involves extrapolating ordinal relations to new cases. For example, if Bill is shorter than Susan, and Jim is taller than Susan, we can deduce that Jim is taller than Bill. Children below age 6 or 7 often have difficulty solving these problems. Piaget attributed this failure to the young children lacking reversibility. More recently, two alternative interpretations have been proposed. One attributes the young children's difficulty to their not remembering the premises. The other suggests that it is due to their not forming an appropriate representation.

First consider the memory-difficulty hypothesis. To solve transitivity problems, children need to memorize the pairwise relations (e.g., A > B). Without doing this, they cannot draw the proper inference even if they understand transitive relations. If children in fact understand the logic of transitivity, but fail transitivity problems because they cannot remember the premises, then insuring that children remember the premises should allow them to draw appropriate inferences as well.

Bryant and Trabasso (1971) directly tested the memory-difficulty interpretation. Preschoolers were shown five sticks of varying length, each of a different color. They learned which of the sticks in a given pair of adjacent-size sticks was longer (e.g., the red stick [the second longest] is longer than the green stick [the third longest]). After children learned the individual pairs, they were presented in random order all four adjacent-size pairs until they answered consistently correctly. Finally, children were questioned not only about the original pairs, but also about pairs whose relations they could only infer (e.g., the second and fourth longest sticks).

Bryant and Trabasso predicted that once the preschoolers learned the orders of the individual pairs, they also would do well on the untrained pairs where they could infer the ordering. This prediction proved accurate. Children who memorized the original pairs generally drew appropriate inferences.

What representation might allow children to draw such inferences? The answer seems to be that they represent the lengths as a simple row, in which stimuli are ordered from shortest to longest. Given such a representation, answering the question "Which is longer?" is easy; simply locate the two asked-about stimuli and choose the one closer to the tall end of the row (Trabasso, Riley, & Wilson, 1975).

The main source of development in drawing transitive inferences seems to be in the range of conditions under which children form these useful representations. As was the case in young children's use of memory strategies (Chapter 7), quite subtle sources of difficulty can lead to failure to use the strategies. For example, rather than training 4-year-olds by asking them to memorize both which stick in a given pair was longer and which stick was shorter, Riley and Trabasso (1974) always asked either only which stick was longer or only which stick was shorter. They found that always asking the question in one form led to much less learning. Of the 4-year-olds trained with both phrasings, 87% learned consistently to solve the problems. Of those trained with only one, 35% learned.

This difference in learning may have been due to young children encoding the relations differently in the two conditions. Children who were always asked one question may have encoded the relation absolutely (Stick 2 is long; Stick 3 is short) rather than relatively (Stick 2 is longer than Stick 3). A given stick eventually would be found to be both long and short. Such contradictory encodings could not be shaped into an integrated rowlike representation of the stick lengths.

In sum, failing to form an appropriate representation (an ordered row) may be the main reason why young children do not consistently solve transitive-inference problems. This interpretation accounts for Riley and Trabasso's finding of preschoolers failing to memorize all the pairwise relations when only one comparative adjective was used in training, with Piaget's original position that preschoolers fail because they have difficulty seeing that an individual stick can simultaneously be smaller and larger than other sticks, and with several other recently advanced interpretations of young children's difficulty on transitivity problems (Brainerd & Kingma, 1984; Halford, 1984). As on the magnitude-comparison task discussed earlier in this chapter, forming an appropriate representation greatly reduces the amount of memorizing needed to solve the problems, and therefore allows young children to succeed on them.

Evaluation of content-oriented approaches. The research on children's understandings of numbers, causality, hierarchical classification, and transitive inference illustrates both strengths and weaknesses of content-oriented approaches to conceptual understanding. They can reveal a large part of children's knowledge of particular concepts. They also can aid understanding of how children's representations come to resemble increasingly closely the underlying structure of the concept. Form-oriented approaches do not yield comparable information about children's knowledge of particular concepts.

The largest disadvantage of approaches that emphasize content is part and parcel with their largest advantage. Investigating children's knowledge of particular concepts yields a huge mass of information. Much of this information is relevant only to the particular concept on which it is obtained. Thus, the approaches only can be used with concepts that are thought to be especially important in and of themselves. It seems quite appropriate, therefore, that much of the research of this type has been devoted to a small number of critical concepts, among them time, speed, and distance (Acredolo & Schmid, 1981; Friedman, 1978, 1982; Levin, 1982; Richards, 1982; Weinreb & Brainerd, 1975; Wilkening, 1982), space (Lockman & Pick, 1984; Acredolo, 1979; Huttenlocher & Newcomb, 1984; Rieser, 1979), and proportionality (Ferretti, Butterfield, Cahn, & Kirkman, 1985; Siegler & Vago, 1978; Strauss, 1982; Surber & Gzesh, 1984).

Although content-oriented approaches focus on particular concepts, they have revealed considerable unity in development across different concepts as well as numerous concept-specific findings. One recurring theme is the importance of the closely-related concepts of representation and encoding. Children's representation and encoding skills strongly influence both the quality of their performance and their ability to learn new information. In comparing numerical magnitudes, children divided numbers into groups, which made good performance possible with considerably less memorization than would have been needed to memorize each pair of numbers separately. On transitive-inference problems, children represented the stick lengths as ordered items in a row to memorize the pairs efficiently and to draw appropriate inferences. The Chapter 3 discussions of the role of encoding in children's solving of analogy and balance-scale problems and the Chapter 7 discussions of the role of representations in memories for baseball, chess, and dinosaurs reinforce this conclusion.

A second common theme is that development does not necessarily end when children perform a task consistently correctly. Development can continue in the direction of greater generality and greater efficiency. This pattern was evident on the number-conservation task. Children progressed from counting or pairing objects in the two rows to using the more general transformation rule, which could be applied to liquid and solid quantity conservation. It also was evident on the class inclusion task. Children initially performed correctly by counting the objects in the subset and superset. Only later did they rely on the logical relation.

The number-conservation and class-inclusion research also illustrates a third trend, that toward greater use of logical rather than empirical means for solving problems. In both cases, children first solved problems through the empirical process of counting. Only later did they logically deduce that a certain answer must be true regardless of the numbers of objects in the problem.

These discoveries of unities are an encouraging sign. They suggest that content-oriented approaches to conceptual development, like their close cousins, the knowledge-oriented approaches to memory development, can help us better understand children's thinking.

SUMMARY

Two approaches to conceptual development have been used: form-oriented and content-oriented approaches. Approaches that emphasize form reflect an attempt to draw generally valid conclusions about children's conceptual representations. They usually have been used to study object concepts. Content-oriented approaches are efforts to illustrate in detail how children represent particular concepts. They have been employed most often to study abstract ideas and relational concepts that people often use and that are of long-standing philosophical interest.

Children seem to use three main forms to represent concepts. One is defining-features representations, which involve a few necessary and sufficient features. Another form that they use is probabilistic representations, in which many features are associated with the concept to varying degrees, but no feature or group of features is necessary and sufficient. A third form that they use is exemplar-based representations, that include particularly memorable or important instances of the concept.

Piaget and Vygotsky have formulated versions of the representational development hypothesis. This hypothesis states that the form of children's conceptual representations changes as the children become older. Within this view, young children cannot form representations based on necessary and sufficient features, but later in development, they not only can but generally do.

Several considerations argue against the view that young children's concepts are fundamentally unlike those of older children and adults, however. If young children's concepts were fundamentally different, it would be much more difficult to communicate with them than it is. Children's sorting of objects, which often is interpreted as supporting the representational development hypothesis, may reflect what they find interesting rather than what they know. Even young children have proved capable of relying on necessary and sufficient features with familiar concepts. Even adults may not in general represent concepts in terms of necessary and sufficient features.

Many of both children's and adults' representations are built on probabilistic connections between features and concepts. Even infants are sensitive to cue validities and to correlations among features. Even toddlers form basic level categories, though superordinate and subordinate level concepts often are not formed until years later. Finally, young children as well as adults form prototypes, that incorporate characteristic patterns of features even if the prototype itself has never been encountered.

Examples also seem to play a large role in children's conceptual representations. Because of the complexity of many concepts, it seems extremely useful for children to retain detailed information about early-encountered examples of a concept. These examples are especially useful for correcting false impressions about the nature of the concept. Evidence exists that examples play a larger role in early conceptual representations than in later ones.

The second major strategy for studying conceptual development emphasizes the content rather than the form of children's conceptual representations. This approach has been applied to knowledge of numbers. Even infants understand certain cardinal and ordinal properties of numbers, as is evident in their ability to discriminate among sets with different numbers of objects, and in their counting. By the end of the preschool period, children supplement these early understandings with knowledge of magnitudes, number conservation, counting, and similarities among numbers. Young children appear to represent numbers in part as falling into discrete categories and use these categories to compare numerical magnitudes, to solve number-conservation problems, and to judge how similar different numbers are. From an early age, children may integrate these varied aspects of the number concept into a single representation that can be acted on by different processes. Representing the number concept in this way would be efficient, and would also be advantageous for learning and for drawing generalizations from existing knowledge.

Children have considerably greater knowledge of many relational concepts, such as causality, hierarchical classification, and transitivity, than once was thought. Improvement beyond this initial competence is found in the ease with which they form appropriate representations, in increasing reliance on logical rather than empirical relations, and in the use of increasingly efficient and general solution processes even beyond the point of consistent, correct responding.

RECOMMENDED READINGS

Keil, F. C., & Batterman, N. (1984). A characteristic-to-defining shift in the development of word meaning. *Journal of Verbal Learning and Verbal Behavior, 23,* 221–236. A clever and convincing demonstration of the shift between ages 5 and 9 from an emphasis on characteristic features to an emphasis on defining features.

Markman, E. M. (1978). Empirical versus logical solutions to part-whole comparison problems concerning classes and collections. *Child Development, 49,* 168–177. A striking demonstration of how many problems which to adults seem to be matters of logic are empirical questions for young children.

Mervis, C. B., & Rosch, E. (1981). Categorization of natural objects. *Annual Review of Psychology, 32,* 89–115. Reviews the accumulated evidence for the roles of basic level categories, correlations among features, and cue validities in children's conceptual development. One of the most important and influential lines of work in the study of thinking.

Shultz, T. R. (1982). Rules of causal attribution. *Monographs of the Society for Research in Child Development, 47,* Whole No. 194. Children have much greater understanding of cause and effect relations than they are usually credited with having; this monograph demonstrates a large number of these capabilities.

Siegler, R. S., & Robinson, M. (1982). The development of numerical understandings. In H. Reese & L. P. Lipsitt (Eds.), *Advances in child development and behavior: Vol. 16.* New York: Academic Press. An effort to document the many different understandings that children have of number by the time they enter school, together with a model of how they integrate the different understandings.

Trabasso, T., Riley, C. A., & Wilson, E. G. (1975). The representation of linear order and spatial strategies in reasoning: A developmental study. In R. J. Falmagne (Ed.), *Reasoning: Representation and process.* Hillsdale, NJ: Erlbaum. A classic analysis of children's representations and processes for solving transitive inference problems.

9
DEVELOPMENT
OF ACADEMIC SKILLS

I struggled through the alphabet as if it had been a bramble-bush; getting considerably worried and scratched by every letter. After that, I fell among those thieves, the nine figures, who seemed every evening to do something new to disguise themselves and baffle recognition. But, at last I began, in a purblind groping way, to read, write, and cipher, on the very smallest scale. (Pip, in Dickens's *Great Expectations*).

Traditionally, children's thinking in school and out of school has been treated as two separate subjects. Researchers considered themselves either educational psychologists or developmental psychologists, but not both. They published in different journals. They spoke to different audiences. They were interested in different problems.

Recently this distinction has been breaking down. The reason is that the inherent concerns of the two fields overlap in important ways. Both are concerned with the types of reasoning children are capable of at different ages. Both are concerned with how children acquire new information. Both are concerned with the relation between what children already know and the way in which they learn.

It is not surprising, then, that differences between the two fields are eroding. At one time the fields were distinguished by whether they emphasized conceptual form or conceptual content. Cognitive-developmental psychology focused on conceptual form, educational psychology on content.

As seen in the last chapter, however, cognitive development now includes approaches that emphasize the contents of children's thought, as well as the forms of their conceptual representations.

Another type of distinction that gradually has blurred concerns which aspects of children's thinking were studied. At one time, cognitive development focused on parts of children's thinking that were believed to be essentially unaffected by the environments in which the children grew up. Educational psychology focused on how children learned material that they were taught.

Although some distinction can still be made on this basis, it is becoming increasingly apparent that the ways children acquire information in and out of school are fundamentally similar. For example, children's understanding of conservation, which once was thought to reflect purely internal developmental processes, is now known to be influenced by formal and informal educational experiences as well. Children of potters in Mexico, who are used to working with clay, understand conservation of solid quantity several years earlier than do other children (Price-Williams, Gordon, & Ramirez, 1969). Complementarily, what children learn from instruction in school often bears little resemblance to what they are taught. For example, children instructed in school to do arithmetic problems in one way often develop a different approach to solve the problems. Resnick and Glaser (1975) referred to many of children's understandings of mathematical concepts as "inventions," because they were so far removed from the instruction the children received. Thus, aspects of children's thinking that are presumed to depend purely on "development" can depend heavily on experience, and aspects of children's thinking that are believed to depend purely on the type of instruction received can depend heavily on more general developmental processes.

I believe the blurring of the lines between educational and cognitive-developmental psychology will lead to a better understanding of children's thinking. Each approach to children's thinking has much to offer. Cognitive development offers a variety of powerful theoretical ideas, methods, and representational languages. These techniques can increase our understanding of how children learn mathematics, reading, and other academic skills and can suggest ideas about how their learning can be improved. The benefits flow in the other direction as well. Reading, writing, and mathematics are among the most important skills children learn; they are important not only in and of themselves, but also because they allow children to gain additional information about the world when they are not at school. A comprehensive account of children's thinking thus requires understanding of what and how children learn at school.

Organization of the chapter. This chapter will examine children's knowledge and learning of the traditional three R's: reading, writing, and arithmetic. The discussion of arithmetic will examine children's development of two computational skills—addition and subtraction—and one noncom-

TABLE 9-1   Chapter Outline

I. Acquisition of Mathematical Skills
A. Addition
B. Subtraction
C. Estimation
II. How Children Learn to Read
A. The Typical Chronological Progression
B. Prereading Skills
C. Identifying Individual Words
D. Comprehension of Larger Units of Prose
III. Acquiring Competence in Writing
A. The Initial Drafting Process
B. The Revision Process
IV. Summary

putational skill—estimation. The discussion of reading will first focus on the prereading skills believed to be prerequisites for learning to read, then on the word-identification skills that are the major challenge in early reading, and finally on the comprehension skills that play an increasingly important role in later reading and that are the true goal of learning to read. The discussion of writing first addresses the general question of why writing is more difficult than speaking, then examines the initial drafting process, and finally examines how children revise (or fail to revise) already-written papers. In all three areas we also will consider the implications of the research for teaching children to learn more effectively. In some of the areas, these implications are already being used to shape new instructional programs, with encouraging results. (Those interested in more extensive discussions of these areas should see Carpenter, Moser, and Romberg [1982] and Ginsburg [1983] in the area of arithmetic; Pearson [1984] and Spiro, Bruce, and Brewer [1980] on the subject of reading; and Bereiter and Scardamalia [1982] and Kress [1982] on the development of writing skills.) The chapter's organization is shown in Table 9-1.

Common features across academic skills.   Superficially, it might seem that although children's reading, writing, and arithmetic are interesting topics in their own right, they have little in common. It turns out, though, that the basic questions about how children learn in each area are quite similar:

1. How do children allocate their attentional resources to cope with competing processing demands?
2. How do children choose which strategy to use from among the several that they might use?
3. Should instructors teach children directly the techniques used by experts in an area, or are indirect teaching approaches more effective?
4. What causes individual difference in knowledge and learning?

These questions have led to discoveries of some striking unities in children's thinking in the different subject areas. Consider, for instance, children's strategy choices in addition, reading, and spelling. In all areas, children need to choose between stating answers from memory or reverting to more time-consuming backup strategies. In adding, children need to decide whether to retrieve an answer and state it or to put up their fingers and count them. In reading, they need to decide whether to state a pronunciation for a word that they have retrieved from memory or to sound out the word. In spelling, they need to decide whether to retrieve a sequence of letters and write the word out or to look up the word in a dictionary. Despite the differences among the subject areas, children seem to make all these strategy choices through the same general process. This is but one example of how children's overall ways of thinking lead them to learn different academic skills in similar ways.

ACQUISITON OF MATHEMATICAL SKILLS

Addition

Even before they enter school, many 1980's preschoolers know how to solve addition problems with sums below 10. Their learning of these problems may be accelerated by educational television programs such as *Sesame Street* and *The Electric Company*. Earlier studies (e.g., Ilg & Ames, 1951) did not find similar competence until children were in first grade.

Although children's absolute amount of knowledge may have changed over the years, the process by which they add has in all likelihood stayed the same. One approach that they use in learning to add was named by Groen and Parkman (1972) the min approach. When children use this approach to add two numbers, they select the larger one and count up from it the number of times indicated by the smaller. Thus, if asked to add 2 + 4, a child would select 4 as the larger number and count up 2 numbers from it.

Groen and Parkman made three further assumptions about the min strategy. One was that the only factor influencing solution times on most addition problems was the number of counts demanded by the counting-on process. Each count in the counting-on process would take a certain amount of time, so the more counts, the more time that would be needed. This assumption allowed analyses of the addition problems via the subtractive technique, an experimental method previously encountered in the contexts of Kail, Pellegrino, and Carter's (1980) mental rotation experiment (Chapter 4) and Chi and Klahr's (1975) subitizing and counting experiment (Chapter 8). In this method, each additional execution of the critical process (in this case counting) should take a constant amount of time. Thus, Groen and Parkman predicted that mean solution times on different addition problems would fall on a straight line, with each additional count up to the size of the minimum number requiring a constant amount of time.

Groen and Parkman's second assumption involved a single exception to their first assumption. This exception involved ties, problems with equal first and second numbers, such as "2 + 2" and "3 + 3." Children were said to retrieve answers to these problems directly, at a uniformly rapid rate, so that solution times for all the ties would be as fast as for problems with an addend of 0. The times would be similar because neither ties nor problems with a 0 would require counting-on. Groen and Parkman's third assumption was that children always used the min model when adding numbers.

Several types of evidence supported this model. It accurately predicted the solution times of first graders (Figure 9–1). The larger the minimum number, the longer children took to solve the problem. It also predicted the solution times of Swedish third graders, and, with a small modification, slow-learning older children (Svenson, 1975; Svenson & Broquist, 1975). Children's verbalizations about their ongoing solution processes also often alluded to counting-on from the larger number (Ginsburg, 1977).

Ashcraft (1982) formulated an alternative model of how children add numbers, which focused on their retrieval of number facts from memory. He proposed that children represented addition facts in the form shown in Figure 9–2. The representation is a matrix with one addend heading the columns and the other heading the rows. In this mental table, distances between columns and between rows increase exponentially with increases in the absolute values of the two addends. For example, the distance between

FIGURE 9-1 First graders' solution times on addition problems. As the smaller addend in the problem increases, children take longer to solve the problem (from Groen & Parkman, 1972).

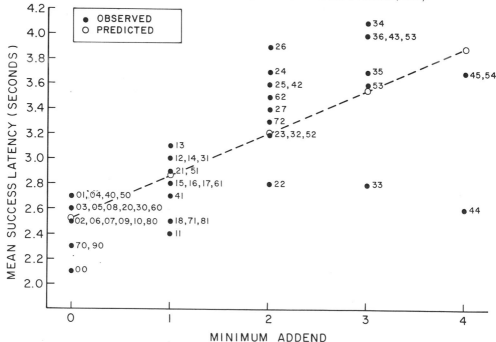

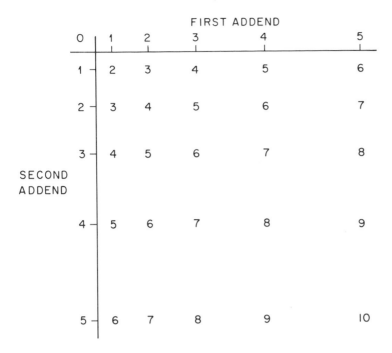

FIRST ADDEND

FIGURE 9-2 Ashcraft's (1982) representation of older children's and adults' addition knowledge.

the third and fourth rows is greater than that between the second and third rows. Children would add by starting at the origin, looking through the columns until they located the first addend, and then traveling down that column until they reached the row indicated by the second addend. The answer would be found at that location (the intersection of the two addends). The farther the distance from the origin to the answer, the larger the solution times would be.

Ashcraft (1982) reported that this fact-retrieval model did not fit first graders' performance as well as did the min model. The two models fit the performance of third graders equally well. The fact-retrieval model fit better the performance of fourth, fifth, and sixth graders. Ashcraft concluded that young children use the min approach and that older children and adults use the fact-retrieval approach. The transition would occur in third grade, during which some children would use one approach and some the other.

These studies have been useful in several ways. They document some of the strategies that children use to add. They also include quite specific hypotheses about the mental processes involved in the strategies. However, they are limited in one crucial respect. Even informal observation of children's addition reveals that many children use a variety of strategies. Sometimes a child will retrieve an answer, sometimes the child will put up his fingers and count them, and so on. Any model that says children of a given age always solve addition problems in a particular way is thus doomed

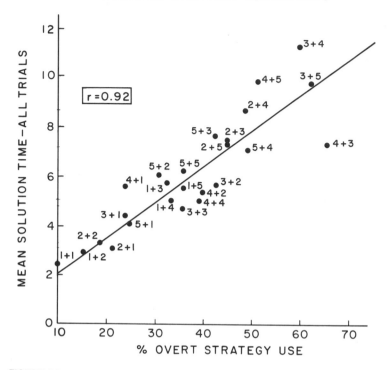

FIGURE 9-3   Relations between percentage overt strategy use and solution times (this page) and percentage overt strategy use and errors (facing page) (Siegler and Shrager, 1984).

to be wrong. A comprehensive model of how children add numbers must indicate what range of strategies children of specific ages use, why they use different strategies, and how they decide which strategy to use on a given occasion.

Strategy choices in addition   Siegler and Shrager (1984) videotaped 4-and 5-year-olds as they added problems with sums of 10 or less. The preschoolers used four strategies. Sometimes they counted their fingers. Sometimes they counted aloud while just gazing into space. Sometimes they put up fingers but answered without counting them. Finally, sometimes they just stated an answer that they retrieved from memory.

The most interesting finding of this experiment was the discovery of the very strong relation shown in Figure 9–3. The harder the problem (measured either by large numbers of errors or long solution times), the more often children used one of the three *overt* strategies: counting fingers, counting, or just putting up fingers.[1]

---

[1]The three strategies were labeled overt strategies because all involved overt audible or visible behaviors.

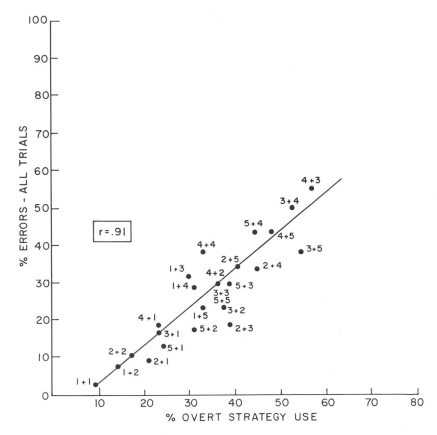

Using overt strategies most often on the hardest problems helped children in two different ways. First, it helped them solve the problems. On 24 of the 25 problems, children were more accurate when they used overt strategies than when they did not. It also was efficient. Children required more than twice as long to solve problems when they used one of the overt strategies as when they retrieved the answer. By only using the overt strategies on the hardest problems, children only expended large amounts of time on the problems where the time was needed.

How did children know when to use overt strategies? The most straightforward possibility was that their factual knowledge of the difficulty of the problems led to their choices. They might hear a problem and think "That's a hard problem, too hard to solve without putting up my fingers. I'd better put up my fingers to solve it." Several considerations made this view unlikely, though. As discussed in the chapter on memory development, preschoolers do not seem to have a great deal of factual knowledge about their thinking. Further, when the 4- and 5-year-olds needed to judge how hard each addition problem was, their judgments did not correlate highly with how often they used overt strategies. The finding suggested that a less-straightforward decision process must be at work.

Siegler and Shrager proposed the distribution of associations model shown in Figure 9–4 to explain how children chose strategies. We will consider this model in detail because it provides a framework for understanding how children choose strategies not only on addition problems but on other academic tasks, such as subtraction and reading, as well.

The model involves a process operating on a representation. First consider the representation (Figure 9–4A). It consists of associations of varying strengths between each problem and possible answers to the problem. The numerical values in the Figure 9–4A matrix are the estimated strengths of these associations. For example, an associative strength of .05 links the problem 1 + 1 and the answer "1," and an associative strength of .86 links 1 + 1 and "2."[2]

The process that operates on this representation can be divided into three phases: retrieval, elaboration of the representation, and counting. As shown in Figure 9–4B, at the outset of the retrieval phase on each problem, the child (who we here imagine to be a girl) sets two guidelines. One is a confidence criterion, indicating how sure she needs to be of an answer to state it. This varies randomly from 0 (not sure at all) to 1 (entirely sure). The second guideline is the search length. This indicates how many retrieval efforts the child will make before taking steps beyond retrieval.

Once these guidelines are set, the child attempts to retrieve an answer. The probability of retrieving any particular answer is proportional to that answer's associative strength relative to all of the answers' associative strengths. Thus, the associative strength .86 linking the problem 1 + 1 and the answer 2 means that 2 will be retrieved 86% of the time when 1 + 1 is presented (the total associative strength of all of the answers to the problem is 1.00.) The child states whatever answer she retrieved if its associative strength exceeds the current confidence criterion. Thus the .86 associative strength will allow the answer 2 to be stated most of the time, since it exceeds most possible confidence criteria. In contrast, the associative strength .05 linking 1 + 1 and the answer 1 means that answer will not be stated very often even on the 5% of trials on which it is retrieved.

If the child cannot retrieve an answer whose associative strength exceeds the confidence criterion, she proceeds to the next step. Here she generates a more elaborate representation of the problem, perhaps by putting up her fingers, and tries again to retrieve an answer. As before, if she is sufficiently confident of the answer she states it. Otherwise, she counts the objects in the representation and states the last number as the answer.

[2]These estimated associative strengths are based on children's performance in a separate experiment. Four-year-olds received simple addition problems and were asked to "just say what you think the right answer is without putting up your fingers or counting." The purpose of these instructions was to obtain the purest possible estimate of the strengths of associations between problems and answers. The numbers in the matrix indicate the proportion of trials on which children advanced a given answer to a given problem. Thus, an associative strength of .86 between 1 + 1 and 2 means that children answered "2" on 86% of trials, indicating a very strong association between the problem and that answer.

A. Representation (Associative Strengths)

PROBLEM	0	1	2	3	4	5	6	7	8	9	10	11	OTHER
1 + 1		.05	.86		.02		.02					.02	.04
1 + 2			.09	.70	.02		.04			.07	.02	.02	.05
1 + 3		.02		.11	.71	.05	.02	.02					.07
1 + 4					.11	.61	.09	.07				.02	.11
1 + 5					.13	.16	.50	.11		.02	.02		.05
2 + 1		.07	.05	.79	.05								.04
2 + 2	.02		.04	.05	.80	.04		.05					
2 + 3			.04	.07	.38	.34	.09	.02	.02	.02			.04
2 + 4		.02		.07	.02	.43	.29	.07	.07				.04
2 + 5		.02		.05	.02	.16	.43	.13			.02		.18
3 + 1		.02		.09	.79	.04		.04					.04
3 + 2			.09	.11	.11	.55	.07						.07
3 + 3	.04			.05	.21	.09	.48		.02	.02	.02		.07
3 + 4				.05	.11	.23	.14	.29	.02				.16
3 + 5				.07		.13	.23	.14	.18		.05		.20
4 + 1			.04	.02	.09	.68	.02	.02	.07				.07
4 + 2			.07	.09		.20	.36	.13	.07		.02		.07
4 + 3				.05	.18	.09	.09	.38	.09		.02		.11
4 + 4	.04			.02	.02	.29	.07	.07	.34		.04		.13
4 + 5					.04	.09	.16	.09	.11	.18	.11	.04	.20
5 + 1			.04		.04	.07	.71	.04	.04		.04		.04
5 + 2			.05	.20	.02	.18	.27	.25	.02		.02		
5 + 3			.02	.11	.09	.18	.05	.16	.23		.05		.11
5 + 4					.11	.21	.16	.05	.11	.16	.04		.16
5 + 5	.04					.07	.25	.11	.02	.04	.34	.04	.11

FIGURE 9-4A The distribution of associations model of how young children solve addition problems (from Siegler & Shrager, 1984).

It may be useful to examine how a child using the model would solve a particular problem. Suppose a girl was presented the problem 3 + 4. Initially, she chooses a confidence criterion and a search length. For purpose of illustration, we will assume that she selects the confidence criterion .50 and the search length 2. Next, she retrieves an answer. As shown in Figure 9-4A, the probability of retrieving 3 is .05, the probability of retrieving 4 is .11, the probability of retrieving 5 is .21, and so on. Suppose that the child retrieves 5. This answer's associative strength, .21, does not exceed the current confidence criterion, .50. Therefore, the girl does not state it as the answer. She next checks whether the number of searches has reached the search length. Since it has not, she again retrieves an answer. This time she might retrieve 7. The associative strength of 7, .29, does not exceed the confidence criterion, .50. Since the number of searches, 2, has reached the allowed search length, the child proceeds to the second phase of the process.

In this second phase, the girl initially represents the problem either by forming a mental image of the objects or by putting up her fingers to re-

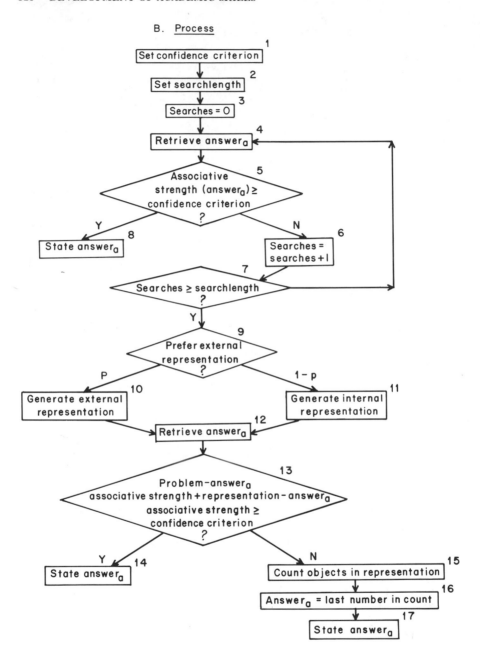

FIGURE 9-4B

present each object. We will assume that she puts up three fingers on one hand and four on the other. Next, she again retrieves an answer. Suppose that the girl retrieves 7. Its associative strength still does not exceed the .50 confidence criterion. Therefore, the girl does not state it. She instead proceeds to the third phase of the process. Here, she counts her fingers and states the last number as the answer to the problem. If she counts correctly, she will say "7."

This model explains the close relations among the percentage of overt strategy use, the percentage of errors, and the mean solution times on each problem. The relations arise because all three dependent variables are functions of the same independent variable: the distribution of associations linking problems and answers. The way in which this dependency operates becomes apparent when we compare the outcomes of a peaked distribution of associations, such as that for 2 + 1 in Figure 9–5, with those of a flat distribution, such as that for 3 + 4. A high percentage of use of retrieval, a low percentage of errors, and a short mean solution time all accompany the peaked distribution. Compared to the flat distribution, the peaked distribution results in (1) more frequent use of retrieval (because the answer most likely to be retrieved—the answer at the peak of the distribution—has very high associative strength, which will allow it to exceed most confidence criteria and be stated); (2) fewer errors (because of the higher probability of retrieving and stating the answer that forms the peak of the distribution, which generally will be the correct answer); and (3) shorter solution times

FIGURE 9-5   A peaked and a flat distribution of associations. The peaked distribution would lead to less frequent need for children to use overt strategies, fewer errors, and shorter solution times (from Siegler, in press).

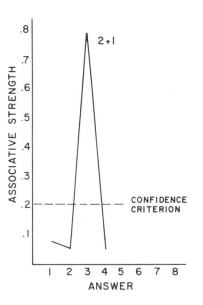
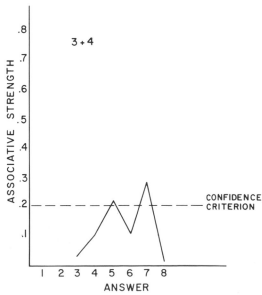

(because the probability of retrieving on an early search an answer whose associative strength exceeds any given confidence criterion is greater the more peaked the distribution of associations). Thus, errors, solution times, and overt strategy use go together because all depend on how peaked the distribution of associations is.

This account raises the question of how distributions of associations develop. Why do children form peaked distributions on some problems and flat ones on others? The central developmental assumption of this model was that children associate whatever answer they state with the problem on which they state it. Therefore, the issue reduced to why children state certain answers to problems. Three factors seemed likely to be influential: preexisting associations from the counting string, frequency of exposure to each problem, and the sum of the addends.

As noted in the Chapter 8 discussion of children's understandings of numbers, most 4- and 5-year-olds know the counting string quite well. This knowledge appears to both help and hurt their addition performance. Counting helps by providing a backup strategy to use when children cannot retrieve an answer that they are sufficiently confident of to state. It can also hurt, however, by suggesting incorrect answers. On all ten ascending series problems (items on which the second addend is the larger one, such as $2 + 3$) and ties (e.g., $3 + 3$) the most frequent error that 4- and 5-year-olds made was to say that the answer was the number one greater than the second addend. That is, they answered that $3 + 3 = 4$ and $3 + 4 = 5$. Hearing the experimenter present problems such as $3 + 4$ may have led to the preschoolers momentarily forgetting that they were adding, and instead reverting to a related procedure they had engaged in many more times, counting.

A second potential influence on which problems develop peaked and which flat distributions of associations was the sum of the addends. Presumably, the more objects children need to represent, and the more objects they then need to count, the more likely they are to err. In line with this view, Gelman and Gallistel (1978) reported that 3- and 4-year-olds' counting errors increased as the sets they counted grew larger.

The third potential influence was exposure to problems. Parents, teachers, and other children may present some problems more often than others. To test this possibility, Siegler and Shrager invited parents of 2- to 4-year-olds to teach their children to solve addition problems, as they might at home. The goal was to see how often parents presented each problem. The results helped explain several otherwise anomalous results. Recall Groen and Parkman's finding that ties were easier than their minimum numbers would suggest. Parents presented ties much more often than other problems with large minimum numbers. Further, children answer " + 1" problems (such as "3 + 1" and "4 + 1") more accurately than corresponding "1 +" problems, such as "1 + 3" and "1 + 4." Parents were found to present " + 1" problems five times as often as the corresponding "1 +" problems (for example, they presented "4 + 1" five times as often as "1 + 4").

To examine how well these three factors accounted for children's addition performance, Siegler and Shrager wrote a computer simulation. The simulation operated in accord with the following principles:

1. The simulation is presented the 25 problems in accord with their relative frequency in the parental input study described above.

2. Before each problem, the simulation randomly generates a confidence criterion and a search length. The confidence criterion ranges from .01 to .99 and the search length from 1 to 3.

3. The probability of retrieving an answer is proportional to its associative strength. A retrieved answer is stated if its associative strength exceeds the current confidence criterion. Retrieval attempts continue until either the associative strength of a retrieved answer exceeds the confidence criterion or the number of searches matches the allowed search length.

4. If the number of retrieval efforts reaches the allowed search length, and no answer has been stated, the program generates an elaborated representation of the number of objects in the two addends. It then retrieves an answer and states it if its associative strength exceeds the confidence criterion.

5. If this last retrieval effort is unsuccessful, the model counts the objects in the elaborated representation. On each count there is a fixed probability of skipping over the object being counted and a fixed probability of counting it twice.

6. Every time the system advances an answer, the association between that answer and the problem increases. The increment is twice as great for correct answers, which presumably are reinforced, as for incorrect answers, which presumably are not.

As shown in Table 9-2, the simulation performed much like the children. Both the correlations among different measures of the simulation's output and the correlations between the simulation's output and the children's behavior on each measure were strong. The four strategies produced by the simulation—retrieval, fingers, counting, and counting fingers—were the same four that children used. The relative solution times of the strategies—retrieval fastest, fingers next fastest, and counting and counting fingers slowest—also was identical to the children's pattern. Most impor-

TABLE 9-2   Computer Simulation's Performance on Addition Problems (after Siegler & Shrager, 1984)

INTRAMODEL CORRELATIONS

Correlation between percentage of errors and percent overt strategy use	$r = .97$
Correlation between percentage of errors and mean solution times	$r = .97$
Correlation between percent overt strategy use and mean solution times	$r = .99$

CORRELATIONS BETWEEN CHILDREN'S AND MODEL'S BEHAVIOR

Correlation between percentage of errors produced by model and children	$r = .87$
Correlation between percent overt strategy use produced by model and children	$r = .85$
Correlation between mean solution times produced by model and children	$r = .82$

tant, the simulation produced the same high correlations among its errors, solution times, and overt strategy use as the children had shown. These similarities supported the view that the mechanisms embodied in the simulation were much like those through which children learn to add.

For me, the model is as interesting for the issues it raises as for the results it has produced. One such issue involves the effects of making errors. When the model advances an answer, the associative strength of that answer increases, regardless of whether the answer is correct or incorrect. The intuition underlying this procedure comes from my experience with spelling. Once I have spelled a word incorrectly a number of times, I often have difficulty remembering whether this misspelling or the correct spelling is right. This holds true even if I have been told numerous times that the misspelling is wrong. I know that one or the other spelling is correct, but not which one.

My experience, which I suspect is quite common, raises the issues of whether we should institute methods for teaching spelling, arithmetic, and other subjects that minimize the number of errors children make during the learning process. Almost a half century ago, B. F. Skinner and others interested in operant conditioning advocated an instructional policy of errorless learning. Their argument was that errors produced emotional reactions that interfered with learning. Perhaps they were right for the wrong reason. Limiting errors to the number necessary to disconfirm incorrect assumptions and beliefs may be effective not because (or not just because) it minimizes children's emotional reactions, but because it minimizes their construction of interfering associations. If this is true, it raises a whole host of other issues. How rapidly do associations grow when children are told an answer is wrong compared to when they are told it is right? Does making the same mistake 10 times (concentrating all the associative strength in a single incorrect answer) have a larger interfering effect than making 10 different mistakes? Does making plausible mistakes, such as spelling *accommodation* as *accomodation* interfere with learning more than making implausible ones, such as spelling it *accommodattion*?

Another issue raised by the model concerns how the context of problem solving influences children's arithmetic. An intriguing study of Brazilian street children suggests that problem-solving contexts may greatly influence children's performance on arithmetic problems (Carraher, Carraher, & Schlieman, 1983). The 9- to 15-year-olds whose problem solving was studied were the sons and daughters of poor migrant workers who had moved to a large city. They contributed to the family financially by working either alone or with other family members as street vendors, selling coconuts, popcorn, corn on the cob, and other goods. Their work required them to add, subtract, multiply, and occasionally divide in their heads (one coconut costs *x* cruzeiros; five coconuts will cost . . .). Despite little formal education, (such children usually attend school for fewer than five years), the children are able to tell customers how much purchases cost and how much change they will get.

In the experiment, the children were asked to solve three types of problems. Some were problems that came up in the context of customer-vendor transactions ("How much do a coconut and a corn-on-the-cob cost?") Others involved similar problem-solving situations but did not involve goods carried by the child's stand (If a banana costs 85 cruzeiros and a lemon costs 63 cruzeiros, how much do the two cost together?). Yet others were numerically identical problems but presented without a problem-solving context (e.g., "How much is 85 + 63?"). The children solved 98 percent of the items involving practical questions that could arise at their stand, 74 percent of the other items that had slightly unfamiliar problem-solving context, and only 37 percent of the items without a problem-solving context. These differences clearly demonstrate that children bring different aspects of their knowledge to bear in different problem-solving situations.

A third issue concerns another educational implication of the model, that the common policy of discouraging children from using their fingers to add is misguided. Many teachers adopt this policy of discouraging children from using their fingers, and they have a certain logic on their side. One of the goals of education is to make younger and less intelligent children more like older and smarter ones. Older and smarter children do not use their fingers, whereas younger and less intelligent children do.

Therefore, by this reasoning, preventing young children from using their fingers will lead them to add more like older children. The distribution of associations model, however, implies that pushing children not to use their fingers may actually retard learning. Older and smarter children do not use their fingers because they possess peaked distributions of associations. These peaked distributions render their using overt strategies unnecessary. Younger and less knowledgeable children, however, use overt strategies precisely because they lack peaked distributions of associations. Forcing them to retrieve answers will lead to many errors, which, since each response adds to the associative strength of that answer, will make their distributions flatter than they were before. Paradoxically, pressuring children not to use their fingers may lead to them needing to use them for a longer time than if they were not pressured.

This account is borne out in teachers' descriptions of the effects of banning overt strategies. Teachers we have interviewed admit that children continue to use overt strategies under their desks and behind their backs even when they have been told not to do this. One teacher responded to my question of how often she had to tell a child in her class not to use his fingers by asking "How many days have there been in the school year?" Thus, it may be useless or worse for teachers to discourage children from using overt strategies. The children will spontaneously abandon the more cumbersome counting strategies when their distributions of associations become sufficiently peaked, that is, when they no longer need them.

Subtraction

Simple subtraction.   In learning to subtract, children use two counting procedures akin to the min strategy in addition. In one procedure, they count up from the smaller number to the bigger one and say that the answer is the number of counts needed to go from the smaller to the larger. For example, on "9-7," they would count up 2 numbers and therefore respond that the answer was 2. In the other procedure, they count down from the bigger number the number of times indicated by the smaller and say that whatever is left is the answer. For example, on "9-2" they would count down 2 numbers from 9 and say that the answer was 7, since that would be how many were left.

Woods, Resnick, and Groen (1975) suggested that children would use whichever procedure required fewer counts for the problem that was presented. For example, they would solve "9-7" by counting up and "9-2" by counting down, because this would be the most efficient way to solve each problem. Woods et al. predicted that the amount of time to solve each problem would increase with each additional count needed to solve the problem using the easier strategy. Thus, "9-2" and "9-7" would take the same amount of time, because both would require 2 counts.

This model accurately predicted the solution times of second and third grade American children on single-digit subtraction problems (Woods et al., 1975). It fit the solution times of Swedish children as well (Svenson & Sjoberg, 1982). Children in both countries at times explicitly cited these strategies to describe how they subtracted.

Complex subtraction.   When children encounter more complex subtraction problems, such as 102 – 69, they often have difficulty remembering exactly how the subtraction formula operates. As a result, many of them develop "bugs" in their solution formulas. These bugs are persistent errors that children make when faced with particular types of problems. Brown and Burton's (1978) description of the bugs, as well as their way of teaching teachers how to diagnose and correct them, were described in Chapter 1, on pages 7 to 9. It may be worthwhile to review them here, where they can be considered in the general context of children's academic skills.

Strategy choices in subtraction.   The strategy choice model described earlier in the context of addition also seems applicable to subtraction. Both the counting strategies described by Woods, Resnick, and Groen and the buggy subtraction rules described by Brown and Burton in Chapter 1 seem likely to be used when people cannot retrieve an answer whose associative strength is sufficient to state it. However, a child or adult who has a peaked distribution of associations for a particular problem will usually state a retrieved answer. Illustratively, experienced grocery cashiers probably would be able to retrieve the answer to 100 or 500 minus any number of cents, though they would have to compute the answer to many other problems.

Siegler and Shrager (1984) observed 5- and 6-year-olds' subtraction performance to test how well the model of strategy choice fit the children's performance. The children's subtraction showed the same strong relation among the frequency of overt strategy use, the frequency of errors, and the length of solution times on each problem that had been present in addition. As shown in Figure 9–6, the harder the problem, the more often children used the overt strategies. Further, a direct measure of the distribution of associations, obtained in the addition experiments (footnote 1; p. 308) indicated that this distribution accurately predicted all three other variables. This and other evidence suggested that in subtraction, as in addition, the peakedness of children's distributions of associations determines whether they use the retrieval strategy.

Estimation

A number of scholarly panels (e.g., Romberg & Stewart, 1983) have recently attempted to answer the question, "Why is mathematics achievement declining in America?" The commissions' reports suggest that several aspects of mathematics instruction in the schools should be changed. One of their primary suggestions is that more emphasis be placed on the ability to estimate accurately, that is, to know roughly what the answer must be even before computing an exact solution. This would help children avoid mistakes such as saying that 1/3 divided by 7/2 is 7/6, because they would know that a larger number cannot possibly go into a smaller number more than one full time.

Newman and Berger (1984) studied young children's estimation strategies in the context of a computer game. The bottom of the screen was labeled with the number 1; the top with the number 23. Children were told that each vertical position between 1 and 23 corresponded to a specific number—the position just above the 1 would be position 2, for example. Since no numbers or markers appeared between the 1 and the 23, children could only estimate what the number for the position would be. On each trial, children saw a target appear somewhere between the 1 and the 23 and needed to estimate what number went with that position. A dart was then shot across the computer screen at the number the child chose. The process continued until the child chose the right number, at which point the dart would land on and destroy the target.

Children used a number of estimation strategies to help them send the dart to the right position. The most common strategy among 6-year-olds was

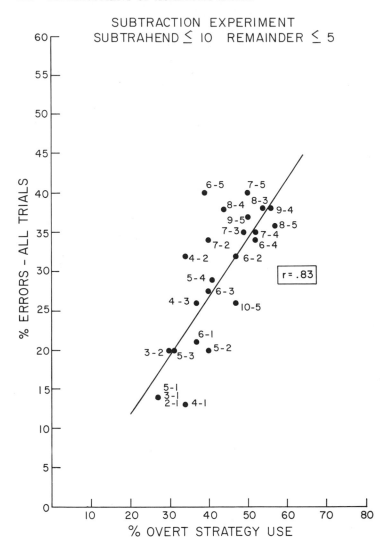

FIGURE 9-6 Relations between percent overt strategy use and errors (this page) and percent overt strategy use and solution times (facing page) (Siegler, in press).

to count from 1 to wherever the target appeared, estimating the sizes of the units. This worked quite well for targets in the lower part of the screen, but not for targets in the middle or top. The most common strategy among 7-year-olds was to count from 1 when the target appeared in the bottom half of the screen and to count backward from 23 when it appeared in the top half. This worked well when the target was near the top or bottom, but not when it was near the middle. The majority of 9-year-olds adopted a third

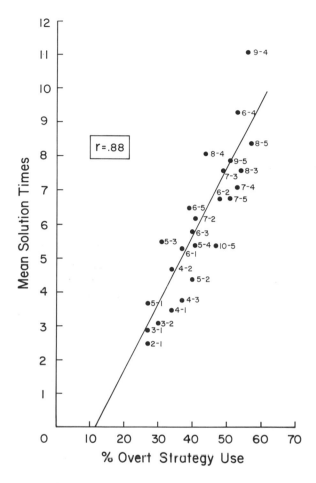

strategy. They counted from the top, the bottom, or an arbitrary benchmark they established in the middle, depending on which was most efficient. This approach worked quite well for all targets.

Why did different-age children adopt different strategies? Newman (1984) suggested that amount of general facility with numbers was critical. Even among children of a single age, those who generally knew more about numbers, even knowledge that had nothing obvious to do with this task, were better at estimating where the spaceship would be. The practical implication is that providing children with a greater variety of experiences with numbers, not just calculation, might improve their ability to estimate. Improved ability to estimate, in turn, might eventually help children generally do better in mathematics by helping them know approximately what the correct answer must be and allowing them to infer that certain of their answers must be wrong. The advantage would be like that of that enjoyed by people knowledgeable about baseball in their memory for a new baseball game (Chapter 7, p. 248).

HOW CHILDREN LEARN TO READ

Children's reading, like many other areas of their cognitive development, can be viewed either chronologically (what happens at particular ages) or topically (how does quality *x* develop). Below we first consider the main types of reading development that occur at different ages. Then we examine three crucial aspects of reading development in greater detail: prereading skills, word identification, and comprehension.

The Typical Chronological Progression

Chall (1979) hypothesized that children progress through five stages in learning to read. The stages oversimplify some complex and overlapping cognitive changes and make reading acquisition seem tidier and neater than it really is. However, they do capture the major developments that occur in learning to read and the ages at which each type of development seems to be most dramatic. They also communicate a sense of the multiple challenges that children must meet to become good readers.

In Stage 0, lasting from birth to the beginning of first grade, children master several prerequisites for reading. Many learn to discriminate among the letters of the alphabet. Many learn to write their names. Some learn to read a few words, typically the names of products such as Coca-Cola and stores such as Sears. As was the case in arithmetic, young children's knowledge of reading seems to be considerably greater than it was 40 or 50 years ago. The improvement may be due to educational programs such as Sesame Street and to often-repeated, attention-grabbing television commercials.

In Stage 1, which usually occupies first and second grade, children acquire *phonological recoding* skills, that is, the skills involved in translating letters into sounds so as to identify words. Children also complete their learning of the letter names and sounds in this stage.

In Stage 2, most commonly occurring in second and third grade, children become able to read fluently. They do not need to spend as much time and mental effort to identify each word. However, Chall indicated that at this stage, reading is not for learning. The demands of word identification on children's processing resources apparently are still sufficiently great that they make difficult the acquisition of new information. This difficulty may contribute to the uninteresting character of most early reading books. Presenting interesting content is difficult when substantial processing resources are required just to identify individual words. The existence of captivating and charming books that children at this level can read, such as *Charlotte's Web*, *Stuart Little*, and the Pippi stories, demonstrates that the limit is not absolute. Nonetheless, it may be even more difficult to write a great story that 7- and 8-year-olds can read than to write a novel of comparable quality for adults.

In Stage 3, which Chall identified with fourth through eighth grade, children become capable of obtaining new information from print. To quote her characterization, "In the primary grades, children learn to read; in the higher grades they read to learn" (p. 42). At this point, however, they only can consider information presented from a single perspective, for example, as an indisputable fact.

In Stage 4, which occupies the high school years, children come to comprehend written information presented from multiple viewpoints. This makes possible much more interesting discussions of history, economics, and politics than was possible previously. It also allows appreciation of the subtleties of great works of fiction, which are presented much more often in high school than in elementary school.

This chronology points to two major themes in children's acquisition of reading skills: the centrality of reading comprehension as the goal of learning to read, and the need for efficient word identification so that the largest possible amount of processing resources are available for comprehending. Before children can even acquire word identification skills, though, they seem to need certain prereading skills. These are discussed in the next section.

Prereading Skills

Children seem to acquire certain important prereading skills effortlessly. They appear to simply absorb that written language proceeds from left to right on a page, that text continues from the extreme right on one line to the extreme left on the next, and that spaces between letter sequences signal the ends and beginnings of words. Two other prerequisites for reading are considerably more difficult for most children to master, though: discriminating between different letters and dividing words into component sounds. These relatively demanding prerequisites are discussed below, along with a group of children of special interest: children who learn to read without formal instruction.

Letter perception.   Even the lowest-level process in reading, recognizing and identifying letters, presents a complex challenge for young children. As discussed in Chapter 7, identification of distinctive features plays a critical role in children's ability to discriminate letters from each other. Once children learn that each letter can be described as a unique combination of curves, horizontal segments, vertical segments, and diagonals, they can more quickly and accurately identify the letters.

Many parents and teachers, as well as researchers, have wondered whether learning letter names helps children learn to read. The picture is complex, but at least a preliminary conclusion is possible. Kindergarteners' ability to name letters predicts their later reading achievement scores, at least into second and third grade, quite well (DeHirsch, Jansky, & Langford, 1966). At first glance, this would seem to indicate that learning letter names helped children. However, teaching young children letter names does not facilitate their learning to read (Venezky, 1978). Together, the two facts suggest that learning the letter names does not directly help children to learn to read. Rather, one or more other variables—interest in print, general intelligence, good perceptual skills, parental interest in their reading, or some combination of the above—probably is responsible both for children learning the letter names and for them later doing well in reading.

Phonemic awareness. Another difficult prerequisite for reading is realizing that words consist of separable sounds. This realization has been labeled *phonemic awareness.* Even after years of speaking a language, most children seem unaware that they are combining separate sounds to make words. Liberman, Shankweiler, Fischer, and Carter (1974) illustrated this point with 4- and 5-year-olds. The children were trained to tap once for each sound in a short word. Thus, they were supposed to tap twice for "it" and three times for "hit." None of the 4-year-olds could perform this task accurately, and only a few of the 5-year-olds could. It is tempting to dismiss the task as being intuitively unlike reading and unimportant to it. Liberman and Shankweiler (1977) and others, however, have reported that how well a child can do on it is an excellent predictor of the child's early reading achievement. Further, training 4- and 5-year-olds to detect which of three words does not share a common phoneme (*cot, pot, hat*) leads to improved reading and spelling performance as much as 4 years later (Bradley & Bryant, 1983).

Why should phonemic awareness be so closely related to, and so helpful in promoting, early reading achievement? Thinking about the process by which children learn to read suggests an answer. When children are taught to read, they learn the sounds that typically accompany each letter. Unless they can blend these sounds into a word, however, the knowledge of these sound-symbol correspondences can do little good. Being able to divide a word into its component sounds, a skill required on phonemic awareness tasks, is the exact inverse of combining those sounds together into a word. Thus, phonemic awareness may accurately predict early reading achievement because it measures how well children will be able to blend sounds together to form words.

Children who read early. Some children learn to read before they begin school. What types of long-term consequences does this have? Contrary to the fears of some educators, it does not seem to have any adverse affects on their later reading and general school performance. Durkin (1966) identified a group of children who knew how to read when they entered school and followed their progress over the next six years. The children maintained their superior level of reading achievement over the six-year period. A number of them did well enough in school to skip a grade. It cannot be concluded that the early reading caused the children to do so well (they were intelligent children in any case), but it certainly does not seem to have done any harm.

What distinguished these children from others? To find out, Durkin interviewed their parents and the parents of other children of comparable IQs and social class background who did not learn to read early. The largest differences seemed to be in interest: interest of the children in learning to read and interest of the parents in their child learning to read. Parents of both early readers and nonreaders said that their children were interested in reading before starting school. However, the parents of the children who learned to read early pointed to several specific sources of interest that were not mentioned as often by the other parents: presence of reading materials in the home, availability of a blackboard for the child at home, and the child being unusually interested in the meaning of words. The children tended to be from middle-class homes, as has been the case with other groups of precocious readers (e.g., Briggs & Elkind, 1977). However, if we can generalize from other studies of individual differences in reading, the responsiveness of the parents to the child, the amount of reading done with the child, and the extent to which the parents themselves read for pleasure were larger factors in the children's learning to read than whether the parents were well-to-do, middle-class, or poor (Wigfield & Asher, 1984).

Identifying Individual Words

As Chall noted in her stage model, reading development in the early grades is mostly the development of the ability to identify individual words. Children use two main methods to identify words: *phonological recoding* (sometimes called decoding) and *visually based retrieval*. In both methods, children first examine printed words and later locate the entry for the word in long-term memory. The central difference concerns what happens in between. When children phonologically recode a word, they translate the visual form into a speechlike one, and use this speechlike representation to identify the word. When they visually retrieve a word, they do not take this step. The two approaches are not quite as distinct as this description suggests; for example, children sometimes phonologically recode the first letter or two and then are able to retrieve the word's identity without further recoding. Despite these mixed cases, the distinction still seems to correspond to a genuine difference in the ways children identify words.

The difference between the two word-identification processes is echoed in the difference between the two main approaches to reading instruction. Whole-word approaches emphasize visual retrieval; phonics-oriented approaches emphasize phonological recoding. Historically, educational practice has gyrated erratically between these two instructional approaches. At the beginning of this century, most teachers emphasized phonics skills. Between the 1920s and the 1950s, they emphasized visual access. In the last twenty years, they again emphasized phonics. Two likely reasons for the switches are that both methods do eventually succeed in teaching most children to read and that neither method succeeds in teaching every child to read. In addition, neither approach has to be pursued in pure form, and most teachers use both. The issue is not whether children need to learn letter/sound relations or whether they need to be able to retrieve words rapidly, but how early and to what extent each skill should be emphasized.

Another reason why the debate has not been resolved is that a good argument can be made for each side. The whole-word argument: Skilled readers rely on visually based retrieval; the goal of reading instruction is to produce skilled readers; therefore, beginning readers should be taught to read like skilled ones. The phonics argument: For children to learn to read, they must be able to identify unfamiliar words; phonological recoding skills allow them to do this; therefore, beginning readers should be taught in a way that will allow them to read independently.

Understanding the processes by which children learn to read may provide an informed basis for choosing between these two arguments. Below we examine phonological recoding, visually based retrieval, and the process by which children choose which of the two approaches to use to identify a particular word. The analysis suggests an explanation for why one of the two approaches to teaching children to read has proven to be more effective than the other.

Phonological recoding.   Everyone who has observed children learning to read has heard them translate letters into sounds and combine the sounds into words. The technique allows them to "sound out" words that they otherwise could not read without help. This advantage underlies the persistent and continuing international trend toward use of alphabetic rather than pictorial writing systems (Gleitman & Rozin, 1977). Simply put, alphabetic systems are easier to learn.

The nature of the reading material that beginning readers encounter makes evident the advantage of an alphabetic system. Firth (1972) examined the 2,747 words that occurred in a basal reader for first and second graders. More than 70% of the words were presented five or fewer times, and more than 40% of the words only once. Some basal readers repeat words more frequently, but more repetitive material tends to degenerate into the remarkably boring primers criticized by so many parents and educators. As long as children encounter large numbers of words that they have rarely seen, skill at phonological recoding is essential.

Beyond allowing children to read independently, phonological recoding ability also may help them to learn to retrieve words visually without recoding them. Jorm and Share (1983) described how this might occur.

Their basic assumption was that children learn the answers that they state; this was the same assumption made by Siegler and Shrager about arithmetic learning. If children lack good phonological reading skills, they will be forced to rely more often on context to infer words' identities. Context is often an undependable guide, and relying on it will lead to many errors. In contrast, accurate sounding out will increase the association between the printed and spoken word, thus increasing the likelihood of the child being able to retrieve the word's identity through purely visual processes. As Jorm and Share commented, "Phonological recoding may be the principal mechanism by which beginning readers learn to use the more efficient visual retrieval route and eventually achieve skilled performance" (p. 114). This view is supported by numerous studies indicating that knowledge of phonetic relations predicts individual differences in elementary school children's reading, even at ages where the children no longer sound out many words (Johnson & Bauman, 1984).

Visually based retrieval processes. It is tempting to describe the development of word identification skills by saying that early in learning to read, children sound out words, and that later in the process they learn to visually retrieve their identities. In fact, the progression is not this simple. Many children can retrieve the identities of a few words even before they know any sound-symbol correspondences. Gough and Hillinger (1980) provided the example of a preschooler who learned to read two words: "Budweiser" and "Stop." The boy learned the first word from beer cans, the second from road signs. Context provided many clues to the words' identities. Some young children, however, also are able to read such words if they are typed on an index card. A girl might know that she knows two words and that "Budweiser" is the long one and "Stop" the short one. Next, she might learn the word "Coors." The long/short distinction would no longer be sufficient. Now she might identify the words on the basis that if the word was long it was "Budweiser," if it was short and started with a letter that had only one curve it was "Coors," and if it was short and started with a letter that had two curves it was "Stop."

Gough and Hillinger's point is an important one: that when first learning to read, children often identify words through individual cues that temporarily provide distinctive features. As they encounter more words, however, this system breaks down. They are forced to look for a more systematic way of identifying words, such as that provided by letter–sound correspondences. Learning these correspondences greatly increases their ability to identify new words.

Just as the letters within a word influence children's retrievals of word identities, so does the surrounding context. This influence can be seen from early in the reading acquisition process, and is especially apparent in beginning readers' errors. Weber (1970) compared the relative frequency of four types of errors: substitutions of one word for another; omissions of a word; insertions of a word; and scrambles, in which the words read corresponded only roughly to those printed on the page.

Most of first graders' errors proved to be substitutions. More than 90 % of these substitutions were consistent with the context. The children spontaneously reread the passage twice as often when their errors were inconsistent with the context as when the errors were consistent with it. Thus, both the errors themselves and the rereading patterns indicated that even beginning readers use context to help identify words.

Among older children, context seems to be especially important in the word identifications of poor readers. Patberg, Dewitz, and Samuels (1981) examined fourth graders' identification of words presented with and without supporting context. Good readers were unaffected by the context; they used visually based retrieval to identify the words in both situations. The fourth graders who were poor readers also used visually based retrieval when the words were presented in context, but fell back on phonological recoding when the context was not present. Stanovich (1983) also found that poor readers' ability to identify words depended more than that of good readers on having a supporting context.

Visually based retrieval might seem like a basic process that could not be analyzed further. In fact, recent experimental findings and computer simulation models of adults' word identification suggest that the process is composed of many separate components (e.g., McClelland & Rumelhart, 1981). Because these models have not yet been extended to children, we will not discuss them in any detail here. One point that seems worth mentioning, though, is that the models postulate a great deal of parallel processing in adults' word identification. That is, numerous types of information are brought to bear on word identification at the same time: information from the particular letters, information from the word as a whole, and information from the surrounding context. It will be interesting to learn whether children's word identification incorporates such parallel processing from the beginning of the learning-to-read process, or whether their processing at first has a more serial character.

Strategy choices in word identification.   Although beginning readers sound out many words, they do not sound out all words. Many of the earliest words that they learn have extremely irregular letter-sound correspondences: *to, the,* and *of,* to name three. These words cannot easily be sounded out. This observation raises the issue of how children know whether to use phonological recoding or visually based retrieval to identify a particular word.

The way in which children decide whether to retrieve a word's identity or to sound it out may be analogous to the procedures they use in addition and subtraction. In this scenario, children form distributions of associations between each word's visual appearance and its identity. Each time they encounter the word, they try to retrieve its identity from this distribution of associations. If the alternative they retrieve has sufficient associative strength, they state it. Otherwise they resort to a backup strategy, such as sounding out the word or asking an older child or adult.

This perspective, combined with Jorm and Share's (1983) position that children become able to use visually based retrieval through prior accurate use of phonological recoding, imply that phonics-based instruction should be superior to the whole-word approach in helping children identify words quickly and accurately. This is in fact what happens. In both classroom and laboratory tests, phonics-based approaches have proven superior (Chall, 1979; Lesgold & Curtis, 1981). The basic cause may be that good phonological recoding skills help children identify words correctly from the beginning of the learning-to-read process. Identifying the words correctly leads to peaked distributions of associations, which facilitate rapid, accurate retrieval.

The reasoning also implies that as in arithmetic, reading teachers should not discourage children from using overt strategies. If a printed word were sufficiently strongly associated with the word's identity, children would use visually based retrieval on their own. The likely impact of telling them that they must not sound out words will be to force them to rely unduly heavily on context, even when the context is an unclear clue to the word's identity. To the extent that this practice results in reading errors, it may delay the time when children can confidently use visually based retrieval.

Comprehension of Larger Units of Prose

Reading comprehension is one of the most complex cognitive activities that is humanly possible. It also is one of the most important cognitive activities in children's lives. It allows them to acquire new information, to pursue all kinds of interests, and, perhaps most important for many children, to escape from boredom. Below we consider four aspects of reading comprehension: what component processes are involved in it, how it is related to listening comprehension, the source of developmental differences in it, and how it can be improved through well-designed instruction.

The components of comprehension. Perfetti (1984) noted that to comprehend written passages, children need to execute four component processes: *lexical access, proposition assembly, proposition integration*, and *text modeling*. Lexical access is another name for word identification. It is the process by which children retrieve the meaning of each printed word from long-term memory. Proposition assembly involves relating words to each other to form meaningful units. For example, in the sentence "The sick boy went home," there are several propositions: "There was a boy," "The boy was sick," and so on. (See Chapter 4, pp. 109–110). Proposition integration involves combining individual propositions into larger units of meaning. Finally, text modeling refers to the processes by which children draw inferences and relate what they are reading to what they already know. Children would draw on knowledge about school nurses, illnesses, and typical distances between homes and schools in interpreting the sentence about the sick boy.

Reading comprehension and listening comprehension.   Perfetti's division of reading comprehension into the four types of processes makes clear the relation between comprehension of written language and speech. Forming propositions, integrating propositions, and constructing a general model of the situation play the same role in comprehending spoken and written language. Lexical access from printed words, however, represents a unique demand of reading comprehension.

This relation between written and spoken language suggests the concept of *reading potential.* The idea is that children's general intelligence, motivation, and knowledge about the particular situation determine how much they comprehend while listening. If children could completely overcome the cognitive demands of lexical access, then they could read as quickly and with as much comprehension as they could listen. Thus, in this view, listening comprehension sets an upper limit on how much they can understand in reading.

The idea of reading potential seems to be a useful way of thinking about children's reading comprehension (Sticht & James, 1984). The gap between children's reading and listening comprehension starts out being extremely large in first and second grade and gradually diminishes through seventh or eighth grade, at which point the two are quite similar. The closeness of the relation between individual differences in listening comprehension and individual differences in reading comprehension also increase substantially over the course of schooling. Children's performance on listening tests is only mildly correlated with their performance on reading tests in first and second grade. By sixth and seventh grade, the relation is more than twice as strong.

The idea of reading potential is not without problems. For example, reading has certain advantages over listening—it allows the reader to look back over the text and to pace the flow of information—which, with difficult material, may allow reading comprehension to exceed the hypothetical upper limit imposed by listening comprehension. At a general level of analysis, though, the idea that reading comprehension gradually approaches its potential as reflected in listening comprehension seems a reasonable way of thinking about changes in comprehension abilities.

What develops in reading comprehension?   Just about every way in which 5- to 20-year-olds develop probably contributes at least something to reading comprehension. However, four types of development seem to be particularly important: automatization of lexical access, ability to hold longer phrases in short-term memory, greater prior knowledge of the material being read, and ability to flexibly adapt reading procedures to the demands of particular tasks.

As suggested by the large differences between beginning readers' listening and reading comprehension, the joint demands of lexical access and higher-level comprehension processes often reach the outer limits of young children's mental resources. Wilkinson (1980) documented this conflict. Elementary school children either read material or listened to the text as it was read to them. Then they were asked questions that either required only memory for literal statements or deeper comprehension.

Children found the task that required reading and deep comprehension of the material to be more difficult than either of the tasks that required only one or the other. Wilkinson noted that the most difficult task created especially great competition for attentional resources. Not only would both lexical access and comprehension create demands, but switching attention between them would create yet additional demands.

Wilkinson's finding points to the importance of *automatization* in the development of reading comprehension. As noted in the discussion of Case's theory (Chapter 3), automatization refers to efficient execution of cognitive processes. When processes are automatized, they require little if any memory capacity or attention. In the case of reading, as word identification becomes more automatic, greater amounts of attention and memory capacity can be devoted to comprehension. This is one reason why older children comprehend written material better than younger ones.

A second, related source of development of reading comprehension involves the amount of material children can hold in short-term memory. If children can hold longer phrases in short-term memory, they have a better chance to integrate previous and new ideas and to infer connections between them. Daneman (1981) cleverly illustrated this point by showing "garden path" paragraphs to second through sixth graders. These paragraphs received their name because their context suggests an interpretation of a particular word that later proves to be inaccurate. Thus, readers are led down the garden path. The following was one of the paragraphs:

> The little girl was sad because her clothes were torn. She was upset because she couldn't go to the party. She began to cry. There were big tears in her brown dress. She didn't know what to do.

The word "tears" has two pronunciations, each associated with a distinct meaning. The immediately preceding sentence, "She began to cry," implies that "tears" refers to droplets, but the later part of the phrase, "the tears were in the dress," reveals that "tears" actually referred to rips. Daneman suggested that children's short-term memory capacity determined whether they could keep in mind the verbatim phrasing of the sentence long enough to reinterpret it if their initial interpretation proved to be incorrect.

Daneman analyzed children's eye movements and oral readings of paragraphs such as the one about the tears. Figure 9–7 illustrates one fifth grader reading the sentence described above. The child's sequence of eye fixations is indicated by the integers above and below the words. The words indicate what the boy said aloud.

As indicated by eye fixations 1–7, the boy read from left to right until he encountered the word "dress." He initially pronounced "tears" to indicate droplets. While reading "dress" (gaze 7), he detected an incongruity between his initial interpretation and the later phrasing of the sentence. Therefore, he tried to clarify the meaning by looking back at the preceding words even while continuing to recite his first reading of the sentence (gazes 8–11). Then he started the sentence over, this time pronouncing "tears" to indicate the meaning "rips" (gazes 14–15).

Daneman found clear differences in the reading patterns of children with short and long memory spans. Children with long spans looked for more time at the disambiguating word ("dress" in the above sentence) when it conflicted with their initial interpretation of the sentence than when it was consistent with it. By contrast, children with short spans looked longer at the disambiguating word than at other terms only when the disambiguating word followed immediately after the term they had misinterpreted. Presumably, the children with short memory spans had difficulty identifying

FIGURE 9-7 A fifth grader's sequence of eye movements, durations of eye fixations, and words stated in the course of reading a garden path sentence. Words in large letters at the middle of the figure indicate the sentence as it appeared on the screen. Words in small letters indicate the words the child stated while reading the sentence. The numbers 1–15 indicate the sequence of eye fixations. The child's oral pronunciations indicate that he initially interpreted *tears* as (tirs), meaning *salty water droplets,* and then changed his interpretation to (ters), meaning *rips.*

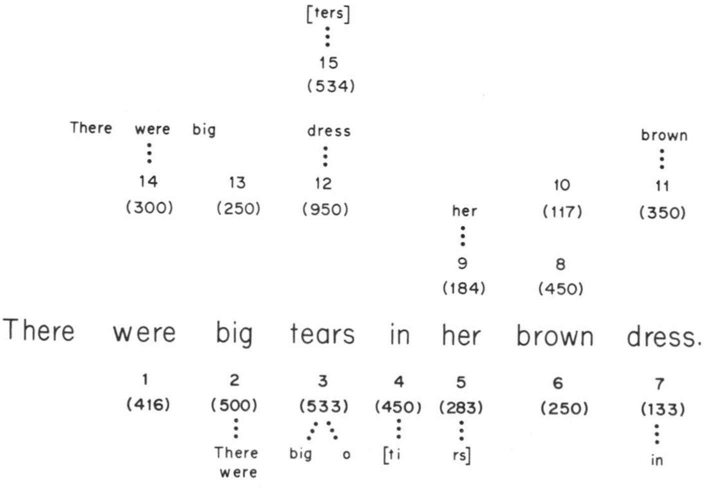

the source of their confusion when the word they misinterpreted occurred farther back. It is easy to see how children who could preserve literal phrasings for a longer time would have a leg up in interpreting many types of difficult or unclear reading material.

A third source of the development of reading comprehension skills is increasing knowledge of the material being read. What is important is that children possess organized systems of knowledge, not that they possess large numbers of unorganized individual facts. The importance of such structured knowledge has been discussed in connection with Piaget's theory, in connection with children's scripts for remembering the way that mealtimes go at their day care center, and in connection with memory for baseball. Children who have scripts, schemas, or other organized systems of knowledge can check the plausibility of what they remember against what they already know. They can also draw reasonable inferences about the ways things probably went in the past and the ways they probably will go in the future.

The importance of organized knowledge for reading comprehension is apparent in situations where even young readers comprehend well because they possess efficient ways for organizing the material. One such case arises in their ability to comprehend fairy tales. Mandler and Johnson (1977) and Stein and Glenn (1979) demonstrated that even 6- and 7-year-olds recall material well when it conforms to standard fairy tale form. The children draw reasonable inferences about the likely causes of the characters' actions and form sensible expectations about what will happen next when they can organize new stories into the fairy tale format.

What does children's organization of fairy tales look like? Stein and Glenn (1979) suggested that it includes two main parts: a setting and an episode. The setting introduces the main character and the environment in which the story occurs. Sentences beginning with "Once upon a time" usually serve as setting statements. The episode includes five types of information. First an initiating event occurs. This event causes the main character to desire some goal that would necessitate a change in the initial state of affairs. Then an internal response occurs, in which the main character establishes the goal and plans how to obtain it. Next, the character attempts to obtain the goal. The attempts lead to consequences—either success, failure, or a mix of the two in reaching the goal. Finally, the reaction phase closes the story. Here, the narrator or one of the characters evaluates the effects of the main characters' actions. If things have gone well, the reaction is the comforting "they lived happily ever after."

Even quite inexperienced readers comprehend such stories. They usually include all or almost all of the essential points when they retell the story. The finding demonstrates the importance of general as well as specific knowledge in comprehension.

A fourth source of the development of reading comprehension skills involves children's increasingly flexible adaptation of reading strategies to the particular task. Reading comprehension is not one task but many. This is evident in comparing the way we read a novel, a mathematics textbook, a newspaper, and the instructions for assembling a new bicycle.

Kobasigawa, Ransom, and Holland (1980) documented the growth of one frequently adaptive skill: skimming, Children of ages 10, 12, and 14 were presented a two-paragraph story. Their task was to find the answer to a question that was posed before they started reading. The first paragraph of the story was irrelevant to the answer, whereas the second paragraph was relevant. Reading of the first sentence of each paragraph, in each case a clear topic sentence, was sufficient to indicate the irrelevance of the first paragraph and the potential relevance of the second.

The 12- and 14-year-olds progressed through the first (irrelevant) paragraph faster under these conditions than under conditions in which they were simply told to read the whole story. However, the 10-year-olds did not. Only when the 10-year-olds were explicitly told to search for particular words relevant to the question did they skim the first paragraph. These results indicate that children as young as 10 can adjust their reading styles to meet task demands. However, they require more direct suggestions than older children to make the adjustments.

Implications for classroom instruction.   How can reading comprehension be improved? One way seems to be to build up children's content knowledge that is relevant to the story they will read *before* they read the story. Beck and McKeown (1984) noted that many stories children read in elementary school presume considerable background knowledge that they in fact do not have. Recognizing the importance of content knowledge for remembering and learning (Chapter 7), they reasoned that explaining underlying concepts in advance might help children organize what they read in a more meaningful way.

The story in question appeared in a second grade text; it was called "The Raccoon and Mrs. McGinnis." Mrs. McGinnis, a poor but good-hearted farmer, wishes on a star for a barn in which to house her animals. Instead, a gang of bandits comes and steals the animals. A raccoon, who habitually looks for food at night on Mrs. McGinnis's doorstep, sees the bandits, follows them, and then climbs a tree to be safe from them. The bandits see the raccoon's masked face and mistake it for another bandit. Frightened, the bandits release the animals and inadvertently drop a bag of money they had stolen from someone else. The raccoon picks up the money bag, returns to Mrs. McGinnis's doorstep to continue looking for food, and drops the bag of money on the doorstep. The next morning, Mrs. McGinnis finds the money and attributes her good fortune to her wish of the night before being answered.

The teachers' guide for this story suggested several preparatory activities. Children were to be told that the story was about Mrs. McGinnis and a raccoon; that raccoons were clever, intelligent, and mischievous; and that unusual things would happen to Mrs. McGinnis and the raccoon. Beck and McKeown reasoned that these were not the critical concepts needed for comprehension. Instead, they introduced children to the story by discussing two concepts more closely related to the story's deeper meaning: coincidence and habit. That is, they explained how coincidences involve two events just happening to occur together, with neither causing the other, and how habits often lead to people and animals repeatedly engaging in the same activity. They also introduced several specific facts that would serve as useful background knowledge: that the dark circles around raccoons' eyes look like masks, that raccoons habitually hunt for food at night, and that raccoons often pick up objects and carry them to other locations.

The background knowledge provided by Beck and McKeown helped the children not to misinterpret what happened. Second graders who received the background information, unlike many of their peers, did not conclude that the raccoon was trying to help Mrs. McGinnis get her money back. The emphasis on the concept of coincidence also helped children form accurate interpretations. A number of children who received the background, but almost none who did not, explicitly contrasted what Mrs. McGinnis thought had happened with what actually had.

The investigators' general recommendations were that teachers not just introduce stories in general terms, but that they also explain to children critical background knowledge that the children might lack. To introduce stories in this way requires careful analysis both of what concepts are critical to the meaning of the story and what children already know. Beck and McKeown also recommended that with young children, stories should be divided into small units (one to three pages each), and concepts relevant to the upcoming segment should be discussed just before children read the segment. These seem to be wise suggestions, based on both research findings and common sense.

Palincsar and Brown (1984) integrated a different set of psychological principles into a program for teaching reading comprehension to seventh graders. The success their program has met with is perhaps the most impressive demonstration to date of how knowledge of children's thinking can be useful in the classroom. The children who were involved were seventh graders from disadvantaged backgrounds. Although their decoding skills were at the expected grade level, their comprehension skills were two to three years behind. Palincsar and Brown hypothesized that the source of the children's difficulty was that they were not monitoring their own comprehension sufficiently well.

The seventh graders received instruction in four skills that might help them monitor their comprehension of what they had read: summarization, clarification, questioning, and anticipating future questions. After reading a paragraph, they needed to summarize it. Then they needed to clarify any ambiguities in their summaries or in the paragraph they had summarized. Next, they needed to anticipate what question the teacher might ask about the paragraph. Finally, they needed to predict what the next paragraph might be about. These four elements—summarizing, clarifying, anticipating questions, and predicting future content—were the heart of the instruction.

To help the seventh graders learn these skills, the teacher took turns with the student. After both the student and the teacher read a paragraph, the teacher would summarize it, point to material that needed clarification, anticipate likely questions, and predict what would happen next in the story. On the next paragraph, the student would carry out these activities. Then it would be the teacher's turn. This turn taking was essential because at first students were quite inept in executing the skills. For example, at the beginning of the training, only 11% of students' summary statements captured the main idea of the paragraph. By the end of the more than twenty instructional sessions, 60% of their statements did so.

The instruction had all kinds of good effects on the seventh graders' reading comprehension. Every day after the instruction, they read new paragraphs and answered from memory ten questions about the paragraphs. On a pretest, before the instruction, the children averaged 20% correct on the test. At the end of instruction, they averaged more than 80% correct. The improved comprehension for such paragraphs was still evident when the seventh graders were retested six months after the instruction ended. Even more impressive, on tests that were part of the regular classwork in science and social studies, the trained children improved from the 20th percentile of their school to the 56th percentile. The instruction later proved just as effective when carried out in natural group settings by the children's regular teachers.

What general implications can we draw from this success story? One key element, according to Palincsar and Brown (1984), was that the comprehension skills were taught within the exact context in which they would be used—reading of passages. Another key element was the interaction between student and teacher. The teacher could model the types of thinking that were desired and could adjust the instruction to the child's existing level. For example, at the beginning, the students were so incompetent at summarizing that the teacher often needed almost to put words in their mouths for them to produce a coherent summary. Later, instruction could be at a much higher level. As the children's competence grew, teachers could phase out their role in the instruction. Finally, the example underlines the importance of comprehension monitoring as a key process in reading comprehension and is consistent with the speculation, made in Chapter 7, that metacognitive skills may be most important in later childhood and adolescence.

ACQUIRING COMPETENCE IN WRITING

A venerable sorrow of teachers and other educators is how badly students write. The difficulty does not end in childhood. For many computer companies, it seems far easier to build a machine capable of performing millions of operations per second than to write a manual that explains in clear English how to get the machine to work. This is particularly unfortunate because of the growing role of writing in modern life. For example, business personnel spend an estimated 19% of their working hours writing memos, letters, and technical reports (Klemmer & Snyder, 1972).

Much less is known about how children learn to write than about how they learn to read or perform arithmetic. However, at least rough pictures are beginning to emerge of the initial drafting process and the process of revision. In each of these areas, the need to pursue multiple goals simultaneously and to automatize lower-level processing so that processing resources can be focused on higher-level goals are central problems for young writers.

The Initial Drafting Process

Most people do not have a good sense of what children's compositions are like. The following essay, actually a better-than-average effort for an 8-year-old, should communicate the flavor:

> I have not got a bird but I know some things about them. They have tow nostrils and They clean Ther feather and They eat seeds, worms, bread, cuddle fish, and lots of other things. and they drink water. When he drinks he Puts his head up and it gose down. A budgie (birdie) cage gets very dirty and peopel clean it. (Kress, 1982, pp. 59–60)

This story illustrates not only the quality of children's writing but several reasons why writing is so difficult. There is the need to think of what to say. Then there is the need to place the retrieved ideas in a sensible order. This need entails a difficult choice. If children wait to write their stories until they have retrieved all relevant information that they possess, they probably will forget some important points that they earlier recalled. If they write the ideas in the order in which they recall them, the essay will often sound either disconnected or illogical. Then there are many types of lower-level processes that are needed; as the 8-year-old's essay indicates, producing correct spelling, capitalization, punctuation, and grammar pose major challenges for children. It is no wonder they find writing to be difficult.

Just as reading can be compared to listening, so can writing be compared to speaking. In contrast to the first comparison, where only the single process of lexical access separates reading from listening, writing imposes many demands that speaking does not. Bereiter and Scardamalia (1982) noted three major types of differences: the kinds of topics that are discussed, the ways in which goals are generated, and the mechanical demands of writing.

Demands of unfamiliar topics.   To write a story, children must first activate information in long-term memory that is relevant to the topic. In many cases this is difficult because they have never thought about the topic they are assigned to write about (e.g., "Why I like winter"). Under such conditions, they must pull together material from diverse parts of their memory and organize the material into a sensible argument. The 8-year-old's essay on birds exemplifies what often happens. The last sentence of the story seems to have little to do with the rest of the composition; it probably was retrieved later and never integrated with the earlier portion.

Demands of multiple goals.   Writing often entails many or all of the following goals: to amuse, to convince, to inform, to arouse, to write enough material, not to write too much material, and to communicate enthusiasm. Intonations and nonverbal gestures, which can achieve some of these purposes in speech, are unavailable to the writer. Beyond this, other people's questions and comments often suggest new goals and paths to pursue in conversations. Writers' feedback during the initial drafting process is ordinarily limited to their own reactions to what they have written. Thus, writing demands formulating goals independently, keeping them in mind for long time periods, and figuring out how to meet them.

How do children cope with the need to pursue multiple goals simultaneously? Scardamalia and Bereiter (1984) labeled children's typical approach as the *knowledge-telling strategy.*   This strategy simplifies the writing task to the point where only a single goal needs to be considered at any given time. The basic organization of the strategy includes only two parts. First, give a direct reaction to the question that was asked. Second, write down relevant information from memory in the order that it is retrieved. The 8-year-old's story described above exemplifies this approach. Initially, she answered a question about birds, "I do not have a bird, but I know some things about them." Then she listed several facts she knew about birds. The limited goals of the knowledge-telling strategy may account for the brevity of most schoolchildren's compositions.

The difficulty of keeping multiple goals in mind over extended time periods may also account for the lack of internal connections in young children's essays. McCutchen and Perfetti (1982) noted that typically, second and fourth graders' stories are organized only in the sense that all the statements relate to the topic sentence; this is the structure of the knowledge-telling strategy, for example. In contrast, sixth graders' essays are more richly textured. Later sentences in stories refer not only to the topic sentence but also to other sentences within the story. Creating such internal connections requires keeping in mind both the point of the original topic sentence and the particulars of other sentences. Thus, it creates a greater memory load than the knowledge-telling strategy. However, it also creates more of the feel of a story, in which steady progress is made toward some end, rather than a grocery list.

With experience in writing, children come to organize goals into standard sequences, which help them cope with the memory demands of writing. An unusual natural experiment reported by Waters (1980) demonstrated how skills in coordinating multiple goals develop with practice. Waters analyzed 120 essays written by a second-grade girl (herself) during a school year. All the essays were written in response to a "class news" assignment. Each day, students were to write about that day's events.

Waters intensively examined five essays she had written on consecutive days at the beginning of the year, five in the middle, and five at the end. As shown in Table 9–3, story contents at first were limited to the date, weather, and class activities. Later, they also included information about peers, duties, and materials brought to school

Most important, the later stories showed a greater number and variety of goals than the earlier ones. In the later essays, each time the child recalled an event, she seemed to immediately form the goal of noting the time at which the event occurred. After writing about the time of the event, she moved on to pursuing the goal of describing her reaction to the event. These

TABLE 9-3 Stories Written at Beginning, Middle, and End of Year for Class News Assignment (Waters, 1980)

SEPTEMBER 24, 1956

> Today is Monday, September 24, 1956. It is a rainy day. We hope the sun will shine. We got new spelling books. We had our pictures taken. We sang Happy Birthday to Darbara.

JANUARY 22, 1957

> Today is Tuesday, January 22, 1957. It is a foggy day. We must be careful crossing the road.
> This morning, we had music. We learned a new song.
> Linda is absent. We hope she come back soon.
> We had arithmetic. We made believe that we were buying candy. We had fun.
> We work in our English work books. We learned when to use *is* and *are*.

MAY 27, 1957

> Today is Monday, May 27, 1957. It is a warm, cloudy day. We hope the sun comes out.
> This afternoon, we had music. We enjoyed it. We went out to play.
> Carole is absent. We hope she comes back soon.
> We had a spelling lesson, we learned about a *dozen.*
> Tomorrow we shall have show and tell.
> Some of us have spelling sentences to do for homework.
> Danny brought in a cocoon. It will turn into a butterfly.

prearranged sequences of goals reduced the processing demands of the writing task by suggesting context beyond the sheer occurrence of events. They resemble the story grammars used by children to recall fairy tales in their use of organized knowledge to aid processing.

Facility in managing less-stereotyped sequences of goals also develops during the elementary school years. Goldman (1983) presented fourth and sixth graders with two-paragraph stories and asked them to summarize the stories in a single sentence. When the story contained a clear topic sentence, children of both ages used it as the summary. When the story lacked a topic sentence, sixth graders usually generated one of their own. Fourth graders, however, rarely generated their own topic sentences. Presumably, the older children focused more clearly on the paragraph's goal, and this enabled them to capture the point of the paragraph in a single sentence. More generally, ability to separate goals from details, and to state the goals clearly, may be a key part of what develops in the acquisition of writing skills.

Helping young elementary school children to consider two or more goals simultaneously and to relate these goals to each other may help them overcome their problems of not writing enough material and not writing sufficiently interconnected material. Bereiter and Scardamalia (1982) found that a surprisingly simple instructional device was useful in achieving these goals. The approach involved giving children a deck of cards with common sentence openings on them: "Further," "For example," "Even though," and so on. Children were asked to use these prompts when they could not think of what to say next. The prompts led to more content and more richly interconnected content, even though they did not tell children what content to add.

Mechanical demands.   The third type of difficulty involved in writing but not in speaking involves the mechanical demands of forming letters, ordering the letters into correctly spelled words, and putting punctuation marks in the right places. In addition to posing yet another goal that writers need to meet, these mechanical demands also create a different type of obstacle: They force many children to proceed so slowly that losing their train of thought becomes a distinct possibility. To test the possible harmful effects of both mechanical demands and slow rate of production, Bereiter and Scardamalia asked fourth and sixth graders to compose essays under one of three conditions. In the first condition, children wrote as they ordinarily would, thus encountering both the mechanical demands of writing and its slow rate. In the second, they dictated their essays to a scribe trained to write at each child's typical writing speed. This released the children from the mechanical demands of writing but not from its slow rate. In the third condition, the children dictated at their normal speaking rate into a tape recorder. This released them from both the mechanical and the rate demands of ordinary writing.

Children in the normal dictation condition produced the highest-quality compositions; children in the slow dictation condition produced the next best; and children in the standard writing condition the worst. In other words, children unburdened by either mechanical demands or slow rate produced the best essays, children burdened only by slow rate the next best, and children burdened by both the worst. The findings suggests that if children became skillful in typing or in using word processors, the quality of their writing might improve. The hypothesis certainly seems worth testing.

The Revision Process

After people draft essays, usually they must revise them. Revision involves a comparison between some unit of text, such as a word or sentence, and an internal representation of the intended meaning or grammatical properties. For most of us, this is a difficult process. One frequently advanced explanation is that psychological and temporal closeness to the composition interferes with efforts at revision. Therefore, writing teachers often advise students to defer revising their work until they can look at it objectively.

Such advice may not get to the heart of the problem, though. The quality of fourth to twelfth graders' revisions is no better when they revise the work a week after writing than when they revise it immediately (Bereiter & Scardamalia, 1982). The educational implication is that children might as well begin revising their essays as soon after writing them as is convenient. Waiting, in and of itself, does no good.

Another common belief is that elementary-school-age children's egocentrism interferes with their ability to revise their essays. Just as earlier in their lives they were unable to see the ambiguity in their oral communications (Chapter 2), they now would experience a similar problem in their writing. Bartlett (1982) found that children do experience difficulty separating what they themselves know from what their readers could reasonably be expected to know. Fifth graders were asked to write short narrative stories for a class anthology. The children then needed to revise either their own essay or an essay written by another child. Bartlett was interested in how well children detected two types of errors: grammatical mistakes and ambiguous references. She reasoned that if the problem was egocentrism, children would have more difficulty detecting ambiguous references ("The policeman and the robber fought. He was killed.") in their own stories; after all, they knew who the "he" referred to. In revising other children's essays, however, there was no particular reason to expect this type of mistake to be harder to correct than the grammatical errors.

The children's revisions followed exactly this pattern. Children were quite good at noticing other children's referential ambiguities, but were much less good at noticing their own. The difference in detecting grammatical errors in their own and other children's stories was considerably less great, though it was still present to some extent. Thus, a major part of development of revising skills may be ability to separate one's own perspective from that of the reader. Training similar to that provided by Sonnenschein and Whitehurst (1984) to help children overcome their problems in oral referential communication (p. 57) might also help them detect comparable ambiguities in their writing.

The general themes revisited.   Early in the chapter, four recurring issues were listed: how children allocate attentional resources, how they choose strategies, the relative worth of direct and indirect teaching techniques, and the sources of individual differences. It may be worthwhile to consider the lessons that can be drawn about these issues.

Allocation of attentional resources seemed to play an especially large role in children's reading and writing. Wilkinson discussed the trade-offs in reading between identifying individual words and trying to comprehend larger units of meaning. Perfetti ascribed the importance of automaticity of lexical access to its freeing up attentional resources that then could be devoted to comprehension. Bereiter and Scardamalia emphasized the conflicts inherent between the mechanical demands of writing, the need to communicate in the absence of gestures and intonations, and the formation of grammatical sentences. Waters attributed her improved writing in the class news assignment to her organizing goals more effectively, thereby reducing the memory demands of the tasks.

Children's strategy choices appeared to exert a large influence on both their arithmetic and their reading performance. The Siegler and Shrager model explained how children chose addition and subtraction strategies in a way that led to their using the most effortful strategies only where such strategies were most needed. The model also accounted for why children use the strategies that they do and why they require more time to execute some strategies than others. The Jorm and Share model explained similar phenomena in reading. The strong correlation between children's phonological recoding skills and their reading comprehension, and the general superiority of instructional approaches that directly teach sounding-out skills, also were consistent with the strategy-choice models.

Whether teaching directly to the ultimate goal is invariably the most effective instructional strategy also was discussed most extensively in the contexts of reading and arithmetic. In reading, the reasoning was that even though advanced readers rely most heavily on visually based retrieval, telling beginning readers to do this would be counterproductive. The beginning readers would be forced to advance many incorrect answers. If they learned the incorrect answers that they stated, they would ultimately take longer to learn to retrieve the words efficiently. The same reasoning led to the view that discouraging children from using their fingers to add and subtract would slow their learning.

Individual differences were examined most thoroughly in reading. Very early in learning to read, knowledge of letter names seems the best predictor of subsequent individual differences in reading. This seems attributable to knowledge of letter names being related to children's and their parents' interest in learning to read. Somewhat later, phonological recoding skills are the best predictors of individual differences. Still later, general comprehension skills become most important. This latter change seems attributable to the larger amount of phonological recoding that beginning readers do, and to the greater comprehension demands of the material that advanced readers encounter. Palincsar and Brown demonstrated, however, that instruction in comprehension monitoring can change around the pattern of individual differences that children show. Seventh graders who initially were in the bottom 20% of their class on comprehension tests made so much progress during the instructional program that they eventually exceeded the average score in their school on such tests.

SUMMARY

The separation between cognitive development and educational psychology is steadily diminishing. The reason is that children's thinking outside of the classroom seems to have a great deal in common with their thinking inside it. This can be seen in each of the 3 R's: reading, writing, and arithmetic.

Young children use a variety of methods to add and subtract. Sometimes they retrieve an answer from memory and state it. Other times they put up their fingers and count them. Yet other times they put up their fingers but answer without counting, or they count aloud but without putting up their fingers.

Which strategy children use to solve particular problems seems to be determined by the distribution of associations between problems and possible answers. When associative strength is concentrated in one answer (a peaked distribution), children usually retrieve that answer and state it. When associative strength is divided among several answers (a flat distribution), children more often use a backup strategy such as putting up their fingers and counting them. Among the factors that create peaked distributions of associations are helpful associations from the counting string, a low sum, and frequent exposure to the problem.

In learning to read, children need to learn to identify letters and words and to comprehend larger units of meaning. Among the most important prereading skills are letter perception and phonemic awareness. Quick and accurate letter perception demands knowledge of distinctive features that distinguish letters from each other, such as large curves, small curves, and vertical and diagonal lines. Phonemic awareness involves the ability to isolate sounds that comprise words. The degree to which children possess these types of knowledge when they start school predicts quite well how well they will do in reading in the first few grades.

Children use two main word-identification methods: phonological recoding and visually based retrieval. Both methods begin with examination of the printed word and end with location of the word's meaning and pronunciation in long-term memory. Phonological recoding also involves an intermediate step in which letters are translated into sounds. The two skills are related in that accurate phonological recoding may aid development of strong associations between the printed word and its long-term memory entry and thus aid visually based retrieval. In addition, clues from the surrounding context may aid word identification, especially of beginning or poor readers. However, the price of needing such aid may be reduced comprehension, due to the need to devote processing resources to drawing the inferences.

Reading comprehension, the purpose of reading, draws on virtually all the intellectual skills children possess. As children become increasingly efficient in identifying words, their reading comprehension becomes increasingly closely linked to their listening comprehension. Among the other especially important sources of development in reading comprehension are ability to hold longer phrases in short-term memory, greater prior knowledge of the material being read, ability to flexibly adapt reading procedures to the demands of particular tasks, and automatization of lexical access.

Writing is a challenging task for most children. They have difficulty establishing clear goals in the absence of the prompts that conversation usually provides. They also have difficulty reconciling the competing demands of executing the mechanics of writing, forming grammatical sentences, expressing meanings, and keeping the reader's reaction in mind. Children in the early and middle elementary school grades often adopt a knowledge-telling strategy to cope with these demands. The strategy involves stating a reaction to the question that was posed and then listing supporting evidence in the order in which it is retrieved from memory. The strategy produces coherent but uninspiring compositions. A major change that occurs with age and experience at writing is improved ability to coordinate goals so as to produce more extensive and more interesting essays. Skill at revising also improves as children come to separate their own knowledge as writers from what the reader would know just from having read the text.

RECOMMENDED READINGS

Beck, I. L., & McKeown, M. G. (1984). Application of theories of reading to instruction. *American Journal of Education, 93,* 61–81. A successful instructional program in reading, based on a detailed analysis of the hidden prerequisites for understanding the story.

Palincsar, A. S., & Brown, A. L. (1984). Reciprocal teaching of comprehension-monitoring activities. *Cognition and Instruction, 1,* 117–175. Perhaps the most successful application of cognitive psychological principles to the task of improving learning in the schools. Seventh graders with serious reading comprehension problems became able to comprehend at an above-average level through this program.

Scardamalia, M., & Bereiter, C. (1984). Written composition. In M. Wittrock (Ed.), *Handbook of Research on Teaching*, (3rd ed.) (in press). An excellent summary of what is known about the psychology of children's writing and how to improve it.

Siegler, R. S., & Shrager, J. (1984). A model of strategy choice. In C. Sophian (Ed.), *Origins of cognitive skills.* Hillsdale, NJ: Erlbaum. Raises the issue of how children choose among alternative strategies and presents a model that explains how they do so in addition and subtraction.

Waters, H. S. (1980). "Class news": A single-subject longitudinal study of prose production and schema formation during childhood. *Journal of Verbal Learning and Verbal Behavior, 19,* 152–167. Documents the progress of one girl learning to write throughout a school year. Illustrates the importance of organized sequences of goals in the learning process.

10
CONCLUSIONS
FOR THE PRESENT /
CHALLENGES
FOR THE FUTURE

"So how *do* children think?"
A 7-year-old, reacting to a description of research on children's thinking

Previous chapters have focused separately on perception, language, memory, conceptualization, and other areas of cognitive development. The division has made it easier to consider the unique properties of children's thinking in each area. However, such a division also can obscure the qualities that all aspects of children's thinking share in common. The two main goals of this chapter are to discuss conclusions that unify research in all the areas and to identify issues that seem likely to be central in the future.

Several types of commonalities will be emphasized in this effort to sketch out a "big picture" of cognitive development. One commonality involves issues. The largest issues in the study of problem solving, conceptualizing, memorizing, and the other capabilities are quite similar. A second commonality involves empirical findings. Research in all of the areas has revealed a number of consistent patterns. A third commonality involves mechanisms. Children's perception, memorization, problem solving, conceptualization, and use of language are products of the same developing cognitive system. It should not be surprising that the processes that produce them often are the same.

Toward the end of the very first chapter of this book, eight themes were listed that would apply to many different aspects of children's think-

TABLE 10-1 Chapter Outline

    I.   The two questions that stand out as the most basic in the study of children's thinking are "What Develops?" and "How Does Development Occur?"
         A.   Current knowledge about what develops and how development occurs
         B.   Future issues

   II.   Development is about change. Four change processes that seem to be particularly large contributors to cognitive development are automatization, encoding, generalization, and strategy construction.
         A.   Current knowledge about change processes
         B.   Future issues

  III.   A major challenge children face is how to deploy limited processing resources to deal effectively with cognitively demanding situations.
         A.   Current knowledge about children's deployment of processing resources
         B.   Future issues

  IV.   Changes in children's thinking do not occur in a vacuum. What children already know about material they encounter influences not only *how much* they learn but also *what* they learn.
         A.   Current knowledge about the effects of existing knowledge
         B.   Future issues

   V.   Knowledge of the adult cognitive system is useful for studying changes in children's thinking. It is much easier to study development when we know where the development is going.
         A.   Current contributions of knowledge of adults' thinking
         B.   Future issues

  VI.   Differences between age groups tend to be ones of degree rather than kind. Young children are more cognitively competent than they often are depicted as being, and older children and adults are not so cognitively competent as we often think.
         A.   Current knowledge about differences between age groups
         B.   Future issues

  VII.   Children's thinking develops within a social context. Parents, peers, teachers, and the overall society influence what children think about, as well as how and why they come to think in particular ways.
         A.   Current knowledge of social influences on children's thinking
         B.   Future issues

  VIII.   We have learned quite a bit about cognitive development, but there is far more left to learn.

  IX.   Summary

ing. These themes also provide an appropriate framework for organizing this concluding chapter. The chapter is divided into eight sections, with each section focusing on a single theme. The first part of each discussion is used to summarize what is known at present that is relevant to the theme. The second part is used to consider what questions should be asked in the future and to speculate about what answers may be found. The chapter's organization is summarized in Table 10–1.

1. The two questions that stand out as the most basic in the study of children's thinking are "What develops?" and "How does development occur?"

When investigators of children's thinking write in journal articles, "The purpose of this investigation is . . . ," they almost never complete the sentence with "to try to find out what develops" or "to try to find out how development occurs." Modesty, and the realization that no one study is likely to go far toward resolving these issues, prevent researchers from mentioning them. Yet these are the deepest motivations of research on children's thinking. Always keeping them in mind is critical to understanding what the research is all about.

Current Knowledge About What Develops and How Development Occurs

On a few occasions, investigators have tried to address directly the question of what develops. In one of these instances, Brown and DeLoache (1978) noted four potential answers in the domain of memory development: growth of basic capacities, strategies, metacognition, and content knowledge. These potential sources of memory development provide a useful guide for thinking about all aspects of cognitive development.

Many examples attest to the generality of these sources of development. Improvements in basic capacities were not only invoked to explain improved functioning of the sensory, short-term, and long-term memory stores. They also were used to explain changes in the complexity of the stimuli infants prefer to look at (Banks & Salapatek, 1981), in the analogy problems that children can solve (Sternberg & Rifkin, 1979), and in the ambiguous "garden path" sentences that children can read and interpret (Daneman, 1981). Similarly, changes in strategies were seen in contexts other than rehearsal, organization, and the other mnemonic strategies. They also emerged as a source of development in children's increasing success in solving conservation, class inclusion, and missing addend problems (Anderson & Cuneo, 1978; Case, 1981; Markman & Siebert, 1976), in their use of overgeneralized "ed" endings such as "runned" and "hitted" (Brown, Cazden, & Bellugi, 1969), in their visual scanning of houses to see if they are identical (Vurpillot, 1968), and in their use of predesignated sequences of goals to prompt their writing of "class news" assignments (Waters, 1980). Improved metacognition allowed high school students to take more useful notes than junior high school students on material they were studying (Brown, Smiley, & Lawton, 1978) and allowed normal children to plan problem-solving approaches more effectively than retarded children (Sternberg, 1984) as well as allowing them to evaluate more accurately their memory capacity. Finally, superior knowledge of the content under consideration also facilitated many cognitive activities besides remembering. It enabled toddlers to identify causes more successfully (Shultz, 1982), preschoolers to add more efficiently

(Siegler & Shrager, 1984), first graders to read more efficiently (Jorm & Share, 1983), and high school students to use formal operational reasoning in areas they were knowledgeable about (Piaget, 1972).

Hypotheses about how development occurs, like hypotheses about what develops, reflect the interconnectedness of different aspects of cognitive development. Recall some of the diverse contexts in which encoding and related processes were used to explain changes in children's thinking. Gibson, Schapiro, and Yonas's (1968) explanations of how children learn to discriminate among letters of the alphabet and Gough and Hillinger's (1980) explanation of how they learn to read their first words emphasized encoding of distinctive features. Klahr's (1984) explanation of how children acquire the concept of number, and Siegler's (1976) explanation of acquisition of knowledge about balance scales also emphasized encoding. So did Clark's (1973) explanation of the development of early vocabulary terms (children gradually increase the number of critical features that they encode) and Ericsson, Chase, and Faloon's (1980) explanation of S. F.'s prodigious memory feats (he learned to encode numbers as running times and then developed complex hierarchies of encodings).

Future Issues

Perhaps the most urgent need for improving our understanding of children's thinking is new theories that are both broadly applicable and precisely stated. Such theories are valuable even if they are not correct in all their particulars. They focus attention on a particular set of issues, raise questions that have not been considered before, and serve as a point of departure from which new ideas can be developed.

For many years, Piaget's theory served these purposes. For much of the 1960s and 1970s, arguments between "pro-Piagetians" and "anti-Piagetians" dominated journals, books, and conferences. Such theoretically motivated questions as whether 5-year-olds could be taught to conserve liquid quantity assumed an almost unreal importance. An outgoing editor of the journal *Child Development* noted that in one year of his tenure, he received enough conservation-training-study submissions that he need not have published anything else to fill all of the journal's pages (Jeffrey, 1975 and personal communication).

Those days are past. Very few researchers today would argue that it is impossible for children to learn conservation, class inclusion, or other concrete operational concepts before age 7. Equally few would argue that young children's difficulty in succeeding on the standard versions of these tasks is due to some artifact of the methodology. Instead, most have adopted the more moderate position that children encounter genuine difficulty understanding these concepts, but that they can learn to do so with appropriate experience.

Moderation has its virtues, but also its costs. Piaget was right in some of his views and wrong in others, but right or wrong, his theory lent coherence to findings about many aspects of children's thinking. What is needed now is a successor that has the virtues of Piaget's theory while surmounting at least some of the drawbacks. That is, a theory is needed that, like Piaget's, incorporates the entire age range from infancy to adolescence; that addresses areas as diverse as problem solving, memory, and moral judgments; and that uncovers numerous heretofore unknown developmental changes in children's thinking. Beyond this, our ideal theory of children's thinking would add precise analyses of change mechanisms and/or extensive analysis of how input from the external world contributes to development. It also would not make predictions inconsistent with known data.

In previous chapters we have encountered a number of efforts at formulating such broad yet detailed theories—among them, the theories advanced by Case, Klahr, and Sternberg. Each of these theories has added to our understanding of cognitive development, but no one of them has captured the imagination of the field as Piaget's theory did. It is possible that we simply know too much today, that no one theory can capture all that is known about children's thinking. However, predictions that something cannot be done have a bad track record. Thirty years ago, experts believed that no human being would ever run a four-minute mile. Since then, literally hundreds of runners have done so. Closer to home, we need only consider S. F.'s prodigious memory feats; he learned to memorize three or four times as many numbers as had been thought possible. Thus, I would not be at all surprised if just the type of encompassing but precise theory that seems needed were to emerge in the near future.

2. Development is about change. Four change processes that seem to be particularly large contributors to cognitive development are automatization, encoding, generalization, and strategy construction.

Current Knowledge About Change Processes

Perhaps the single greatest obstacle to generating more advanced theories of what develops and how development occurs is our underdeveloped knowledge of change processes. Current hypotheses about developmental mechanisms seem to be generally in the right direction, but are too imprecise to generate satisfying predictions or explanations. A symptom of the problem is that investigators trying to characterize change mechanisms often use different terms to describe ideas that are clearly related, and that may be identical. Until the ideas are worked out in greater detail, it will remain impossible to know exactly how they relate to each other.

Although current understanding is not all we would like, considerable evidence testifies to the importance of four broad classes of change processes: *automatization, encoding, generalization,* and *strategy construction.* Automatization refers to increasingly efficient execution of a procedure that frees mental resources for other purposes. Parallel processing and increased rate of processing are related terms. Encoding refers to identification of a set of features for internally representing objects and events. Ideas that overlap with encoding include identification of critical features, discrimination, differentiation, and assimilation. Generalization refers to extrapolating observed relations to new cases. Similar concepts include induction, abstraction, and regularity detection. Strategy construction involves putting together the results of the other processes to adapt to task demands. Related ideas include rule formation, accommodation, combination, and adaptation.

These processes seem to produce a wide range of cognitive developments. Automatization makes possible simultaneous performance of tasks that previously had to be performed successively. A memorable example here is how, with enough practice, people learned to read and write simultaneously (Spelke, Hirst, & Neisser, 1976). Improved encoding allows children to take into consideration additional variables that may be important for their understanding of objects and events. Recall how 5-year-olds, taught to encode distance as well as weight on balance-scale problems, could then learn from experiences that did not help peers who were not taught to encode distance (Siegler, 1976). Generalization allows children to extend relations among encoded variables to novel situations. Maratsos' (1982) description of German children learning that masculine nouns for which you use the term *der* also take the term *sie* nicely illustrates how development can stem from detection of consistent patterns. Finally, strategy construction involves children's attempts to use these consistent patterns to adapt to the task environment. Children's use of rehearsal strategies to memorize words exemplifies this type of change. Preschoolers did not rehearse; 8-year-olds, who had learned that rehearsal produced better performance, rehearsed the most recently presented word in isolation; 11-year-olds, who had learned which types of rehearsal were most effective, rehearsed more- and less-recently presented words together (Ornstein, Naus, & Liberty, 1975). Additional examples of each process's influence on diverse areas of cognitive development are listed in Table 10-2.

This set of processes seems important not only for each process's individual contribution to development, but also for their joint contribution. The processes can be viewed as being hierarchically related to each other. Constructing new strategies, the most global process, requires children to generalize to new cases the connections they have made between their own actions and the outcomes that follow. Generalizing in turn requires encoding of the units that consistently go together. Finally, encoding new units often depends on execution of other processes being sufficiently automatized to free cognitive resources for noticing new features to encode.

To get a feel for how these four hierarchically related processes might produce development in a particular area, think about the min strategy for adding numbers (Chapter 9, p. 303). This strategy involves choosing the larger addend and counting up from it the number of times indicated by the

TABLE 10-2   Some Demonstrations of the Importance of Automatization, Encoding, Generalization, and Strategy Construction

PROCESS	DOMAIN	INVESTIGATORS
Automatization	Writing of essays	Bereiter and Scardamalia (1982)
	Reading comprehension	Wilkinson (1980)
	General theory of development	Case (1978)
	General theory of cognition	Shiffrin (1976)
Encoding	Solving analogy problems	Sternberg and Rifkin (1979)
	Identifying letters of the alphabet	Gibson, Schapiro, & Yonas (1968)
	General theory of development	Siegler (1984)
	General theory of cognition	Craik and Lockhart (1972)
Generalization	Acquisition of phonology and syntax	MacWhinney (1978)
	Learning of concepts	Rosch and Mervis (1975)
	General theory of development	Klahr and Wallace (1976)
	General theory of cognition	Skinner (1957)
Strategy Construction	Strategies for remembering	Flavell (1970)
	Buggy strategies for solving subtraction problems	Brown and Van Lehn (1982)
	General theory of development	Sternberg (1985)
	General theory of cognition	Newell and Simon (1972)

smaller addend. On 2 + 5 and 5 + 2, for example, a child using the min strategy would note that 5 was the larger addend, count up 2 numbers from it, and answer, "7."

Each of the four processes likely contributes to acquisition of the min strategy. Constructing the strategy depends on having previously formed the generalization that adding a + b always yields the same answer as adding b + a. Otherwise, there would be no basis for always counting up from the larger number, regardless of the ordering of the addends. Forming this generalization, in turn, depends on appropriate encoding. To learn that the order of the addends is irrelevant, children need to encode a feature of "first addend" and a feature of "second addend," as well as the particular numbers within each problem. Finally, encoding not only the particular numbers being added but also the abstract categories of "first addend" and "second addend" would seem to require a high degree of automatization of the execution of all other processes. That is, execution of other processes used to add, such as counting, must be sufficiently automatized that it does not require all the child's processing resources. Only then will encoding of new, potentially useful features be possible.

Future Issues

Many challenges need to be overcome before change processes will be well understood. The most urgent need is probably for more precise analyses of how particular change processes operate. Efforts toward this goal are not very far along, but progress is being made.

Holland and Reitman's (1981) analysis of encoding exemplifies this progress. These investigators drew an explicit analogy between the development of improved encodings and biological evolution. New encodings, like new life forms, would be created by the joint operation of random mutation and environmental selection.

Holland and Reitman began by characterizing knowledge in the form of a production system. Each production included a string of 1's and 0's on the condition side (the system's encoding of the environment), and another string of 1's and 0's on the action side (the response the system would make if the current contents of short-term memory matched that encoding). Productions were associated in varying strengths with attainment of the system's goal. A given production's association with the goal would increase when the production "fired" as part of a sequence that led to attainment of the goal.

Improved encoding would be produced in the following way. Periodically, two productions that had different 1's and 0's from each other on the condition side, but that had the same sequence of 1's and 0's as each other on the action side, would be selected to be "parent productions." The condition sides of the two parent productions would be "cut" at a randomly chosen place, for example between the second and third symbol. Then a new production would be formed by combining the symbols to the left of the cut in condition side of one production with the symbols to the right of the cut in the other. The new production would encode the environment in a way related to the encoding of each parent production but not identical to either one.

This abstract description of the creation of new encodings can be made more concrete by an example. Suppose that the two parent productions were:

$$101 \longrightarrow 010 \quad \text{and} \quad 000 \longrightarrow 010.$$

Making a cut between the second and third symbols on the condition sides of these two productions, and recombining the symbols to the left of the cut in one with those to the right of the cut in the other, would give birth to the new productions

$$001 \longrightarrow 010 \quad \text{and} \quad 100 \longrightarrow 010.$$

These newborn productions would replace existing productions that were the most weakly associated with goal attainment. The replacement process would represent a form of survival of the fittest within the cognitive system, since "weak" productions would be replaced by new, potentially stronger ones. The new productions, like the previous ones, would survive if, and only if, they became positively correlated with attainment of the system's goals.

Holland and Reitman reported that this mechanism for creating new encodings greatly increased the efficiency with which their model learned to solve several simple operant conditioning problems. Goldberg (1983) used the same type of model in a more complex applied setting: as a self-modifying expert system to help gas companies solve pipeline transmission problems. Goldberg's system learned to adjust the flow of gas for seasonal variations, to adjust for variations in usage at different times of day, and even to locate leaks in the pipeline. Computer simulations incorporating similar mechanisms for improving encoding have learned to form cognitive maps of spatial layouts and to play excellent games of poker (Goldberg, 1983).

A second challenge for future research on change processes is to explain how physiological development interacts with children's experiences to produce cognitive development. Some of the most convincing explanations of developmental change have been analyses of such interactions. One of these was Banks and Salapatek's (1981) explanation of how increasingly sharp visual acuity contributes to infants' preference for looking at increasingly complex patterns. Another was Aslin and Dumais's (1980) account of how the development of bifoveal fixation, fusion, and stereopsis enable infants to use binocular depth cues. At present, however, analyses that compellingly connect physiological and cognitive changes are limited to perceptual development in the first year of life.

Although the brain develops particularly dramatically in the first year, it does not stop developing then. Further, the growth of the brain influences memory development, conceptual development, and other facets of children's thinking as well as perceptual development. It would be invaluable to know just how these contributions are made.

Heightened understanding of the contribution of physiological maturation to cognitive development may also serve another purpose. It could help tie together hypothesized large-scale change processes such as equilibration, assimilation, accommodation, and increases in M-space, with smaller-scale change processes such as automatization, encoding, generalization, and strategy construction. At present, the evidence for the existence of the large-scale change processes is not sufficiently conclusive to have convinced all investigators of their reality. Even among those who are convinced that they play a role in cognitive development, many are dissatisfied with existing analyses of what they are supposed to do and how they are supposed to work.

My best guess is that they do exist and that they do contribute in large ways to cognitive development. Until we better understand the role of physiological maturation in cognitive development, however, I doubt that we will be able to say anything very useful about them. Again, future theories of children's thinking can only benefit from additional knowledge of how changes in the brain's structure and functioning influence cognitive activity.

3. A major challenge children face is how to deploy limited processing resources to deal effectively with cognitively demanding situations.

Current Knowledge About Children's Deployment of Processing Resources

The tension between children possessing limited cognitive resources, yet wanting to achieve ambitious goals that tax these resources, has been described in numerous contexts. To speak, children must divide their processing capacity among the demands of enunciating clearly, ordering words grammatically within sentences, and communicating intended meanings. To write, they must not only order words grammatically and express intended meanings but must also cope with the mechanical demands of writing and with the lack of usual communicative aids such as intonations, gestures, and facial expressions. To accurately perceive events going on around them, they must attend to the aspects of the situation that are most likely to be informative and must ignore other aspects.

Children succeed in adapting to the demands of complex task environments in at least three senses. First, as they develop, they represent task environments increasingly completely. Their representations include more and more of the relevant features of concepts and problems. Second, their processing becomes increasingly flexible. They match their cognitive procedures more and more closely to the demands of the particular task. Third, the match becomes increasingly robust. Children come to employ appropriate representations and processes under a widening range of circumstances (see Sophian, 1984, for a similar view).

Empirical examples of each trend are easy to find. First consider the trend toward understandings becoming increasingly complete reflections of the task environment. Early understandings in a number of areas capture parts of the task environments. For example, 5- and 6-year-olds think that whichever of two tumblers includes more orange juice will taste more strongly like orange juice (Case, 1978). Cognitive growth comes when they add understanding of remaining parts of the task environment, in this instance the influence of the amount of water in the two tumblers. A similar trend can be seen in Salapatek's (1975) finding that 1-month-olds scan only the contours of objects, whereas 2- and 3-month-olds scan the interiors as well. It also is evident in Bowerman's (1982) finding that not until years after children learn the meaning of verbs such as *kill* and *drop* do they add the understanding that these words imply a specific causal agent, unlike *fall* and *die.* The studies of development of expertise in playing chess, knowing about dinosaurs, and memorizing digits also reflect the role of increasingly complete representation of the task environment (Ericsson, Chase, & Faloon, 1980; Chi, 1978; Chi & Koeske, 1983).

Evidence for children's increasing flexibility in pursuing particular goals within an environment also comes from many areas of children's thinking. One source is Kobasigawa, Ransom, and Holland's (1980) study of children's skimming of written passages. Older children read through a paragraph quickly when they learned that it was unlikely to prove important for their task. Younger children read the paragraph no faster than usual. Hagen (1972) established a similar point about increasing flexibility in the context of memory research. When children were told that they needed to remember some pictures and not others, older children remembered far more of the pictures described as important than did younger children. However, there were no differences between older and younger children's memory for the pictures that were said to be unimportant.

The third sense in which adaptations to task environments become increasingly successful is robustness. Children's initial conceptual understandings are often quite fragile. They appear only on the simplest experimental tasks and under the most favorable circumstances for application of the concept. These initial understandings are followed by a protracted period of development. During this period, children apply the concept in increasing numbers of circumstances and apply it increasingly well. Acredolo's (1978) findings about the increasing number of situations in which infants remember where objects are, despite changes in their own spatial positions, is one example of this increasing robustness. Another is Barton's (1978) description of toddlers' progress in making and remembering phonemic distinctions in the context of unfamiliar as well as familiar words. Markman's (1979) report of the decreasing number of prompts children need before they realize that they do not understand instructions about how to make baked Alaska is one more example.

Future Issues

One of the largest mysteries about children's adaptations to different situations is why effective adaptation requires such differing amounts of time in different domains. By age 4 months, infants possess a large variety of perceptual skills; by age 4 years, children possess a large variety of language skills. Yet at both of these ages, children's problem-solving skills seem much less advanced; they rarely use memory strategies; their metacognitive knowledge is severely limited; and teaching them to read or to solve any but the simplest arithmetic problems is difficult.

Domain-specific learning mechanisms. One intriguing hypothesis about why the adaptations take such differing amounts of time attributes the differences to the existence of *domain-specific learning mechanisms.* In this view, children not only possess general learning mechanisms such as automatization, encoding, and generalization; they also are seen as possessing learning mechanisms specifically adapted for acquiring particular skills. These specific learning mechanisms would help children deploy their processing resources especially effectively in the areas where the mechanisms operate.

Several proposals concerning domain-specific learning mechanisms were mentioned in the chapter on language development. Among these were Chomsky's (1957) proposal that young children possess a language-acquisition device specialized for acquiring the types of grammars that appear in natural languages, Slobin's (1983) proposal that young children are predisposed to acquire grammatical constructions that conform to a basic child grammar, Lenneberg's (1967) proposal of a critical period during which special acquisition mechanisms allow language to be mastered especially rapidly, and Bickerton's (1983) similar explanation for why immigrant children exposed only to pidgin languages could invent creoles where older immigrants could not.

Recently, investigators have extended the idea of domain-specific learning mechanisms to conceptual development and to intelligence as a whole. One of the most thought-provoking efforts in this direction is that of Keil (1981). Keil suggested that children possess specific learning mechanisms that allow them to quickly classify new concepts as being of a particular type. He illustrated his ideas in greatest detail as they related to *predicability*, the study of which predicates can be used in which sentences. As may be recalled from long-ago grammar lessons, the predicate is the part of the sentence that includes the verb and its complement. In the sentence "The monster is now alive," "The monster" is the subject, and "is now alive" is the predicate.

The phenomenon that motivated Keil's interest was children's ability to distinguish between statements that contain nonsensical predicates and statements whose predicates render the sentence untrue but sensible. Even if the speaker is mistaken in saying, "The monster is now alive," the sentence still is comprehensible. However, it is more than false to say "The monster is now an hour"; it is meaningless. The predicate "is now alive" can be used to describe living creatures, whereas the predicate "is now an hour" cannot. Even preschoolers discriminate between the two types of statements. The question is how they do so.

Keil assumed that children innately divide their experiences into certain basic categories of existence, and that they know these categories are related to each other in a hierarchical fashion. He also assumed that children are biologically predisposed to generate certain hypotheses about the categories into which their experiences can be placed. These assumptions were embodied in his proposal that children's ability to distinguish between mistaken and meaningless statements reflects the existence of a hierarchy like that shown in Figure 10-1. The hierarchy incorporates both categories of ex-

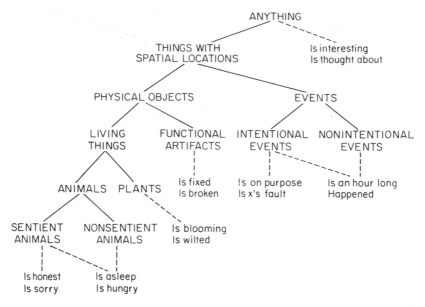

FIGURE 10-1   Part of Keil's (1981) predicability hierarchy indicating which categories of objects can be described by which types of predicates. Categories of objects are in capitals; predicates that can be used to describe words in that category are in lowercase letters. Early in development, children only make distinctions shown at top of tree. Gradually they make distinctions found lower and lower in the tree. The full tree represents adults' knowledge of predicability.

istence and predicates that can be used with all subjects that fall into each category.

The hierarchy divides both categories of existence and their potential predicates into classes of decreasing generality. The classes toward the top apply very widely. Any object, event, or idea can be said to be interesting, for example. The classes of predicates toward the bottom, in contrast, apply much more narrowly. Only humans and a few other animals can be said to "feel sorry" or to "be honest."

Keil's claim was not that the full predicability tree shown in Figure 10-1 is present at birth. Rather, he argued that the form of the conceptual organization is always a treelike hierarchy, and that children make the topmost distinctions in the tree before the bottommost ones. As children develop, they make more of the distinctions that they are predisposed to make eventually. For example, even kindergarteners distinguish between living things and functional artifacts, such as cars and stoves. Second graders make these distinctions and divide living things into animals and plants. Sixth graders further distinguish among various types of animals; people can be described as being honest or sorry, but rabbits cannot be.

How would such predicability trees contribute to conceptual development? Keil advanced the following scenario. Suppose a girl in sixth grade who did not know the word *tempest* encountered the sentence "The tempest lasted for an hour." If she possessed the tree typical of sixth graders (the full Figure 10–1 tree), the predicate "for an hour" would indicate that tempests are events of some type. By contrast, a child who made only the distinctions typically made by kindergarteners (just the top few levels of the tree in Figure 10–1) would know only that tempests were either inanimate solid objects, liquids, events, or abstractions. The more detailed predicability tree would allow the typical sixth grader to draw more precise inferences than the typical kindergartener and thus to learn faster. In this way, the predicability tree would serve as a domain-specific mechanism useful for learning new concepts.

Multiple intelligences. Gardner (1983) proposed an even more radical version of domain-specific learning mechanisms. In his theory of multiple intelligences, he suggested that intelligence itself consists of seven domains: linguistic, musical, logical-mathematical, spatial, bodily-kinesthetic, self-understanding, and social-understanding. He further suggested that each intelligence is based on a distinct symbol system and includes separate change mechanisms.

What criteria must a cognitive domain meet in order to be considered a separate intelligence? Gardner suggested several indicators. One is the existence of idiot savants or prodigies in the area: individuals whose excellence in the domain far exceeds what would be expected from other aspects of their intelligence. Thus, the existence of a Mozart, composing music before being old enough to attend elementary school, though not being especially precocious in other ways, is evidence for a separate musical intelligence. Another type of evidence is a plausible evolutionary history through which the ability could arise and prove adaptive. Since people did not program computers until recently, a separate intelligence for programming would be unlikely. Finally, individual differences in different aspects of a domain should correlate more highly with each other than with aspects of other domains. That is, abilities in different aspects of the domain should hang together.

The existence of idiot savants and prodigies seems especially dramatic evidence for the existence of separate intelligences. Gardner cites cases of severely retarded children, who had had no instruction in music, being able to play by ear pieces on the piano that they had just heard for the first time. The same children exhibited only the most primitive learning abilities in other domains, suggesting that they learned music through different mechanisms than they learned other skills.

Gardner also saw evidence for the operation of distinct intelligences in the exceptionally strong motivation that some children have to exercise particular talents. When the great mathematician Pascal was a child, his father forbade him to talk about mathematics and severely discouraged him from reading about it. In spite of this harsh reaction, Pascal marked with charcoal the walls of his room, trying to find ways of constructing triangles with equal sides and angles. He invented names for mathematical concepts, since he did not know the conventional words. He developed an axiomatic system for geometry and, in so doing, reinvented much of Euclid. He even dreamed of theorems and axioms—all of this in the face of a hostile environment.

The ideas of domain-specific learning mechanisms and separate intelligences are not without their problems. Knowledge of predicability may be acquired through the same learning mechanisms as many other types of knowledge. Few people would argue that people possess domain-specific mechanisms for learning to discriminate among the letters of the alphabet. Yet Gibson, Schapiro, and Yonas (1968) found that children's knowledge of the features of the letters is hierarchical (p. 254), just as their knowledge of predicability is. Further, children acquire their hierarchical knowledge of the letters' features within a year after they start reading, at least as quickly as they acquire knowledge of predicability. Thus, neither the existence of hierarchical knowledge about predicability nor the relatively rapid acquisition of the knowledge demands domain-specific learning mechanisms.

The idea of separate intelligences also has problematic aspects. Several of the abilities that Gardner classified as separate intelligences may in fact be related. Relevant data comes from IQ tests. Children's performance on verbal, logical-mathematical, and spatial reasoning subtests correlates positively. The same children who do well on one tend to do well on all three. It is not clear why this should be so if the symbol systems are truly separate. Further, the existence of prodigies and idiot savants in an area may be more closely related to the isolation of the area from other aspects of life than to whether the ability could plausibly have been evolutionarily advantageous. There are prodigies in chess; there are idiot savants who can quickly calculate what the day of the week will be on January 19, 6593. Neither of these activities would seem to confer any evolutionary benefit.

Despite these problems, the ideas of separate intelligences and domain-specific learning mechanisms are exciting. They seem intuitively reasonable and point in the direction of greater connection between people's innate endowments and their subsequent learning. Thus, they may constitute important building blocks for improving understanding of change processes and for creating new theories of children's thinking.

4. Changes in children's thinking do not occur in a vacuum. What children already know about material they encounter influences not only how much they learn but also what they learn.

Current Knowledge About the Effects of Existing Knowledge

There can be little doubt that people find it easier to learn, remember, and understand in areas where they already have some expertise. Inhelder, Sinclair, and Bovet (1974) and Strauss (1972) demonstrated that children who already had some knowledge about conservation and class inclusion more easily learned to master the concept than did less knowledgeable children. Chi (1978) found that 10-year-old chess experts remembered more about new chess positions than did adults less knowledgeable about the game. Mandler and Johnson (1977) and Stein and Glenn (1979) demonstrated that 6- and 7-year-olds understood more of the content of stories that followed standard fairy tale forms than stories in less-familiar forms.

Prior content knowledge influences what people learn as well as how much they learn. Such effects are especially evident in the rare cases where knowledge interferes with learning and remembering. Spilich, Vesonder, Chiesi, and Voss (1979) found that adults knowledgeable about baseball generally remembered more than others about a new baseball game. However, the knowledgeable people remembered less about details irrelevant to the progress of the game, such as the attendance and the particular songs played on the organ. Werker, Gilbert, Humphrey, and Tees (1981) demonstrated that adults' general knowledge of which phonemic contrasts were important in English interfered with their perception of Hindi contrasts. Seven-month-olds who were growing up in English-speaking homes, but who were less familiar with the English language, could perceive these same contrasts.

Prior content knowledge does not operate as a factor apart from the previously mentioned change processes, such as encoding, generalization, and strategy construction. Rather, the prior knowledge, along with incoming information, provides the data on which the change processes operate. Put another way, the prior content knowledge helps to determine what the change processes do, that is, what features children encode, what generalizations they draw, and what strategies they construct. The nature of the change processes, however, determines how they do it.

Several studies illustrate the ways in which content knowledge influences what features children encode, what generalizations they draw, and what strategies they form. First consider encoding. Siegler (1976) taught 5-year-olds that distance from the fulcrum was an important variable on balance-scale problems. The knowledge that distance was important, along with the acquisition of procedures for remembering distances, led the children to encode distance as well as weight. Later, the improved encoding enabled them to learn from experiences with balance-scale problems that previously had not enabled age peers to learn.

The effects of content knowledge on generalization were illustrated by Bowerman's (1982) studies of how children learn which verbs can take the prefix "un." Some terms, such as "cover" and "buckle," can; other terms, such as "spill" and "give," cannot. Only after children possess detailed knowledge of the exact meanings of the particular verbs can they detect the regularity that exists: Verbs involving either contact between objects or enclosing of objects generally can take the prefix; other verbs cannot. Given the subtlety of this regularity, it is not surprising that precise knowledge of verb meanings must be attained before children reach the proper generalization.

With regard to strategy construction, it was no accident that S. F. learned complex hierarchical retrieval strategies in the context of numbers, a context he knew well. More generally, experts in particular content areas have been found to invent a whole host of strategies for dealing with their particular area of expertise (Chase, in press). They typically do not invent comparable strategies in other areas.

I am not aware of similar demonstrations of the effects of prior knowledge on the operation of automatization. However, it seems likely that children would more rapidly automatize procedures if they learned them on familiar content. Illustratively, it seems likely that an 8-year-old girl, making the transition from printing to writing, could more rapidly automatize handwriting skills if she was writing about well-known material than if she was writing about an unfamiliar area.

Future Issues

What becomes of children's early knowledge about a topic when they acquire more advanced, later knowledge about it? Flavell (1972) proposed a taxonomy in which he divided the relations between early and later knowledge into five categories: addition, substitution, inclusion, modification, and mediation. The taxonomy raises several issues for future consideration.

First consider the five relations themselves. In *addition* relations, the second unit of knowledge coexists with the first, with neither influencing the other. First learning $4 - 3$ and then learning $17 - 9$ provides one example. *Substitution* involves a later unit of knowledge replacing an earlier one. In liquid quantity conservation, children first "know" that the glass with the taller liquid column has more water. Later, the knowledge that pouring water never affects its quantity replaces this earlier knowledge. *Inclusion* involves an earlier acquired cognitive entity being subsumed within a later acquired one. Children might first learn a route from their home to their school. Later the route might be included within an overall cognitive map of the neighborhood. *Modification* involves an earlier acquisition being altered in some way by a later acquisition, but still existing in recognizable form. Children might differentiate their writing styles from a general all-purpose approach into specific styles for writing letters, essays, and book reports, all of which maintained some aspects of the original approach. Finally, *mediation* involves the first unit of knowledge serving as a bridge to the second but not becoming part of it. In number conservation, for example, counting the number of objects in each row serves as a bridge to the knowledge that the type of transformation determines the relation between initial and later quantities.

One issue raised by this taxonomy concerns an implication of the substitution category. Flavell's description of this category suggests that at times, earlier knowledge is totally replaced by later knowledge. Yet recall Bahrick, Bahrick, and Wittlinger's (1975) study in which an experimenter showed senior citizens photos of classmates from high school yearbooks. The results of that study suggested that knowledge in long-term memory is never erased; it continues to exist, though at times it is difficult to find.

To make the issue concrete, consider what happens to children's early beliefs that the taller liquid column must have more water. If the belief still exists somewhere in long-term memory, why are older children and adults so surprised to hear that they once thought in this way? Or is it possible that different types of knowledge have different status in long-term memory? Might factual knowledge reside there indefinitely, while problem-solving procedures are "written over" when clearly better procedures are learned?

Flavell's taxonomy also suggests an interesting point about when children will generalize their existing knowledge to new situations. Educators often have lamented that children do not draw all the implications from their earlier knowledge that they might. The educators have derived only small comfort from learning that adults are similar in often failing to generalize their knowledge to new situations (Kotovsky, 1983).

Flavell's modification and mediation categories suggest a type of generalization that may more realistically be expected of children. In neither category does the first type of knowledge automatically transform itself into the second type. Rather, the role of the existing knowledge is to facilitate the acquisition of new or broader knowledge when potential learning experiences arise. The point is that generalizations may be more apparent in savings of time and effort in future learning than in direct extension of knowledge to new domains without intervening experiences with those domains.

5. Knowledge of the adult cognitive system is useful for studying changes in children's thinking. It is much easier to study development when we know where the development is going.

Current Contributions of Knowledge of Adults' Thinking

Ideas that arise in trying to understand one subject often advance understanding of other subjects as well. This certainly has been the case with cognitive development. Cognitive psychologists interested in adults have contributed theories, methods, and empirical findings with important implications for children's thinking. Researchers in other cognitive disciplines, such as philosophy, artificial intelligence, and linguistics, also have contributed insights about the nature of thought in general, and thus have contributed to our appreciation of cognitive development.

One major benefit that has come from looking outward has been useful theoretical ideas. Atkinson and Shiffrin's (1968) division of the cognitive system into sensory, short-term, and long-term stores has proven convenient for organizing ideas about children's thinking, just as it has in the context of the adult system. Their hypotheses about limited capacities and speed of processing of these stores have stimulated both theoretical proposals and empirical experiments about the limits on children's processing capacities. Hoving, Spencer, Robb, and Schulte (1978) reported that 7-year-olds enter information into the sensory store more slowly than adults. Morrison, Holmes, and Haith (1974) demonstrated that the capacity of 5-year-olds' sensory stores is similar to that of adults. Keating and Bobbitt (1978) found that the speed of children's retrieval from the long-term store increases between ages 9 and 17 years. These findings have led to general acceptance of the view that the speed of processing may increase with development but the capacity of memory does not.

Newell and Simon's (1972) theory also has exercised a pervasive influence. Their general view of cognition as an effort to deploy limited mental resources to cope with complex task environments is one major contribution. This is evident in the entire discussion of the third theme of this chapter. Their emphasis on computer simulations as a good way to characterize cognitive activity has also been influential. J. S. Brown and Van Lehn's (1982) simulation of Buggy subtraction rules, Klahr and Wallace's (1976) simulation of the development of conservation and class-inclusion concepts, Greeno, Riley, and Gelman's (1984) simulation of children's understanding of counting principles, and McClelland and Rumelhart's (1981) simulation of word identification in reading testify to this influence. Research on differences between experts and novices, such as Chi's (1978) research on chess, Chi and Koeske's (1983) research on knowledge of dinosaurs, and Ericsson, Chase, and Faloon's (1980) research on S. F., also shows a strong influence of Newell and Simon's theory.

Philosophers, computer scientists, and linguists have contributed other insights relevant to children's thinking. One of the most important of these is the philosopher Wittgenstein's view of the nature of concepts. Wittgenstein contended that most concepts lack defining features. His argument inspired Rosch and Mervis's (1975) demonstration that both preschoolers' and adults' representations of concepts often are based on correlations among attributes, prototypic instances, and basic-level categories, rather than on defining features. The work was extremely influential, in part because it undermined all strong forms of the representational-development hypothesis. If neither children nor adults represent most concepts in terms of defining features, it is impossible to maintain that children's representations differ from adults' in lacking such features.

Work on artificial intelligence has been influential in contributing languages for characterizing cognition. Semantic networks have been used to characterize how children count, add, and compare numerical magnitudes (Siegler & Robinson, 1982), how they differentiate between similar words such as *buy* and *sell*, (Gentner, 1975), and how they identify words in reading (McClelland & Rumelhart, 1981). Scripts have been used to characterize children's knowledge about the meals they eat in different settings (Nelson, 1978) and their knowledge of the typical course of stories that they hear (Mandler & Johnson, 1977; Stein & Glenn, 1979). Production systems have been used to characterize the development of understanding of conservation (Klahr & Wallace, 1973), counting (Greeno, Riley, & Gelman, 1984), and balance scales (Klahr & Siegler, 1978).

As might be expected, linguistics has exercised its most direct effects on language development research. Research motivated by a desire to elaborate on Chomsky's proposal that children possess an innate language-acquisition device was discussed in the above section on domain-specific learning mechanisms. Other research has been done to counter Chomsky's contention by showing that no mechanism specifically designed for language learning needs to be postulated. Snow and Hoefnagel–Hohle's (1978) study of immigrants to Holland demonstrated that adult immigrants actually learn new grammars faster than children. Premack's (1976) research on chimpanzees showed that the capacity to learn at least some parts of grammar and meaning is not limited to human beings. MacWhinney's (1978; 1982) models of language acquisition indicated that computer programs, equipped only with general learning mechanisms, also can acquire important aspects of phonology and syntax. Although the issue is far from settled, there is little question that Chomsky's proposal has advanced understanding of language acquisition. It has motivated consideration of exactly what a language-acquisition device might look like, has motivated consideration of how general learning mechanisms might contribute to language learning, and has expanded the range of facts on which new theories of language development can be based.

Future Issues

There is little question that knowledge of the adult system is useful for studying development. Knowledge of children's thinking has also proven useful for understanding of adults; this is evident in recent textbooks on adults' thinking (e.g., Anderson, 1983). It is interesting to think about where knowledge of development might make especially significant further contributions to understanding of adults' thinking.

One natural place for developmentalists to contribute is in the study of change processes. Researchers interested in adult cognitive psychology, linguistics, artificial intelligence, and philosophy can focus on people's existing competence, how they do what they do. Understanding how changes occur is useful in these disciplines, but is not their inherent focus. In contrast, development fundamentally concerns change; to not understand change is to not understand development. This fundamental concern may motivate developmentalists to devise increasingly sophisticated analyses of how changes occur, which will benefit people in other disciplines as well.

A second potential contribution of cognitive-developmental research would be to explain findings with adults that are baffling when developmental data are not taken into account. Consider one, admittedly speculative, analysis of this type. The analysis rests on two repeated findings. One finding is that even after adults have learned to solve certain types of problems perfectly, they still take longest to solve the same items on which children most often err. The second finding is that in a number of these cases, the pattern of data follows quite naturally from the strategies that children are known to use, but is difficult to understand from the perspective of the adults' strategies. Could it be that the problems on which children make many errors remain difficult into adulthood precisely because of the early errors?

Several of the tasks for which children's strategies have been described can be used to illustrate the parallels between children's patterns of errors and adults' patterns of solution times. Groen and Parkman (1972) noted that adults take longer to solve addition problems with higher minimum addends; Ilg and Ames (1951) noted that 6-year-olds most frequently err on the same problems. Moyer and Landauer (1967) observed that adults take longer to solve numerical magnitude comparison with relatively large numbers. Siegler and Robinson (1982) observed the same pattern in 4- and 5-year-olds' error patterns. Jorm and Share (1983) described a similar close relation between which words require long lexical access time in adults and which words children often misread.

The reasons for the children's pattern of errors on these tasks are often quite straightforward. If 6-year-olds are asked how they solved an addition problem such as 3 + 4, they often say they counted up from the larger number. Use of this min strategy explains why they err more often on problems with large minimum numbers. The larger the minimum number, the more internal counting is required. For example, 3 + 4 should be and is more difficult than 2 + 4.

On the other hand, adults almost never say that they solved simple addition problems by counting. Why they take longer to solve 3 + 4 than 2 + 4 is not nearly as easy to understand.

One possible explanation is that stating incorrect answers leads to those answers becoming associated with the problem on which they are stated and thereafter interfering with efforts to retrieve the correct answer. Within this account, the more often children state incorrect answers to a problem, the more difficult it becomes to retrieve the correct answer to that problem even when the min strategy is no longer used. Returning to the addition example, the frequent errors children make in executing the min strategy on some problems would be the cause of adults' relatively long solution times on those same problems. They would interfere with the adults' efforts to retrieve the correct sum. Thus, the parallels between the two patterns would be no accident.

This explanation of the resemblance between children's error patterns and adults' solution-time patterns is only one of several possible accounts. Another explanation of the addition results, for example, is that adults sometimes use the min procedure, just as children do, but do not do so as often (Groen & Parkman, 1972). The fact of the parallels seems incontrovertible, however, as does the allure of finding an explanation for them. More generally, a variety of surprising patterns within adult cognition may ultimately be found to have their explanations in the developmental process. By explaining how these parallels came to be, those interested in children's thinking can also make large contributions to understanding of adults' thinking.

6. Differences between age groups tend to be ones of degree rather than kind. Young children are more cognitively competent than they often are given credit for, and older children and adults are not quite so cognitively competent as we often think.

Current Knowledge About Differences Between Age Groups

What does not develop? As mentioned above, developmentalists often ask "What develops?" Increasingly, they also are identifying capabilities that *do not* develop, because the capabilities are so advanced from early in life. Infants less than a year old have many more capabilities than was suspected until recently.

These capabilities were discussed in chapters on many different aspects of children's thinking. Probably the greatest number emerged in the chapter on perceptual development. Among these were looking rules that help infants to locate informative parts of the environment (Haith, 1979), ability to discriminate among the voices of different speakers (DeCasper & Fifer, 1980), use of vision to guide reaching (von Hofsten, 1982), and ability to perceive coordinated biological motion (Fox & McDaniel, 1982). The memory-development chapter included demonstrations that infants can form associations, generalize, and perhaps show insight (Rovee & Fagan, 1976). The language-development chapter documented infants' ability to discriminate among sounds much as adults do (Eimas, Siqueland, Juscyk, & Vigorito, 1971) and to produce all the sounds in the world's languages (Kaplan & Kaplan, 1971). The conceptual-development chapter added the abilities to discriminate between small sets having different numbers of objects (Strauss & Curtis, 1984) and to note correlations among features (Younger & Cohen, 1983). Clearly, some important cognitive capabilities are present at very early ages.

Other capabilities are not present in infancy, but begin developing far earlier than was previously suspected. Consider just Piagetian tasks and concepts that were once thought impossible for children below age 7. Four- and

5-year-olds can solve certain conservation problems (Gelman, 1972), class inclusion problems (Markman & Siebert, 1976), and transitive inference problems (Trabasso, Riley, & Wilson, 1975). When 4-year-olds talk to 2-year-olds, they take into account differences between their knowledge and that of their listeners; thus they are not totally egocentric (Shatz & Gelman, 1973). Preschoolers know that causes should precede effects, that contiguity is a useful clue in attributing causation, and that mechanistic processes connect causes with their effects (Sedlak & Kurtz, 1981). They also know a great deal about numbers: They can solve conservation of number problems, add and subtract small numbers, identify the larger of two numbers, and count in a way that reflects understanding of the structure of the counting string (Siegler & Robinson, 1982).

Limitations of adults' reasoning.   At the other end of the age spectrum, adults' reasoning may not be quite so rational as was once thought. Even high school and college students rarely solve Piagetian formal operations problems without training. These difficulties are not limited to Piaget's tasks or to scientific reasoning problems. Shaklee (1979) reviewed a whole host of irrational aspects of adults' thinking. Adults will bet more on a cut of a deck of cards when playing against a nervous opponent than when playing against a relaxed one. They become more confident of their ability to play a game of pure chance when they have had time to practice it. When asked to judge which of two sentences of random events are more likely, they ignore the randomness if one sentence sounds more representative (they say that a sequence of births in a family of "girl, girl, girl, boy, boy, boy" is less likely than one of "girl, boy, boy, girl, boy, girl"). In short, while infants act like budding scientists in some contexts, educated adults ignore the most basic logical considerations in others.

Future Issues

Discoveries of young children's previously unsuspected capacities and of adults' previously unsuspected irrationalities have doomed many explanations of development. It is no longer tenable to believe that preschoolers' inherent egocentrism makes it impossible for them to take other people's perspectives. Nor is it tenable to believe that their mediation deficiencies make it impossible for them to benefit from using memory strategies, or that their example-based representations make it impossible for them to form concepts with defining features. These falling dominos, in turn, threaten another long-held belief about children's thinking: that it is possible to state a single age at which children acquire a particular cognitive capability. It seems increasingly probable that for most concepts and reasoning skills, there is no single age at which the acquisition is made.

It was once possible to believe that the age at which most children mastered a particular task was the age at which they understood the concept associated with that task. For example, children were said to understand number conservation when they could solve Piaget's number-conservation problem. As investigators devised additional tasks corresponding to the same concept, however, it became clear that the age at which children could solve the different tasks varied dramatically. For example, they could solve some number-conservation problems by age 3, but could not solve others until age 6. At what age, then, did they understand number conservation?

One plausible approach to answering this question was to identify conceptual understanding with the earliest form of understanding. Children who did not yet understand any task corresponding to a concept would be said not to understand the concept. Children who could pass one or more tasks that demanded understanding of the concept would be said to understand it. Braine (1959) argued for this view when he wrote, "If one seeks to state an age at which a particular type of response develops, the only age that is not completely arbitrary is the earliest age at which this type of response can be elicited. . . ." (p. 16).

Braine's statement is entirely reasonable, as far as it goes. When one considers the long time period separating initial and mature understanding of concepts, however, a paradox becomes evident. Adopting the initial-competence criterion puts us in the position of saying that many concepts develop at young ages, yet also of saying that children fail many reasonable indices of understanding for years thereafter. Stated another way, much—perhaps most—conceptual growth would be seen as occurring after the concept "develops."

Brown (1976) argued for an alternative criterion for conceptual understanding: that of stable usage. Children would not be viewed as understanding a concept until they could use it in most or all situations in which the concept applies. The problem here is evident in Braine's comment. What exactly does a child understand when he or she can use a concept in some situations but not in others? It does seem arbitrary to identify understanding with anything other than the earliest form of understanding. However, it seems misleading to identify it with the earliest form of understanding.

One alternative to stating an age at which children acquire a cognitive capability is to produce more encompassing models of whatever knowledge they have at different ages that is relevant to that capability. These models would not only specify how children of a particular age perform on various tasks associated with a concept. They also would indicate the conditions under which children applied various types of knowledge that they had. Number conservation again can be used to illustrate. As documented by Gelman (1972), Siegler (1981), and Winer (1974), from age 3 years, children sometimes try to solve number-conservation problems by counting the objects in each row and sometimes by comparing the lengths of the rows. First they count the objects in each row only when there are small numbers of objects in the rows and something has been added to or subtracted from one of them. Then they count any time there are small numbers of objects in the rows. Slightly later, they count either if there are small numbers of objects or if there are large numbers of objects and something has been added or subtracted. Yet later, they count in all situations. Finally, they switch from counting to solving the problems on the basis of the type of transformation performed.

The example illustrates the excess involved in saying that preschoolers do not understand number conservation. It also indicates the misleadingness of saying that they understand number conservation as soon as they can consistently succeed on any type of number-conservation problem. Both the range of problems they can handle and the thought processes by which they handle them change greatly from age 3 to age 6. Given the complexity of cognitive development, it often will prove impossible to provide a meaningful statement about *the* age at which children acquire a cognitive capability. Models that specify both how children think and the conditions under which they think in various ways seem needed to deal with this complexity.

7. Children's thinking develops within a social context. Parents, peers, teachers, and the overall society influence what children think about, as well as how and why they come to think in particular ways.

People are profoundly social animals. This social nature is what makes much of cognitive development possible. A child growing up without access to other people or to the skills developed by previous generations could not hope to learn as much about the world as children ordinarily do.

The relation between cognitive development and the social world can be approached in two ways. One way, probably the more common, is to view the social world as one of the many things children come to understand as they develop. Children think about their friends, parents, and teachers, about what is fair, what is moral, and so on. Their understanding of these people and social issues shows considerable development with age and experience. Thus, the understandings could reasonably be viewed as part of cognitive development, since children think about the topics and the sophistication of their thoughts about them develops. My own view, though, is that these topics fall more properly under the heading of social development. To the extent that they differ from other forms of cognition, the differences arise precisely because the thoughts are about people and their social inventions. In any case, plentiful information about research in these areas is already available. High-quality reviews of this literature have been provided by Shantz (1983), Rest (1983), and Damon (1978).

An alternative approach is to emphasize the effects that parents, teachers, peers, and the general culture exercise on children's thinking. The influence is evident in at least three ways. First, they influence *what* children think about. In Japan, most children learn to operate abacuses; in the United States, very few do. Second, they influence *how* children acquire information. Parents in Western societies encourage their children to learn by asking questions; parents in many parts of Africa do not. Third, they influence *why* children learn. Peers, parents, teachers, and societal attitudes are important motivators of children's thinking.

Understanding how the social environment exercises these influences represents a major future challenge for people interested in cognitive development. Information about the influence of the social world has only begun to be integrated with the relatively detailed analyses of children's thinking that have been discussed in other places in this book. If we are to understand fully the process of cognitive growth, this situation must change. Children's thinking does not develop in a vacuum. Understanding how it develops demands an understanding of the context within which it develops.

Current Knowledge of Social Influences on Children's Thinking

Although social influences have not been emphasized in previous chapters, they have been discussed in a few places. Palincsar and Brown (in press) described an instructional program through which teachers greatly improved the comprehension skills of seventh graders. The program involved the teachers initially taking the lead in illustrating how to summarize passages and how to anticipate likely questions about the material. Gradually, the teachers faded into the background as the children assumed increasing responsibility for these activities. Thus, the successful teachers, in a sense, did themselves out of a job.

The contribution of parents was evident in Kaye and Charney's (1980) description of parental strategies for eliciting conversation from young children. For example, in answering 2-year-olds' questions, parents often built new questions into their replies. These questions were more effective than simple statements for motivating the children to continue talking. Durkin's (1966) analysis of how home background contributed to children learning to read before entering school and Rogoff, Ellis, and Gardner's (1984) description of how parents teach children to deploy cognitive resources effectively are other examples of parental contributions.

Shatz and Gelman (1973) demonstrated the influence of peers. They found that 4-year-olds adjusted their language to 2-year-olds' cognitive capacities so that the 2-year-olds could grasp what they were saying.

Finally, the influence of the society as a whole was evident in the existence of Chapter 9, the chapter on the development of academic skills. Children's acquisition of reading and writing skills can only be studied in those cultures that have developed these competencies.

Future Issues

Social influences on what children think about.   The most obvious impact of the social environment on children's thinking is on what they think about. It influences whether they acquire certain cognitive skills at all, the degree of proficiency they attain with other skills that everyone masters to some degree, and the contexts within which they can use various skills. A few recent studies of development in other cultures illustrate how these connections are beginning to be made.

Children's acquisition of abacus skills exemplifies how the larger society influences whether children acquire some cognitive skills at all. Abacuses are commonly used in the Orient to solve arithmetic problems, though they rarely are used in other areas of the world. Although the advent of calculators and computers might seem to make these devices obsolete, their popularity among children as well as adults remains great. In several Asian countries, abacus training is a part of every schoolchild's curriculum. Many children take additional lessons after school to gain extra proficiency on the abacus. Winners of national abacus competitions become quite famous and are greatly respected.

Figure 10–2 illustrates the type of abacus most commonly used. Its columns represent a base 10 notation, like that used in standard computation. The column at one end (it can be either end) is the 1's column, the next column inward is the 10's column, the next column inward is the 100's column, and so on. Each column is divided into the single bead above the divider and the four beads below. The bead above the divider represents a value of five; each of the four beads below it represents a value of one.

Here is how the abacus can be used to represent and add numbers. When the value of a column is zero, the 5's bead is at the top of the abacus and the four 1's beads are at the bottom. To represent numbers greater than zero, the operator moves beads toward the divider in the middle. Thus, to represent 1, a girl would move a 1's bead up toward the divider. To represent 8, she would move the 5's bead down toward the divider and would move three 1's beads up toward it. To add 4 + 3, she would first push four 1's beads from below the divider up toward the middle with an upward finger motion (to represent the 4). When her finger reached the top of the

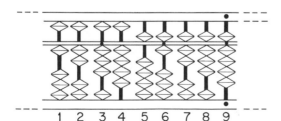

FIGURE 10-2   The number 123,456,789 as represented on an abacus. The number 1 is represented on the leftmost bar and the number 9 on the rightmost bar (from Stigler, 1984).

column, she would make a downward motion, pushing the 5's bead down toward the middle and returning two of the 1's beads that had been pushed up near the divider to their original position. This would leave the 5's bead and two 1's beads in the middle, indicating the answer, 7.

Stigler (1984) studied the addition performance of 11-year-old Taiwanese children who had become abacus experts. He presented them with problems ranging from quite simple (adding two numbers, each having two digits) to quite demanding (adding five numbers, each having five digits). The children needed to solve the problems on one occasion in their heads and on another occasion on their abacuses.

The 11-year-olds' addition on the abacus was quick and accurate; this does not seem especially surprising, given that they were practicing abacus arithmetic in school every day and after school at least three days a week. Their mental arithmetic performance was surprising, though. They correctly solved more than 90% of problems, even quite difficult ones such as adding four numbers each having four digits. Further, they actually added more rapidly in their heads than on the abacus.

What might the children's abacus expertise have to do with their exceptionally skillful mental arithmetic? Following an hypothesis advanced by Hatano, Miyake, and Binks (1977), Stigler argued persuasively that the children formed a mental image of the abacus and imagined carrying out the same finger movements on it that they would on a real abacus. Two characteristics of the 11-year-olds' error patterns supported this interpretation. A disproportionate number of the children's errors were off by exactly five in a column. This type of error is easy to make on the abacus, because only the single 5's bead discriminates between 2 and 7, 3 and 8, and so on. Second, the Taiwanese children were three times more likely than American undergraduate and graduate students to err by leaving out a column altogether. If an answer to a problem was 43,296, a common type of error for the Taiwanese was 4396. This type of error would occur if the Taiwanese children read their answers from a mental image of an abacus, in which adjacent columns had blurred together.

Hatano and Osawa (1983) studied Japanese abacus experts and demonstrated another benefit of expertise of this type. Abacus experts possess digit spans far beyond those of nonexperts. Again, they seem to represent the digits in terms of a mental image of an abacus. The data supporting this view involves some of the strongest evidence for the existence of mental imagery yet collected. Asking the abacus experts simultaneously to remember digits and perform another visual imagery task lowered their digit span markedly. The same visual imagery task did not interfere with the digit span of other people, who followed the typical strategy of auditorially rehearsing the digits. Conversely, asking the abacus experts to simultaneously remember digits and perform a task that taxed auditory memory did not lower the abacus experts' digit span. It did reduce the digit span of the other people, who used auditory rehearsal rather than visual imagery to maintain the digits in memory.

Cultures not only influence what their members think about, but also to what degree they develop certain skills. The abacus studies demonstrate this in a fairly specific domain: numbers. Abacus experts not only know about abacuses but also are unusually proficient at remembering numbers and at performing mental calculations, skills that people in other cultures possess, but to lesser degrees. Studies of aborigines who live in the western desert of Australia make the point with regard to a broader skill, spatial ability. These aborigines have followed a seminomadic hunting and gathering life-style for the past 30,000 years (Kearins, 1981). On most tests of cognitive functioning, aboriginal children do far less well than children of the same ages in Europe and North America. For example, they do not demonstrate understanding of the concrete operational concepts studied by Piaget until ages 9 to 11 years. A considerable proportion fail to solve the problems even then (Dasen, 1973).

Kearins (1981) suggested that a different picture might emerge if the focus was on skills of everyday importance in the lives of the aborigines. Much of aboriginal life is a series of treks between widely spaced wells and creeks. Whether a particular well or creek has water depends on capricious rainfall patterns. Few obvious landmarks exist in the stony desert to indicate where the wells and creeks are, and the shifting rainfall patterns create continuous needs to approach water holes from new directions.

Kearins contrasted the spatial location skills of aboriginal children raised in the desert with those of white Australian children raised in a city. She presented twenty objects arranged in a five-by-four rectangle. After 30 seconds, the experimenter picked up all the objects and asked children to rearrange them as they had been before. In some arrays, the objects were chosen for being familiar to the white Australian children (erasers, scissors, etc.). In others, the objects were chosen for being familiar to the aborigines (feathers, rocks, etc.).

The aboriginal children outperformed the white Australian children on all the spatial location tasks. In addition, the familiarity of the objects exerted different influences on the two groups. The city-dwelling white Australian children recalled the location of familiar objects considerably better than unfamiliar ones. The aboriginal children did as well locating unfamiliar objects as familiar ones. Thus, it appears that the nature of aboriginal life leads children to develop spatial skills to a greater extent than children in other cultures. The skills become sufficiently abstract that they do not depend on the particular objects the children need to locate.

A third sense in which the social world influences what children think about involves the contexts in which their cognitive skills manifest themselves. Lave's (1977) study of Liberian tailors and their apprentices illustrates this point. The tailors and their apprentices ranged from 10 to 40 years old, had gone to school for between 0 and 10 years, and had between a few months and 25 years of tailoring experience. Lave presented them with arithmetic tasks, some of which involved questions and numbers like those arising in tailoring work, others of which involved questions and numbers like those appearing in standard elementary school textbooks.

Amount of tailoring experience proved to be the major determinant of performance on those problems where the particular questions and numbers were like those that arise in tailoring. Number of years in school was the largest determinant of performance where the questions and numbers were like those in textbooks. The point seems clear. Much of people's thinking is quite specific to the situation in which they learn. Even with skills that could easily be generalized, the context of learning often influences where the thinking is used effectively.

Social influences on how children think.   In considering social influences on how children think, it is important to distinguish between different levels of analysis. At a fine-grained level of analysis, there seems little doubt that the processes that lead to cognitive development are the same in all social environments. Regardless of the particular people, technologies, and institutions a boy encounters, he will develop by automatizing his processing, by encoding more and more of the critical features, by generalizing, and by forming improved strategies. Surber (1980) and Fiske and Taylor (1984) have documented numerous similarities in the processes used to reason in social and nonsocial situations.

At a more general level of analysis, though, social factors do alter the process of cognitive growth. Children's questions illustrate this point. Asking questions is one of the most powerful and generally applicable tools for learning that children possess. The effectiveness with which children encode features of situations, generalize to new situations, and use other basic processes certainly influences whether they ask questions and which questions they ask. However, the social environment also contributes. Comparisons among different cultures once again are illuminating. Greenfield and Lave (1982) noted that in Ghanian, Kenyan, and Liberian tribes, children are discouraged from asking questions and only rarely do so. In the West, asking questions is not only tolerated but often encouraged. Thus, in the Western societies, asking questions would influence how development occurs to a greater extent than in the African societies.

Asking questions is not the only general level acquisition process whose use is influenced by the social environment. Recall from Chapter 2 that formal operations reasoning is correlated with taking science courses and that it is absent altogether from some societies. Presumably, the abilities to design experiments that separate the influence of different variables and to interpret such experiments correctly are learned in science classes through direct instruction and observation. Once they are acquired, they can be applied to acquiring new knowledge in many additional situations. Formal deductive logic, statistics, and reading are other general-level skills whose acquisition depend critically on the social environment and that once acquired, themselves become powerful aids for acquiring more knowledge.

These examples might convey an impression that the influence of the social environment is a one-way process, with the world imparting learning skills to children. Actually, the process is reciprocal, with children's cognitive capabilities influencing the input they receive, as well as the input influencing their thinking. This reciprocity can be seen in the earliest interactions of babies and their parents. Babies coo and gurgle considerably more often in the presence of their parents than when they are alone. Parents, in turn, speak to the babies in motherese, which seems to engage their attention more than other forms of speech (Aslin, Pisoni, & Jusczyk, 1983). Parents also adapt their words for describing objects to the infants' existing understandings. For example, mothers of 13-month-olds describe a variety of objects to their babies as "balls": round candles, round banks, oranges, and so on (Mervis & Mervis, 1982). This is not due to the time spent around the infants having rotted the mothers' minds; when talking to adults, they use the usual terms to describe the objects. Rather, the mothers adapt to the infants' limited vocabularies by using words that the infants already know and that have important features in common with the new objects.

In this discussion, the influence of the social environment on what children think about has been considered separately from its influence on how they think. The distinction is useful for analyzing the separate influences, but it also is important to remember that the two are complexly entwined. The point can be illustrated with regard to the Kearins (1981) study of aboriginal children's spatial skills. Kearins made a number of observations indicating how these spatial skills manifested themselves. The two groups of children behaved quite differently while they viewed the matrix of objects that they later would need to reproduce. The aboriginal children studied in silence. When they subsequently were asked how they remembered where the objects had been, they often said that they remembered the "look of it." In contrast, the city-dwelling children could be heard whispering and saying aloud the names of the objects while they studied them. They explained their performance by such statements as "I described them to myself."

Why might the city children have used the more verbal strategy? The fact that they attended school and the aboriginal children did not is one likely explanation. Similar differences have emerged among schooled and unschooled populations in other parts of the world and on other tasks. For example, Sharp, Cole, and Lave (1979) contrasted the performance on conceptual and memory development tasks of Mexican Indians who had and had not attended school. The advantage of the schooled group was greatest on the tasks where verbal strategies were the most useful. The schooled children tended to use the verbal strategies; the unschooled children tended not to.

Azuma (1984) noted that the way in which school influences children depends on the relation between the children's personalities and the qualities the school values. He presented Japanese and American preschoolers with two types of problems. One was a standard problem-solving task that required a certain amount of insight. The other was a more unusual task: Children were told to draw a circle as slowly as they possibly could, while still moving their pencil continually.

To an American like myself, the findings with the American preschoolers do not seem surprising. Their performance on the standard problem-solving task predicted their later school achievement quite well. Their ability to draw the circle slowly was not highly correlated with their subsequent success in school. The findings with the Japanese preschoolers seem more surprising, though. How slowly they could draw the circle was a good predictor of later school success. How well they could solve the problem, on the other hand, was not nearly as good a predictor.

How can this result be explained? Azuma suggested that the different priorities of schools in the two countries might account for the differences. American teachers emphasize problem solving, insight, and originality as especially valuable traits. Children who possess these traits are best equipped to do well in school. Japanese teachers emphasize perseverance, effort, and obedience. Drawing the circle very slowly would call for all of these qualities. Thus, the influence of the social environment on children's thinking may profitably be thought of as an interaction between children's social and intellectual qualities and the values of the societies in which they grow up.

Social influences on children's motivations for thinking. Many differences in what children think about and in how they think about various topics are due to motivational factors. Some of these motivational influences are quite obvious. A boy who is praised for his skill in writing stories is more likely to develop his talent further than one whose writing is ignored or criticized. Other motivational influences are more subtle though. Two of these more subtle influences are prior interest in a topic and reactions to negative experiences.

Just as prior knowledge contributes to cognitive growth, so does prior interest. Renninger and Wozniak (1985) demonstrated some of the ways that interest affects preschoolers' attention and memory. They first observed 3-year-olds at a nursery school to see which objects they played with most often. Each child was observed for two hours. The children varied considerably in their favorite objects: One child preferred a toy bear, another a train, another a ball, and so on.

Later in the study, the experimenter presented the children cards with pictures of two objects and a colored dot in the middle. The task was for the child to indicate what color the dot was. What the experimenter was really interested in, though, was which object the child attended to after identifying the color. It was found that the 3-year-olds consistently looked at the object they most often played with, rather than the alternative.

Next, the children were shown a set of pictures which they were told depicted presents a child received at his birthday party. Then the experimenter presented these pictures and others, and asked the 3-year-olds to separate the pictures of birthday presents from the other pictures. The children more often remembered whether or not their favorite object had been a birthday present than whether the other objects had. They also were considerably more likely to indicate the status of their favorite object first, before any other object, than would have been expected by chance.

The study suggests a means by which even small initial differences in interest might lead to large later differences in both interest and knowledge. Children attend more to objects that attract their interest and remember more about them. Attending and remembering more lead to greater knowledge about these objects, which is likely to be intrinsically rewarding. The greater knowledge also may attract praise, if the particular type of knowledge is valued. The knowledge also will make future learning about the subject easier. Thus, early-developing interests, formed for quite idiosyncratic reasons, may snowball into significant factors in children's lives.

Another quite subtle influence on children's motivation for thinking is their reaction when things go wrong. Reactions to seemingly discouraging circumstances can be quite different than might be anticipated. Albert and Runco (1985), in studying the development of exceptionally intelligent boys (IQs above 160), noted that parental disagreement, discord, and even divorce had some surprising positive consequences. In particular, such familial strife was associated with especially high creativity among these boys.

Most people's intuition is that pleasant, concordant homes provide the most secure bases from which to explore the world and to be creative. Another line of reasoning also is possible, though. Homes that support a gifted child's creativity are not necessarily ones where parents get along with each other. One or both parents may become *more* invested in a child's success as other aspects of family relationships founder. Alternatively, strife-torn homes may lead some children to withdraw from social acitivies and to substitute a passion for creative breakthroughs in some other area. As in many aspects of the issue of what motivates cognition, not enough is known to confidently delineate how lack of parental harmony leads gifted boys to unusually high creativity. The topic certainly would seem to merit further consideration, though.

One of the few areas in which motivational influences on cognition are relatively well understood involves children's reactions to failure. For this, we have to thank a series of elegant experiments by Dweck and her colleagues. The research is not only interesting theoretically, it also provides an intriguing explanation of a socially important phenomenon: "math phobia" among women.

Dweck's research grew out of investigations of learned helplessness. People and other animals, when given a series of unsolvable problems, tend to react by giving up. Even after the series of unsolvable problems ends, they often are unable to solve problems that they otherwise would easily figure out. They also tend to regress to less-sophisticated hypotheses than they previously formed, and generally to do less than their best thinking.

Dweck and Goetz (1978) noted that some children defy this pattern. They react to failure by maintaining their efforts or by trying even harder than before. Their problem solving and hypothesis formation remain at least as successful as previously.

What differentiates these children from others? It is not their intelligence; their IQs are similar to those of their peers. Rather, they differ most dramatically in their attributions of their failure. When they fail, they believe the reason was that they did not try hard enough. Presumably, greater effort would bring success. Children who become helpless in the face of failure, on the other hand, tend to attribute their failures to a lack of ability. With this attribution, they see greater effort as being of limited value.

Girls and boys differ in their most typical reactions to failure. Girls tend to blame their own ability. Boys tend to blame other people, such as unfair teachers, and also chance factors, such as bad luck.

Dweck and Licht (1980) suggested that types of feedback that girls and boys receive in classrooms may contribute to these different reactions. Girls and boys receive the same amount of negative comments, but the nature of the comments differs. Teachers' criticisms of girls' work focuses consistently on the intellectual quality of the work. Their criticisms of boys' work sometimes focuses on intellectual quality and sometimes on neatness, conduct, or effort.

Dweck and Licht suggested that these differing comments might lead girls to blame their limited abilities and boys to blame other factors for failures. Boys can attribute teachers' negative reactions to any number of considerations, since the teachers fault a variety of aspects of their work. Girls, on the other hand, cannot easily blame sloppiness, bad conduct, or lack of effort, since teachers do not criticize them on these qualities. Adding to the imbalance, both girls and boys view teachers as liking girls better. This adds another attribution that boys can make but girls cannot.

To test this interpretation, Dweck and Licht presented 10-year-olds negative feedback that either resembled the type of feedback girls typically get or the type that boys do. In the "girl" feedback, only the correctness of the work was faulted. In the "boy" feedback, neatness as well as correctness was. Both boys and girls reacted as expected. Those who received the "girl" feedback blamed their own lack of ability for their failure on the task. Those who received the "boy" feedback blamed insufficient effort or the unfairness of the experimenter.

These differing attributions of failure may especially influence reactions to mathematics. In reading, social studies, and most other subjects, children make relatively steady progress toward mastery. From the beginning, children understand some of the information being presented. Mathematics is different. Often, people's first reaction to a new mathematical concept is total bewilderment. Even beyond this point, the precision of mathematics makes it clear just how many wrong answers the learner is making. This quality may lead those children who become helpless in the face of failure to give up on mathematics.

Licht and Dweck (1984) tested this interpretation, that it was the tendency to become helpless following failure experiences that led girls to do badly following initial failures. They presented 10-year-old girls and boys with a questionnaire concerning their likely reactions to hypothetical failures. On the basis of this questionnaire, they divided children into helpless and mastery-oriented groups. They then presented boys and girls within each group with one of two conditions. They first gave some children a confusing task, designed to elicit reactions like those that accompany presentation of a new mathematics concept. Then they presented children in both groups with a set of eminently solvable problems.

As illustrated in Figure 10–3, mastery-oriented children's problem solving was not adversely affected by prior exposure to the confusing task. However, children who reacted helplessly to failure solved problems much less effectively following exposure to the confusing task. The findings were similar for girls and boys who were initially classified as helpless and for girls

FIGURE 10-3   Percentage of helpless and mastery-oriented children in different learning conditions who solved the test problem. Encountering the confusing problem adversely affected the helpless children's later performance, but not the performance of the mastery-oriented children (data from Licht and Dweck, 1984).

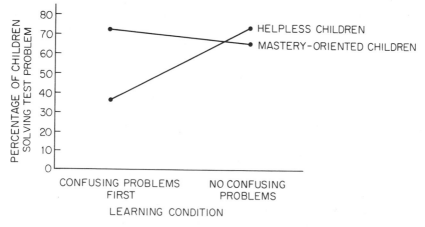

and boys classified as mastery-oriented. The primary difference between the sexes was in the percentage of children initially classified in each way.

The conclusion that "math phobia" among women is attributable to motivational factors was buttressed by a recent comparison between gifted Oriental and Caucasian children. Campbell, Connolly, Bologh, and Primavera (1984) reported that Asians as a group are unusually strong in mathematics and science achievement. For example, although the population of New York is less than 2% Oriental, the group accounts for almost 20% of the region's Westinghouse Science Contest winners. Of special interest in the present context, the percentage of women winners differed for the ethnic groups. Among Caucasians, 27% of the winners were female; among Orientals, 46% were.

Why are Oriental girls more likely than their Caucasian counterparts to achieve at a superior level in mathematics and science? Lee, Stigler, and Stevenson (1984) suggested that differences in parents' beliefs about the roles of ability and effort might be fundamental. Caucasian parents emphasize ability as a primary reason for success and failure on intellectual tasks. Oriental parents emphasize effort as the critical factor. Uememoto (1984) characterized the difference in this way: "We [Japanese] are more sentimental about our abilities, always wanting to have hope that they can be improved with effort" (p. 10). The observation lends us hope that with increasing understanding of motivational influences on children's thinking, the current high incidence of "math phobia" among women can become a thing of the past.

8. We have learned quite a bit about cognitive development, but there is far more left to learn.

Some statements need no explanation.

SUMMARY

The development of perception, language, memory, problem solving, and conceptualization have a great deal in common. Important unities exist in the issues, empirical findings, and mechanisms that produce changes in all aspects of children's thinking.

The largest issues in the study of children's thinking are "What develops?" and "How does development occur?" Four commonly advanced hypotheses about what develops are basic capacities, strategies, metacognition, and content knowledge. Each of these types of changes seemed to be connected with cognitive improvements in many areas and at many ages.

The greatest need for future research on these issues is more advanced theories of cognitive development. Ideally, new theories would preserve the strengths of Piaget's approach—great breadth, applicability to all periods of childhood, interesting empirical observations—while explaining change processes in greater detail and not making predictions inconsistent with known data.

Four change processes that seem to be especially large contributors to cognitive development are automatization, improved encoding, generalization, and construction of new strategies. Automatization involves increasingly efficient execution of procedures that allows cognitive resources to be devoted to other purposes. Improved encoding involves identification of features that are useful for internally representing objects or events. Generalization involves detecting regular patterns and extrapolating them to new instances. Strategy construction involves using the products of the other processes to adapt to task demands. Among the greatest future challenges in the study of these change mechanisms is more detailed analysis of exactly how the cognitive system produces change.

Much of cognitive development is a process of deploying limited processing resources increasingly effectively to meet task demands. Children adapt to the demands of task environments in at least three senses. They represent the task environments increasingly completely; their processing becomes increasingly flexible; and they apply their most sophisticated processing to a widening range of situations. Research is just beginning on the issue of why children adapt to some task environments so much faster than others. Among the most promising ideas that have been proposed are domain-specific learning mechanisms and multiple intelligences.

Existing knowledge exerts a pervasive influence on the acquisition of new knowledge. Having a large amount of existing knowledge about a topic increases the amount of new knowledge that is acquired from particular experiences. It also influences what children learn by leading them to focus on the material most likely to prove important. Relations between earlier and later knowledge can be grouped into five categories: addition, substitution, inclusion, modification, and mediation. The relations raise such issues as whether newer knowledge can ever simply replace older knowledge, and whether generalization of existing knowledge is more likely to be seen in the form of faster learning than as direct transfer from one domain to another.

Knowing about the adult cognitive system greatly facilitates understanding of cognitive development. Among the contributions from other cognitive disciplines to the story of cognitive development have been theories of the overall cognitive system, methods for studying thinking, empirical findings that hold true with children as well as adults, languages for characterizing cognition, and philosophical insights that have altered perspectives on long-standing debates about children's thinking. Analyses of children's thinking, in turn, may inform these other areas about the nature of change processes and about how otherwise inexplicable patterns within adult cognition came to be.

The gap between children's and adults' thinking no longer seems to be as wide as once was thought. The narrowing has come from both ends. Infants have a variety of previously unsuspected capabilities, particularly in perception, conceptualization, and some aspects of memory. Young children demonstrate some understanding of other concepts that previously were thought to be totally beyond their grasp. At the other end of the age spectrum, adults have been shown to think less rationally and scientifically than had been believed. These developments have made it clear that in many cases, there is no single age at which children acquire a cognitive capability. The future need is for more encompassing models that indicate both how children think about particular topics and the conditions under which they apply various modes of thinking.

Children's thinking develops within a social context of parents, peers, teachers, and the society in general. These social agents profoundly influence what children think about. They influence whether children acquire some cognitive skills at all, such as operating an abacus. They also influence the degree to which they acquire other abilities, such as the ability to locate objects in space. They further influence the context in which the skills are manifested, as in the study about African tailors.

The social world also influences how children acquire information. It influences the extent to which children use techniques that can help them learn: among them asking questions, reading, understanding statistics, and reaching correct logical deductions. Attending school also seems to have a general effect of promoting use of verbal strategies for learning. Children's success within a given social environment is influenced by the interaction between the child's personality and environmental values, as evidenced by the differing predictors of school success in the United States and Japan.

Finally, many differences in what children think about are due to motivational factors. Prior interest is one pervasive influence. Children pay greater attention to materials that already interest them and also remember more about those materials. Another important motivational influence is reactions to negative experiences. In the face of failure, some people give up and become helpless, whereas others double their efforts. The reactions seem to be tied to people's attributions of the causes of the failures. People who attribute their failures to lack of ability tend to give up, whereas those who attribute their failures to lack of effort try harder the next time. Reactions to failure may be especially important in learning about mathematics, since the introduction of mathematical concepts so frequently produces at least initial failures. The types of feedback girls receive at school may lead to their attributing failures to lack of ability and thus being especially prone to develop "math phobia." Greater emphasis on effort as the primary cause of success may help alleviate this problem.

RECOMMENDED READINGS

Gardner, H. (1983). *Frames of mind. The theory of multiple intelligences.* New York: Basic Books. A stimulating and provocative proposal that people have multiple intelligences based on fundamentally different types of representations. Almost every reader will find points of disagreement, but there also are a number of real insights here.

Hatano, G., & Osawa, K. (1983). Digit memory of grand experts in abacus-derived mental calculation. *Cognition, 15*, 95–110. Describes how abacus experts form "mental abacuses" that enable them to perform exceptionally rapid and accurate calculations even when the abacus is not physically present.

Kearins, J. M. (1981). Visual spatial memory in Australian Aboriginal children of desert regions. *Cognitive Psychology, 13*, 434–460. An unusual study documenting the superior spatial skills that Australian aboriginal children develop in the course of their long treks through the desert.

Keil, F. C. (1981). Constraints on knowledge and cognitive development. *Psychological Review, 88*, 197–227. People in general, and children in particular, may be predisposed to learn in certain ways. This article persuasively describes how such predispositions may operate and help children to acquire concepts rapidly.

Licht, B. G., & Dweck, C. S. (1984). Determinants of academic achievement: The interaction of children's achievement orientations with skill area. *Developmental Psychology, 20*, 628–636. Children's social environments exert important influences on their thinking. This article compellingly illustrates how feelings of helplessness may interfere with women's efforts to learn mathematics.

REFERENCES

Acredolo, C., & Schmid, J. (1981). The understanding of relative speeds, distances, and durations of movement. *Developmental Psychology, 17*, 490–493.

Acredolo, L. P. (1978). The development of spatial orientation in infancy. *Developmental Psychology, 14*, 224–234.

Acredolo, L. P. (1979). Laboratory versus home: The effect of environment on the 9-month-old infant's choice of spatial reference system. *Developmental Psychology, 15*, 666–667.

Acredolo, L. P., & Hake, J. L. (1982). Infant perception. In B. J. Wolman (Ed.), *Handbook of developmental psychology*. Englewood Cliffs, NJ: Prentice-Hall.

Adams, R. J., & Maurer, D. (1984). *The use of habituation to study newborns' color vision.* Paper presented at the 4th International Conference on Infant Studies, New York, NY.

Aitken, S., & Bower, T. G. R. (1982). Intersensory substitution in the blind. *Journal of Experimental Child Psychology, 33*, 309–323.

Albert, R. S., & Runco, M. A. (in press). The achievement of eminence: A model based on a longitudinal study of exceptionally gifted boys and their families. In R. J. Sternberg & J. Davidson (Eds.), *Conceptions of giftedness*. New York: Cambridge University Press.

Anderson, J. R. (1983). *The architecture of cognition*. Cambridge, MA: Harvard University Press.

Anderson, J. R., Boyle, C. F., & Yost, G. (in press). The geometry tutor. *International Joint Conference on Artificial Intelligence.*

Anderson, N. H., & Cuneo, D. O. (1978). The height + width rule in children's judgments of quantity. *Journal of Experimental Psychology: General, 107*, 335–378.

Anglin, J. M. (1977). *Word, object, and conceptual development*. New York: W. W. Norton.

Antell, S. E., & Keating, D. P. (1983). Perception of numerical invariance in neonates. *Child Development, 54*, 695–701.

Ashcraft, M. H. (1982). The development of mental arithmetic: A chronometric approach. *Development Review, 2*, 213–236.

Aslin, R. N. (1977). Development of binocular fixation in human infants. *Journal of Experimental Child Psychology, 23*, 133–150.

Aslin, R. N., & Dumais, S. T. (1980). Binocular vision in infants: A review and a theoretical framework. In L. P. Lipsitt & H. W. Reese (Eds.), *Advances in child development and behavior*. New York: Academic Press.

Aslin, R. N., Pisoni, D. P., & Jusczyk, P. W. (1983). Auditory development and speech perception in infancy. In P. H. Mussen (Ed.), *Handbook of child psychology: Infancy and developmental psychobiology, Vol. II*. New York: Wiley.

Atkinson, R. C., & Shiffrin, R. M. (1968). Human memory: A proposed system and its control processes. In K. W. Spence & J. T. Spence (Eds.), *Advances in the psychology of learning and motivation research and theory, Vol. 2*. New York: Academic Press.

Azuma, H. (1984). *Socialization and motivation: Some thoughts about "receptive diligence" implicitly encouraged in Japanese education.* Paper presented at American Educational Research Association Conference, New Orleans, April.

Bahrick, H. P., Bahrick, P. O., & Wittlinger, R. P. (1975). Fifty years of memory for names and faces: A cross-sectional approach. *Journal of Experimental Psychology, 104,* 54–75.

Baillargeon, R. (1984). *Object permanence in the five month old infant.* Paper presented at the Conference on Conceptual Constraints, University of Pennsylvania, Philadelphia, PA.

Baker, L., & Brown, A. L. (1984). Metacognitive skills and reading. In P. D. Pearson (Ed.), *Handbook of reading research Part 2.* New York: Longman.

Banks, M. S. (1980). The development of visual accommodation during early infancy. *Child Development, 51,* 646–666.

Banks, M. S., Aslin, R. N., & Letson, R. D. (1975). Sensitive period for the development of human binocular vision. *Science, 190,* 675–677.

Banks, M. S., & Salapatek, P. (1981). Infant pattern vision: A new approach based on the contrast sensitivity function. *Journal of Experimental Child Psychology, 31,* 1–45.

Baron, J. (1978). Intelligence and general strategies. In G. Underwood (Ed.), *Strategies in information processing.* New York: Academic Press.

Bartlett, E. J. (1982). Learning to revise: Some component processes. In M. Nystrand (Ed.), *What writers know. The language, process, and structure of written discourse.* New York: Academic Press.

Bartlett, F. C. (1932). *Remembering.* Cambridge, England: Cambridge University Press.

Barton, D. (1978). The discrimination of minimally different pairs of real words by children aged 2; 3 to 5; 11. In N. Waterson & C. Snow (Eds.), *The development of communication.* Chichester, England: Wiley.

Beck, I. L., & McKeown, M. G. (1984). Application of theories of reading to instruction. *American Journal of Education, 93,* 61–81.

Bellugi, U. (1965). The development of interrogative structures in children's speech. In K. Riegel (Ed.), *The development of language functions.* Ann Arbor: University of Michigan Language Development Program.

Belmont, J. M., & Butterfield, E. C. (1977). The instructional approach to developmental cognitive research. In R. V. Kail, Jr. & J. W. Hagen (Eds.), *Perspectives on the development of memory and cognition.* Hillsdale, NJ: Erlbaum.

Bem, D. J., & Allen, A. (1974). On predicting some of the people some of the time: The search for cross-situational consistencies in behavior. *Psychological Review, 81,* 506–520.

Bereiter, C., & Scardamalia, M. (1982). From conversation to composition: The role of instruction in a developmental process. In R. Glaser (Ed.), *Advances in instructional psychology.* Hillsdale, NJ: Erlbaum.

Berko, J. (1958). The child's learning of English morphology. *Word, 14,* 150–177.

Bertenthal, B. I., Proffitt, D. R., Septner, N. B., & Thomas, M. A. (1985). Development of infant sensitivity to biomechanical motion. *Child Development, 56,* 531–543.

Best, C. T., Hoffman, H., & Glanville, B. B. (1982). Development of infant ear asymmetries for speech and music. *Perception & Psychophysics, 31,* 75–85.

Bickerton, D. (1983). Creole languages. *Scientific American, 249,* 116–122.

Billman, D., & Shatz, M. (1981). *A longitudinal study of the development of communication skills in twins and unrelated peers.* Unpublished manuscript, University of Michigan, Ann Arbor.

Bjorklund, D. F., & Zeman, B. R. (1982). Children's organization and metamemory awareness in their recall of familiar information. *Child Development, 53,* 799–810.

Bloom, L. (1970). *Language development: Form and function in emerging grammars.* Cambridge, MA: MIT Press.

Bloom, L., Rocissano, L., & Hood, L. (1976). Adult-child discourse: Developmental interaction between information processing and linguistic knowledge. *Cognitive Psychology, 8,* 521–552.

Bonvillian, J. D., Orlansky, M. D., & Novack, L. L. (1983). Developmental milestones: Sign language acquisition and motor development. *Child Development, 54,* 1435–1445.

Borkowski, J. C. (1980). *Signs of intelligence: Strategy generalization and metacognition.* Paper presented at Gatlinburg Conference on Mental Retardation, Gatlinburg, TN.

Bornstein, M. H. (1976a). Infants are trichromats. *Journal of Experimental Child Psychology*, *21*, 425–445.

Bornstein, M. H. (1976b). Infants' recognition memory for hue. *Developmental Psychology*, *12*, 185–191.

Bornstein, M. H. (1978). Chromatic vision in infancy. In H. W. Reese & L. P. Lipsitt (Eds.), *Advances in child development and behavior*. New York: Academic Press.

Bower, T. G. R. (1965). Stimulus variables determining space perception in infants. *Science*, *149*, 88–89.

Bower, T. G. R. (1979). The origins of meaning in perceptual development. In A. Pick (Ed.), *Perception and its development: A tribute to Eleanor J. Gibson*. Hillsdale, NJ: Erlbaum.

Bower, T. G. R., & Wishart, J. G. (1972). The effects of motor skill on object permanence. *Cognition*, *1*, 165–172.

Bowerman, M. (1973). *Early syntactic development: A cross-linguistic study with special reference to Finnish*. Cambridge, MA: Harvard University Press.

Bowerman, M. (1980). The structure and origin of semantic categories in the language-learning child. In M. Foster & S. Brandes (Eds.), *Symbol as sense: New approaches to the analysis of meaning*. New York: Academic Press.

Bowerman, M. (1982). Starting to talk worse: Clues to language acquisition from children's late speech errors. In S. Strauss (Ed.), *U-Shaped behavioral growth*. New York: Academic Press.

Brackbill, Y. (1971). The role of the cortex in orienting: Orienting reflex in an anencephalic infant. *Developmental Psychology*, *5*, 195–201.

Bradley, L., & Bryant, P. E. (1983). Categorizing sounds and learning to read—a causal connection. *Nature*, *301*, 419–421.

Braine, M. D. S. (1959). The ontogeny of certain logical operations: Piaget's formulation examined by nonverbal methods. *Psychological Monographs*, *73*, (Whole No. 475).

Braine, M. D. S. (1963). The ontogeny of English phrase structure: The first phrase. *Language*, *39*, 1–13.

Braine, M. D. S. (in press). A model of distributional learning. In B. MacWhinney (Ed.), *Mechanisms of language acquisition*. Hillsdale, NJ: Erlbaum.

Brainerd, C. J. (1973). Order of acquisition of transitivity, conservation, and class inclusion of length and weight. *Developmental Psychology*, *8*, 105–116.

Brainerd, C. J. (1978). The stage question in cognitive developmental theory. *Behavioral and Brain Sciences*, *1*, 173–213.

Brainerd, C. J. & Kingma, J. (1984). Do children have to remember to reason? A fuzzy-trace theory of transitivity development. *Developmental Review*, *4*, 311–377.

Bransford, P. W. (1979). *Human cognition. Learning, understanding and remembering*. Belmont, CA: Wadsworth.

Brener, R. (1940). An experimental investigation of memory span. *Journal of Experimental Psychology*, *26*, 467–482.

Brennan, W. M., Ames, E. W., & Moore, R. W. (1966). Age differences in infants' attention to patterns of different complexity. *Science*, *151*, 354–356.

Briggs, C., & Elkind, D. (1977). Characteristics of early readers. *Perceptual and Motor Skills*, *14*, 1231–1237.

Bronson, G. W. (1974). The postnatal growth of visual capacity. *Child Development*, *45*, 873–890.

Brown, A. L. (1976). Semantic integration in children's reconstruction of narrative sequences. *Cognitive Psychology*, *8*, 247–262.

Brown, A. L., Bransford, J. D., Ferrara, R. A., & Campione, J. C. (1983). Learning, remembering, and understanding. In P. H. Mussen (Ed.), *Handbook of child psychology: Cognitive development, Vol. III*. New York: Wiley.

Brown, A. L., & Campione, J. C. (1972). Recognition memory for perceptually similar pictures in preschool children. *Journal of Experimental Psychology, 95,* 55–62.

Brown, A. L., & DeLoache, J. S. (1978). Skills, plans, and self-regulation. In R. S. Siegler (Ed.), *Children's thinking: What develops?* Hillsdale, NJ: Erlbaum.

Brown, A. L., & Scott, M. S. (1971). Recognition memory for pictures in preschool children. *Journal of Experimental Child Psychology, 11,* 401–412.

Brown, A. L., Smiley, S. S., & Lawton, S. C. (1978). The effects of experience on the selection of suitable retrieval cues for studying texts. *Child Development, 49,* 829–835.

Brown, J. S., & Burton, R. B. (1978). Diagnostic models for procedural bugs in basic mathematical skills. *Cognitive Science, 2,* 155–192.

Brown, J. S., & Van Lehn, K. (1982). Towards a generative theory of 'bugs.' In T. Romberg, T. Carpenter, & J. Moser (Eds.), *Addition and subtraction: A developmental perspective.* Hillsdale, NJ: Erlbaum.

Brown, R. (1973). *A first language. The early stages.* Cambridge, MA: Harvard University Press.

Brown, R., Cazden, C., & Bellugi, U. (1969). The child's grammar from I to III. In J. P. Hill (Ed.), *Minnesota symposium on child psychology.* Minneapolis: University of Minnesota Press.

Brown, R., & McNeill, D. (1966). The "tip of the tongue" phenomenon. *Journal of Verbal Learning and Verbal Behavior, 5,* 325–337.

Bruce, B., & Newman, D. (1978). Interacting plans. *Cognitive Science, 2,* 195–234.

Bruner, J. S., Oliver, R. R., & Greenfield, P. M. (1966). *Studies in cognitive growth.* New York: Wiley.

Bryant, P. E. (1974). *Perception and understanding in young children.* New York: Basic Books.

Bryant, P. E., & Trabasso, T. (1971). Transitive inferences and memory in young children. *Nature, 232,* 457–459.

Buckhalt, J. A., Mahoney, G. J., & Paris, S. G. (1976). Efficiency of self-generated elaborations by EMR and nonretarded children. *American Journal of Mental Deficiency, 81,* 93–96.

Bullock, M., & Gelman, R. (1979). Preschool children's assumptions about cause and effect: Temporal ordering. *Child Development, 50,* 89–96.

Bullock, M., Gelman, R., & Baillargeon, R. (1982). The development of causal reasoning. In W. J. Friedman (Ed.), *The developmental psychology of time.* New York: Academic Press.

Butterfield, E., Siladi, D., & Belmont, J. (1980). Validating theories of intelligence. In H. W. Reese & L. P. Lipsitt (Eds.), *Advances in child development and behavior.* New York: Academic Press.

Butterworth, G. E. (1978). A review of "A primer of infant development." *Perception, 7,* 363–364.

Callanan, M. A. (1985). *Object labels and young children's acquisition of categories.* Paper presented at Society for Research in Child Development Conference, Toronto, April.

Campbell, J. R., Connolly, C., Bologh, R., & Primavera, L. (1984, April). *Impact of ethnicity on math and science among the gifted.* Paper presented at the Annual Meeting of the American Educational Research Association, New Orleans.

Campione, J. C., & Brown, A. L. (1978). Toward a theory of intelligence: Contributions from research with retarded children. *Intelligence, 2,* 279–304.

Campos, J., Hiatt, S., Ramsay, D., Henderson, C., & Svejda, M. (1978). The emergence of fear on the visual cliff. In M. Lewis & L. Rosenblum (Eds.), *The origins of affect.* New York: Plenum Press.

Carey, S. (1978). A child's concept of animal. Unpublished manuscript.

Carey, S. (in press). Are children fundamentally different kinds of thinkers and learners than adults? In S. Chipman, J. Segal, & R. Glaser (Eds.), *Thinking and learning skills.* Hillsdale, NJ: Erlbaum.

Caron, A. J., Caron, R. F., & Carlson, V. R. (1979). Infant perception of the invariant shape of objects varying in slant. *Child Development, 50,* 716–721.

Carpenter, G. (1974). Visual regard of moving and stationary faces in early infancy. *Merrill-Palmer Quarterly, 20,* 181–194.

Carpenter, T. P., Moser, J. M., & T. A. Romberg (Eds.). (1982). *Addition and subtraction: A cognitive perspective.* Hillsdale, NJ: Erlbaum.

Carraher, T. N., Carraher, D. W., & Schliemann, A. D. (1983). *Mathematics in the streets and in schools.* Unpublished manuscript, University of Recife, Brazil.

Carver, S. M., & Klahr, D. (1985). *Developmental progress in the use of weak methods: From hill climbing to subgoaling.* Paper presented at the Society for Research in Child Development Conference, Toronto, Canada.

Carver, C. S., & Scheier, M. F. (1981). *Attention and self-regulation: A control-theory approach to human behavior.* New York: Springer-Verlag.

Case, R. (1972). Validation of a neo-Piagetian capacity construct. *Journal of Experimental Child Psychology, 14,* 287–302.

Case, R. (1978). Intellectual development from birth to adulthood: A neo-Piagetian approach. In R. S. Siegler (Ed.), *Children's thinking: What develops?* Hillsdale, NJ: Erlbaum.

Case, R. (1981, April). *The search for horizontal structure in children's development.* Paper presented at the Society for Research in Child Development Conference, Boston.

Case, R. (1985). *Intellectual development: A systematic reinterpretation.* New York: Academic Press.

Case, R., Kurland, D. M., & Goldberg, J. (1982). Operational efficiency and the growth of short-term memory span. *Journal of Experimental Child Psychology, 33,* 386–404.

Cavanaugh, J. C., & Perlmutter, M. (1982). Metamemory: A critical examination. *Child Development, 53,* 11–28.

Cazden, C. B. (1968). The acquisition of noun and verb inflections. *Child Development, 39,* 433–438.

Chall, J. S. (1979). The great debate: Ten years later, with a modest proposal for reading stages. In L. B. Resnick & P. A. Weaver (Eds.), *Theory and practice of early reading.* Hillsdale, NJ: Erlbaum.

Chase, W. G. (in press). Visual information processing. In K. R. Boff, L. Kaufman, & J. P. Thomas (Eds.), *Handbook of perception and human performance.* New York: Wiley.

Chi, M. T. H. (1978). Knowledge structures and memory development. In R. S. Siegler (Ed.), *Children's thinking: What develops?* Hillsdale, NJ: Erlbaum.

Chi, M. T. H. (1981). Knowledge development and memory performance. In J. P. Das & N. O'Conner (Eds.), *Intelligence and learning.* New York: Plenum Press.

Chi, M. T. H., Feltovich, P. J., & Glaser, R. (1981). Categorization and representation of physics problems by experts and novices. *Cognitive Science, 5,* 121–152.

Chi, M. T. H., & Klahr, D. (1975). Span and rate of apprehension in children and adults. *Journal of Experimental Child Psychology, 19,* 434–439.

Chi, M. T. H., & Koeske, R. D. (1983). Network representation of a child's dinosaur knowledge. *Developmental Psychology, 19,* 29–39.

Chomsky, N. A. (1957). *Syntactic structures.* The Hague: Mouton.

Chomsky, N. A. (1959). Verbal behavior: A review of Skinner's book. *Language, 35,* 26–58.

Chomsky, N. A. (1968). *Language and mind.* New York: Harcourt, Brace & World.

Clancy, P. M. (1984). How children learn language: Getting it from the input to the output. Review of "E. Wanner and L. R. Gleitman (Eds.), Language acquisition: The state of the art." *Contemporary Psychology, 29,* 489–491.

Clark, E. V. (1973). What's in a word? On the child's acquisition of semantics in his first language. In T. E. Moore (Ed.), *Cognitive development and the acquisition of language.* New York: Academic Press.

Clark, E. V. (1978). Strategies for communicating. *Child Development, 49,* 953–959.

Clark, E. V. (1981). Lexical innovations: How children learn to create new words. In W. Deutsch (Ed.), *The child's construction of language.* New York: Academic Press.

Clark, E. V. (1983). Meanings and concepts. In P. H. Mussen (Ed.), *Handbook of child psychology: History, theory, and methods, Vol. I.* New York: Wiley.

Clifton, R. K., Morrongiello, B. A., Kulig, J. W., & Dowd, J. M. (1981). Newborns' orientation toward sound: Possible implications for cortical development. *Child Development, 52*, 833–838.

Cohen, L. B. (1972). Attention getting and attention holding processes of infant visual preference. *Child Development, 43*, 869–879.

Cohen, L. B., & Strauss, M. S. (1979). Concept acquisition in the human infant. *Child Development, 50*, 419–424.

Cole, M., & Scribner, S. (1974). *Culture and thought.* New York: Wiley.

Condon, W., & Sanders, L. (1974). Synchrony demonstrated between movements of the neonate and adult speech. *Child Development, 45*, 456–462.

Conrad, R. (1964). Acoustic confusions in immediate memory. *British Journal of Psychology, 55*, 75–84.

Conrad, R. (1971). The effect of vocalizing on comprehension in the profoundly deaf. *British Journal of Psychology, 62*, 147–150.

Cooper, L. A., & Regan, D. (1982). Attention, perception, and intelligence. In R. Sternberg (Ed.), *Handbook of human intelligence.* New York: Cambridge University Press.

Cooper, R. G. (1984). Early number development: Discovering number space with addition and subtraction. In C. Sophian (Ed.), *Origins of cognitive skills.* Hillsdale, NJ: Erlbaum.

Corman, H. H., & Escalona, S. K. (1969). Stages of sensorimotor development: A replication study. *Merrill-Palmer Quarterly, 15*, 351–361.

Corrigan, R. (1975). A scalogram analysis of the development of the use and comprehension of "because" in children. *Child Development, 46*, 195–201.

Craik, F. I. M., & Lockhart, R. S. (1972). Levels of processing: A framework for memory research. *Journal of Verbal Learning and Verbal Behavior, 11*, 671–684.

Craik, F. I. M., & Watkins, M. J. (1973). The role of rehearsal in short-term memory. *Journal of Verbal Learning and Verbal Behavior, 12*, 599–607.

Crosby, F. (1976). Early discourse agreement. *Journal of Child Language, 3*, 125–126.

Cultice, J. C., Somerville, S. C., & Wellman, H. M. (1983). Preschoolers' memory monitoring: Feeling-of-knowing judgments. *Child Development, 54*, 1480–1486.

Cuvo, A. J. (1975). Developmental differences in rehearsal and free recall. *Journal of Experimental Child Psychology, 19*, 65–78.

Dale, P. S. (1976). *Language development.* New York: Holt, Rinehart, and Winston.

Dallago, M. L., & Moely, B. E. (1980). Free recall in boys of normal and poor reading levels as a function of task manipulations. *Journal of Experimental Child Psychology, 30*, 62–78.

Damon, W. (Ed.). (1978). *New directions for child development: Vol. 1. Social cognition.* San Francisco: Jossey-Bass.

Daneman, M. (1981). *The integration processes of reading: Individual and developmental differences.* Doctoral dissertation, Carnegie-Mellon University, Pittsburgh.

Dasen, P. R. (1973). Piagetian research in Central Australia. In G. E. Kearney, P. R. de Lacey, & G. R. Davidson (Eds.), *The psychology of Aboriginal Australians.* Sydney: Wiley.

Day, R. H., & McKenzie, B. E. (1981). Infant perception of the invariant size of approaching and receding objects. *Developmental Psychology, 17*, 670–677.

DeCasper, A. J., & Fifer, W. P. (1980). Of human bonding: Newborns prefer their mothers' voices. *Science, 208*, 1174–1176.

de Hirsch, K., Jansky, J., & Langford, W. (1966). **Predicting reading failure.** New York: Harper & Row.

DeLoache, J. S. (1980). Naturalistic studies of memory for object location in very young children. *New Directions for Child Development, 10*, 17–32.

DeLoache, J. S. (1984). Oh where, oh where: Memory-based searching by very young children. In C. Sophian (Ed.), *Origins of cognitive skills.* Hillsdale, NJ: Erlbaum.

DeLoache, J. S., & Brown, A. L. (1983). Very young children's memory for the location of objects in a large-scale environment. *Child Development, 54*, 888–897.

DeLoache, J. S., Rissman, M. D., & Cohen, L. B. (1978). An investigation of the attention-getting process in infants. *Infant Behavior and Development, 1*, 11–25.

DeVries, R. (1969). Constancy of generic identity in the years three to six. *Society for Research in Child Development Monographs, 34,* (Whole No. 127).

Dobson, V. (1983). Clinical applications of preferential looking measures of visual acuity. *Behavioural Brain Research, 10,* 25–38.

Dobson, V., & Teller, D. Y. (1978). Visual acuity in human infants: A review and comparison of behavioral and electrophysiological studies. *Vision Research, 18,* 1469–1483.

Dodwell, P. E. (1960). Children's understanding of number and related concepts. *Canadian Journal of Psychology, 14,* 191–205.

Donaldson, M., & Balfour, G. (1968). Less is more: A study of language comprehension in children. *British Journal of Psychology, 59,* 461–472.

Donaldson, M., & Wales, R. J. (1970). On the acquisition of some relational terms. In J. R. Hayes (Ed.), *Cognition and the development of language.* New York: Wiley.

Durkin, D. (1966). *Children who read early.* New York: Teachers College Press.

Dweck, C. S., & Goetz, T. E. (1978). Attributions and learned helplessness. In. J. H. Harvey, W. Ickles, & R. F. Kidd (Eds.), *New directions in attribution research, Vol. 2.* Hillsdale, NJ: Erlbaum.

Dweck, C. S., & Licht, B. G. (1980). Learned helplessness and intellectual achievement. In J. Garber & M. E. P. Seligman (Eds.), *Human helplessness: Theory and applications.* New York: Academic Press.

Eimas, P. D., Siqueland, E. R., Jusczyk, P., & Vigorito, J. (1971). Speech perception in infants. *Science, 171,* 303–306.

Elkind, D. (1961a). Children's discovery of the conservation of mass, weight, and volume: Piaget replications study II. *Journal of Genetic Psychology, 98,* 37–46.

Elkind, D. (1961b). The development of quantitative thinking: A systematic replication of Piaget's studies. *Journal of Genetic Psychology, 98,* 37–46.

Elliot, A. J. (1981). *Child language.* Cambridge, England: Cambridge University Press.

Ellis, S., & Rogoff, B. (1982). The strategies and efficiency of child versus adult teachers. *Child Development, 53,* 730–735.

Ericsson, K. A., Chase, W. G., & Faloon, S. (1980). Acquisition of a memory skill. *Science, 208,* 1181–1182.

Ericsson, K. A., & Simon, H. A. (1980). Verbal reports as data. *Psychological Review, 87,* 215–251.

Ervin-Tripp, S. (1970). Discourse agreement: How children answer questions In J. R. Hayes (Ed.), *Cognition and the development of language.* New York: Wiley.

Estes, W. K. (1956). The problem of inference from curves based on group data. *Psychological Bulletin, 53,* 134–140.

Fabricius, W. V., & Hagen, J. W. (1984). Use of causal attributions about recall performance to assess metamemory and predict strategic memory behavior in young children. *Developmental Psychology, 20,* 975–987.

Fagan, J. F. (1984). The intelligent infant: Theoretical implications. *Intelligence, 8,* 1–9.

Fagan, J. F., & Singer, L. T. (1983). Infant recognition memory as a measure of intelligence. In L. P. Lipsitt (Ed.), *Advances in infancy research. Vol. 2.* Norwood, NJ: Ablex.

Fantz, R. L. (1958). Pattern vision in young infants. *Psychological Record, 8,* 43–47.

Fantz, R. L. (1961). The origin of form perception. *Scientific American, 204,* 66–72.

Fantz, R. L., Fagan, J. F., & Miranda, S. B. (1975). Early perceptual development as shown by visual discrimination, selectivity, and memory with varying stimulus and population parameters. In L. B. Cohen & P. Salapatek (Eds.), *Infant perception: From sensation to cognition.* New York: Academic Press.

Farah, M. J., & Kosslyn, S. M. (1982). Concept development. In H. W. Reese & L. P. Lipsitt (Eds.), *Advances in child development and behavior.* New York: Academic Press.

Fernald, A. (1981). *Four-month-olds prefer to listen to "motherese."* Paper presented at the meeting of the Society for Research in Child Development, Boston.

Ferretti, R. P., Butterfield, E. C., Cahn, A., & Kerkman, D. (1985). The classification of children's knowledge: Development on the balance-scale and inclined-plane tasks. *Journal of Experimental Child Psychology, 39,* 131–160.

Field, D. (1977). The importance of the verbal content in the training of Piagetian conservation skills. *Child Development, 48,* 1583–1592.

Firth, I. (1972). Components of reading disability. Unpublished doctoral dissertation, University of New South Wales.

Fischer, K. W. (1980). A theory of cognitive development: The control and construction of hierarchies of skills. *Psychological Review, 87,* 477–531.

Fiske, S. T., & Taylor, S. E. (1984). *Social cognition.* Reading, MA: Addison-Wesley.

Flavell, J. H. (1970). Developmental studies of mediated memory. In H. W. Reese & L. P. Lipsitt (Eds.). *Advances in child development and behavior.* New York: Academic Press.

Flavell, J. H. (1971). Stage-related properties of cognitive development. *Cognitive Psychology, 2,* 421–453.

Flavell, J. H. (1972). An analysis of cognitive-developmental sequences. *Genetic Psychology Monographs, 86,* 279–350.

Flavell, J. H. (1982). On cognitive development. *Child Development, 53,* 1–10.

Flavell, J. H. (1984). Discussion. In R. J. Sternberg (Ed.), *Mechanisms of cognitive development.* New York: W. H. Freeman.

Flavell, J. H. (1985). *Cognitive development.* Englewood Cliffs, NJ: Prentice-Hall.

Flavell, J. H., Beach, D. R., & Chinsky, J. M. (1966). Spontaneous verbal rehearsal in a memory task as a function of age. *Child Development, 37,* 283–299.

Flavell, J. H., Flavell, E. R., & Green, F. L. (1983). Development of the appearance-reality distinction. *Cognitive Psychology, 15,* 95–120.

Flavell, J. H., Friedrichs, A. G., & Hoyt, J. D. (1970). Developmental changes in memorization processes. *Cognitive Psychology, 1,* 324–340.

Flavell, J. H., Speer, J. R., Green, F. L., & August, D. L. (1981). The development of comprehension monitoring and knowledge about communication. *Monographs of the Society for Research in Child Development, 46* (Whole No. 192).

Flavell, J. H., & Wellman, H. M. (1977). Metamemory. In R. V. Kail, Jr. & J. W. Hagen (Eds.), *Perspectives on the development of memory and cognition.* Hillsdale, NJ: Erlbaum.

Flavell, J. H., Zhang, X. D., Zou, H., Dong, Q., & Qi, S. (1983). A comparison between the development of the appearance-reality distinction in the People's Republic of China and the United States. *Cognitive Psychology, 15,* 459–466.

Fodor, J. (1972). Some reflections on L. S. Vygotsky's *Thought and language. Cognition, 1,* 83–95.

Ford, M. E. (1985). Two perspectives on the validation of developmental constructs: Psychometric and theoretical limitations in research on egocentrism. *Psychological Bulletin, 97,* 497–501.

Fox, R., Aslin, R. N., Shea, S. L., & Dumais, S. T. (1980). Stereopsis in human infants. *Science, 207,* 323–324.

Fox, R., & McDaniel, C. (1982). The perception of biological motion by human infants. *Science, 218,* 486–487.

Fraiberg, S. (1977). *Insights from the blind: Comparative studies of blind and sighted infants.* New York: Basic Books.

Freud, S. (1953). Three essays on the theory of sexuality. In J. Strachey (Ed.), *The standard edition of the complete psychological works of Sigmund Freud: Volume 7.* London: Hogarth.

Friedman, W. J. (1978). Development of time concepts in children. In H. W. Reese & L. P. Lipsitt (Eds.), *Advances in child development and behavior.* New York: Academic Press.

Friedman, W. J. (1982). Conventional time concepts and children's structuring of time. In W. J. Friedman (Ed.), *The developmental psychology of time.* New York: Academic Press.

Gallagher, T. M. (1981). Contingent query sequences within adult-child discourse. *Journal of Child Language, 8,* 51–62.

Ganz, L. (1975). Temporal factors in visual perception. In E. C. Carterette & M. P. Friedman (Eds.), *Handbook of perception*. New York: Academic Press.

Gardner, H. (1983). *Frames of mind. The theory of multiple intelligences*. New York: Basic Books.

Garner, R., & Reis, R. (1981). Monitoring and resolving comprehension obstacles: An investigation of spontaneous text lookbacks among upper-grade good and poor comprehenders. *Reading Research Quarterly, 16*, 569–582.

Garnica, O. K. (1973). The development of phonemic speech perception. In T. E. Moore (Ed.), *Cognition and the acquisition of language*. New York: Academic Press.

Gelman, R. (1969). Conservation acquisition: A problem of learning to attend to relevant attributes. *Journal of Experimental Child Psychology, 7*, 167–187.

Gelman, R. (1972). The nature and development of early number concepts. In H. W. Reese & L. P. Lipsitt (Ed.), *Advances in child development and behavior*. New York: Academic Press.

Gelman, R. (1978). Cognitive development. *Annual Review of Psychology, 29*, 297–332.

Gelman, R., & Gallistel, C. R. (1978). *The child's understanding of number*. Cambridge, MA: Harvard University Press.

Gentner, D. (1975). Evidence for the psychological reality of semantic components: The verbs of possession. In D. A. Norman & D. E. Rumelhart (Eds.), *Explorations in cognition*. San Francisco: Freeman.

Gibson, E. J., Schapiro, F., & Yonas, A. (1968). *Confusion matrices for graphic patterns obtained with a latency*. (Tech. Rep. No. 5-1213). Ithaca, NY: Cornell University and U. S. Office of Education.

Gibson, J. J. (1966). *The senses considered as perceptual systems*. Boston: Houghton Mifflin.

Ginsburg, H. (1977). *Children's arithmetic: The learning process*. New York: D. Van Nostrand.

Ginsburg, H. P. (1983). *The development of mathematical thinking*. New York: Academic Press.

Gleitman, L., & Rozin, P. (1977). The structure and acquisition of reading I: Relations between orthographies and the structure of language. In A. Reber & D. Scarborough (Eds.), *Toward a psychology of reading: Proceedings of the CUNY conference*. Hillsdale, NJ: Erlbaum.

Goldberg, D. E. (1983). *Computer-aided gas pipeline operation using genetic algorithms and rule learning*. Doctoral dissertation, University of Michigan.

Goldin-Meadow, S. (1979). Structure in a manual communication system developed without a conventional language model: Language without a helping hand. In H. Whitaker & H. A. Whitaker (Eds.), *Studies in neurolinguistics, Vol 4*. New York: Academic Press.

Goldin-Meadow, S., & Morford, M. (1985). Gesture in early child language: Studies of deaf and hearing children. *Merrill-Palmer Quarterly. 31*, 145–176.

Goldman, S. R. (1983, November). *Toward procedures for summarizing text*. Presented at the Psychonomic Society.

Goodnow, J. J. (1962). A test of millieu differences with some of Piaget's tasks. *Psychological Monographs, 76*, (Whole No. 555).

Gough, P. B., & Hillinger, M. L. *(1980).* Learning to read: An unnatural act. *Bulletin of the Orton Society, 30*, 171–196.

Graham, F. K., Leavitt, L. A., Strock, B. D., & Brown, J. W. (1978). Precocious cardiac orienting in human anencephalic infants. *Science, 199*, 322–324.

Granrud, C. E., Haake, R. J., & Yonas, A. (in press). Infants' sensitivity to familiar size: The effect of memory on spatial perception. *Perception and Psychophysics*.

Greenberg, D. J., & O'Donnell, W. J. (1972). Infancy and the optimal level of stimulation. *Child Development, 43*, 639–645.

Greenfield, P. M., & Lave, J. (1982). Cognitive aspects of informal education. In D. A. Wagner & H. W. Stevenson (Eds.), *Cultural perspectives on child development*. San Francisco: Freeman.

Greenfield, P. M., & Smith, J. (1976). *The structure of communication in early language development.* New York: Academic Press.

Greeno, J. G. (1976). Cognitive objectives of instruction: Theory of knowledge for solving problems and answering questions. In D. Klahr (Ed.), *Cognition and instruction.* Hillsdale, NJ: Erlbaum.

Greeno, J. G., Riley, M. S., & Gelman, R. (1984). Conceptual competence and children's counting. *Cognitive Psychology, 16,* 66–94.

Groen, G. J., & Parkman, J. M. (1972). A chronometric analysis of simple addition. *Psychological Review, 79,* 329–343.

Gruber, H. E., & Voneche, J. J. (1977). *The essential Piaget: An interpretive reference and guide.* New York: Basic Books.

Guttentag, R. E., & Ornstein, P. A. (1985). *Transitions in the development of memory skills.* Paper presented at the Society for Research in Child Development Conference, Toronto, April.

Hagen, J. W. (1972). Strategies for remembering. In S. Farnham-Diggory (Ed.), *Information processing in children.* New York: Academic Press.

Hagen, J. W., & Hale, G. A. (1973). The development of attention in children. In A. D. Pick (Ed.), *Minnesota symposia on child psychology, Vol. 7.* Minneapolis: University of Minnesota Press.

Hagen, J. W., Hargrove, S., & Ross, W. (1973). Prompting and rehearsal in short-term memory. *Child Development, 44,* 201–204.

Haith, M. M. (1979). Visual cognition in early infancy. In R. B. Kearsley & I. E. Sigel (Eds.), *Infants at risk: Assessment of cognitive functioning.* Hillsdale, NJ: Erlbaum.

Haith, M. M., Bergman, T., & Moore, M. J. (1977). Eye contact and face scanning in early infancy. *Science, 198,* 853–855.

Halford, G. S. (1982). *The development of thought.* Hillsdale, NJ: Erlbaum.

Halford, G. S. (1984). Can young children integrate premises in transitivity and serial order tasks? *Cognitive Psychology, 16,* 65–93.

Halford, G. S. (1985). Children's utilization of information: A basic factor in cognitive development. *Unpublished manuscript,* University of Queensland, Australia.

Harris, P L. (1983). Infant cognition. In P. H. Mussen (Ed.), *Handbook of child psychology: Infancy and developmental psychobiology, Volume II.* New York: Wiley.

Hasher, L., & Zacks, R. T. (1984). Automatic processing of fundamental information: The case of frequency of occurrence. *American Psychologist, 39,* 1372–1388.

Hatano, G., Miyake, Y., & Binks, M. G. (1977). Performance of expert abacus calculators. *Cognition, 5,* 57–71.

Hatano, G., & Osawa, K. (1983). Digit memory of grand experts in abacus-derived mental calculation. *Cognition, 15,* 95–110.

Hayes, C. (1951). *The ape in our house.* New York: Harper & Row.

Haynes, H., White, B. L., & Held, R. (1965). Visual accommodation in human infants. *Science, 148,* 528–530.

Hebb, D. O. (1949). *The organization of behavior.* New York: Wiley.

Herman, L. M., Richards, D. G., & Wolz, J. P. (1983). *Comprehension of sentences by bottlenosed dolphins.* Unpublished manuscript.

Herodotus. (About 450 B.C.). *The history of Herodotus.*

Hoffer, A. (1981). Geometry is more than proof. *Mathematics Teacher,* 11–18.

Holland, J. H., & Reitman, J. S. (1981). *Cognitive systems based on adaptive algorithms.* Unpublished manuscript, University of Michigan, Ann Arbor.

Hood, L., & Bloom, L. (1979). What, when, and how about why: A longitudinal study of early expressions of causality. *Monographs of the Society for Research in Child Development, 44,* (Whole No. 181).

Hoving, K. L., Spencer, T., Robb, K. Y., & Schulte, D. (1978). Developmental changes in visual information processing. In P. A. Ornstein (Ed.), *Memory development in children.* Hillsdale, NJ: Erlbaum.

Hume, D. (1911). *A treatise of human nature.* (Original work published 1739–1740). London: Dent.

Humphrey, G. K., & Humphrey, D. E. (in press). The use of binaural sensory aids by blind infants and children: Theoretical and applied issues. In F. Morrison & C. Lord (Eds.), *Applied Developmental Psychology, Vol. 2.* New York: Academic Press.

Hunt, J. M. (1961). *Intelligence and experience.* New York: Ronald Press.

Huttenlocher, J., & Burke, D. (1976). Why does memory span increase with age? *Cognitive Psychology, 8,* 1–31.

Huttenlocher, J., & Newcombe, N. (1984). The child's representation of information about location. In C. Sophian (Ed.), *Origins of cognitive skills.* Hillsdale, NJ: Erlbaum

Ilg, F., & Ames, L. B. (1951). Developmental trends in arithmetic. *Journal of Genetic Psychology, 79,* 3–28.

Inhelder, B., & Piaget, J. (1958). The growth of logical thinking from childhood to adolescence. New York: Basic Books.

Inhelder, B., & Piaget, J. (1964). *The early growth of logic in the child.* London: Routledge and Kegan.

Inhelder, B., Sinclair, H., & Bovet, M. (1974). *Learning and the development of cognition.* Cambridge, MA: Harvard University Press.

Jakobson, R. (1981). Why "mama" and "papa"? *Selected writings. Phonological studies.* The Hague, Paris: Mouton.

Javal, E. (1878). Essaie sur la physiologie de la lecture. *Annales d'oculistique, 79,* 97.

Jeffrey, W. E. (1975). Editorial. *Child Development, 46,* 1–2.

Johnson, C. N., & Wellman, H. M. (1982). Children's developing conceptions of the mind and brain. *Child Development, 53,* 222–234.

Johnson, D. D., & Baumann, J. F. (1984). Word identification. In P. D. Pearson (Ed.), *Handbook of reading research: Part 3.* New York: Longman.

Jorm, A. F., & Share, D. L. (1983). Phonological recoding and reading acquisition. *Applied Psycholinguistics, 4,* 103–147.

Jusczyk, P. W., Rosner, B. S., Cutting, J. E., Foard, F., & Smith, L. B. (1977). Categorical perception of non-speech sounds by two-month-old infants. *Perception & Psychophysics, 21,* 50–54.

Just, M. A., & Carpenter, P. A. (1980). A theory of reading: From eye fixations to comprehension. *Psychological Review, 87,* 329–354.

Kail, R. (1984). *The development of memory in children: Second edition.* New York: Freeman.

Kail, R., Pellegrino, J., & Carter, P. (1980). Developmental changes in mental rotation. *Journal of Experimental Child Psychology, 291,* 102–116.

Kaiser, M. K., McCloskey, M., & Proffitt, D. R. (in press). Development of intuitive theories of motion: Curvilinear motion in the absence of external forces. *Developmental Psychology.*

Kaplan, E., & Kaplan, G. (1971). The prelinguistic child. In J. Elliot (Ed.), *Human development and cognitive processes.* New York: Holt, Rinehart, and Winston.

Karmiloff-Smith, A., & Inhelder, B. (1977). If you want to get ahead, get a theory. *Cognition, 3,* 195–212.

Katz, H., & Beilin, H. (1976). A test of Bryant's claims concerning the young child's understanding of quantitative invariance. *Child Development, 47,* 877–880.

Kaye, K., & Charney, R. (1980). How mothers maintain dialogue with two-year-olds. In D. Olson (Ed.), *The social foundations of language and thought.* New York: W. W. Norton.

Kearins, J. M. (1981). Visual spatial memory in Australian Aboriginal children of desert regions. *Cognitive Psychology, 13,* 434–460.

Keating, D. P., & Bobbitt, B. L. (1978). Individual and developmental differences in cognitive processing components of mental ability. *Child Development, 49*, 155–167.

Keenan, E. O. (1977). Making it last: Uses of repetition in children's discourse. In S. Ervin-Tripp, & C. Mitchell-Kernan (Eds.), *Child discourse*. New York: Academic Press.

Keeney, T. J., Cannizzo, S. R., & Flavell, J. H. (1967). Spontaneous and induced verbal rehearsal in a recall task. *Child Development, 38*, 953–966.

Keil, F. C. (1981). Constraints on knowledge and cognitive development. *Psychological Review, 88*, 197–227.

Keil, F. C., & Batterman, N. (1984). A characteristic-to-defining shift in the development of word meaning. *Journal of Verbal Learning and Verbal Behavior, 23*, 221–236.

Kellogg, W. N., & Kellogg, L. A. (1933). *The ape and the child: A study of environmental influence upon early behavior*. New York: McGraw-Hill.

Kelman, P. J., & Spelke, E. S. (1983). Perception of partially occluded objects in infancy. *Cognitive Psychology, 15*, 483–524.

Kendall, C. R., Borkowski, J. G., & Cavanaugh, J. C. (1980). Metamemory and the transfer of an interrogative strategy by EMR children. *Intelligence, 4*, 255–270.

Kendler, H. H., & Kendler, T. S. (1962). Vertical and horizontal processes in problem solving. *Psychological Review, 69*, 1–16.

Kennedy, B. A., & Miller, D. J. (1976). Persistent use of verbal rehearsal as a function of information about its value. *Child Development, 47*, 566–569.

Klahr, D. (1982). Nonmonotone assessment of monotone development: An information processing analysis. In S. Strauss (Ed.), *U-shaped behavioral growth*. New York: Academic Press.

Klahr, D. (1984). Transition processes in quantitative development. In R. J. Sternberg (Ed.), *Mechanisms of cognitive development*. New York: Freeman.

Klahr, D., & Siegler, R. S. (1978). The representation of children's knowledge. In H. W. Reese & L. P. Lipsitt (Eds.), *Advances in child development*. New York: Academic Press.

Klahr, D., & Wallace, J. G. (1973). The role of quantification operators in the development of conservation of quantity. *Cognitive Psychology, 4*, 301–327.

Klahr, D., & Wallace, J. G. (1976). *Cognitive development: An information processing view*. Hillsdale, NJ: Erlbaum.

Klemmer, E. T., & Snyder, F. W. (1972). Measurement of time spent communicating. *Journal of Communication, 22*, 142–158.

Kobasigawa, A., Ransom, C. C., & Holland, C. (1980). Children's knowledge about skimming. *Alberta Journal of Educational Research, 26*, 169–182.

Kossan, N. (1981). Developmental differences in concept acquisition strategies. *Child Development, 52*, 290–298.

Kotovsky, K. (1983). *Tower of Hanoi problem isomorphs and solution processes*. Unpublished doctoral dissertation, Carnegie-Mellon University, Pittsburgh.

Krauss, R. M., & Glucksberg, S. (1969). The development of communication: Competence as a function of age. *Child Development, 40*, 255–266.

Kress, G. (1982). *Learning to write*. Boston: Routledge & Kegan Paul.

Kreutzer, M. A., Leonard, C., & Flavell, J. H. (1975). An interview study of children's knowledge about memory. *Monographs of the Society for Research in Child Development, 40* (Whole no. 159).

Kuczaj II, S. A. (1981). More on children's initial failures to relate specific acquisitions. *Journal of Child Language, 8*, 485–487.

Kuhl, P. K., & Miller, J. D. (1975). Speech perception by the chinchilla. *Science, 190*, 69–72.

Kun, A. (1978). Evidence for preschoolers' understanding of causal direction in extended causal sequences. *Child Development, 49*, 218–222.

Lamb, M. E., & Campos, J. J. (1982). *Development in infancy: An introduction*. New York: Random House.

Lange, G. (1973). The development of conceptual and rote recall skills among school age children. *Journal of Experimental Child Psychology, 15*, 394–407.

Lange, G. (1978). Organization-related processes in children's recall. In P. A. Ornstein (Ed.), *Memory development in children*. Hillsdale, NJ: Erlbaum.

Larkin, J. H., Heller, J. I., & Greeno, J. G. (1980). Instructional implications of research on problem solving. In W. J. McKeachie (Ed.), *Cognition, college teaching, and student learning*. San Francisco, Jossey-Bass.

Lasky, R. E., Syrdal-Lasky, A., & Klein, R. E. (1975). VOT discrimination by four to six-and a half-month-old infants from Spanish environments. *Journal of Experimental Child Psychology, 20*, 215–225.

Lave, J. (1977). Tailor-made experiments and evaluating the intellectual consequences of apprenticeship training. *Quarterly Newsletter of the Institute of Comparative Human Development, 1*, 2.

Lee, S., Stigler, J. W., & Stevenson, H. W. (1984). *Beginning reading in Chinese and English*. Unpublished manuscript. University of Michigan, Ann Arbor.

Lenneberg, E. H. (1967). *Biological foundations of language*. New York: Wiley.

Lepofsky, D. (1980, November). Consumer corner: Edited transcript from a speech. Wormald International: Sensory Aids Report.

Lesgold, A. M., & Curtis, M. E. (1981). Learning to read words efficiently. In A. M. Lesgold & C. A. Perfetti (Eds.), *Interactive processes in reading*. Hillsdale, NJ: Erlbaum.

Levin, I. (1977). The development of time concepts in children: Reasoning about duration. *Child Development, 48*, 435–444.

Levin, I. (1979). Interference of time-related and unrelated cues with duration comparisons of young children: Analysis of Piaget's formulation of the relation of time and speed. *Child Development, 50*, 469–477.

Levin, I. (1982). The nature and development of time concepts in children: The effects of interfering cues. In W. J. Friedman (Ed.), *The developmental psychology of time*. New York: Academic Press.

Levin, I., Wilkening, F., & Dembo, Y. (1984). Development of time quantification: Integration and nonintegration of beginnings and endings in comparing durations. *Child Development, 55*, 2160–2172.

Liben, L. (1975). Evidence for developmental differences in spontaneous seriation and its implications for past research on long-term memory improvement. *Developmental Psychology, 11*, 121–125.

Liben, L. S. (1977). Memory from a cognitive-developmental perspective: A theoretical and empirical review. In W. F. Overton & J. M. Gallagher (Eds.), *Knowledge and development: Vol. 1. Advances in research and theory*. New York: Plenum Press.

Liberman, I. Y., & Shankweiler, D. (1977). Speech, the alphabet and teaching to read. In L. B. Resnick & P. A. Weaver (Eds.), *Theory and practice of early reading*. Hillsdale, NJ: Erlbaum.

Liberman, I. Y., Shankweiler, D., Fischer, F. W., & Carter, B (1974). Explicit syllable and phoneme segmentation in the young child. *Journal of Experimental Child Psychology, 18*, 201–212.

Licht, B. G., & Dweck, C. S. (1984). Determinants of academic achievement: The interaction of children's achievement orientations with skill area. *Developmental Psychology, 20*, 628–636.

Lindberg, M. A. (1980). Is knowledge base development a necessary sufficient condition for memory development? *Journal of Experimental Child Psychology, 30*, 401–410.

Lockman, J. J., & Pick, H. L. (1984). Problems of scale in spatial development. In C. Sophian (Ed.), *Origins of cognitive skills*. Hillsdale, NJ: Erlbaum.

Lovell, K. (1961). A follow-up study of Inhelder and Piaget's *The growth of logical thinking*. *British Journal of Psychology, 52*, 143–153.

Macnamara, J. (1982). *Names for things: A study of human learning*. Cambridge, MA: MIT Press.

MacWhinney, B. (1978). Processing a first language: The acquisition of morphophonology. *Monographs of the Society for Research in Child Development, 43* (Whole No. 174).

MacWhinney, B. (1982). Levels of syntactic acquisition. In S. Kuczaj (Ed.), *Language development: Syntax and semantics*. Hillsdale, NJ: Erlbaum.

Mandler, J. M., & Johnson, N. (1977). Remembrance of things parsed: Story structure and recall. *Cognitive Psychology*, 9, 111–152.

Maratsos, M. P. (1982). The child's construction of grammatical categories. In L. Gleitman & H. E. Wanner (Eds.), *Language acquisition: The state of the art*. Cambridge, MA: The University Press.

Maratsos, M. P. (1983). Some current issues in the study of the acquisition of grammar. In P. H. Mussen (Ed.), *Manual of child psychology: Cognitive development, Vol. III*. New York: Wiley.

Markman, E. M. (1973). Facilitation of part-whole comparisons by use of the collective noun 'family'. *Child Development*, 44, 837–840.

Markman, E. M. (1978). Empirical versus logical solutions to part-whole comparison problems concerning classes and collections. *Child Development*, 49, 168–177.

Markman, E. M. (1979). Realizing that you don't understand: Elementary school children's awareness of inconsistencies. *Child Development*, 50, 643–655.

Markman, E. M., & Callanan, M. (1983). An analysis of hierarchical classification. In R. Sternberg (Ed.), *Advances in the psychology of human intelligence*. Hillsdale, NJ: Erlbaum.

Markman, E. M., & Hutchinson, J. E. (1984). Children's sensitivity to constraints on word meaning: Taxonomic vs. thematic relations. *Cognitive Psychology*, 16, 1–27.

Markman, E. M., & Seibert, J. (1976). Classes and collections: Internal organization and resulting holistic properties. *Cognitive Psychology*, 8, 561–577.

Martorano, S. C. (1977). A developmental analysis of performance on Piaget's formal operations task. *Developmental Psychology*, 13, 666–672.

Masur, E. F., McIntyre, C. W., & Flavell, J. H. (1973). Developmental changes in apportionment of a study time among items in a multitrial free recall task. *Journal of Experimental Child Psychology*, 15, 237–246.

Maurer, D., & Lewis, T. L. (1979). A physiological explanation of infants' early visual development. *Canadian Journal of Psychology*, 33, 232–252.

McCall, R. B., Kennedy, C. B., & Applebaum, M. I. (1977). Magnitude of discrepancy and the distribution of attention in infants. *Child Development*, 48, 772–786.

McCarthy, D. (1954). Language development in children. In L. Carmichael (Ed.), *Manual of child psychology*. New York: Wiley.

McCutchen, D., & Perfetti, C. A. (1982). Coherence and connectedness in the development of discourse production. *Text*, 2, 113–139.

McClelland, J. L., & Rumelhart, D. E. (1981). An interactive model of the effect of context in perception: Part 1. *Psychological Review*, 88, 375–407.

McGarrigle, J., & Donaldson, M. (1974). Conservation accidents. *Cognition*, 3, 341–350.

Marschark, M., & West, S. H. (1985). Creative language abilities of deaf children. *Journal of Speech and Hearing Research*, 28, 73–78.

Medin, D. L., & Schaffer, M. (1978). Context theory of classification learning. *Psychological Review*, 85, 207–238.

Mendelson, M. J., & Haith, M. M. (1976). The relation between audition and vision in the human newborn. *Monographs of the Society for Research in Child Development*, 41 (Whole No. 167).

Mendelson, R., & Schultz, T. R. (1976). Covariation and temporal contiguity as principles of causal inference in young children. *Journal of Experimental Child Psychology*, 13, 89–111.

Menig-Peterson, C. L. (1975). The modification of communicative behavior in preschool-aged children as a function of the listener's perspective. *Child Development*, 46, 1015–1018.

Mervis, C. B., & Mervis, C. A. (1982). Leopards are kitty-cats: Object labeling by mothers for their thirteen-month-olds. *Child Development*, 53, 267–273.

Mervis, C. B., & Rosch, E. (1981). Categorization of natural objects. *Annual Review of Psychology*, 32, 89–115.

Milewski, A. E. (1976). Infants' discrimination of internal and external pattern elements. *Journal of Experimental Child Psychology, 22*, 229–246.

Miller, K., & Gelman, R. (1983). The child's representation of number: A multidimensional scaling analysis. *Child Development, 54*, 1470–1479.

Miller, P. H. (1983). *Theories of developmental psychology.* San Francisco: Freeman.

Miller, S. A. (1976). Nonverbal assessment of conservation of number. *Child Development, 47*, 722–728.

Moely, B. E. (1977). Organizational factors in the development of memory. In R. V. Kail & J. W. Hagen (Eds.), *Perspectives on the development of memory and cognition.* Hillsdale, NJ: Erlbaum.

Moely, B. E., Olson, F. A., Halwes, T. G., & Flavell, J. H. (1969). Production deficiency in young children's clustered recall. *Developmental Psychology, 1*, 26–34.

Molfese, D. L., & Molfese, V. J. (1979). Hemisphere and stimulus differences as reflected in the cortical responses of newborn infants to speech stimuli. *Developmental Psychology, 15*, 505–511.

Morrison, F. J., Holmes, D. L., & Haith, M. M. (1974). A developmental study of the effects of familiarity on short-term visual memory. *Journal of Experimental Child Psychology, 18*, 412–425.

Morse, P. A. (1972). The discrimination of speech and nonspeech stimuli in early infancy. *Journal of Experimental Child Psychology, 14*, 477–492.

Moyer, R. S., & Landauer, T. K. (1967). The time required for judgments of numerical inequality. *Nature, 215*, 1519–1520.

Moynahan, E. D. (1973). The development of knowledge concerning the effect of categorization upon free recall. *Child Development, 44*, 238–246.

Muir, D., Abraham, W., Forbes, B., & Harris, L. (1979). The ontogenesis of an auditory localization response from birth to four months of age. *Canadian Journal of Psychology, 33*, 320–333.

Muller, E., Hollien, H., & Murray, T. (1974). Perceptual responses to infant crying: Identification of cry. *Journal of Child Language, 1*, 89–95.

Murray, F. B. (1972). Acquisition of conservation through social interaction. *Developmental Psychology, 6*, 1–6.

Mussen, P. H., Conger, J. J., Kagan, J., & Geiwitz, J. (1979). *Psychological development: A life-span approach.* New York: Harper & Row.

Naus, M. J., & Ornstein, P. A. (1983). Development of memory strategies: Analysis, questions, and issues. In M. T. Chi (Ed.), *Trends in memory development research.* New York: Karger.

Naus, M. J., Ornstein, P. A., & Aivano, S. (1977). Developmental changes in memory: The effects of processing time and rehearsal instructions. *Journal of Experimental Child Psychology, 23*, 237–251.

Neimark, E. D. (1975). Intellectual development during adolescence. In F. D. Horowitz (Ed.), *Review of child development research, Vol. 4.* Chicago: University of Chicago Press.

Nelson, D. L. (1978). Remembering pictures and words: Significance and appearance. In L. S. Cermak & F. I. M. Craik (Eds.), *Levels of processing and human memory.* Hillsdale, NJ: Erlbaum.

Nelson, K. (1973). Structure and strategy in learning to talk. *Monographs of the Society for Research in Child Development, 38*, Serial No. 149.

Nelson, K. (1978). How children represent knowledge of their world in and out of language: A preliminary report. In R. S. Siegler (Ed.), *Children's thinking: What develops?* Hillsdale, NJ: Erlbaum.

Nelson, K., & Ross, G. (1980). The generalities and specifics of long term memory in infants and young children. In M. Perlmutter (Ed.), *New directions for child development: Children's memory.* San Francisco: Jossey-Bass.

Newell, A. (1968). *En calcul et formilisation dans les sciences de l'homme,* (On the analysis of human problem-solving protocols). Paris: ENRS.

Newell, A., & Simon, H. A. (1972). *Human problem solving.* Englewood Cliffs, NJ: Prentice-Hall.

Newman, R. S. (1984). Children's numerical skill and judgments of confidence in estimation. *Journal of Experimental Child Psychology, 37,* 107–123.

Newman, R. S., & Berger, C. F. (1984). Children's numerical estimation: Flexibility in the use of counting. *Journal of Educational Psychology, 76,* 55–64.

Newport, E. L. (1982). Task specificity in language learning? Evidence from speech. In E. Wanner & L. R. Gleitman (Eds.), *Language acquisition: The state of the art.* Cambridge, MA: Cambridge University Press.

Nisbett, R. E., & Wilson, T. D. (1977). Telling more than we can know: Verbal reports on mental processes. *Psychological Review, 84,* 231–259.

Nodine, C. F., & Steurle, N. L. (1973). Development of perceptual and cognitive strategies for differentiating graphemes. *Journal of Experimental Psychology, 97,* 158–166.

Odom, R. D. (1978). A perceptual-salience account of decalage relations and developmental change. In L. S. Siegel & C. J. Brainerd (Eds.), *Alternatives to Piaget.* New York: Academic Press.

O'Hara, E. (1975). Piaget, the six-year-old child, and modern math. *Today's Education, 64,* 33–36.

Olson, G. M. (1976). An information-processing analysis of visual memory and habituation in infants. In T. J. Tighe & R. N. Leaton (Eds.), *Habituation.* Hillsdale, NJ: Erlbaum.

Ornstein, P. A., Naus, M. J., & Liberty, C. (1975). Rehearsal and organizational processes in children's memory. *Child Development, 26,* 818–830.

Palermo, D. S. (1973). More about less: A study of language comprehension. *Journal of Verbal Learning and Verbal Behavior, 12,* 211–221.

Palincsar, A. S., & Brown, A. L. (1984). Reciprocal teaching of comprehension-monitoring activities. *Cognition and Instruction, 1,* 117–175.

Paris, S. G. (1975). Integration and inference in children's comprehension and memory. In F. Restle, R. Shriffrin, J. Castellan, H. Lindman, & D. Pisoni (Eds.), *Cognitive theory, Vol. 1.* Hillsdale, NJ: Erlbaum.

Paris, S. G., & Lindauer, B. K. (1977). Constructive aspects of children's comprehension and memory. In R. V. Kail, Jr., & J. W. Hagen (Eds.), *Perspectives on the development of memory and cognition.* Hillsdale, NJ: Erlbaum.

Paris, S. G., & Myers, M. (1981). Comprehension monitoring, memory, and study strategies of good and poor readers. *Journal of Reading Behavior, 13,* 5–22.

Pascual-Leone, J. A. (1970). A mathematical model for transition in Piaget's developmental stages. *Acta Psychologica, 32,* 301–345.

Patberg, J., Dewitz, P., & Samuels, S. J. (1981). The effect of context on the size of the perceptual unit used in word recognition. *Journal of Reading Behavior, 13,* 33–48.

Patterson, C. J., & Kister, M. C. (1981). The development of listener skills for referential communication. In W. P. Dickson (Ed.), *Children's oral communication skills.* New York: Academic Press.

Pearson, P. D. (Ed.). (1984). *Handbook of reading research.* New York: Longman.

Pellegrino, J. W., & Glaser, R. (1982). Analyzing aptitudes for learning: Inductive reasoning. In R. Glaser (Ed.), *Advances in instructional psychology, Vol. 2.* Hillsdale, NJ: Erlbaum.

Perfetti, C. A. (1984). *Reading ability.* New York: Oxford University Press.

Perlmutter, M. (Ed.). (1980). *New directions for child development: Children's memory.* San Francisco: Jossey-Bass.

Perlmutter, M., & Lange, G. A. (1978). A developmental analysis of recall-recognition distinctions. In P. A. Ornstein (Ed.), *Memory development in children.* Hillsdale, NJ: Erlbaum.

Perry, D. G., & Bussey, K. (1979). The social learning theory of sex differences: Imitation is alive and well. *Journal of Personality and Social Psychology, 37,* 1699–1712.

Piaget, J. (1946a). *The development of children's concept of time.* Paris: Presses Universitaires de France.

Piaget, J. (1946b). *Les notions de mouvement et de vitesse ches l'enfant.* Paris: Presses Universitaires de France.

Piaget, J. (1951). *Play, dreams, and imitation in childhood.* New York: W. W. Norton.

Piaget, J. (1952). *The child's concept of number.* New York: W. W. Norton.

Piaget, J. (1954). *The construction of reality in the child.* New York: Basic Books.

Piaget, J. (1969). *The child's conception of physical causality.* Totowa, NJ: Littlefield, Adams & Co.

Piaget, J. (1971). *The construction of reality in the child.* New York: Ballantine.

Piaget, J. (1972). Intellectual evolution from adolescence to adulthood. *Human Development, 15,* 1–12.

Piaget, J., & Inhelder, B. (1973). *Memory and intelligence.* New York: Basic Books.

Premack, D. (1976). *Intelligence in ape and man.* New York: Wiley.

Pressley, M. (1982). Elaboration and memory development. *Child Development, 53,* 296–309.

Pressley, M., Borkowski, J. G., & O'Sullivan, J. T. (in press). Metamemory and the teaching of learning strategies. In D. L. Forrest-Pressley, E. MacKinnon, & T. G. Waller (Eds.), *Metacognition, cognition, and human performance.* New York: Academic Press.

Pressley, M., Forrest-Pressley, D. L., Elliott-Faust, D., & Miller, G. (1985). Children's use of cognitive strategies: How to teach strategies, and what to do if they can't be taught. In M. Pressley & C. J. Brainerd (Eds.), *Cognitive learning and memory in children.* New York: Springer-Verlag.

Pressley, M., & Levin, J. R. (1977). Developmental differences in subjects' associative learning strategies and performance: Assessing a hypothesis. *Journal of Experimental Child Psychology, 24,* 431–439.

Pressley, M., & Levin, J. R. (1980). The development of mental imagery retrieval. *Child Development, 51,* 558–560.

Price, G. G. (1984). Mnemonic support and curriculum selection in teaching by mothers: A conjoint effect. *Child Development, 55,* 659–668.

Price-Williams, D., Gordon, W., & Ramirez, M. (1969). Skill and conservation: A study of pottery-making children. *Developmental Psychology, 1,* 769.

Quine, W. V. O. (1960). *Word and object.* Cambridge, MA: MIT Press.

Rabinowitz, M., & Chi, M. T. H. (1985). An interactive model of strategic processing. *Unpublished manuscript,* University of Illinois, Chicago.

Rader, N., Bausano, M., & Richards, T. E. (1980). On the nature of the visual-cliff avoidance response in human infants. *Child Development, 51,* 61–68.

Reese, H. W. (1962). Verbal mediation as a function of age level. *Psychological Bulletin, 59,* 502–509.

Reese, H. W. (1977). Imagery and associative memory. In R. V. Kail & J. W. Hagen (Eds.), *Perspectives on the development of memory and cognition.* Hillsdale, NJ: Erlbaum.

Renninger, K. A., & Wozniak, R. H. (1985). Effect of interest on attentional shift, recognition, and recall in young children. *Developmental Psychology, 21,* 624–632.

Rescorla, L. (1976). *Concept formation in word learning.* Unpublished doctoral dissertation.

Resnick, L. B., & Glaser, R. (1976). Problem solving and intelligence. In L. B. Resnick (Ed.), *The nature of intelligence.* Hillsdale, NJ: Erlbaum.

Rest, J. R. (1983). Morality. In P. H. Mussen (Ed.), *Handbook of child psychology: Cognitive development, Vol. III.* New York: Wiley.

Reyna, V. F. (1985). Figure and fantasy in children's language. In M. Pressley & C. J. Brainerd (Eds.), *Cognitive learning and memory in children.* New York: Springer-Verlag.

Richards, D. D. (1982). Children's time concepts: Going the distance. In W. J. Friedman (Ed.), *The developmental psychology of time.* New York: Academic Press.

Richards, D. D., & Siegler, R. S. (1984). The effects of task requirements on children's life judgments. *Child Development, 55,* 1687–1696.

Richman, C. L., Nida, S., & Pittman, L. (1976). Effects of meaningfulness on child free-recall learning. *Developmental Psychology, 12,* 460–465.

Rieser, J. (1979). Spatial orientation of six-month-old infants. *Child Development, 50,* 1078–1087.

Riley, C. A., & Trabasso, T. (1974). Comparatives, logical structures, and encoding in a transitive inference task. *Journal of Experimental Child Psychology, 45,* 972–977.

Robinson, E. J., & Robinson, W. P. (1981). Egocentrism in verbal referential communication. In M. Cox (Ed.), *Is the young child egocentric?* London: Concord.

Rodgon, M. M. (1979). Knowing what to say and wanting to say it: Some communication and structural aspects of single-word responses to questions. *Journal of Child Language, 6,* 81–90.

Romberg, T. A., & Stewart, D. M. (Eds.). (1983). *School mathematics: Options for the 1990s, Proceedings of the Conference, Madison, Wisconsin.* Washington, D.C.: U.S. Department of Education.

Rosch, E., & Mervis, C. B. (1975). Family resemblances: Studies in the internal structure of categories. *Cognitive Psychology, 7,* 573–605.

Rosch, E., Mervis, C. B., Gray, W. D., Johnson, D. M., & Boyes-Braem, P. (1976). Basic objects in natural categories. *Cognitive Psychology, 8,* 382–439.

Rogoff, B., Ellis, S., & Gardner, W. (1984). The adjustment of adult-child instruction according to child's age and task. *Developmental Psychology, 20,* 193–199.

Rovee, C. K., & Fagen, J. W. (1976). Extended conditioning and 24-hour retention in infants. *Journal of Experimental Child Psychology, 21,* 1–11.

Ruff, H. A., & Kohler, C. J. (1978). Tactual-visual transfer in six-month-old infants. *Infant Behavior and Development, 1,* 259–264.

Salapatek, P. (1975). Pattern perception in early infancy. In L. B. Cohen & P. Salapatek (Eds.), *Infant perception: From sensation to cognition.* New York: Academic Press.

Salatas, H., & Flavell, J. H. (1976). Behavioral and metamnemonic indicators of strategic behaviors under instructions to remember in first grade. *Child Development, 47,* 81–89.

Scardamalia, M., & Bereiter, C. (1984). Written composition. In M. Wittrock (Ed.), *Handbook of research on teaching,* 3rd ed.

Schank, R. C. (1975). *Conceptual information processing.* New York: Elsevier.

Schlesinger, I. M. (1971). Production of utterances and language acquisition. In D. I. Slobin (Ed.), *The ontogenesis of grammar.* New York: Academic Press.

Schneider, B. A., Trehub, S. E., & Bull, D. (1979). The development of basic auditory processes in infants. *Canadian Journal of Psychology, 33,* 306–319.

Sedlak, A. J., & Kurtz, S. T. (1981). A review of children's use of causal inference principles. *Child Development, 52,* 759–784.

Seidenberg, M. S., & Petitto, L. A. (1979). Signing behavior in apes: A critical review. *Cognition, 7,* 177–215.

Shaklee, H. (1979). Bounded rationality and cognitive development: Upper limits on growth? *Cognitive Psychology, 11,* 327–345.

Shantz, C. U. (1983). Social cognition. In P. H. Mussen (Ed.), *Handbook of child psychology: Cognitive development, Vol. III.* New York: Wiley.

Sharp, D., Cole, M., & Lave, C. (1979). Education and cognitive development: The evidence from experimental research. *Monographs of the Society for Research in Child Development, 44* (Whole No. 178).

Shatz, M. (1978). On the development of communicative understandings: An early strategy for interpreting and responding to messages. *Cognitive Psychology, 10,* 271–301.

Shatz, M. (1983). Communication. In P. H. Mussen (Ed.), *Manual of child psychology: Cognitive development, Vol. III* (J. H. Flavell and E. M. Markman (Eds.)). New York: Wiley.

Shatz, M., & Gelman, R. (1973). The development of communication skills: Modifications in the speech of young children as a function of listener. *Monographs of the Society for Research in Child Development, 38* (Whole No. 152).

Shepard, R. N., & Metzler, J. (1971). Mental rotation of three-dimensional objects. *Science, 171,* 701–703.

Sherrod, L. R. (1979). Social cognition in infants: Attention to the human face. *Infant Behavior and Development, 2,* 279–294.

Shiffrin, R. M. (1976). Capacity limitations in information processing, attention, and memory.

In W. Estes (Ed.), *Handbook of learning and cognitive processes*. Hillsdale, NJ: Erlbaum.

Shultz, T. R. (1982). Rules of causal attribution. *Monographs of the Society for Research in Child Development, 47* (Whole No. 194).

Siegler, R. S. (1976). Three aspects of cognitive development. *Cognitive Psychology, 8,* 481–520.

Siegler, R. S. (1978). The origins of scientific reasoning. In R. S. Siegler (Ed.), *Children's thinking: What develops?* Hillsdale, NJ: Erlbaum.

Siegler, R. S. (1981). Developmental sequences within and between concepts. *Monographs of the Society for Research in Child Development, 46* (Whole No. 189).

Siegler, R. S. (1983). Five generalizations about cognitive development. *American Psychologist, 38,* 263–277.

Siegler, R. S. (1984). Mechanisms of cognitive growth: Variation and selection. In R. J. Sternberg (Ed.), *Mechanisms of cognitive development*. New York: Freeman.

Siegler, R. S., & Richards, D. (1979). Development of time, speed, and distance concepts. *Developmental Psychology, 15,* 288–298.

Siegler, R. S., & Robinson, M. (1982). The development of numerical understandings. In H. W. Reese & L. P. Lipsitt (Eds.), *Advances in child development and behavior*. New York: Academic Press.

Siegler, R. S., & Shrager, J. (1984). Strategy choices in addition and subtraction: How do children know what to do? In C. Sophian (Ed.), *Origins of cognitive skills*. Hillsdale, NJ: Erlbaum.

Siegler, R. S., & Vago, S. (1978). The development of a proportionality concept: Judging relative fullness. *Journal of Experimental Child Psychology, 25,* 371–395.

Simon, H. A. (1981). *The sciences of the artificial*. Cambridge, MA: MIT Press.

Siqueland, E. R., & Lipsitt, L. P. (1966). Conditioned head turning in human newborns. *Journal of Experimental Child Psychology, 3,* 356–376.

Skinner, B. F. (1957). *Verbal behavior*. New York: Appleton-Century-Crofts.

Slobin, D. I. (1983, April). *Crosslinguistic evidence for basic child grammar*. Paper presented at the Biennial Meeting of The Society for Research in Child Development, Detroit.

Smiley, S. S., & Brown, A. L. (1979). Conceptual preference for thematic or taxonomic relations: A nonmonotonic age trend from preschool to old age. *Journal of Experimental Child Psychology, 28,* 249–257.

Smith, C. L. (1979). Children's understanding of natural language hierarchies. *Journal of Experimental Child Psychology, 27,* 437–458.

Smith, E. E., & Medin, D. L. (1981). *Categories and concepts*. Cambridge, MA: Harvard University Press.

Smith, M. E. (1926). An investigation of the development of the sentence and the extent of vocabulary in young children. *University of Iowa Studies in Child Welfare, 3,* (Whole No. 5).

Smith, N. V. (1973). *The acquisition of phonology: A case study*. Cambridge, England: Cambridge University Press.

Snow, C. E., & Hoefnagel-Hohle, M. (1978). The critical period for language acquisition: Evidence from second language learning. *Child Development, 49,* 1114–1128.

Sokolov, E. N. (1963). *Perception and the conditioned reflex*. New York: Macmillan.

Sonnenschein, S., & Whitehurst, G. J. (1984). Developing referential communication: A hierarchy of skills. *Child Development, 55,* 1936–1945.

Sophian, C. (1984). Developing search skills in infancy and early childhood. In C. Sophian (Ed.), *Origins of cognitive skills*. Hillsdale, NJ: Erlbaum.

Sophian, C., & Stigler, J. W. (1981). Does recognition memory improve with age? *Journal of Experimental Child Psychology, 32,* 343–353.

Spear, N. E. (1984). Ecologically determined dispositions control the ontogeny of learning and memory. In R. Kail & N. E. Spear (Eds.), *Comparative perspectives on the development of memory*. Hillsdale, NJ: Erlbaum.

Spelke, E. (1976). Infant's intermodal perception of events. *Cognitive Psychology, 8,* 553–560.

Spelke, E., Hirst, W., & Neisser, U. (1976). Skills of divided attention. *Cognition, 4,* 215–230.

Spence, M. J., & DeCasper, A. J. (1982). *Human fetuses perceive maternal speech.* Paper presented at the meeting of the International Conference on Infant Studies, Austin, TX.

Sperling, G. (1960). The information available in brief visual presentations. *Psychological Monographs, 74* (Whole No. 176).

Spilich, G. J., Vesonder, G. T., Chiesi, H. L., & Voss, J. (1979). Text processing of domain-related information for individuals with high and low domain knowledge. *Journal of Verbal Learning and Verbal Behavior, 18,* 275–290.

Spiro, R. J., Bruce, B. C., & Brewer, W. F. (Eds.). (1980). *Theoretical issues in reading comprehension.* Hillsdale, NJ: Erlbaum.

Standing, L., Conezio, J., & Haber, R. N. (1970). Perception and memory for pictures: Single trial learning of 2560 visual stimuli. *Psychonomic Science, 19,* 73–74.

Stanovich, K. E. (1983, April). *The interactive-compensatory model of reading: A confluence of developmental, experimental and educational psychology.* Paper presented at the meeting of the Society for Research in Child Development, Detroit.

Starkey, P., & Cooper, R. S. (1980). Perception of numbers by human infants. *Science, 210,* 1033–1035.

Stein, N., & Glenn, C. (1979). An analysis of story comprehension in elementary school children. In R. Freedle (Ed.), *New directions in discourse processing, Vol. 2.* Norwood, NJ: Ablex, Inc.

Stern, D. N., Spieker, S., & MacKain, C. (1982). Intonation contours as signals in maternal speech to prelinguistic infants. *Developmental Psychology, 18,* 727–735.

Sternberg, R. J. (1977). *Intelligence, information processing, and analogical reasoning.* Hillsdale, NJ: Erlbaum.

Sternberg, R. J. (1984). Mechanisms of cognitive development: A componential approach. In R. J. Sternberg (Ed.), *Mechanisms of cognitive development.* New York: Freeman.

Sternberg, R. J. (1985). *Beyond IQ: A triarchic theory of human intelligence.* New York: Cambridge University Press.

Sternberg, R. J., & Davidson, J. E. (1983). Insight in the gifted. *Educational Psychologist, 18,* 52–58.

Sternberg, R. J., & Rifkin, B. (1979). The development of analogical reasoning processes. *Journal of Experimental Child Psychology, 27,* 195–232.

Sternberg, S. (1966). High-speed scanning in human memory. *Science, 153,* 652–654.

Sticht, T. G., & James, J. H. (1984). Listening and reading. In P. D. Pearson (Ed.), *Handbook of reading research: Part 2.* New York: Longman.

Stigler, J. W. (1984). "Mental Abacus": The effect of abacus training on Chinese children's mental calculation. *Cognitive Psychology, 16,* 145–176.

Stokoe, W. C., Jr. (1960). Sign language structure: An outline of the visual communications system of the American deaf. *Studies in Linguistics, Occasional Papers,* Vol. 8.

Strauss, M. S., & Cohen, L. P. (1978). *Infant immediate and delayed memory for perceptual dimensions.* Unpublished manuscript, University of Illinois, Urbana.

Strauss, M. S., & Curtis, L. E. (1981). Infant perception of numerosity. *Child Development, 52,* 1146–1152.

Strauss, M. S., & Curtis, L. E. (1984). Development of numerical concepts in infancy. In C. Sophian (Ed.), *The origins of cognitive skills.* Hillsdale, NJ: Erlbaum.

Strauss, S. (1972). Inducing cognitive development and learning: A review of short-term training experiments I. The organismic-developmental approach. *Cognition, 1,* 329–357.

Strauss, S. (Ed.). (1982). *U-shaped behavioral growth.* New York: Academic Press.

Strelow, E. R., Kay, N., & Kay, L. (1978). Binaural sensory aid: Case studies of its use by two children. *Journal of Visual Impairment and Blindness, 72,* 1–9.

Sullivan, M. W., Rovee-Collier, C. K., & Tynes, D. M. (1979). A conditioning analysis of infant long-term memory. *Child Development, 50,* 152–162.

Supalla, T. (1982). *The acquisition of morphology of American Sign Language verbs of motion and location.* Unpublished doctoral dissertation, University of California, San Diego.

Surber, C. F. (1980). The development of reversible operations in judgments of ability, effort, and performance. *Child Development, 51,* 1018–1029.

Surber, C. F., & Gzesh, S. M. (1984). Reversible operations in the balance scale task. *Journal of Experimental Child Psychology, 38,* 254–274.

Svenson, O. (1975). Analysis of time required by children for simple additions. *Acta Psychologica, 39,* 289–302.

Svenson, O., & Broquist, S. (1975). Strategies for solving simple addition problems. *Scandinavian Journal of Psychology, 16,* 143–151.

Svenson, O., & Sjoberg, K. (1982). Solving simple subtractions during the first three school years. *Journal of Experimental Education, 50,* 91–100.

Terrace, H. S., Petitto, L. A., Sanders, R. J., & Bever, J. G. (1983). Can an ape create a sentence? *Science, 26,* 891–902.

Tighe, T. J., Glick, J., & Cole, M. (1971). Subproblem analysis of discrimination-shift learning. *Psychonomic Science, 24,* 159–160.

Torgeson, J. K., & Goldman, T. (1977). Verbal rehearsal and short-term memory in reading disabled children. *Child Development, 48,* 56–60.

Trabasso, T., Isen, A. M., Dolecki, P., McLanahan, A. G., Riley, C. A., & Tucker, T. (1978). How do children solve class-inclusion problems? In R. S. Siegler (Ed.), *Children's thinking: What develops?* Hillsdale, NJ: Erlbaum.

Trabasso, T., Riley, C. A., & Wilson, E. G. (1975). The representation of linear order and spatial strategies in reasoning: A developmental study. In R. J. Falmagne (Ed.), *Reasoning: Representation and process.* Hillsdale, NJ: Erlbaum.

Trehub, S. E. (1973). Infant's sensitivity to vowel and tonal contrasts. *Developmental Psychology, 31,* 102–107.

Tuddenham, R. D. (1962). The nature and measurement of intelligence. In L. Postman (Ed.), *Psychology in the making.* New York: Alfred A. Knopf.

Tulving, E. (1983). *Elements of episodic memory.* New York: Oxford University Press.

Turnure, J., Buium, N., & Thurlow, M. (1976). The effectiveness of interrogatives for promoting verbal elaboration productivity in young children. *Child Development, 47,* 851–855.

Uememoto, T. (1984, September). Cross-cultural study of achievement calls for changes in home. *APA Monitor,* p. 10.

Uzgiris, I. C. (1964). Situational generality of conservation. *Child Development, 35,* 831–841.

Venezky, R. (1978). Reading acquisition: The occult and the obscure. In F. Murray, H. Sharp, & J. Pikulski (Eds.), *The acquisition of reading: Cognitive, linguistic and perceptual prerequisites.* Baltimore: University Park Press.

von Hofsten, C. (1982). Eye-hand coordination in newborns. *Developmental Psychology, 18,* 450–461.

Vurpillot, E. (1968). The development of scanning strategies and their relation to visual differentiation. *Journal of Experimental Child Psychology, 6,* 632–650.

Vygotsky, L. S. (1934). *Thought and language.* New York: Wiley.

Walk, R. D. (1979). Depth perception and a laughing heaven. In A. D. Pick (Ed.), *Perception and its development: A tribute to Eleanor J. Gibson.* Hillsdale, NJ: Erlbaum.

Walk, R. D., & Gibson, E. J. (1961). A comparative and analytical study of visual depth perception. *Psychological Monographs, 75* (Whole No. 519).

Wallace, J. G., Klahr, D., & Bluff, K. (in press). A self-modifying production system for conservation acquisition. In D. Klahr, P. Langley, & R. Neches (Eds.), *Self-modifying production systems: Models of learning and development.* Cambridge, MA: MIT Press.

Waters, H. S. (1980). "Class news": A single-object longitudinal study of prose production and schema formation during childhood. *Journal of Verbal Learning and Verbal Behavior, 19,* 152–167.

Waters, H. S., & Andreassen, C. (1983). Children's use of memory strategies under instruction. In M. Pressley & J. R. Levin (Eds.), *Cognitive strategies: Developmental, educational, and treatment-related issues.* New York: Springer-Verlag.

Waters, H. S., & Tinsley, V. S. (1985). Evaluating the discriminant and convergent validity of developmental constructs: Another look at the concept of egocentrism. *Psychological Bulletin, 97,* 483–496.

Weber, R. M. (1970). First graders' use of grammatical context in reading. In H. Levin & J. P. Williams (Eds.), *Basic studies of reading.* New York: Basic Books.

Weinreb, N., & Brainerd, C. J. (1975). A developmental study of Piaget's groupement model of the emergence of speed and time concepts. *Child Development, 46,* 176–185.

Wellman, H. M. (1983). Metamemory revisited. In M. T. Chi (Ed.), *Trends in memory development research.* New York: Karger.

Wellman, H. M., Ritter, R., & Flavell, J. H. (1975). Deliberate memory behavior in the delayed reactions of very young children. *Developmental Psychology, 11,* 780–787.

Wellman, H. M., & Somerville, S. C. (1980). Quasi-naturalistic tasks in the study of cognition: The memory-related skills of toddlers. In M. Perlmutter (Ed.), *New directions for child development: Children's memory, No. 10.* San Francisco: Jossey-Bass.

Wellman, H. M., & Somerville, S. C. (1984). The development of human search ability. In M. E. Lamb & A. L. Brown (Eds.), *Advances in developmental psychology.* Hillsdale, NJ: Erlbaum.

Werker, J. F., Gilbert, J. H. V., Humphrey, K., & Tees, R. C. (1981). Developmental aspects of cross-language speech perception. *Child Development, 52,* 349–355.

Werner, J. S., & Siqueland, E. R. (1978). Visual recognition memory in the preterm infant. *Infant Behavior and Development, 1,* 79–94.

Wertheimer, M. (1961). Psychomotor coordination of auditory-visual space at birth. *Science, 134,* 1692.

Wexler, K. (1982). A principle theory for language acquisition. In L. Gleitman & H. E. Wanner (Eds.), *Language acquisition: The state of the art.* Cambridge, MA: The University Press.

Whimbey, A. (1975). *Intelligence can be taught.* New York: Dutton.

Whitehurst, G. J., & Sonnenschein, S. (1981). The development of informative messages in referential communication: Knowing when vs. knowing how. In W. P. Dickson (Ed.), *Children's oral communication skills.* New York: Academic Press.

Wigfield, A., & Asher, S. R. (1984). Social and motivational influences on reading. In P. D. Pearson (Ed.), *Handbook of reading research: Part 2.* New York: Longman.

Wilkening, F. (1981). Integrating velocity, time, and distance information: A developmental study. *Cognitive Psychology, 13,* 231–247.

Wilkening, F. (1982). Children's knowledge about time, distance, and velocity interrelations. In W. J. Friedman (Ed.), *The developmental psychology of time.* New York: Academic Press.

Wilkinson, A. C. (1980). Children's understanding in reading and listening. *Journal of Educational Psychology, 72,* 561–574.

Williams, K. G., & Goulet, L. R. (1975). The effects of cuing and constraint instructions on children's free recall performance. *Journal of Experimental Child Psychology, 19,* 464–475.

Winer, G. A. (1974). An analysis of verbal facilitation of class inclusion reasoning. *Child Development, 45,* 224–227.

Winer, G. A. (1980). Class-inclusion reasoning in children: A review of the empirical literature. *Child Development, 51,* 309–328.

Winner, E., McCarthy, M., & Gardner, H. (1980). The ontogenesis of metaphor. In R. Honeck & R. Hoffman (Eds.), *Cognition and figurative language.* Hillsdale, NJ: Erlbaum.

Winner, E., Rosensteil, A. K., & Gardner, H. (1976). The development of metaphoric understanding. *Developmental Psychology, 12,* 289–297.

Wittgenstein, L. (1970). *Philosophical investigations.* New York: Macmillan.

Woods, S. S., Resnick, L. B., & Groen, G. J. (1975). Experimental test of five process models for subtraction. *Journal of Educational Psychology, 67,* 17–21.

Yonas, A., and Granrud, C. E. (in press). The development of sensitivity to kinetic, binocular, and pictorial depth information in human infants. In D. Ingle, D. L. Jeannerod, & M. Jeannerod (Eds.), *Brain Mechanisms and Spatial Vision.* Amsterdam: Martinus Nijhoff Press.

Younger, B. A., & Cohen, L. B. (1983). Infant perception of correlations among attributes. *Child Development, 54,* 858–867.

Zimiles, H. (1966). The development of conservation and differentiation of number. *Monographs of the Society for Research in Child Development, 31* (Whole No. 108).

Zimmerman, B. J., & Rosenthal, T. L. (1974). Conserving and retaining equalities and inequalities through observation and correction. *Developmental Psychology, 10,* 260–268.

AUTHOR INDEX

SUBJECT INDEX